DRUG DEPENDENT PATIENTS

DRUG DEPENDENT PATIENTS

Treatment and Research

Edited by

ROBERT J. CRAIG, Ph.D.

Chief, Drug Dependence Treatment Program
West Side VA Medical Center
Chicago, Illinois
and
University of Illinois at the Medical Center
School of Public Health

and

STEWART L. BAKER, M.D.

Associate Director, Mental Health and Behavioral Sciences
for Alcohol and Drug Dependence
Department of Medicine and Surgery
VA Central Office
Washington, D.C.
and
Clinical Professor
Department of Psychiatry
Uniformed Services University of the Health Sciences
Bethesda, Maryland

CHARLES C THOMAS • PUBLISHER

Springfield • Illinois • U.S.A.

Published and Distributed Throughout the World by
CHARLES C THOMAS • PUBLISHER
2600 South First Street, Springfield, Illinois 62717, U.S.A.

©*1982, by* CHARLES C THOMAS • PUBLISHER

ISBN 0-398-04562-3

Library of Congress Catalog Card Number: 81-8807

With THOMAS BOOKS careful attention is given to all details of manufacturing and design. It is the Publisher's desire to present books that are satisfactory as to their physical qualities and artistic possibilities and appropriate for their particular use. THOMAS BOOKS will be true to those laws of quality that assure a good name and good will.

Library of Congress Cataloging in Publication Data

Main entry under title:

Drug dependent patients, treatment and research.

Includes bibliographies and index.
1. Drug abuse – Treatment. 2. Drug abuse – Treatment – Evaluation.
I. Craig, Robert J., 1941-   . II. Baker, Stewart L. [DNLM: 1. Substance
abuse — Therapy. 2. Substance dependence — Therapy. WM 270.D794]
RC564.D782   616.86'3   81-8807
ISBN 0-398-04562-3   AACR2

Printed in the United States of America

AF-RX-I

**To Our Staff,
Who Taught Us,**

**To Our Patients,
Who Educated Us.**

CONTRIBUTORS

David L. Bachrach, Ed.D., — Director, Pain Management Clinic, Psychology Service, Boston VA Medical Center, Boston, Massachusetts.

Stewart Baker, M.D., — Associate Director, Mental Health and Behavioral Sciences for Alcohol and Drug Dependence, VA Central Office, Washington, D.C., and Clinical Professor, Department of Psychiatry, Uniformed Services University of the Health Sciences, Bethesda, Maryland.

Richard N. Bale, Ph.D., — Chief, Drug Dependence Evaluation and Referral, Palo Alto VA Medical Center, Palo Alto, California, and Assistant Clinical Professor, Department of Psychiatry and Behavioral Sciences, Stanford University Medical School.

Dale A. Callner, Ph.D., — Director, Child and Family Services, Seattle Mental Health Institute, Seattle, Washington.

Robert J. Craig, Ph.D., — Chief, Drug Dependence Treatment Program, West Side VA Medical Center, Chicago, Illinois, and University of Illinois at the Medical Center, School of Public Health.

Robert L. Custer, M.D., — Chief, Treatment Services Division, Mental Health and Behavioral Sciences Service, VA Central Office, Washington, D.C.

Walter Dorus, M.D., — Chief, Alcohol and Drug Dependence Treatment Programs, Hines VA Hospital, Hines Illinois, and Associate Professor of Psychiatry, Stritch School of Medicine, Loyola University of Chicago.

Richard Heilman, M.D., — Chief, Chemical Dependence Treatment Program, Minneapolis VA Medical Center, Minneapolis, Minnesota, and Assistant Professor, University of Minnesota, Department of Psychiatry, School of Public Health.

John A. Hermos, M.D., — Medical Director, Substance Abuse Treatment Program, Boston VA Medical Center, Boston, Massachusetts, and Assistant Professor of Medicine, Boston University School of Medicine.

Henry Lahmeyer, M.D., — Consultant, Drug Dependence Treatment Center, West Side VA Medical Center, Chicago, Illinois, and Assistant Professor of Psychiatry, Department of Psychiatry, University of Illinois School of Medicine.

James E. Lewis, Ph.D., — Director of Research, The Kingsbury Center, Washington, D.C.

Theodore W. Lorei, MSW, — Social Service Analyst, Health Service Research and Development Division, Department of Medicine and Surgery, VA Central Office, Washington, D.C., and Lecturer, School of Social Service, Catholic University of America.

Paul A. Mider, — Chief, Drug Dependence Treatment Center, F.D.R. VA Hospital, Montrose, New York, and Member, Adjunct Faculty, School of New Resources, College of New Rochelle.

Walter Penk, Ph.D., — Research Psychologist, Dallas VA Medical Center, Dallas, Texas.

Ralph Robinowitz, — Chief, Drug Dependence Treatment Program, Dallas VA Medical Center, Dallas, Texas, and Clinical Assistant Professor of Psychology, University of Texas Health Science Center at Dallas.

Steven M. Ross, Ph.D., — Chief, Substance Abuse Treatment Units, VA Medical Center, Salt Lake City, Utah, and Assistant Professor, Department of Psychiatry, University of Utah Medical Center.

M. Duncan Stanton, Ph.D., — Director of Family Therapy and Consultant, Drug Dependence Treatment Program, Philadelphia VA Hospital, Philadelphia, Pennsylvania, and Associate Professor of Psychology in Psychiatry, University of Pennsylvania School of Medicine.

Richard Wang, M.D., Ph.D., — Chief, Drug Dependence Treatment Program, Chief, Clinical Pharmacology Section, Wood VA Medical Center, Wood, Wisconsin, and Adjunct Professor of Pharmacology and Toxicology, Clinical Professor of Psychiatry, Associate Clinical Professor of Medicine, Medical College of Wisconsin.

Vincent Zarcone, Jr., M.D., — Director, Substance Abuse Treatment Unit, Palo Alto VA Medical Center, Palo Alto, California, and Professor of Clinical Psychiatry and Behavioral Sciences, Department of Psychiatry, Stanford University School of Medicine.

ACKNOWLEDGMENTS

This book has been a labor of love. It has provided us with an opportunity to relate with a group of mental health specialists who have applied their expertise and knowledge towards the amelioration of drug dependency and drug abuse. It afforded us with an occasion to interact with these specialists in a common endeavor to bring into public scrutiny the work that each has been involved with over a major portion of their professional life. It has developed into a network of interrelationships that will last beyond the publication of this book.

A majority of participants and contributors to this compendium spend their primary focus working within VA health care facilities, e.g. in hospitals, in medical centers, in outpatient clinics, and in a range of residential treatment programs. Many have both administrative and clinical functions while serving in the capacity as directors of programs in drug abuse. Several others are consultants to VA-Drug Dependence Treatment Programs and apply their special skills in a blend that is often unique and synergistic with the daily accomplishments of program staff. A few are researcher-clinicians operating out of drug abuse programs, conducting important studies to advance our understanding of drug dependent patients and ways to effectively treat them. Still others are collegeal personnel working on special projects under the auspices of drug dependence programs. Finally, some are located in the VA Central Office, coordinating the VA network of drug abuse programs in the nationwide VA health care system. Despite this diversity, there is a common thread — almost all are employed by the largest health care network in America, e.g. the Veterans Administration. They are among the most active public servants working in the drug abuse field today. The contributors to this volume have summarized their observations on drug abuse-related subject areas in which they have been working over extensive periods of time, either as clinicians, researchers, administrators, consultants, or a combination of these various roles. They are among the best. This has been a labor of love. This collection of papers present a reasonable codicil of work that have been recently ongoing in VA facilities. One word of disclaimer. This work does not represent the official position of the Veterans Administration concerning its treatment or research on drug dependence. However, it presents insights and program-related ideas from a number of VA clinicians and researchers.

This book could not have been completed without the help of others. Payne Thomas was patient and understanding throughout this project. The editorial staff is to be commended for their meticulous care in the editing process.

The senior author (R.J.C.) has the great fortune to work for and with Roy J. Korn, M.D., Chief of Staff at West VA Medical Center, Chicago. He has created an atmosphere of professionalism and mutual respect that I deeply appreciate. Alton Pruitt, Charles Paulk, and Alvis Carr served, at various periods of time, as Directors of our medical center. In this capacity, they were quite supportive and allowed our staff to function in a professional manner and without unnecessary intrusion. George Meschel, Ph.D., Chief of Psychology Service at West Side VA, has always been supportive and encouraging throughout this effort, and he has my gratitude. Lynne Morris, Chief of Library Service at West Side VA, was able to acquire many needed resources after personal efforts were at a standstill. The staff in our drug abuse program here has taught me much and often work diligently and without much recognition. Yet, they perform a meaningful and worthwhile service for which we are all thankful. Ed Nightengale, Ph.D., Joe O'Donnell, Ph.D., John Mendoza, Ph.D., and Ramon Stoner critically reviewed selected portions of the manuscript and their comments were quite helpful. However, the editors accept responsibility for the finished product. Finally, Patricia Crunican, Barbara Kendra, and Joan Wantrobski typed selected sections of this manuscript. Without their efforts this book still would be only an idea.

Many of the individual contributors included acknowledgment sections that were deleted by the editors. We hope these contributors will understand and find acceptable ways of expressing their appreciation to those that matter to them.

For over forty years the treatment of drug addiction had been primarily located with the U.S. Public Health Department at the Lexington and Fort Worth Hospitals. In 1974, the community-based approach for the treatment of drug addiction was officially sanctioned by the United States Government and these hospitals were closed. An account of the history and the important clinical work that went on at these facilities has been documented in the NIDA publication entitled *Drug Addiction and the U.S. Public Health Service,* which was published in 1978 and is available through the U.S. Government Printing Office.

The Veterans Administration now operates the largest program under direct management for delivering care to drug addicts. The publication of this book in some ways reflects the knowledge that has accrued in a decade of assuming this responsibility. We hope that this report will pique your interests in the work that is going on in the drug abuse field today and will provide the reader with important material and references for further study.

CONTENTS

DRUG DEPENDENT PATIENTS

Part I
Treatment Modalities

In treating drug dependent patients, the eventual goal is for them to live a nonaddicting and nonabusing life-style. Therefore, the initial chapter presents methods and techniques to withdraw a patient from opioid drugs. An unusual aspect of this presentation is the careful review of treatment outcomes with the various methods described in the paper. All too often, methods of detoxification are given without a balanced discussion of the effectiveness of these methods. Dorus presents a description of the abstinence syndrome (both early and protracted), discusses rapid versus gradual withdrawal, presents innovative alternatives to traditional physician-controlled detox schedules, deals with outpatient versus inpatient settings for detoxification, and reviews the newer medications that may be used in the detoxification process. We agree with Dorus that detoxification is only an initial step in the rehabilitation process. There are many methods to safely detoxify a patient without serious complications. Thus, the technology of detoxification is not an issue. The more salient concern is to learn how we can prevent relapse and maintain abstinence. It is in these areas that more research is needed.

Methadone maintenance seems to have outgrown the controversy that surrounded it during its introduction to the field. This may be due to the many benefits that this approach has brought to its patients and practitioners. Lahmeyer describes the early development of methadone as a treatment for drug addiction and then takes us through the "nuts and bolts" of this modality. An important realization is that methadone alone is insufficient to ameliorate drug addiction, and it must be supplanted with additional clinical services to improve outcome. The outcome results, including relevant patient and program variables, are summarized and its use with special populations, such as pregnant women and adolescents, is presented with professional objectivity.

Residential treatment approaches, typically referred to as therapeutic communities or "TCs," are among the most popular treatment modalities for drug dependent patients and commonly utilize individual and group treatment approaches. Thus, a TC is more of a philosophical approach than an actual treatment modality. Zarcone uses a gestalt-psychoanalytic orientation to describe the Satori Program under the auspices of the Palo Alto VA Hospital. He discusses the therapeutic processes utilized in this "house" stressing individuation and separateness, amidst contracting (a behavioral approach) in treating immature character defenses so common among drug addicts.

Ross and Callner describe the application of behavioral technology and behavior therapy approaches to the treatment of drug addicts. They discuss the role of learning and reinforcement and the etiology and maintenance of addiction and report the various methods of conducting a behavioral assessment or, more accurately, a "functional analysis of behavior." Behavior therapy is really a class of therapies and several of these are described by the authors, together with some research studies that have applied these methods to drug addicts. These various treatments are grouped according to whether they attempt to intervene at the stage of antecedent cues that set the stage for drug-taking behavior, the drug-taking behavior itself, or the reinforcing consequences that maintain drug abuse. The paper concludes with the authors' recommendations for a model treatment program utilizing behavioral methodology.

Although group therapy is endemic to most drug treatment programs, it is surprising to know how little attention has been given to group treatment of drug addiction in the professional literature. Craig argues that, irrespective of etiology and genesis, addict behavior is surprisingly similar across settings and can effectively be understood and conceptualized using a "game" analysis and approach. Traditional group therapy approaches have been modified when treating drug addicts and these various modifications, such as confrontation, marathon groups, goal-oriented styles and existential methods, are described, together with a discussion concerning their comparative effects. We are not at a stage of development in our knowledge of group treatment of addicts to state which approach is more efficacious. However, Craig highlights a number of structural problems in conducting group therapy with addicts that require special norms reflecting the limit-setting principles necessary in treating acting-out disorders.

Stanton focuses our attention away from the individual patient and urges us to adopt a family perspective to understand and treat drug-dependent patients. He describes the family treatment program at the Philadelphia VA Hospital, which was both a research and a clinical program testing the efficacy of family therapy with VA drug patients. Following the structural model of Minuchin and the strategic approaches popularized by Jay Haley, Stanton and his colleagues developed a treatment approach emphasizing treatment of the nuclear family of the drug addict. An important and unusual feature of this approach was that, with the cooperation of VA physicians, the family therapist maintained control over methadone dosages. In this way, power struggles were avoided and manipulations were undercut. Stanton describes both the method and the results of this highly successful innovation. Also included in this paper are twenty-one recruitment principles that maximize the entrance of the family into treatment.

An emerging trend within the substance abuse field is the combined treatment of alcoholics and drug addicts. Once thought impossible on theoretical and practical grounds, new insights and reformulations have resulted in growing considerations to such approaches. Four basic approaches seem possible: (1) we can treat drug addicts and alcoholics separately, (2) we can combine alcoholics and drug addiction programs administratively but not clinically, (3) we can co-mingle both populations into a single treatment program, or (4) we can administratively combine programs and treat the patients heterogeneously or homogeneously based on the needs of the individual patient. Heilman describes the alternative of co-mingling the two populations and, as readily apparent from a perusal of his paper, is a strong advocate of this approach. He describes the events leading up to the decision to treat addicts and alcoholics in a combined setting and discusses the experiences with this organizational and clinical alignment. It is a refreshingly personal appeal that is consistent with humanistic and holistic concepts presently in vogue.

CHAPTER 1

WITHDRAWAL FROM OPIOID DRUGS: A REVIEW OF TECHNIQUES AND OUTCOMES

Walter Dorus

Withdrawal from opioid drugs is one of the safest and simplest of procedures in medicine. The signs and symptoms (referred to as the opioid abstinence syndrome) experienced by the patient during withdrawal are short-lived and self-limited; most symptoms disappear within a few weeks after the last dose of opioid drug is taken. Withdrawal almost never results in complications or in death (Lipkowitz, Schwartz, and Lazarus, 1971).

In addition to being safe and simple, withdrawal, considered alone, is also perhaps the most unimportant phase of the rehabilitation of opioid addict; it only assumes importance in the context of the total treatment intervention plan for the patient. Therefore, our objective in discussing withdrawal is not only to review specific techniques, but to indicate how the withdrawal is incorporated into the total treatment plan for the patient: Is withdrawal, in the absence of any other intervention, justified as a treatment of narcotic addiction? Which type of withdrawal plan is most likely to facilitate the treatment process and hoped-for recovery of the patient?

A relevant consideration is the setting in which withdrawal occurs. Whether the withdrawal is done in a hospital or other controlled environment or whether it is done on an outpatient basis has a profound impact on the process. The characteristics of the patients themselves may be important in selecting a withdrawal plan. Young patients with mild habits may have different needs than "hard-core" addicts with high levels of tolerance and dependence and many years of addiction. Obviously the state of health of the patient, and the possibility of pregnancy in female patients, are important variables. The psychiatric and socioeconomic conditions of the patient need to be considered. A patient, for example, with a severely symptomatic psychiatric disturbance may use opioids to relieve unbearable anxiety or to temporarily obliterate psychological chaos. Such a patient might not be a good candidate for withdrawal. A patient who is stable and successfully functioning in most other areas of his life may be able to tolerate the stress of withdrawal better and be able to remain abstinent.

BACKGROUND

Kolb and Himmelsbach (1938) reviewed the literature on opioid withdrawal technique published to that time. They were careful to distinguish between the withdrawal process and outcome. None of the techniques of withdrawal advocated at that time had much impact on the natural course or outcome of addiction. No matter what technique was used, high rates of relapse were always encountered. Unfortunately, this fact is often forgotten. Even today many therapists as well as patients continue to confuse withdrawal with remission or cure.

In discussing withdrawal techniques, Kolb and Himmelsbach distinguish between two basic approaches to the withdrawal process. Slow withdrawal, gradually reducing patient's dose of opioid drug, lasting a month or more, had been the traditional appoach until the turn of the century. Rapid withdrawal, usually lasting less than a month, was the type of withdrawal most favored at the time their report was written. It is the approach upon which is grafted various pharmacological and somatic cures. The authors lucidly critiqued the impressionistic research prevalent at the time and pointed out the need for appropriate subject selection criteria and control groups. They concluded that none of the special treatments, which included belladonna, water balance, lipoid, endocrine, immunity, hypnosis, and prolonged barbiturate-induced sleep, were of any benefit to patients; indeed some were harmful.

Kolb and Himmelsbach's paper is a landmark in psychiatric literature. In addition to being an excellent discussion on the problems of withdrawal, it is one of the reports that lays the groundwork for modern psychiatric clinical research. The tradition of leadership in psychiatric research in the area of addictions has continued through the years.

The Acute Abstinence Syndrome and the Himmelsbach Scale for Assessing Its Severity

The signs and symptoms of narcotic withdrawal are characteristic; they are essentially the same regardless from which opioid the patient is withdrawing. The time course may be somewhat longer and the intensity of symptoms less severe in a long-acting opioid, such as methadone hydrochloride (methadone), than in the short-acting drugs, heroin and morphine.

Patients present a wide range of intensity of symptoms when in acute withdrawal. For some patients the experience is no more severe than a mild case of the flu and moderate insomnia. Others suffer much more. The factors that contribute to these differences are the level of dependence (the severity of the "habit"), the patient's expectation, and the patient's general health. The level of use of other drugs, especially alcohol and sedative-hypnotics, also influences the symptoms.

Patients experiencing acute withdrawal from heroin or morphine develop symptoms within eight to twelve hours. They appear anxious, irritable, apprehensive and demanding. The pupils are dilated, the most conspicuous sign in patients with blue eyes. Lacrimation is often present. Sniffing and sneezing, along with rhinorrhea, are other common signs. Piloerection is often observed. Intestinal hypermobility is present; in more severe cases vomiting and nausea may be present during the first two to four days. In some cases sweating may be profuse. Finally, it is common to observe mild increases in body temperature, pulse, respiration, and systolic and diastolic blood pressure. Clinically, recovery from these acute symptoms is usually complete within fourteen days.

The typical patient's most frequent complaint is of aching

pains in the joints, bones, and muscles. For some patients pain in the lower back, in large muscles of the leg, and hip and knee joints predominates. A smaller number will complain of pain and stiffness in their hands. Insomnia is the next most frequent complaint; it also tends to be the most persistent. Other frequent complaints include stomach cramps, hot and cold flashes, and anorexia.

A point system for assessing the severity of the acute abstinence syndrome developed by Himmelsbach appears in Table 1-I. This rating scheme utilizes observable signs that may be quantified by an observer. It ignores symptoms reported by patients that are subjective and may be influenced by mood, psychological lability, or clinical setting.

TABLE 1-I

POINT SYSTEM FOR MEASURING ABSTINENCE SYNDROME INTENSITY

	Points	Maximum
Yawning	1	1
Lacrimation	1	1
Rhinorrhea	1	1
Perspiration	1	1
Mydriasis	3	3
Tremor	3	3
Gooseflesh	3	3
Anorexia (40 percent decrease in caloric intake)	3	3
Restlessness	5	5
Emesis (each spell)	5	—
Fever (for each 0.1°C rise over mean addiction level)	1	—
Hyperpnea (for each resp./min. rise over mean addiction level)	1	—
Rise in AM systolic B.P. (for each 2 mmHg over mean addiction level)	1	15
Weight loss (AM) (for each pound from last day of addiction)	1	—

This system of rating severity of withdrawal remains useful clinically in estimating the severity of a patient's addiction. About 20 percent of patients presenting for treatment will exhibit a moderate or severe clinical picture of withdrawal. Eighty percent of addicts have "habits" that are too weak to result in severe symptoms during withdrawal, a situation which is unchanged for over forty years.

The acute *methadone* abstinence syndrome is quite similar to the morphine abstinence syndrome, although the onset is slower and the duration longer (Martin et al., 1973). Symptoms develop between twenty-four and forty-eight hours after the last dose of methadone. The maximum intensity of the symptoms occurs between the third and eighteenth day. Decreases in symptomatology begin typically during the third week of abstinence, with symptoms fluctuating widely from day to day. For most patients, symptoms of early abstinence largely disappear by the end of eight weeks. Table 1-II compares the morphine and methadone abstinence syndromes. Mydriasis, tremor, and piloerection are more prominent in methadone withdrawal than in withdrawal from short-acting opioids.

TABLE 1-II

RELATIVE PERCENTAGE AND RANK SCORES FOR
MORPHINE AND METHADONE ABSTINENCE SYNDROMES

	MORPHINE		*METHADONE*	
	% of Total Points	*Rank*	*% of Total Points*	*Rank*
Yawning Lacrimation Rhinorrhea Perspiration	4.4	6	14.7	4
Mydriasis Tremor Gooseflesh	9.3	5	20.6	1
Caloric Intake	1.9	8	3.4	7
Restlessness	0.8	9	2.2	9
Emesis	2.8	7	3.0	8
Fever	12.3	3	11.9	5
Hyperpnea	31.1	1	18.2	2
Systolic Blood Pressure	25.5	2	17.6	3
Weight loss (AM)	11.5	4	8.4	6

Protracted Abstinence

Following the resolution of the stormy acute abstinence syndrome, the patient enters a period characterized by more subtle signs and symptoms. This collection of signs and symptoms has been called the protracted abstinence syndrome. It was described by Himmelsbach (1942). He reported on twenty-one patients who were followed for nine months after abrupt withdrawal of opioids in a study that focused on physiological parameters. The results of this study indicated blood glucose returned to normal within one month; body temperature, caloric intake, sleep, and respiration required two to three months to return to normal; BMR, blood pressure, hematocrit, and sedimentation rate required four to six months. The protracted abstinence following the withdrawal of methadone is similar to the morphine protracted abstinence syndrome (Martin et al., 1973).

Subjective symptoms during the protracted abstinence syndrome tend to be varied and mild to moderate, and it is difficult to describe a distinct set of symptoms. In general, there is a trend for patients to feel tired and weak, to be withdrawn, apathetic, hypochondriacal, critical of others, to feel less efficient and popular and to have decreased feelings of well-being. It appears that these symptoms tend to wax and wane at irregular intervals during this period, although the general trend is towards improvement. Very often the patients will switch from insomnia to hypersomnia during protracted abstinence. These vague and unpleasant feelings may be related to the high risk of relapse during the early months of abstinence. Additional research is needed on the physiological and psychological aspects of the protracted abstinence syndrome's relationship to natural history of addiction.

Federal Regulations Relevant to Opioid Withdrawal

Before reviewing any of the current research on withdrawal it is necessary to outline the policy of the United States Food and Drug Administration (FDA) and Drug Enforcement Administration, which defines and prescribes certain aspects of treatment for addicted patients. Clinicians involved in treatment need to be familiar with three documents, which appeared in the *Federal Register:* (1) "Methadone — Listing as New Drug with Special Requirements and Opportunity for Hearing" (1972), (2) "Dextropropoxyphene Scheduled as Narcotics" (1980), and (3) "Methadone for Treating Narcotic Addicts; Joint Revision of Conditions for Use" (1980).

According to the regulations only methadone may be used for either the maintenance or withdrawal of narcotic addict patients. "Detoxification" is defined as dispensing for a period not in excess of twenty-one days of a narcotic drug in decreasing doses to an individual in order to bring the individual to a narcotic drug-free state within such a period. Any treatment that extends beyond twenty-one days is automatically defined as "maintenance treatment." This distinction is of considerable, practical importance since there are large numbers of patients who according to the regulations, are ineligible for maintenance treatment but for whom detoxification treatment may be very difficult. Any person who either is under the age of eighteen or who has a history of addiction dating back less than one year is not eligible for methadone maintenance treatment, and is only eligible for what has become popularly known as FDA twenty-one-day detoxification. Patients who fail at detoxification, that is patients who either are not helped sufficiently symptomatically or who relapsed to drug use, are required to wait a period of at least one week before they are allowed to begin a second course of detoxification. Patients must "fail" two detoxification attempts before they can be considered for a longer term withdrawal or maintenance program. The detoxification time limit has been a controversial regulation. The intent of the regulation was to prevent patients with minimal addiction histories from becoming more dependent on methadone. The length of time allowed would appear to be sufficient based on the inpatient studies conducted at Lexington Hospital. However, detoxification almost exclusively occurs today in nonprisoner outpatient treatment clinics. Several studies, which will be reviewed later, raised serious doubts as to the wisdom of this regulation. It is also important to note that physicians are prohibited from treating narcotic addicts as outpatients with methadone, either for detoxification or maintenance, except under the auspices of a federally licensed drug abuse treatment clinic.

WITHDRAWAL IN A GENERAL HOSPITAL SETTING

If a patient has been hospitalized for a medical problem other than opioid dependence, that problem should be treated first.

The patient's level of dependence should be determined and the patient should be kept on a dose of methadone adequate to maintain that level of addiction (Fultz et al., 1976).

House staff members have difficulty resisting the temptation to withdraw a patient, particularly when the patient seems sincerely well motivated. However, the probability of failure of the withdrawal under these circumstances are high. As soon as the withdrawal is under way, the patient's anxiety level and irritability level increase dramatically. The patient becomes difficult to manage and troublesome to the staff continually complaining and requesting medication. Typicaly, the patient changes his mind about being withdrawn but is afraid to tell this to his physician. Other patients convince themselves that they are successfully withdrawing, not taking into account the "small" doses of heroin visitors have begun to supply. As soon as the heroin use is discovered, the patient is discharged from the hospital following an angry confrontation among patients, nursing staff, physicians, and hospital security guards. The results of this often repeated drama include the fact that the patient's primary medical problem, which was serious enough to require hospitalization, may remain inadequately treated. The patient's expectation of poor treatment by hospital staff members is confirmed, and the staffs' notion regarding the impossibility of working with heroin addicts reinforced.

Hospital staff members must remember that patients with narcotic addiction experience the same feelings of impotence, anxiety, and loss of autonomy when they are hospitalized as do other patients. In fact, many narcotic addicts suffer a greater anxiety and sense of helplessness in this situation. The demands, arguments, and threats sometimes used by opioid dependent patients represents a fairly fragile defense aginst these feelings.

In summary, it is inappropriate to withdraw a patient who is in need of inpatient medical treatment for another problem. The best approach to the treatment of the dependent is to maintain the patient and arrange a referral to an inpatient or outpatient methadone treatment program where the patient can have his addiction managed under favorable conditions following the hospitalization.

However, there are times when withdrawal must be attempted while the patient is hospitalized. If,for example, there is no local drug abuse facility, or the nature or severity of the patient's condition preclude participation in such a program, withdrawal may begin only after the primary illness is well under control. The patient should be free of pain and not taking narcotic analgesics. Dose decreases should not exceed 5 mg of methadone a day. Larger dose decrements will almost certainly result in the emergence of withdrawal symptoms, which are difficult to control. The necessity for patient participation and cooperation in this procedure cannot be overemphasized. Without patient knowledge of the fact that he is being withdrawn and his active support in participation in the plan, a plan is likely to result in failure. Even if the patient's dose is reduced to zero, the chances are high that he will resume narcotic use at his first opportunity. Withdrawal does not equal remission or cure.

Because of the high rate of relapse and expense of inpatient withdrawal, this type of treatment is seldom indicated today. Exceptions to this general policy include physicians and nurses who are under great peer pressure from their colleagues to remain abstinent. Addicts in the medical profession are usually better able to make beneficial use of psychotherapy, particularly when their drug use following hospital discharge is carefully monitored by the local professional society.

A Comparison of Outpatient versus Hospital Methadone Detoxification

Wilson et al., (1975) reported their experience comparing inpatient hospital ten-day detoxification with an identical schedule for outpatients without complicating medical disorders. Patients were detoxified without any period of stabilization on methadone or specific psychological preparation. Ten patients were hospitalized and thirty were outpatients. One of the ten inpatients remained for the entire ten-day course. Six of the thirty outpatients completed ten days. Aproximately two-thirds of each group were followed up for three months following completion of the detoxification (the other were lost to follow-up). None of the hospitalized patients had remained drug-free and two of the outpatients remained drug-free. The authors conclude that patients received little benefit from either treatment approach and could report no significant difference between treatments. Only a few patients achieved a drug-free state, and of those who did all but one returned to narcotic use within two months.

SHORT-TERM OUTPATIENT DETOXIFICATION

The data to be reviewed in this section concern attempts to withdraw opioid dependent patients at the beginning of treatment. These detoxification procedures are rapid, generally lasting from seven to thirty days. Outpatient rapid detoxification programs have been viewed as either very successful or as total failures depending upon the point of view of the author and the outcome measures the author chooses to utilize. The most positive support of the detoxification programs come from Newman (1978), who stresses the relatively low cost, safety, and accessibility to patients of this procedure. Newman suggests that the goal of detoxification should be to provide symptomatic relief from the withdrawal syndrome while the body adjusts to a drug-free state. In his discussion, however, he provides no data to support the notion that the detoxification procedure used provides symptomatic relief and no data that any of the patients approach a drug-free state. Perhaps because of this he also suggests an even more limited goal for detoxification: to provide a safe, legal alternative to heroin for patients on those days which they come to the clinic. He states that a major justification for detoxification is that of consumer acceptance. Detoxification programs, especially those in New York City, have attracted many clients who it is claimed would not have participated in other types of programs. In fact, popularity has very little to do with effectiveness or benefits. Wesson and Smith (1974) consider detoxification a success "even if the individual resumes drug use on the first day following withdrawal."

Silsby and Tennat (1974) report on a seven-day ambulatory detoxification program for soldiers stationed in West Germany. This study is particularly noteworthy since, because of their active duty status in the army, follow-up was obtainable on all subjects. Of twenty-one patients studied, eight dropped out before completion of the seven-day treatment program. Thirteen (62%) completed the course but experienced symptoms that included nausea, vomiting, restlessness, sleeplessness, and rhinorrhea. At six-month follow-up two (9.5%) of the patients were opiate-free.

A much larger study by Canada (1972) in a civilian setting has findings similar to those of Silsby and Tennant. Canada used a thirty-day detoxification schedule. No attempt was made to select patients on the basis of length or severity of addiction. No data were reported on the course of detoxification, but intensive efforts were made to interview patients six months after their completion of their detoxification. One hundred and fifty-seven patients were successfully contacted; of these eleven (7%) were thought to be drug-free. Other studies (Wilson et al., 1974; Berle and Nyswander, 1964; Katon et al., 1972), each with minor modifications on the length of detoxification, supportive services offered, and patient demographic characteristics, have all resulted in similar unsatisfactory results when continuation of treatment or abstinence from opioid drugs are considered outcomes of interest. Finally, comprehensive review of clinic data from all federally funded treatment programs in this country lead Sells et al. (1978) to conclude that detoxification was not an effective treatment modality.

Addict patients and the general public have come to believe that rapid outpatient detoxification is a beneficial and efficacious form of treatment of opioid dependence. With the exception of Newman (1979) the almost universal conclusion has been that the approach is not effective. The advent of methadone maintenance detoxification programs has not changed the observation of Himmelsbach that detoxification is easy but that is an unimportant phase of the rehabilitation of opioid dependent persons. In terms of quality of the patients' lives, an opportunity for rehabilitation, and cost to society, the use of rapid outpatient detoxification, especially in the patient group for whom it has been mandated by the FDA, may be antitherapeutic.

The Rapid Detoxification Process

The studies reviewed have been descriptive studies that primarily focused on patient outcomes. Recently we (Dorus et al., 1981) compared FDA-mandated twenty-one-day detoxification of recently addicted individuals with a more gradual ninety-day schedule. We were interested in the patients' subjective experiences, heroin use during treatment, length of treatment, and global rating of the detoxification experience. Patients were randomly assigned to a standard twenty-one-day detoxification schedule or to an eighty-four-day schedule under double-blind conditions. The length of the study was ninety days. Patients assigned to the twenty-one-day detoxification received decreasing doses of methadone according to a predetermined schedule of twenty-one days followed by placebo the remaining sixty-nine days. Patients assigned to the eighty-four-day schedule received methadone for the eighty-four days and placebo for the final week. The mean starting dose for each group was 20 mg of methadone. None of the subjects were eligible for methadone maintenance because of addiction histories of less than two years.

The mean length of treatment for the twenty-one-day detoxification goup was 23.2 days; for the eighty-four-day group the mean length of treatment was 42.6. This difference is significant (p < .001). All twenty-one-day detoxification patients had dropped out of treatment by the end of week nine, when thirteen (35%) of the eighty-four-day patients remained in treatment. All five patients who remained in treatment at the end of the double-blind were in the eighty-four-day group. Symptom levels for each group begun were essentially the same for the first three weeks. Beyond three weeks the patients in the twenty-one-day group reported more severe symptoms than the eighty-four-day group. For example, at week six the twenty-one-day group had statistically significant (p < .05) reports on eleven symptoms, including abdominal cramps, chills, nausea, insomnia, sneezing, irritability, and depression. Overall, counselors rated seventeen (50%) of the patients in the twenty-one-day groups as having moderate to severe observable withdrawal symptoms compared to six (16.7%) of the patients in the eighty-four-day group. At a one-year follow-up of patients who were in treatment, twenty-two of the thirty-five patients in the twenty-one-day group had returned and were in treatment and twenty-four (64.9%) of the eighty-four-day group were in treatment. All followed-up patients in the twenty-one-day group were receiving methadone treatment; four of the twenty-four patients in the eighty-four-day group were abstinent from all drug use. The results of this study indicate that the twenty-one-day group dropped out of treatment earlier, had a higher percent of urine positive from morphine, reported higher levels of symptomatology, and were less likely to remain drug-free than patients in the more gradual withdrawal detoxification group. On the other hand, the percentage of patients reaching abstinence and remaining drug-free was not large in either group. The FDA's justification for the twenty-one-day detoxification time limit is that it reduced a potential from minimally addicted individuals to become more severely dependent upon methadone than they had been on heroin. The results of this study demonstrated that the gradual schedule does not result in a greater number of patients continuing or returning to methadone treatment. Modern methadone maintenance treatment has become part of the comprehensive approach, which may include counseling, legal assistance, family therapy, and employment training. However, in order for any of these treatment components to occur, the patient must cease heroin use and must be relatively free from withdrawal symptoms (Bourne and Slade, 1974). Our study indicates that to a certain extent this is possible for patients who were detoxified on the eighty-four-day schedule; clearly, patients treated with methadone for twenty-one-days missed the opportunity for the social and interpersonal aspects of treatment to occur.

GRADUAL WITHDRAWAL OF SUCCESSFULLY METHADONE-MAINTAINED PATIENTS

The Role of Rate and Expectation in Withdrawal From Methadone

We (Senay et al., 1977) evaluated the variables of rate and expectation in withdrawal from methadone maintenance in patients who had been successfully maintained on methadone maintenance treatment for at least one year. Unlike patients who had been studied earlier in inpatient facilities where rapid or abrupt detoxification was utilized, they had benefited from outpatient maintenance treatment. Among the questions we addressed was whether or not these people should continue to be maintained. If they attempted withdrawal, what is the optimum rate at which it should be undertaken? We studied the role of expectation, following up the observations that withdrawal symptoms were often objectively mild and, although subjectively severe, may be difficult for some patients to discriminate between ordinary anxiety and withdrawal symptoms. One hundred and twenty-seven patients were randomly divided into four study groups:

Group I: *Known maintenance.* These patients were maintained throughout the thirty-week experimental period.

Group II: *Blind maintenance.* This group was maintained on their starting dose during the study but both subject and staff were blind to their status.

Group III: *Rapid withdrawal.* This group was withdrawn from methadone over a period of ten weeks with dose reductions of 10 percent per week under double-blind conditions.

Group IV: *The gradual withdrawal.* This group was withdrawn over thirty weeks under double-blind conditions.

There was a statistically significant difference between groups in the percent of patients completing the study: 70 percent of known maintenance, 94 percent of blind maintenance, 24 percent of the rapid withdrawal groups, and 53 percent of the gradual withdrawal group completed the study (p < .001). The average weekly methdone dose for each group is illustrated in Figure 1-1. This figure shows that for the gradual withdrawal group the deviation from the projected rate and actual rate was not large. For the rapid withdrawal group, however, the discrepancy was large and subjects as a group were not able to adhere to the 10 percent dose decrement schedule. The figure indicates that the schedule was maintained for the first five weeks but became more gradual because of patient requested interruptions (which were allowed on a weekly basis) when an average dose of 16 mg was reached. We also reported a statistically significant difference among groups on an average weekly symptoms score (p < .05), with the rapid group having the highest rate of symptoms and the known maintenance the lowest. Especially noteworthy was the fact that 43 percent of the gradual withdrawal group never reported an urge to get high during the thirty-week study compared to 18 percent of the rapid withdrawal group (p < .001). There was also a significant difference between groups in the rate of positive urine reports for opiates and quinine (an adulterant frequently used to dilute heroin). The known maintenance group had an average rate of 10 percent positive urines, followed by the blind maintenance group, 13 percent, gradual withdrawal 17 percent, and rapid withdrawal 26 percent (p < .05).

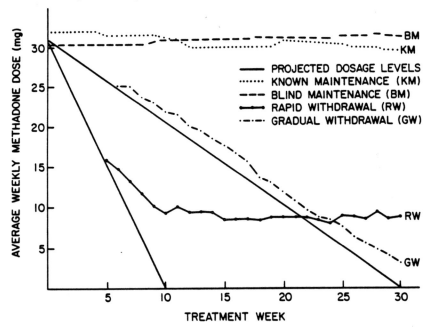

Figure 1-1. Average weekly methadone (mg) and projected dosage decrement by treatment group (N=127). (From *Archives of General Psychiatry, 34*:4, 361-367, 1977. Copyright 1977, American Medical Association.)

This study indicates that *the withdrawal process from outpatient methadone maintenance should be carried out with dose decrements of approximately 3 percent per week.* Large dose decrements were associated with increased dropout rates, illicit narcotics use, and subjective distress. The moderately large differences between the blind maintenance and known maintenance groups in these outcome measures suggests that formal treatment procedures should be developed for reducing the variance attributable to expectation. In general, the notion of "the slower the better" withdrawal of methadone outpatients has become generally accepted since publication of this paper. However, this study has certain important limitations. First, only the process of withdrawal itself was studied. This study shed little light on the post-withdrawal course of these patients. We were never able to determine, for example, what percentage of each group of patients continued in a successful remission and what percentage relapsed to opioid use. Second, it was not possible to conduct a follow-up comparison of the group of patients who were maintained on methadone with those who attempted withdrawal. Additional research on this question is needed.

Patient-Regulated Withdrawal from Opioids

It has been commonly believed that the narcotic addict patient's psychological status contributed so much to the withdrawal syndrome that the patient would be better off if kept blind to his dosage. In this way, withdrawal effects attributable to expectation might be minimized. Razani et al.,(1975) have referred to this as a "kind but paternalistic and authoritarian approach." Typically, the physician plans a schedule of methadone dose decreases ordered once or twice each week. Very often patients continue on placebo for one to several weeks after the completion of withdrawal. Patients generally have to make an appointment to see the physician to interrupt or discontinue the withdrawal. In many clinics, especially those in which counselors measure success in terms of how little methadone a patient is taking, interrupting withdrawal results in embarrassment and feelings of failure for the patient. Some patients elect to resume illicit drug use rather than admit to clinic staff members that they cannot tolerate the withdrawal.

Early in the history of methadone maintenance treatment, investigators began to systematically examine the necessity for blind dose levels in maintenance and withdrawal. Renault (1973) in a controlled experiment demonstrated that patients' knowledge of dose did not lead to requests for increases or frequent dose changes. Later, Goldstein (1975) allowed methadone-maintained patients to adjust their own dose levels within certain parameters. This study demonstrated positive, responsible behavior by the vast majority of patients with little difference in mean dose between physician-regulated and self-regulated patient.

Partial Patient Regulation of Withdrawal in Day Care and Inpatient Settings

The first report of active patient participation in withdrawal was published by Raynes and Patch (1973). They compared two groups of day care patients who were "mostly" active heroin addicts, although some methadone-maintained patients were included. Patients in the control group were withdrawn at the rate of 5 mg of methadone per day; the experimental group was reduced automatically 5 mg every three days, but they had the option of requesting 5 mg decreasing on days when no decrease was scheduled. Mean stabilization doses (62.2 mg for study patients, 50.7 mg for controls) were not significantly different. Twenty of thirty-nine experimental patients compared to ten of thirty-five control patients completed withdrawal. The difference is statistically significant ($p < .05$). The mean length of stay in treatment was twenty-one days for the experimental group and approximately 15.5 days for the control group. No data on concurrent heroin use was reported, nor were any follow-up data presented. Nevertheless, the study demonstrated that narcotic addicts would cooperate in their own withdrawal and do so with better results than a similar group entirely physician-regulated. The authors observed that the more successful group took longer to withdraw than the controlled group and longer on the average than the FDA twenty-one-day limit for detoxification. They suggest that the FDA time limit may be somewhat antitherapeutic since if the period was extended it might allow more patients to be successfully treated by detoxification.

Razani et al., (1975) described their experience with thirty heroin addicts who were judged to have habits too severe to permit the nonmedically managed abrupt withdrawal to which other applicants were assigned. These patients were hospitalized and allowed to ask for as much methadone as they needed, up to 20 mg per twelve-hour period. Methadone was dispensed in 5 mg doses. Patients were told that they should withdraw as quickly as they could comfortably do so. None of the patients had medical conditions that complicated their treatment. This procedure resulted in very successful withdrawal: twenty-eight patients completed withdrawal within seven days, twenty-two reported their experience as satisfactory or very satisfactory. The authors point out that these patients took a shorter time to complete detoxification than patients on schedules determined solely by physician based on clinical judgment. "The active role that patients took in their own detoxification enhanced their self-esteem and feeling of mastery in controlling their habits." The research was conducted in an acute psychiatric unit where patients' access to drugs could be controlled. Thus, removal from the regular environment and control over the possibility of obtaining drugs were critical factors in the success of this research. Although the authors state that this method of withdrawal could be utilized in any inpatient setting, my experience indicates that it would be successful only in settings that offer considerably more control and surveilance than a typical general hospital ward could offer.

Self-regulated Withdrawal in Outpatients

Fulwiler et al., (1979) were the first to publish a comparison of self-regulated rapid withdrawal on an outpatient basis. Their patients were active heroin addicts who were stabilized on 40 mg of methadone for two days prior to beginning the study. Patients were assigned to one of three groups: (1) In the physician-controlled group, patients were detoxified on a fixed schedule with 5 mg decreases every other day. (2) In the self-regulated group, patients were allowed 12 days to regulate their dosage. All changes were limited to 5 mg daily and within a range of 0 to 5 mg total daily dose. Patients in this group who failed to detoxify within fourteen days were converted to a physician-regulated schedule and detoxified at the rate of 5 mg per day. (3) In the third (modified self-regulated) group the patients were scheduled for 5 mg decreases each day but only received it if they agreed. Each day the nurse would ask them "Do you wish a dose decreased today?" None of the patients, either the self-regulated group or the modified self-regulated group, completed detoxification within the planned fourteen days, and all were ultimately detoxified on the physician-controlled schedule. However, the self-regulated groups had a significantly lower percentage of positive urinalysis tests for opiates than the physician-controlled group during days three to fourteen, and patients in the self-regulated groups continued in treatment longer than the physician-controlled group. All patients dropped out of treatment within twenty-two days. No follow-up data were given. The authors conclude that their results indicated that simple self-regulation in outpatient conditions on newly enrolled patients will usually "encourage maintenance rather than detoxification." They suggest that treatment policy should not pressure addicts to begin detoxification, at least during their first few days of treatment.

Recently we (Dorus et al., 1980) presented a preliminary report on self-regulated withdrawal in successfully methadone-maintained outpatients. This research was primarily designed to determine if self-regulated withdrawal was feasible for the growing numbers of patients who seemed interested in a short-time methadone maintenance program rather than an open-ended maintenance treatment contract. In order to qualify for this study patients had to have a stable dose of methadone for a minimum of thirty days and a maximum of ninety days. Prior to beginning withdrawal, patients were required to have opioid-free urinalysis for four consecutive weeks and not to have missed more than two consecutive treatment days. Patients in the self-regulated group were allowed to change their dose a maximum of 5 mg each day. Patients could raise or lower their dose level but they were not allowed to raise their dose higher than their starting level. Patients in the self-regulated group were allowed twenty-two weeks to complete their withdrawal. Concurrently, a control group of patients was withdrawn on a predetermined schedule of 5 percent dose decreases per week, which enabled them to complete withdrawal in approximately twenty weeks.

The most interesting finding of this study was the lack of difference between the self-regulated and the physician-regulated group (Figure 1-2). Sixteen (32%) of the self-regulated patients completed withdrawal during the twenty-two-week trial period. Five more (10%) completed withdrawal under physician control within a few weeks after the end of the study. The findings of this study are consistent with those of Renault (1973) and Goldstein (1975), who were impressed by the lack of difference in the pharmacological aspect of treatment when patient participation was increased. The counselors at the clinic felt that patients participating in the study believed that self-regulation was a definite improvement, this despite the fact that initially 62 percent of the patients indicated that they would prefer to be withdrawn on a physician-planned schedule. The group of patients studied here were on the average highly motivated to withdraw and had demonstrated a good response to initial methadone stabilization therapy. Patients who had evidence of even rare heroin use or who missed treatment frequently were not allowed to participate. The staff were well versed on the research that indicated the advantages of small dose decrements and a slow overall withdrawal schedule. We had no doubt that this knowledge accounted in part for the gradual schedule that patients, on the average, chose to follow. This self-regulation scheme might not be as successful in the absence of such a specifically trained supportive staff. We were unable to provide any information on the patients following their participation in the research.

Although none of the research on patient-regulated withdrawal from narcotics is entirely satisfactory, a review of this literature indicates that in the proper inpatient or outpatient settings this approach is as successful or more successful than the traditional physician-regulated treatment. However, none of the research addresses the overall impact of this procedure on the

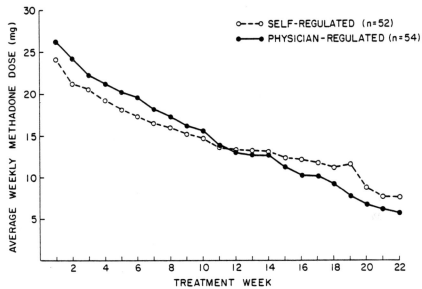

AVERAGE WEEKLY METHADONE DOSE FOR
SELF-REGULATED AND PHYSICIAN REGULATED GROUPS (n=106)

Figure 1-2. Average weekly methadone dose for self-regulated and physician regulated groups (N=106.)[2] (From *Archives of General Psychiatry, 28*: 286-295, Copyright 1973, American Medical Association.)

natural history of the patient's addiction. In one study (Fulwiler et al., 1979), most of the patients never achieved a remission based on the high rate of urine positive for opioids. The other reports give little or no data on the patients' concurrent use of narcotics or post-treatment course.

Non-specific Supports During Withdrawal

Clinicians have developed a variety of ways to deal with patients' complaints, concerns, and symptoms during withdrawal. Several descriptions have been published (Chappel et al., 1973; Kleber, 1977), but to my knowledge there has been no research comparing efficiencies of any of the possible group and individual counseling activities that could be helpful.

Similarly, the use of adjunctive medications has received little study. Over the years, the use of little extra doses of opioids has been reported (Himmelsbach, 1942; Martin et al., 1973) during withdrawal, and even after the completion of withdrawal (Kleber, 1977). Beyond confounding the data on the signs and symptoms of withdrawal, it is unclear whether this practice has any useful impact.

In my experience patients complain most bitterly about insomnia and irritability during withdrawal. Typically, patients request diazepam for these symptoms. In addition to its anti-anxiety effects, there are two additional reasons why patients may request this drug: (1) patients can feel the "rush" from diazepam because of its rapid absorption, and (2) diazepam apparently inhibits methadone metabolism (Spaulding et al., 1974). There is no research regarding efficacy of prescribing diazepam or other benzodiazepines during withdrawal. Whenever I do prescribe benzodiazephines, I arrange to have it dispensed by the clinic nurse along with the patient's methadone. The nurse dispenses the number of tablets the patient will require until his next clinic visit. This is an automatic procedure with all patients who receive prescriptions and not related to prior patient behavior or judgments about patient's trustworthiness. This procedure eliminates the possibility of diversion (lost prescriptions) and overdose. In addition, it represents a tangible additional support supplied by the clinic, which the patient carries.

Propoxyphene napsylate (Darvon®) has been proposed as an alternative agent for withdrawal. Because of propoxyphene's weak narcotic agonist effects it was hoped that it would be preferable to methadone in patients with mild heroin dependence. Tennant et al., (1975) reported on the results of double-blind comparison of methadone and propoxyphene in two groups of 36 outpatient heroin addicts using the FDA 21-day withdrawal schedule. There were few differences in outcome between groups with most of the patients relapsing to heroin use or entering maintenance programs. The groups did differ significantly in two ways: (1) the methadone group had significantly lower daily average ($p < .001$) of withdrawal symptom scores than the propoxyphene group; (2) the methadone group remained in treatment longer (18.4 vs. 15.2 days, $p < .05$).

Recently, the Drug Enforcement Administration reclassified

propoxyphene as a class IV narcotic substance (Dextropropoxyphene Scheduled as Narcotics, 1980). This classification made it illegal to use propoxyphene for the treatment of narcotic addiction, leaving methadone as the only currently approved drug.

Tricyclic antidepressants and major tranquilizers have not been particularly successful in treating withdrawal symptoms and little research on their use has been published. Because of the toxicity of these compounds and the difficulty of treating overdoses, it is prudent to avoid their use as general supportive medication during withdrawal.

NEW NON-OPIOID PHARMACOLOGIC AGENTS

Clonidine

Clonidine is a centrally active alpha-2-adrenergic agonist which is used in the treatment of hypertension. The alpha-adrenergic activity results in an inhibition of certain central nervous system centers. One of these centers, the locus coeruleus, is an important center for modulation of emotions, behaviors, and symptoms of the type suppressed by opioid drugs (Gold et al., 1979). The locus coeruleus is inhibited both by opioids and alpha-2-adrenergic stimulation. During withdrawal the locus coeruleus is released from opioid suppression, which results in an enormous burst of sympathetic activity: lacrimation, rhinorrhea, insomnia, fever, piloerection, etc. (Cohen, 1980). Gold and his associates speculated that administering clonidine could diminish these symptoms by inhibiting the locus coeruleus with alpha-adrenergic activity. They administered clonidine to hospitalized methadone-maintained and heroin addict patients following abrupt withdrawal. Initially, twelve patients were studied. All patients reported marked relief of subjective distress. There was also a reduction in objective withdrawal signs. Clonidine produced no "high" or euphoria. The only persistent symptoms were sleep disturbance and a feeling of sluggishness. Ten of the original twelve patients were opioid- and clonidine-free at two-week follow-up. In a more recent report Gold et al., (1980) demonstrated that clonidine was equally successful in suppressing symptoms and signs of abrupt withdrawal in patients maintained on 15, 50, and 75 mg of methadone. The only symptoms reported were irritability and difficulty in falling asleep.

The first outpatient clinical trial of clonidine was reported by Washton and Resnick (1980). Seventy patients were studied: fifty-nine were methadone maintained and eleven were heroin using. Twenty of the methadone-maintained patients received clonidine in conjunction with gradual methadone dose reduction; the remaining patients were abruptly withdrawn from opioids. Successful outcome was defined as remaining opioid free for ten days. The most successful group was the abruptly withdrawn methadone maintenance patients; thirty-five (70%) of these patients successfully completed the treatment. The least successful group was the heroin using patients; four (36%) successfully completed treatment. Most patients complained that insomnia, lethargy, lightheadedness, and dizziness was a problem on at least one occasion. Six of the seventy patients could not tolerate even low doses of clonidine because of hypotensive episodes or excessive sedation. For most patients a regimen of 0.1 mg or 0.2 mg every four to six hours provided adequate suppression of withdrawal symptoms with an unacceptable level of side effects.

It seems apparent that clonidine will become a useful adjunct in the withdrawal of opioid dependent patients. However, certain limitations to its use are emerging. First is the fact that tolerance to the withdrawal-suppressing effects of clonidine develops quickly. After ten to fourteen days clonidine loses most of its effectiveness. We have observed patients who initially respond well to clonidine but who occasionally continued to use heroin and who have moderate to severe withdrawal symptoms reemerge despite their continued clonidine use. A second problem is the marked effects on blood pressure the drug possesses. Hypotensive episodes during clonidine administration and potentially dangerous episodes of hypertension if the drug is abruptly withdrawn are serious concerns. Finally, since clonidine is helpful only for a few days following the withdrawal, it will not have much impact on the natural course of addiction. A potential important use of clonidine may be found if the narcotic antagonist naltrexone is approved for clinical use. Clonidine may help bridge the gap between the termination of methadone maintenance and the induction of patients on naltrexone. The utilization of clonidine in this regard is currently being investigated.

BUPRENORPHINE

Buprenorphine is a partial opioid agonist and partial antagonist and as such combines in one drug the characteristics of both methadone and naltrexone (Mello and Mendelson, 1980). The subjective effects of buprenorphine are similar to those of morphine, and former heroin addict patients report that they like the drug as well as morphine. In addition, buprenorphine effectively antagonizes high doses of morphine for twenty-four to thirty-six hours. Most interesting is the fact that termination of maintenance with high doses of buprenorphine results in mild and short-lived withdrawal signs and symptoms. It is too early to determine if this drug will be effective either as a maintenance or withdrawal agent. Appropriate clinical studies have not yet been carried out or are incomplete. In addition, an oral preparation of this substance had not yet been developed. Nevertheless, its unusual combination of actions has stimulated a great deal of interest in researchers and clinicians.

POST-WITHDRAWAL COURSE OF SUCCESSFULLY METHADONE-MAINTAINED PATIENTS

There is little doubt remaining about the success of methadone maintenance. Thousands of ex–heroin addicts are now able to lead essentially normal, conventional lives in every respect while maintained on methadone. The patients, their families, and society have benefited from this treatment. Successful methadone-maintained patients face a dilemma. Must they commit themselves to a lifetime of maintenance? Do they risk losing their slowly won gains by attempting to achieve abstinence? The central issue is not how many patients can be gotten to zero dose of methadone. Numerous methods for doing so have been described in this chapter. Under proper conditions every one can be withdrawn from methadone. Where our data have been lacking is in the description of successfully maintained patients' postwithdrawal course. The information that has been available has often been confusing and contradictory and involved only very short periods of follow-up. Chappel et al., (1973) were able to follow-up 127 patients one year after completing withdrawal. They report that 22 percent of these patients remained abstinent for fifty-two weeks. The highest rate of success were among patients who were therapeutically withdrawn and who attended regular withdrawal group meetings. Stimmel and Rabin (1974) followed up 198 withdrawn maintenance patients. Thirty-four (20%) were identified as drug-free. However, the follow-up period for patients varied with some of the follow-ups being very short. Cushman (1974) reviewed follow-up data on 396 withdrawn patients to determine how many had reached a stable narcotic-free state. Time of interview was fourteen (± 5) months after the last methadone dose. Forty-eight (12%) of the patients were judged to be functioning very well. Factors associated with successful detoxification included slow detoxification, full-time employment, positive motivation for detoxification, and high degree of assimilation into the nondrug world. Factors associated with the narcotic-free state were positive motivation for detoxification, high degree of assimilation into the nondrug world, and satisfactory completion of detoxification. The most positive results in a more or less typical group of heroin addicts were recorded by Riordan et al. (1976). They reported a follow-up of thirty-eight successfully withdrawn methadone-maintenance patients, an average of 19.5 months following completion of withdrawal (range 6 to 44 months). Of this group twenty-six (68%) had remained drug free. Of the remaining twelve patients (32%), five had returned to methadone treatment and seven were actively using drugs. The patients who were best able to maintain abstinence following withdrawal were black and had lower income and lesser social achievement at the time of admission to treatment. The authors speculate that their program, which treats drug dependence behavior in terms of social rehabilitation, may make a greater impact on these individuals. The more successful patients were also older and had shorter courses of addiction. The mean length of withdrawal for all patients was seven months, preceded by a mean length of methadone maintenance of twenty-five months in the group that successfully withdrew versus nineteen months in the group that relapsed to drug use. The results of this study are more positive than the results of other studies. It is difficult to imagine why these patients have done so much better, on the average, than patients reported in other studies. The high employment rates both on admission and at follow-up and the small-town setting in which the study took place may have been contributed to the patients' success.

Dole and Newman (1980) summarized a follow-up of persons in New York City who had participated in methadone-maintenance programs. This study was conducted on a random sample of 1,513 names chosen from the approximately 96,500 names in New York City's methadone-maintenance registry. Ninety-five percent of this sample were ultimately contacted. The results indicated that 83 percent of the patients did well so long as they were receiving methadone maintenance. The majority of them relapsed after termination of methadone maintenance, usually within two months. Overall, 8 percent of the patients who had completed withdrawal could be considered in satisfactory condition, while 63 percent of patients remaining in treatment were free from all drug and behavioral problems. Approximately 20 percent of the patients entering treatment were considered to have achieved social rehabilitation by staff members at the time of discharge. One hundred and sixty-seven patients leaving treatment were so classified. Of this group fifty-eight (34%) had not relapsed to opioids or developed other major problems during the period between discharge and follow-up. Dole and Newman summarize their findings: "Methadone, given in an adequate daily dose, enables many otherwise intractable addicts to live a normal life, but does not cure their disease. When maintenance is terminated, the majority of patients will relapse to illicit narcotics."

Thus, although we have learned a great deal about the technique and process of withdrawal from opioid drugs, we have not developed a technology of rehabilitation or therapy that enables the majority of opioid dependent persons to avoid quickly relapsing. Only after our rehabilitation treatment develops to the point where patients may reasonably be assured of continued remission following withdrawal should we encourage successfully maintained patients to withdraw.

REFERENCES

Bass, U. F.; and Brown, B. S.: Methadone maintenance and methadone detoxification: A comparison of retention rates and client characteristics. *Int J Addict, 8*:6, 889-895, 1973.

Berle, B.; and Nyswander, M: Ambulatory withdrawal treatment in heroin addicts. *NY State J Med, 64*:1846-1948, 1964.

Bourne, P. G.; and Slade, J. D.: Methadone: The mechanism of its success. *J Nerv Ment Disorders, 159*:5, 371-375, 1974.

Canada, A. T., Jr.: Methadone in a 30-day detoxification program for narcotic addicts: A critical review. *Int J Addict, 7*:4, 613-617, 1972.

Chappel, J.; Skolnick, C. J.; and Senay, E.: Techniques of withdrawal from Methadone-maintained patients. In *Proceedings of the Fifth National Conference on Methadone Treatment, Washington, D.C.,* 1973. New York: NAPAN, 1973, pp. 482-489.

Cohen, S.: Clonidine (Catapress): Nonopiate detoxification. *Drug Abuse Alcoholism Newsletter, 9*:6, July, 1980.

Cushman, P., Jr.: Detoxification of rehabilitated methadone patients: frequency and predictors of long-term success. *Am J Drug Alcohol Abuse, 1*:3, 393-408, 1974.

Cushman, P., Jr.; and Dole, V. P.: Detoxification of rehabilitated Methdone-maintained patients. *JAMA, 226*:7, 747-752, 1973

Dextrotropoxyphene Scheduled as Narcotics, June, 1980. *Federal Register,* Part 1308, *41*:123.

Dole, V. P., and Newman, R.: Methadone maintenance treatment of narcotic addiction. *Medical Tribune,* p. 12, July 2, 1980.

Dorus, W.; Joseph, M. L.; Senay, E. C.; and Krystal, J.: Self-regulated withdrawal in outpatient methadone-maintenance programs. In Faulkinberry, R. (Ed.): *Drug Problems of the 70's, Solutions for the 80's.* Lafayette, La., Endac Enterprises, 1980, pp. 315-319.

Dorus, W.; Senay, E. C.; and Showalter, C. V.: Short term detoxification with methadone. *Ann NY Acad Sci,* in press, 1981.

Fultz, J. M.; Rouda, S.; and Senay, E. C.: Treatment of hospitalized narcotic addicts. *Ill Med J, 149*:454-460, 1976.

Fulwiler, R. L.; Hargreaves, W. A.; and Bortman, R. A.: Detoxification from heroin using self vs physician regulation of methadone dose. *Int J Addict, 14*:2, 289-298, 1979.

Gold, M. S.; Pottash, A. L. C.; Sweeney, D. R.; and Kleber, H. D.: Effect of methadone dosage on clonidine detoxification efficacy. *Am J Psychiat, 137*:3, 375-376, 1980.

Gold, M. S.; Redmond, D. E.; and Kleber, H. D.: Noradrenergic hyperactivity in opiate withdrawal supported by clonidine reversal of opiate withdrawal. *Am J Psychiat, 136*:1, 100-102, 1979.

Goldstein, A.; Hansteen, R. W.; and Horns, W. H.: Control of methadone dosage by patients. *JAMA, 234*:7, 734-737, 1975.

Himmelsbach, C. K.: Clinical studies of drug addiction. *Arch Int Med, 69*:766-772, 1942.

Himmelsbach, C. K.: The morphine abstinence syndrome: Its nature and treatment. *Ann Int Med, 15*:829-839, 1941.

Katon, R.; Dupont, R.; and Rubenstein, R.: Methadone detoxification of heroin addicts. In *Proceedings: Fourth National Conference on Methadone Treatment.* San Francisco, NAPAN, 1972, pp.181-186.

Kleber, H. D.: Detoxification from methadone maintenance: The state of the art. *Int J Addict, 12*:7, 807-820, 1977.

Kolb, L.; and Himmelsbach, C. K.: Clinical studies of drug addiction, III. *Am J Psychiat, 94*:2, 759-799, 1938.

Lipkowitz, M. H.; Schwartz, D. W.; and Lazarus, R. J.: Abrupt withdrawal of maintenance methadone. *JAMA, 217*:13, 1860-1861, 1971.

Martin, W. R.; Jasinski, D. R.; Haertzen, C. A.; Kay, D. C.; Jones, B. E.; Mansky, P. A.; and Carpenter, R. W.: Methadone — A reevaluation. *Arch Gen Psychiat, 28*:286-295, 1973.

Mello, N. K.; and Mendelson, J. H.: Buprenorphine suppresses heroin use by heroin addicts. *Science, 207*:8, 657-659, 1980.

Methadone for Treating Narcotic Addicts; Joint Revision of Conditions for Use, September 19, 1980. *Federal Register, Part III, 45*:184, pp. 62694-62718.

Methadone — Listing as New Drug with Special Requirements and Opportunity for Hearing, December 15, 1972. *Federal Register, Part III, 37*:242, pp. 26790-26907.

Newman, R. G: Detoxification treatment of narcotic addicts. In Dupont, R. L.; Goldstein, A.; and O'Donnell, J (Eds.): *Handbook on Drug Abuse.* Rockville, Md., National Institute on Drug Abuse, 1979.

Raynes, A. E.; and Patch, V. D.: An improved detoxification technique for heroin addicts. *Arch Gen Psychiat, 29*:417-419, 1973.

Razani, J.; Chisholm, D.; Glasser, M.; and Kappeler, T.: Self-regulated methadone detoxification of heroin addicts. *Arch Gen Psychiat, 32*:909-911, 1975.

Renault, P. F.: Methadone maintenance: The effect of knowledge of dosage. *Int J Addict, 8*:1, 41-47, 1973.

Riordan, C. E.; Mezritz, M.; Slobetz, F.; and Kleber, H. D.: Successful detoxification from methadone maintenance. *JAMA, 235*:24, 2604-2607, 1976.

Sells, S.; Demaree, R.; and Hornick, C.: *The Comparative Effectiveness of Methadone Maintenance, Therapeutic Community, Outpatient Drug Free, and Outpatient Detoxification Treatments for Drug Users in the DARP: Cohort 1-2*

Followup Study. IBR Report 78-4. Ft. Worth, Texas Christian University, Institute of Technical Research, 1978.

Senay, E. C.; Dorus, W.; Goldberg, F.; and Thornton, W.: Withdrawal from methadone maintenance. *Arch Gen Psychiat, 34*:361-367, 1977.

Sheffet, A.; Quinones, M.; Lavenhar, M. A.; Doyle, K.; and Prager, H.: An evaluation of detoxification as an initial step in the treatment of heroin addiction. *Am J Psychiat, 133*:3, 337-340, 1976.

Silsby, H.; and Tennant, F. S., Jr.: Short-term, ambulatory detoxification of opiate addicts using methadone. *Int J Addict, 9*:1, 167-170, 1974.

Spaulding, T. C.; Minium, L.; Kotake, A. N.; and Takemori, A. I.: The effect of diazepam on the metabolism of methadone by the liver of methadone-dependent rats. *Drug Metab Disposition, 2*:458-463, 1974.

Stimmel, B., and Rabin, J.: The ability to remain abstinant upon leaving methadone maintenance: A prospective study. *Am J Drug Alcohol Abuse, 1*: 379–391, 1974.

Tennant, F. S.; Russell, B. A.; Casas, S. K.; and Bieich, R. N.: A comparison of propoxyphene and methadone. *JAMA, 232*:10, 1019-1022, 1975.

Washton, A. M.; and Resnick, R. B.: Clonidine for opiate detoxification: Outpatient clinical trials. *Am J Psychiat, 137*:9, 655-659, 1980.

Wesson, D. R.; and Smith, D. E.: A conceptual approach to detoxification. *J Psychedelic Drugs, 6*:2, 161-168, 1974.

Wilson, B. K.; Elms, R. R.; and Thomson, C. P.: Low-dosage use of methadone in extended detoxification. *Arch Gen Psychiat, 31*:233-236, 1974.

Wilson, B. K.; Elms, R. R.; and Thomson, C. P.: Outpatient vs. hospital methadone detoxification: An experimental comparison. *Int J Addict, 10*:1, 13-21, 1975.

CHAPTER 2

METHADONE MAINTENANCE

Henry Lahmeyer

HISTORICAL PERSPECTIVE

Methadone was synthesized in the early 1940s. It was first used as an analgesic and sedative agent with properties similar to morphine. The use of long-lasting narcotics as a maintenance agent was not considered and indeed did not appear as a concept in this country until 1964 when Dole and Nyswander initiated the use of oral methadone as a maintenance agent in the treatment of chronic heroin addiction (1965). This situation was somewhat different in England, where prior to 1964 maintenance heroin clinics had been established; although many problems developed with this form of treatment, this modality continues today (Cohen and Stimmel, 1978).

Marie Nyswander, a psychiatrist who had worked with narcotic addicts extensively, felt that psychologically based therapies were inadequate to treat heroin addicts and collaborated with Vincent Dole of the Rockefeller University in a pilot study treating twenty-two patients who were addicted to heroin with oral methadone and found that the methadone relieved "narcotic hunger" and seemed to "block" the euphoric effects of the average heroin dose. They also provided a program of employment rehabilitation, helped clients return to school, and to become reconciled with their families. This study reported remarkable results with most of the twenty-two patients obtaining employment or returning to school. Methadone dosage in this study was from 10 to 180 mg per day.

The concept of methadone maintenance spread from New

York to other large metropolitan areas including Chicago, Philadelphia, St. Louis, Los Angeles, etc. By 1969, programs were established in twenty-three cities throughout the country treating more than 60,000 persons.

The administration of these drug abuse programs has come from several sources. In 1974, Public Law 93-281 (the Narcotic Treatment Act) firmly established the legal basis for the federal government's control of methadone maintenance. Under this act the Secretary of Health, Education, and Welfare was required to publish treatment standards for the use of methadone. All practitioners engaged in maintenance or detoxification of narcotic addicts were required to obtain annual registration from the Drug Enforcement Agency (DEA), the Bureau of the Department of Justice which was given the responsibility of enforcing the federal guidelines with respect to registration. The FDA also took action to discourage prolonged use of methadone as a maintenance agent by stating that methadone maintenance should be discouraged beyond two years of initiation of treatment, unless clinical judgement indicated that maintenance should be continued for a longer period of time. This specific regulation has aroused great controversy because of the difficulty many addicts have in remaining abstinent. Another liability of the close federal intervention in drug abuse maintenance programs has been the data banks of patient information and the problems of confidentiality (see Dole, 1973, for further review of these issues). Dole and Nyswander (1976) note that the problem of diversion of methadone has arisen over the past ten years and has led to tighter regulation of "take home medication." The current requirement that patients return to the clinic, unless they have nearly perfect records while in the clinic or are working regularly, has led many clients to drop out of treatment.

Dole and Nyswander, in giving their general impressions after ten years of experience in methadone maintenance, note that the majority of heroin addicts in our cities remain on the streets and that programs have lost the ability to attract these addicts to treatment. Further they add "an unfortunate consequence of the early enthusiasm for methadone treatment is today's general disenchantment with chemotherapy for addicts. What was not anticipated at the outset was the nearly universal reaction against the concept of substituting one drug for another . . ."

Dole and Nyswander's pessimism addresses the inability of current programs to completely alleviate the problems of heroin addiction. The early reports do not clearly spell out, however, realistic *and* unrealistic goals of methadone maintenance, so "failure" was inevitable. Many problems that are not therapeutic issues remain unsolved. It must be admitted that many therapeutic issues have yet to be adequately resolved. This will become easier when circumscribed problems are attacked.

Epidemiology

It is estimated that the number of heroin users range somewhere between 200,000 and 800,000 in this country (Rittenhouse, 1977). The number of these users who were enrolled in methadone maintenance is currently estimated to be 71,000 (NIDA) but most observers agree that the percentage of heroin users that are now on methadone maintenance is dropping and that the composition is changing to an older population (McLellan et al., 1979).

The loss of human productivity secondary to heroin abuse is difficult to measure, but clearly is very great. Not only are addicts mostly unemployed but they kill, steal from, and injure other productive individuals. One estimate of the human tragedy is the mortality rate among heroin addicts. In New York City, heroin was the single leading cause of death in young men between the ages of thirteen and thirty-five during 1970 (Concool et al., 1979).

The racial composition is shifting to an increased number of Hispanics.

The drugs of abuse are shifting from heroin to polydrugs and other narcotics (Simpson, 1974; Lahmeyer and Steingold, 1980).

THE GENERAL OPERATION OF METHADONE MAINTENANCE PROGRAMS

It should be stated from the outset that federal regulations have put considerable constraints on the variability of treatment modalities available so that the structure from clinic to clinic is fairly constant, although energy and creativity of the staff may vary from clinic to clinic. The basic goals of all programs are (1) to establish or maintain a level of methadone sufficient both to keep an individual comfortable on maintenance and produce tolerance to effects of street heroin; (2) to reduce antisocial behavior; and (3) to increase social productivity. Some clinics may also emphasize psychological health or insight into their problems, although most clinics place less emphasis on this goal.

Staff Composition

This varies considerably but most clinics in the United States now have a physician medical director who may be the overall director of the program or may have a nonphysician administrator as the overall director of the program. The staff consists of counselors, nurses, staff physicians who are often part-time, and, in some clinics, vocational counselors, social workers, and educators.

Criteria for Intake Into the Program

The patient (1) must be over eighteen years of age (if the patient is between the ages of sixteen and eighteen he or she must have a documented history of two or more unsuccessful detoxification attempts); (2) must not be enrolled in another methadone program; and (3) must have a narcotic addiction history of at least one year duration. The induction process includes obtaining a detailed history of drug usage, previous treatments, medical and psychiatric history, urinanalysis for drugs of abuse, and physical examination. If the client has no symptoms of narcotic withdrawal and has negative urine, then other evidence of addiction must be obtained, usually in the form of confirmation of addiction from relative or friend. Appropriate laboratory work is obtained usually including a CBC, urinanalysis, chest x-ray, and other appropriate lab tests.

Exclusion Criteria

In general, clients suffering from severe psychiatric symptoms and those clients who seem to be dominated by polydrug abuse or severe alcohol abuse can be excluded or could be co-enrolled in two modalities of treatments simultaneously.

Once a client is accepted for treatment, methadone is usually initiated at 10 to 20 mg per day under close observation by the staff. If there are no adverse reactions such as nausea or vomiting that are intolerable, the dosage is gradually increased until the client feels stable. Usually this occurs when the methadone dosage is in the range of 30 to 50 mg daily. As previously mentioned the half-life of methadone is twenty-five hours, and, therefore, steady-state plasma levels with a constant dose of methadone is achieved after six to seven days. Consequently, patients during this period will require psychological intervention and reassurance that they will be able to achieve stabilization. They also need to be counseled that they will not achieve euphoria from methadone.

Soon after initiation of methadone it is often useful to obtain an in-depth history from the client regarding social-psychological issues, developmental issues, and current psychological status. Contrary to some popular beliefs, most addicts are not guarded during this period and seem to take the process of methadone maintenance more seriously if they feel the clinic is taking a holistic approach toward their problem.

Baekeland and Lundwall (1975) review the issue of dropping out of treatment in methadone maintenance programs and note that clinics that offer intensive treatment of psychiatrically disturbed addicts reported a very low drop-out rate (5.4%) during fifteen months of clinic operation for that group of patients. This is much below the typical drop-out rate for methadone maintenance patients in general and far below reports of psychiatric patients in this setting. They also outlined several techniques that help in the retention of clients in general in methadone maintenance: (1) the elimination of waiting lists; (2) direct alcoholics to specialized treatment programs as adjuncts; (3) offer as wide a range of ancillary services as possible; (4) tailor the treatment modality to the individual patient; (5) explain clearly to the patient the aims, scope, probable results, side effects, and duration of the kind of treatment to which he is assigned and make sure he understands his role in it; (6) minimize therapist absences and provide adequate substitution during absences; (7) find out why the patient has previously dropped out of treatment — feelings and thoughts about previous drop-outs are the best indicators for future success and also help forge the bond between therapist and client; (8) maintain contact with the addict's significant other — engage his or her help; and (9) in lower-class patients, place major emphasis on rapid symptom relief. Goldstein (1976) emphasizes how universal feelings of ambivalence about treatment are at the initiation of treatment. He again emphasizes the need for immediate symptom relief with particular attention being paid to the patient at induction.

Dosage

Dosage at the initiation of treatment needs to be adjusted to individual needs. In many cities heroin quality is currently extraordinarily low, so that one might assume that very low doses of methadone would be adequate. However, in controlled studies looking at low, moderate, and high dosages of methadone, that is, dosages of 30, 50, 100 mg daily, Goldstein and Judson (1973) found virtually no difference in the 100 and 50 mg dosages, but the 30 mg dose appeared to be marginal in some respects although it was very effective in some patients. This study looks at groups of patients and does not look at individual factors. Plasma levels of methadone were not obtained in this study so that it is possible that lower dosages may be useful for certain patients and higher doses for others. This remains to be determined. Craig (1980b) found that clients maintained on 30 mg of methadone were less likely to remain in treatment than those on higher dosages. Retention and heroin use was significantly better early in treatment in another study by Goldstein (1972) for the 100 mg dose group compared to the 50 and 30 mg groups, but much of this difference had vanished at one year.

Goldstein feels that the dosage must be individualized especially to the phase of treatment. His STEPS program advocates IV heroin early in treatment, followed by methadone, then levo-alpha-acetylmethadol (LAAM) three times per week, followed by naltrexone three times per week for opiate blockade, and finally abstinence. Therapeutically this program probably is more useful than simply shifting methadone dosage but this scheme has not been mandated by federal regulations.

Maintenance on the lowest possible dose of methadone could be of some potential benefit in that detoxification may require a shorter period of time, although this goal of treatment usually is not appropriate until after lengthy stabilization on methadone. Side effects have not generally been associated with dosage levels although this has some theoretical potential. Dosage may be important for pregnant clients because of the withdrawal effects for the newborn (Kron et al., 1973).

Absorption and Distribution

When taken orally in doses of 20 to 100 mg, methadone becomes effective within thirty minutes after ingestion with peak plasma levels occurring at three to four hours. Most of methadone is protein bound with high affinity for organ tissue, which probably explains its persistence after detoxification (Dole and Kreek, 1966). Plasma half-life of methadone is approximately twenty-five hours. Steady-state is achieved in approximately six to seven days after the initiation of a fixed oral dose.

Goldstein (1972) has described in detail the formal pharmacokinetics of methadone and shown that the daily plasma fluctuations of methadone are insignificant so that in dosages above 30 mg per day the addict experiences no or insignificant withdrawal symptoms. This "buffered" system is relatively resistant to increases in opiate dosage either by methadone or heroin so that the addict experiences much less euphoria if he uses illicit heroin while he is taking a regular dose of methadone.

Since methadone is absorbed orally the need for constant injections is eliminated; the long half-life allows for relatively infrequent dosing compared to heroin. This, coupled with the strongly buffered steady-state plasma level and the ability to attenuate the "high" produced by heroin, forms the basis for the concept of methadone maintenance.

Drug Interactions

Diazepam (Valium®) has been shown to inhibit (Spaulding et al., 1974) and phenobarbitol to accelerate (Alvares and Kappas,

1972) metabolic degradation. Therefore, these agents should be used with caution with methadone.

Rifampin has also been shown to affect methadone metabolism with persons maintained on this drug for the treatment of active tuberculosis. The plasma levels undergo marked fluctuations when methadone and rifampin are combined (Cohen and Stimmel, 1978).

There are a number of partial opiate antagonists that compete for narcotic binding. The only drug of this type in use in the United States is pentazocine (Talwan®) and because of this should not be used in narcotic dependent persons (Snyder, 1978).

Methadone and disulfiram (Antabuse®) have been combined in the treatment of alcoholics and heroin addicts and the results show that this can be done safely (Liebson et al., 1973).

Physiological Effects of Methadone

The respiration rate after methadone ingestion has been found to be significantly lower than in both abstinent addicts and controls. Electroencephalographic spectral analysis has shown that the alpha peak occurs at a lower frequency and that there are dose-dependent changes in the EEG (Gritz et al., 1975). These investigators have also shown that persons maintained on methadone perform significantly more poorly than their abstinent fellows on intelligence tests including hidden word test, story recall, and verbal learning. Others have also found that persons maintained on methadone perform significantly more poorly on various psychological tests of intelligence or performance. These changes are, however, subtle and Dole and Nyswander (1976) conclude that over the past ten years there has been little evidence that there are major changes in neuromotor coordination or perceptual acuity that correlates well with the ability of many people on methadone maintenance to hold jobs and attend school.

Many persons experience dizziness, nausea, vomiting, weakness, and drowsiness at the initiation of methadone maintenance. This occurs in approximately 25 percent of patients (Christenson and Gross, 1948).

Constipation is often a very bothersome symptom early in treatment and becomes chronic in approximately 17 percent of those maintained on methadone (Bloom and Butcher, 1970; Kreek, 1973). This problem is often treated by clients themselves with laxatives but for those who are chronically troubled by this symptom stool softener type laxatives are probably preferable. Paralytic ileus is rare but presents a potentially serious problem when present.

Excessive sweating occurs in up to 60 percent of patients but improves after prolonged methadone use (Goldstein, 1970; Kreek, 1973).

Sleep disturbance may present as oversedation or insomnia. Opiates in general are stimulants immediately after a dose is administered but then produce lethargy. This occurs especially after stabilization. Clients also report increased daytime drowsiness but no significant changes in nocturnal EEG sleep are seen (Kay, 1975). Goldstein and Judson (1973) report that insomnia is a common complaint of those maintained on methadone. The subsequent withdrawal phase usually produces poor sleep (Kay, 1975). Common hypnotics such as flurezapam (Dalmane®) seem to be of no use in improving insomnia associated with methadone detoxification (Lahmeyer and Rogalski, 1980). Those clients taking flurezapam slept just as poorly on nights when they took the drug as on other nights and clients who took the drug slept as poorly as those who did not take the hypnotic.

Hyperesthesia of the hands and feet occur in less than one-third of patients (Bloom and Butcher, 1970). Weight gain occurs in 50 to 80 percent (Bloom and Butcher, 1970; Wieland and Yunger, 1970). This may be related to better nutrition habits or unknown factors.

Urinary hesitency and increased frequency have been reported (Dole et al., 1966).

Endocrine

Menstrual periods usually return after institution of methadone maintenance while heroin use terminates regular periods in most women. Women may report lack of sexual interest as well.

Many males report impotence or decreased sex drive. The incidence of sexual problems ranges from 20 to 35 percent while on heroin (Cushman, 1972). Cushman (1973) found plasma testosterone levels to be the same as controls, although higher doses of methadone were associated with lower testosterone levels (Cushman and Kreek, 1974). Cicero et al. (1975) found diminished ejaculate volume, and diminished plasma testosterone levels, although no dosage effect was found. Generally libido is probably better with methadone than while using heroin and other polydrugs in combination, but probably not as good as when detoxified from drugs altogether. In one study clients cited loss of sexual ability as major reason for wanting to withdraw from treatment (Garbutt and Goldstein, 1972). This problem remains as a major stumbling block in client acceptance of methadone maintenance.

Administration of Methadone

Today methadone is usually initiated in the ambulatory setting. One dose per day has been shown to achieve steady-state methadone blood levels, and once methadone plasma levels are above a critical level a two-fold variation in the blood level can be tolerated without withdrawal symptoms (Cohen and Stimmel, 1978). The frequency of take-home medication has produced considerable controversy. The infantalizing aspects of daily attendance to the clinic are clear. Patch et al. (1973) advocated a policy of no take-home and found that many clients dropped out of treatment. Goldstein (1976), on the other hand, has emphasized the absurdity of giving take-home medication to patients who have never been reliable in handling medication, are prone to self-experimentation, and obviously are selling the extra medication. This has led to considerable diversion of methadone and counter-tactics of elaborate means of controlling illicit methadone (Green et al., 1975). From a practical point of view, sufficient commitment to the program of treatment should be evident before take-home medication is given. This is often evidenced by a good relationship with counselor and the absence of narcotics in the urine reports; confirmation of employment by letter or check stubs are also a useful monitoring technique. However, it must be concluded that this strict control of attendance has led to drop-outs and has led Jaffe et al. (1970) and Goldstein (1976) to advocate the use of levo-alpha-acetyl methadol (LAAM) as an alternate treatment modality for those clients who are making satisfactory progress on methadone. The advantage of LAAM is that it can be administered three to four times a week rather than daily without producing withdrawal effects. LAAM is preferred by some addicts but clearly not by others, possibly because of the lack of any sedating effects and feeling on the part of some persons that a narcotic is not being administered.

Clinical Services

Lowinson (1977) has reviewed some of the clinic variables that may influence treatment. She feels that certain minimum standards must be maintained, including the availability of family therapy, group therapy, educational therapy, and family planning guidance. She points out that a clinic serving less than 200 patients might not be able to provide this wide range of rehabilitation services. On the other hand, clinics serving more than 300 patients often are too large to meet the needs of individual patients. These clinics often have the problems of overcrowding, making them unpopular places in local neighborhoods.

Clinic hours need to be adjusted to the needs of the patients, ideally across two work shifts. In general, she advocates that methadone clinics should be open twelve hours a day, six days a week, and should have dispensing capability for Sundays.

She feels that a nurse-client ratio of one to sixty is probably optimum so that some medical relationship can be established between the nurse and the client in order to make trained observations. The ratio of counselor to client varies widely, but optimally would probably be in the range of fifteen to twenty clients for each counselor. This would allow each client to be seen two to three times weekly for brief contacts, and for each client to be involved in a group with his counselor.

The role of the counselor is a very important one since he or she is the interface between "street life" and the "straight life." Most clinics use rehabilitated heroin addicts as counselors, although in recent years nonaddicts have been employed in this position with considerable success. The simple criteria of rehabilitation from heroin addiction is not sufficient to produce a counselor. Additional skills of self-observation, psychological mindedness, and a desire to help clients is essential. The role of counselors has broadened in recent years to the point that expectations of counselors often go beyond their training. One important counselor skill should be the ability to identify and intervene in crisis (Ramer et al., 1971). This is most successfully carried out if a sense of trust and rapport is established previously between client and counselor. It has been shown (Cohen et al., 1980) that outcome is improved if one counselor is assigned to a client and stays with that client through the duration of treatment rather than switching the client from one counselor to another. The content of a counseling sessions should be individualized. Frequent review of the counselor's progress by the supervisory staff or clinic physician or psychiatrist is useful to assist counselors in establishing realistic goals and for developing plans for psychotherapeutic intervention.

Many clinics face economic constraints that prohibit the hiring of skilled therapists to work with clients. These skills have been deemphasized because of past failures in the individual psychotherapeutic mode (Dole and Nyswander, 1965). Baekeland and Lundwall (1975) have noted that research on the problem of heroin addiction has been marked by an almost exclusive emphasis on demographic rather than psychological variables. Much more work needs to be done in the area of client counselor match, successful versus nonproductive interventions, the optimal amount of counselor contact with clients, and outcome research on whether group, family, or individual contact is preferable.

Counselors currently provide invaluable educational information to clients regarding the running of methadone clinics, the effects that methadone will have on them psychologically and physically, and the reactions that family and employers will have. They also provide valuable role models of possible avenues to success for their clients. In addition, certain clients that seem in need of or are receptive to psychotherapeutic interventions should be identified. Counselors working with these clients should receive supervision or work directly with a more skilled psychotherapist. As expectations of counselors increase, a concomitant increase in supervision and continuing education for counselors needs to be provided. This could do much to remedy the problem of sagging staff morale and client drop-outs.

Outreach Services

Clients should be contacted if they miss clinic appointments or methadone dosages. Significant others can be notified at this time as well. As previously mentioned, crisis intervention requires a firm therapeutic alliance, but effective crisis intervention can do much to strengthen the therapeutic alliance.

The Physician's Role in Methadone Maintenance

Often the physician is the medical director of the clinic or director of the overall operation of the clinic. The physician has a role in monitoring methadone dosage and in monitoring the physical status of the patient. The physician has a very important role to play in the education of paraprofessionals, especially with respect to the pharmacology of methadone, medical complications of illicit drug abuse, alcoholism, and in ongoing psychotherapy supervision.

The physician must identify those clients who are having significant psychopathological disturbances and need special attention. Therefore, psychiatric consultation to the clinic is essential. Certain patients must be referred for specific psychiatric treatment, alcohol treatment, and, at times, inpatient treatment for emergency psychiatric illness. A certain percentage of clients use heroin to relieve symptoms of anxiety and depression or to control psychotic symptoms. I have generally found it useful to have these clients seen by a psychiatrist and counselor for brief psychotherapy in the clinic setting to engage the clients in the therapeutic process. If extensive psychopathology is observed, then a period of brief psychotherapy is often critical in allowing the referral process to succeed.

OUTCOME OF PERSONS MAINTAINED ON METHADONE

Initially, results with methadone maintenance were impressive (Dole and Nyswander, 1965), Reported crime decreased from 91 percent pretreatment to 12 percent after entering therapy. Employment rates rose from less than 20 percent to more than 60 percent after one year of treatment. An 80 percent retention rate was achieved. In more recent years, other results have led to more pessimistic conclusion about the success of methadone maintenance.

Maddux and Bowden (1972) reviewed the success of methadone maintenance and criticized many of the studies of outcome because of poor experimental design. They point out that many studies have quoted employment rates based on the remaining sample rather than the samples starting in treatment. On the basis of percentage employed, success rates of those remaining in treatment have ranged from 43 to 62 percent. This compares favorably to a pretreatment level of about 30 percent employed. This is not as impressive as 70 to 90 percent "success rates" that are quoted in some of the studies they criticize but clearcut improvement is being obtained.

In general, measures of outcome have been difficult to define. Should we be interested in abstinence from opiate use as a desirable outcome, absence of criminal behavior, or gainful employment and social rehabilitation as successful outcome measures? Outcome studies that consider all of these variables would be very difficult under the best of circumstances but the high drop-out rate and poor reliability of the data base make those studies very difficult to interpret. Conceptually it is preferable to use abstinence from illicit drug use as the primary desirable outcome and improved employment, decreased criminal behavior, etc. as secondary benefits.

Primary emphasis on social rehabilitation goals and deemphasis of "chemical crutches" has led to zeal for therapeutic communities and other drug-free approaches. In general, methadone maintenance has proved superior to therapeutic communities and ambulatory drug-free clinics as far as retention. In one study, one-year retention rates were 46 percent for methadone maintenance, 13 percent for therapeutic community, and 8 percent for ambulatory drug-free clinic (Gearing and Schweitzer, 1974).

Clearly drug abuse is not simply a metabolic disease, but conceptualizing the problem in this way may make goals clearer to client and treatment staff so that realistic outcomes can be obtained and primary goals separated from secondary benefits.

Heroin addiction parallels other chronic diseases such as schizophrenia in that relapse rates are high and periods of relatively low symptomatology occur, but these periods usually do not indicate cure. As with schizophrenia a rare occurrence of sustained abstinence (apparent cures) do occur (Dole and Nyswander, 1976; Goldstein, 1976). The general rule, though, is relapse.

Hunt and Odoroff (1962) followed up hospitalized detoxified patients and found that 90 percent became re-addicted from one to four and a half years later. Studies have shown that only 6 to 43 percent of persons detoxified from methadone have been able to maintain abstinence (Lowinson and Langrod, 1973; Cushman and Dole, 1973; Cushman, 1974; Stimmel et al., 1976).

There are many reasons for the great difficulty of persons detoxified from methadone remaining opiate free. Animal experiments have revealed that biochemical changes caused by narcotic dependency can persist for prolonged periods of time following detoxification. Such animals have been shown to have greater tendency to readdict themselves when once again exposed to narcotics (Vajda et al., 1975). The secondary symptoms of opiate withdrawal consist of restlessness, irritability, sleep disturbance, malaise, pain, and fatigue and have been observed for many months following detoxification (Cushman and Dole, 1973).

There are many reasons why a client may request detoxification; these range from peer and family pressure to current FDA regulations. However, because of poor outcome results of methadone detoxification, the clinic staff should consider very seriously requests for detoxification. Criteria should be established as prerequisites to detoxification. Those should include stable social rehabilitation, absence of any drug abuse, and motivation on the part of the client to endure the pain detoxification will cause. The client should have an understanding of the need for continued follow-up and the risk of relapse after detoxification. Simpson (1979b) studied 3000 clients in methadone maintenance and showed that the longer clients remained in treatment the better the post-treatment outcome. Clients who spent less than three months in treatment were not significantly different from the detoxification-only group or the intake-only group. This was true in his study whether the clients were on methadone maintenance, therapeutic communities, or drug-free programs. From this study, it appears that the *minimum* length of time in treatment for successful outcome was ninety days for therapeutic communities or drug-free programs, and up to 300 days for methadone maintenance programs. Other studies (Simpson et al., 1979a; Simpson, 1978) have shown that there is a direct relationship between the length of treatment and outcome, that is, the more treatment the better. Since retention and treatment for longer periods of time seems to have salutary effects, we need to know what factors in the clinic and the client lead to retention in treatment.

Client Variables

Psychological variables have been studied with the use of MMPI (Pittel et al., 1972; Stewart and Waddell, 1972). These studies suggest that patients who are more psychopathic, have lower ego strength, are less defensive, and have bizarre symptomatology are more likely to drop out of treatment. Drop-outs also have more somatic complaints (Pittel et al., 1972). Patients who experience more depression are predisposed to dropout (Fisch et al., 1973; Levine et al., 1972). Anxiety and compliance are correlated with success in methadone treatment (Levine et al., 1972).

Demographic variables have been studied to a much greater extent than personality variables (Brown et al., 1973a). Using measures of relapse rather than retention, Henderson (1970), Richman (1966), and Williams and Johnston (1972) found that older patients were more likely to remain in treatment than younger patients. Johnston and Williams (1970) studied a group of patients who were in treatment four years after admission, and found that younger patients were less successful than older patients. Williams and Johnston (1972) and Zahn and Ball (1972) found that individuals who became addicted later in life were more likely to succeed in methadone maintenance. On the other hand, Babst et al. (1971) found that older patients were more likely to fail than younger patients. Several studies reviewed by Szapocznik and Ladner (1977) have shown no effect of age.

Education has been investigated in relation to outcome, with some investigators finding that better educated patients were more likely to succeed in treatment (Berle and Lowinson, 1970; Rosenberg and Patch, 1972) while others (Babst et al., 1971; Sells et al., 1972) were unable to find a relationship between education and methadone maintenance outcome.

Clients who are employed at the time of admission have consistently obtained better outcomes (Babst et al., 1971; Berle and Lowinson, 1970; Chambers et al., 1970; Perkins and Block, 1970).

Ethnicity contributed to outcome in some programs. Blacks dropped out of treatment more frequently than whites in the studies of Berle and Lowinson (1970) and of Rosenberg and Patch (1972). Others (Sells et al., 1972) found no relationship between ethnicity and success in methadone maintenance. Many of these studies are interesting in that no attempt has been made to control for counselor or other therapist variables. Preconceptions among therapeutic staff might account for some of these findings.

Marital status has been positively related to successful outcome in two studies (Chambers et al., 1970; Williams and Johnston, 1972).

A number of investigators have found that multiple drug users and alcoholics were likely to fail (Babst et al., 1971; Perkins and Block, 1970). It is curious that Chambers et al. (1970) found no relationship between these variables. The incidence of alcoholism among patients on methadone maintenance has been reported between 5 and 15 percent (Carrol et al., 1977). Not only is alcohol abuse a possible cause of dropping out of treatment, but also these patients are often kicked out of methadone maintenance programs (Gelb et al., 1979).

The number of criminal convictions has been shown to be a negative influence on methadone maintenance outcome (Babst et al., 1971; Perkins and Block, 1970), but several studies have shown that clients who are on probation for previous offenses and are required to go to methadone maintenance as a condition of parole are often more successful than average (Vaillant and Rasor, 1966; Ball et al., 1970).

Program Variables

Program variables have not been extensively studied, but Dupont (1972) has suggested that programs that have a narrow focus and define the problem as metabolic, advocating that clients should have methadone for the rest of their lives, are more successful than those clinics with a multimodal approach.

Compulsory daily attendance led to increased drop-outs from treatment in the study of Patch et al. (1973).

As previously mentioned, methadone dosage does not have to be of major importance in outcome, except that dosages below 30 mg of methadone per day tends to increase drop-out rates. Szapocznik and Ladner (1977) note that if clients are assigned randomly to dosage without considering clinical variables, attrition rates two to three times normal occur. Whether this is due to lack of clinical concern shown in these situation or a real ability to monitor actual client needs is unknown.

In conclusion, what characteristics would the hypothetically sucessful client have? He (she) would have some anxiety, would tend to be compliant rather than psychopathic or a belligerent alcoholic, would have become addicted later in life, and his education level would be higher or his employment record better. He would be married and heroin would be his primary drug of abuse. He would not have major problems with other drugs or alcohol and have few criminal convictions. If he was under parole, supervision would require methadone maintenance. He would be enrolled in a methadone maintenance program that deemphasized detoxification but emphasized individualized methadone dosage and support during crises.

McLellan et al. (1979) studied a Philadelphia VA population and found that clients today in comparison to 1972 are less employed, older, have less education, more psychopathology, and use more polydrugs. The last finding is confirmed by our Chicago study (Lahmeyer and Steingold, 1980). The client of today does not seem matched to the clinic of today or could be a poorer prognostic risk regardless of treatment modality.

SPECIAL PROBLEMS IN METHADONE MAINTENANCE

Special problems have recently been comprehensively reviewed by Cohen and Stimmel (1978). This section provides only a brief summary of the information in those areas.

Surgical Patients

Several principles should be remembered when treating patients with pain from surgery or other medical illness. First, persons who are maintained on methadone are tolerant to the analgesic effect of the narcotics they are already receiving (Davidson, 1970) so morphine or other narcotic agents must be administered in addition to the methadone they usually take. Morphine in standard analgesic amounts will often suffice, although higher and more frequent dosages of the additional narcotic may be required than would be indicated for nontolerant individuals.

Methadone should be administered as usual through minor surgical procedures. Even for major surgical procedures there is no good reason to lower the dose of methadone and the treatment for pain postoperatively should be with parenteral morphine.

Pentazocine (Talwan®) should never be utilized in persons maintained on methadone, because its partial narcotic antagonist properties could precipitate withdrawal symptoms.

Alcoholics

Previously I have pointed out that alcohol abuse in many studies correlates with poor outcome in methadone maintenance.

Alcohol is the most common drug used by heroin addicts prior to their use of heroin (Simpson, 1973; Stimmel et al., 1972; Brown et al., 1973b; Rosen et al., 1973). Eighty-five percent of persons entering methadone maintenance have been found to consume considerable quantities of alcohol. It is not surprising that they revert to alcohol use or dependency when experiencing difficulty during methadone maintenance treatment or in order to achieve euphoria.

Many observers feel that alcohol consumption increases during methadone maintenance treatment. Gelb et al. (1979), in an attempt to study this problem objectively, found that 12 percent of a large group of addicts used alcohol prior to methadone maintenance at a rate of three or more ounces of alcohol per day, 30 percent drank one ounce or less per day, and 43 percent abstained from alcohol in the three months prior to enrollment. In another study, of the clients followed in methadone maintenance for eight months, 74 percent were found to be using approximately the same amount of alcohol as they had on admission (Simpson, 1973). On the other hand, Bloom and Butcher (1970) reported alcohol abuse to increase 100 percent or more after initiation of methadone maintenance. This has also been confirmed by Maddux and Elliott (1975) and Berman et al. (1976).

Treatment for the alcoholic in methadone maintenance is very problematic. These patients often present behavior problems and often deny their alcoholic problem. Short-term help can be obtained if they are admitted for alcoholic detoxification in a setting where methadone maintenance is possible. Disulfiram (Antabuse®) has been found to be a useful agent in controlling alcoholic patients on methadone therapy and can be dispensed with methadone to those patients who agree to participate (Liebson et al., 1973; Liebson and Bigelow, 1972; Pascarelli and Eaton, 1973). This probably represents a very small percentage of patients. Antabuse must therefore be used judiciously. In summary, it can be said that in general these patients have poor outcomes, but early identification of this problem and aggressive efforts to enroll these patients in specialized treatment programs could improve their outlook.

Adolescents

Clients who apply for treatment under age eighteen must show evidence of at least two attempts at detoxification prior to the institution of methadone maintenance and must have parental consent. Patients under the age of sixteen may not be admitted to methadone maintenance treatment. Many adolescent heroin users are also using a number of other drugs and may only have minimal physical dependence on heroin. On the other hand, many adolescent heroin users have been using for years and have obtained considerable tolerance. This group of adolescents has been successfully treated by low-dose methadone maintenance combined with extensive support services. Many of these clients have been successfully detoxified and been able to maintain abstinence (Millman and Nyswander, 1970; Millman et al., 1972). In general, it has been shown that detoxification of patients maintained on methadone is often unsuccessful. This general rule may not be true among adolescents. Higher success rates for this group have been obtained through withdrawal (Millman and Nyswander, 1970).

Pregnant Women

Fetal distress clearly results in those infants born to heroin or methadone addicts. Attempts have been made to withdraw pregnant women from opiates prior to delivery. Unfortunately, experiences show that heroin addicts will not abstain from narcotics during pregnancy and when detoxified as many as 70 percent will relapse to illicit heroin use prior to delivery (Cohen and Stimmel, 1978).

The optimal dosage of methadone maintenance during pregnancy is unknown although minimum dosage that prevents heroin abuse relapse should be used. It is especially important to avoid abrupt changes in dosage during the last trimester, or to avoid withdrawal during this period since this may be more dangerous for the fetus (Davis and Chappel, 1973).

Infants born to opiate dependent mothers do experience withdrawal symptoms and are usually small for gestational age (Lipsitz and Blatman, 1974). The incidence of fetal distress in carefully controlled methadone maintenance is less than among women using illicit heroin (Stimmel and Adamson, 1975). The long-term effects on infants born to opiate dependent mothers is unknown.

Future of Methadone Maintenance Treatment

The clients of today are getting older partly due to the "aging of America" and partly due to the popularity of polydrugs and the decreasing quality of street heroin. In Chicago, 50 percent of long-term heroin users admitted to the West Side Veterans Hospital detoxification program used pentazocine (Talwan®, "T's") and tripelennamine (Pyribenzamine®, "blues") as the primary drug of choice or as an adjunct to the poor quality street heroin (Lahmeyer and Steingold, 1980). These "T's and blues" users generally do not continue as outpatients in methadone maintenance programs even though they are referred for abstinence. "T and blue" use in Chicago and other large cities has led to a decline in client enrollment. A recent increase in the quality of heroin in New York City, presumably because of heroin from the Middle East, has kept clinic enrollment high there but there is some doubt whether most addicts who switch to polydrugs will switch back to heroin if the quality improves (Gross, 1980). In Chicago, we have found inpatient detoxification to be popular among polydrug-heroin users but outpatient follow-up unpopular (Craig, 1980a). New programs for the changing pattern of addiction are being developed but not as quickly as the behavior changes.

Along with diminshed numbers of clients, community support is poor and federal funds are not increasing for service or research (Brown and Stuart, 1980).

Research could offer many opportunities to boost the badly flagging morale in the methadone maintenance field. Endorphin research could produce much more understanding of the nature of the opiate receptor, the changes that occur at the receptor site after years of exposure to exogenous opiates, and possible new more "physiologic" approaches to heroin addiction than methadone. Intensive worldwide research efforts are being directed toward the "opiate receptor" question. Research in these areas hold much more promise than correlational studies of social variables for providing useful new treatment approaches.

Government regulations will undoubtedly lag behind new ideas so that clinicians must be aggressive in obtaining access to experimental drugs or endorphins. LAAM shows some promise in eliminating the burden of frequent clinic visits for some addicts but clearly leads to relapse in others (Schecter and Schecter, 1978). Other alternatives are needed.

Research is often resisted by paraprofessionals because of fears of "exploitation." This fear is derived from several sources. The first is from lack of knowledge and background in the principles of research. Counselors, not being far removed from the addicted state themselves, vacillate between overidentification and desire to "help" at all costs and the other extreme of rigid limit setting. Lack of clear role delineation between counselor and client can make long-term professional goals seem incompatible with short-term helping goals.

Paraprofessionals often maintain an important characteristic from the days of addiction: the discrepancy between perceived accomplishments and hoped-for dreams seems insurmountable. This internal tension leads to frequent frustration and drop-outs, with a frequency that parallels client drop-outs. Senior clinic personnel and directors must model the ability to modulate this internal tension. Senior staff must take part in a variety of clinic activities so that junior staff not only see how greater experience helps in difficult situations but also how failure can be *tolerated* and transformed into possible solutions.

Clients will question research because it calls upon the client and the counselor to engage on two levels. Can the counselor be trusted to look out for client needs when the counselor might benefit from research results? This question tests the very essence of the therapeutic alliance. Because of the power of this question it may be easier to dodge the whole issue or to blame superiors who might "benefit" from the proposed projects. "Failure" in this situation could occur if the issue was addressed only on the manifest level. The client and the counselor would miss the opportunity to discuss the more important issue — their relationship. In-service education is needed to help paraprofessionals with this issue of therapeutic stance so that overprotectiveness is not confused with empathy. The issue of the therapeutic stance is a very difficult one. Profound concern for the client's ultimate welfare is required if one is to maintain neutrality and remain helpful.

The future of methadone maintenance requires that the therapeutic stance of the treating professionals be more specifically articulated. Treatment goals must likewise be carefully specified and the degree of professional expertise be brought to bear on a specific goal so that "success" is more frequently obtained. All heroin addicts are not treatable. Success with a limited group of clients seems preferable to marginal efforts for everyone.

REFERENCES

Alvares, A. P.; and Kappas, A.: Influence of phenobarbital on the metabolism and analgesic effect of methadone in rats. *J Lab Clin Med, 79*:439, 1972.

Babst, D. V.; Chambers, C. D.; and Warner, A: Patient characteristics associated with retention in a methadone maintenance program. *Br J Addict, 66*:195-204, 1971.

Baekeland, F.; and Lundwall, L.: Dropping out of treatment: A critical review. *Psychol Bull, 82*:738-783, 1975.

Ball, J. C.; Thompson, W. O.; and Allen, D. M.: Readmission rates at Lexington Hospital for 43,215 narcotic drug addicts. *Public Health Reports, 85*:610-616, July 1970.

Berle, F.; and Lowinson, J.: Comparative study of three groups of patients at the Brown State Hospital Methadone Maintenance Program. In *Proceedings of the 3rd National Conference on Methadone Treatment (USPHS No. 2172)*. Washington, D.C.: Government Printing Office, 1970.

Berman, H. S.; Allen, J.; Millman, R. B.; Perez, D.; Clinton, P. J.; and Bihari, B.: Trends and issues in adolescent substance abuse. In J. E. Morgenthau (Ed.): *Adolescent Health Care: A Multi-Disciplinary Approach*. Stamford: Thrush Press, 1976.

Bihari, B.: Alcoholism and methadone maintenance. *Am J Drug Alcohol Abuse, 1*:79, 1974.

Bloom, W. A.; and Butcher, B. T.: Methadone side effects and related symptoms in 200 methadone maintenance patients. In *Proceedings of the 3rd National Conference on Methadone Treatment*. New York: NAPAN, 1970, p. 44.

Brown, B. S.; Dupont, R. L.; Bass, U. F.; Brewster, G. W.; Glendinning, S. T.; Kozel, N. J.; and Meyers, M. B.: Impact of a large-scale narcotics treatment program: A six month experience. *Int J Addict, 8*(1):49-57, 1973a.

Brown, B. S.; Kozel, N. J.; Meyers, M. B.; and Dupont, R. L.: Use of alcohol by addict and non-addict populations. *Am J Psychiatry, 130*:599, 1973b.

Brown, L. S.; and Stuart, J. C.: The federal response to drug abuse: 1976-1980. *J Nat Med Assoc, 72*:753-760, 1980.

Carroll, J. F. X.; Malloy, T. E.; and Kenrick, F. M.: Alcohol abuse by drug-dependent persons: A literature review and evaluation. *Am J Drug Alcohol Abuse, 4*:293-315, 1977.

Chambers, C. D; Babst, D. V.; and Warner, A.: Characteristics predicting long-term retention in a methadone maintenance program. In *Proceedings of the 3rd National Conference on Methadone Treatment (USPHS No. 2172)*. Washington, D.C.: Government Printing Office, 1970.

Christenson, E. M.; and Gross, E. G.: Analgesic effects in human subjects of morphine, meperidine and methadone. *JAMA, 137*:594, 1948.

Cicero, T. J.; Bell, R. D.; Walter, G. W.; Allison, J. A.; Polakoski, K.; and Robbins, E.: Function of the male sex organs in heroin and methadone users. *N Engl J Med, 292*:882, 1975.

Cohen, G. H.; Garey, R. E.; Evans, A.; and Wilchinsky, M.: Treatment of heroin addicts: Is the client-therapist relationship important? *Int J Addic, 15*:207-214, 1980.

Cohen, M.; and Stimmel, B.: The use of methadone in narcotic dependency. In A. Schecter (Ed.): *Treatment Aspects of Drug Dependency.* West Palm Beach, Fla.: CRC Press Inc., 1978.

Concool, B.; Smith, H.; and Stimmel, B.: Mortality rates of persons entering methadone maintenance: A seven year study. *Am J Drug Alcohol Abuse, 6*:345-353, 1979.

Craig, R. J.: Effectiveness of low-dose methadone maintenance for the treatment of inner city heroin addicts. *Int J Addic, 15*:701-710, 1980a.

Craig, R.: Director Drug Dependence Treatment Center, West Side Veterans Aministration Hospital, Chicago. Personal communication, 1980b.

Cushman, P.: Sexual behavior in heroin addiction and methadone maintenance. *NY State J Med, 72*:1261, 1972.

Cushman, P.: Plasma testosterone in narcotic addiction. *Am J Med, 55*:452, 1973.

Cushman, P.: Detoxification of rehabilitated methadone patients: frequency and predictors of long-term success. *Am J Drug Alcohol Abuse, 1*:393, 1974.

Cushman, P.; and Dole, V.P: Detoxification of rehabilitated methadone-maintained patients. *JAMA, 226*:747, 1973.

Cushman, P.; and Kreek, M. J.: Methadone-maintained patients: effect of methadone on plasma testosterone, FSH, LH and prolactin. *NY State J Med, 74*:1970, 1974.

Davidson, M. I.: Medical evaluation and care of the methadone-maintained patient. In *Proceedings of the 3rd National Conference on Methadone Treatment.* New York: NAPAN, 1970, p.78.

Davis, R. C.; and Chappel, J. N.: Pregnancy in the context of narcotic addiction and methadone maintenance. In *Proceedings of the 5th National Conference on Methadone Treatment.* New York: NAPAN, 1973. p. 1146.

Dole, V. P.: Detoxification of methadone patients and public policy. *JAMA, 226*:780, 1973.

Dole, V. P.; and Kreek, M. J.: Methadone plasma level: sustained by a reservoir of drug in tissue. *Proc Natl Acad Sci, 70*:10, 1973.

Dole, V. P.; and Nyswander, M.: A medical treatment for diacetylmorphine (Heroin) addiction. *JAMA, 193*:80-84, 1965.

Dole, V. P.; and Nyswander, M. E.: Methadone maintenance treatment. *JAMA, 235*:2117-2120, 1976.

Dole, V.; Nyswander, M, and Kreek, M.: Narcotic Blockade. *Arch Intern Med, 118*: 304, 1966.

Dupont, R. L.: Trying to treat all the heroin addicts in a community. In *Proceedings of the 4th National Conference on Methadone Treatment.* New York: NAPAN, 1972.

Fisch, A.; Patch, V. D.; Greenfield, A.; and Raynes, A. E.: Depression and self concept as variables in the differential response to methadone maintenance combined with therapy. In *Proceedings of the 5th National Conference on Methadone Treatment.* New York: NAPAN, 1973, p. 440.

Garbutt, G. D.; and Goldstein, A.: Blind comparisons of three methadone dosages in 180 patients. In *Proceedings of the 4th National Conference on Methadone Treatment.* New York: NAPAN, 1972.

Gearing, F. R.; and Schweitzer, M. D.: An epidemiologic evaluation of long term methadone maintenance treatment of heroin addiction. *Am J Epidemiol, 100*:101, 1974.

Gelb, A. M.; Richman, B. L.; and Peyser, N. P.: Alcohol use in methadone maintenance clinics. *Am J Drug Alcohol Abuse, 6*:367-373, 1979.

Goldstein, A.: Blind controlled dosage comparisons with methadone in two hundred patients. In *Proceedings of the 3rd National Conference on Methadone Treatment.* New York: NAPAN, 1970, p. 31.

Goldstein, A.: The pharmacologic basis of methadone treatment. In *Proceedings of the 4th National Conference on Methadone Treatment.* New York: NAPAN, 1972, pp. 27-32.

Goldstein, A.: Heroin addiction. *Arch Gen Psychiatry, 33*:353-358, 1976.

Goldstein, A.; and Judson, B. A.: Efficacy and side effects of three widely different methadone doses. In *Proceedings of the 5th National Conference on Methadone Treatment.* New York: NAPAN, 1973, pp. 21-44.

Green, M. H.; Braun, B. S.; and Dupont, R. L.: Controlling the abuse of illicit methadone in Washington, D.C. *Arch Gen Psychiatry, 32*:221-226, 1975.

Gritz, E. R.; Shiffman, S. M.; Jarvik, M. E.; Huber, J.; Dymond, A. M.; Coger, R.; Charuvastra, V.; and Schlesinger, J.: Physiological and psychological effects of methadone in man. *Arch Gen Psychiatry, 32*:237-242, 1975.

Gross, J.: Illinois Dangerous Drugs Commission, personal communication, 1980.

Henderson, L.: *An Exploration of the Natural History of Heroin Addiction.* Vancouver: Narcotic Addiction Foundation of British Columbia, 1970.

Hunt, G.: and Odoroff, M.: Follow-up study of narcotic drug addicts after hospitalization. *Public Health Rep, 77*:41-54, 1962.

Jaffe, J. H.; Schuster, C. R.; Smith, B. B.; and Blachley, P. H.: Comparison of acetylmethadol and methadone in the treatment of long-term heroin users. *JAMA, 211*:1834-1836, 1970.

Johnston, W.; and Williams, H. R.: Abstinence-relapse patterns among heroin addicts receiving methadone treatment on an outpatient basis. In *Proceedings of the 3rd National Conference on Methadone Treatment.* New York: NAPAN, 1970, p. 61.

Kay, D. C.: Human sleep and EEG through a cycle of methadone dependence. *Encephal Clin Neurophys, 38*:35-43, 1975.

Kreek, M. J.: Physiologic implications of methadone treatment. In *Proceedings of the 5th National Conference on Methadone Treatment.* New York: NAPAN, 1973, p. 824.

Kron, E. E.; Litt, M.; and Finnegan, L. P.: Behavior of infants born to narcotic addicted mothers. Committee on Problems of Drug Dependence. Washington, D.C.: NAS-NRC, 1973.

Lahmeyer, H. W.; and Steingold, R. G.: Pentazocine and tripelennamine: A drug abuse epidemic? *Int J Addic, 15*:1219-1232, 1980.

Lahmeyer, H. W.; and Rogalski, C.: The effect of flurazepam on sleep during heroin and pentazocine detoxification. Submitted for publication, 1980.

Liebson, I.; and Bigelow, G.: A behavioral-pharmacological treatment of dually addicted patients. *Behav Res Ther, 10*:403, 1972.

Liebson, I.; Bigelow, G.; and Flamer, R: Alcoholism among methadone patients: a specific treatment method. *Am J Psychiatry, 130*:483, 1973.

Levine, D. G.; Levin, D. B.; Sloan, I. H.; and Chappel, J. N.: Personality correlates of success in a methadone maintenance program. *Am J Psychiatry, 129*:456-460, 1972.

Lipsitz, P. J.; and Blatman, S.: Newborn infants of mothers on methadone maintenance. *NY State J Med, 74*:994, 1974.

Lowinson, J. H.: Commonly asked clinical questions about methadone maintenance. *Int J Addict, 12*:821-835, 1977.

Lowinson, J. H.; and Langrod, J.: Detoxification of long-term methadone patients. In *Proceedings of the 5th National Conference on Methadone Treatment.* New York: NAPAN, 1973, p. 256.

McLellan, A. T.; MacGahan, J. A.; and Druley, K. A.: Changes in drug abuse clients — 1972-1978: Implications for revised treatment. *Am J Drug Alcohol Abuse, 6*:151-162, 1979.

Maddux, J. F.; and Bowden, C. L.: Critique of success with methadone maintenance. *Am J Psychiatry, 129*:440-446, 1972.

Maddux, J. F.; and Elliott, B. E.: Problem drinkers among patients on methadone. *Am J Drug Alcohol Abuse, 2*:245, 1975.

Millman, R. B.; and Nyswander, M. E.: Slow detoxification of adolescent heroin addicts in New York City. In *Proceedings of the 3rd National Conference on Methadone Treatment.* New York: NAPAN, 1970, p. 88.

Millman, R. B.; Khuri, E. T.; and Nyswander, M. E.: A model for the study and treatment of heroin addiction in an urban adolescent population. In *Proceedings of the 4th National Conference on Methadone Treatment.* New York: NAPAN, 1972, p. 47.

(NIDA) National Institutes on Drug Abuse-Statistical Series — Series D #13. Quarterly-Report provisional data Oct.-Dec. 1979. Published March 1980, Rockville, Md.

Pascarelli, E. F.; and Eaton, C.: Disulfiram in the treatment of methadone maintenance alcoholics. In *Proceedings of the 5th National Conference on Methadone Treatment.* New York: NAPAN, 1973, p. 316.

Patch, V. D.; Fisch, A.; Levine, M. E.; McKenna, G. J.; and Raynes, A. E.: Daily visits, "no-take-home" methadone and seven-day-per-week operation: patient retention and employment patterns subsequent to cessation of "take-home" privileges in a methadone maintenance clinic. In *Proceedings of the 5th National Conference on Methadone Treatment.* New York: NAPAN, 1973, p. 1273.

Perkins, M. E.; and Block, H. I.: Survey of a methadone maintenance program. *Am J Psychiatry, 126*:1389-1396, 1970.

Pittel, S. M.; Weinberg, J. A.; Grevert, P.; and Sullivan, N.: Three studies of the MMPI as a predictive instrument in methadone maintenance. In *Proceedings of the 4th National Conference on Methadone Treatment.* New York: NAPAN, 1972.

Ramer, B. S.; Zaslove, M. D.; and Langan, J.: Is methadone enough? The use of ancillary treatment during methadone maintenance. *Am J Psychiatry, 127*:1040, 1971.

Richman, A.: Follow-up of criminal narcotic addicts. *Can Psychiatr Assoc J, 11*:107-115, 1966.

Rittenhouse, J. D. (Ed.): *The Epidemiology of Heroin and Other Narcotics.* Rockville, Md.: Research Monograph No. 16, Publication No. (ADM) 78-559, National Institute on Drug Abuse, 1977.

Rosen, A.; Ottenberg, D. J.; and Baur, H. L.: Patterns of previous abuse of alcohol in a group of hospitalized drug addicts. In *Proceedings of the 5th National Conference on Methadone Treatment.* New York: NAPAN, 1973, p. 306.

Rosenberg, C. M.; and Patch, V. D.: Twelve month follow-up of adolescent addicts treated with methadone. In *Proceedings of the 4th National Conference on Methadone Treatment.* New York: NAPAN, 1972.

Schecter, A.; and Schecter, M. J.: The role of long-acting methadone (LAAM) in the treatment of opiate dependence. In A. Schecter (Ed.): *Treatment Aspects of Drug Dependence.* West Palm Beach, Fla.: CRC Press Inc., 1978, pp. 33-39.

Sells, S. B.; Chatham, L. R.; and Joe, G. W.: The relation of selected epidemiological factors to retention in methadone treatment. In *Proceedings of the 4th National Conference on Methadone Treatment.* New York: NAPAN, 1972.

Simpson, D. D.: *Use of Alcohol by DARP Patients in Treatment for Drug Abuse: 1969-1971 Admissions.* IBR Report No. 73-7, Texas Christian University, Fort Worth, 1973.

Simpson, D.: *Patterns of Multiple Drug Use.* Institute of Behavioral Research Report No. 72-18, Texas Christian University, Fort Worth, 1974.

Simpson, D. D., et al.: *Evaluation of Drug Abuse Treatments: Based on First Year Follow-up.* Washington, D.C., U.S. Government Printing Office, 1978.

Simpson, D. D.; Savage, L. J.; and Lloyd, M. R.: Follow-up evaluation of treatment of drug abuse during 1969 to 1972. *Arch Gen Psychiatry, 36*:772-780, 1979a.

Simpson, D. D.: The relation of time spent in drug abuse treatment to post-treatment outcome. *Am J Psychiatry, 136*:1449-1453, 1979b.

Snyder, S. H.: The opiate receptor and morphine-like peptides in the brain. *Am J Psychiatry, 135*:645-652, 1978.

Spaulding, T. C.; Minium, L; Kotake, A. N.; and Takermori, A. E.: The effect of diazepam on the metabolism of methadone by the liver of methadone-dependent rats. *Drug Metab Dispos, 2*:458, 1974.

Stewart, G. T.; and Waddell, K.: Attitudes and behavior of heroin addicts and patients on methadone. In *Proceedings of the 4th National Conference on Methadone Treatment.* New York: NAPAN, 1972, p. 141.

Stimmel, B.; Vernace, S.; and Tobias, H.: Hepatic dysfunction in heroin addicts. The role of alcohol. *JAMA, 222*:811, 1972.

Stimmel, B.; and Adamsons, K.: Narcotic Dependency in Pregnancy: The Effects of Methadone Maintenance as Compared to the Use of Street Drugs. Paper presented at the Second National Drug Abuse Conference. New Orleans, April 3-7, 1975.

Stimmel, B.; Rotkopf, E.; and Cohen, M. J.: Parameters Defining the Ability to Remain Abstinent After Detoxification from Methadone: A Six-year Study. Paper presented at the Third National Drug Abuse Conference. New York, March 25-29, 1976.

Szapocznik, J.; and Ladner, R.: Factors related to successful retention in methadone maintenance: A Review. *Int J Addic, 12*:1067-1085, 1977.

Vaillant, G. E.; and Rasor, R. W.: The role of compulsory supervision in the treatment of addiction. *Federal Probation, 30*:53-59, 1966.

Vajda, J. A.; King, M. G.; and Oei, T. P. S.: Methadone dependence in the rat. *Psychopharmacologia, 42*:255, 1975.

Wieland, W. F.; and Yunger, M.: Sexual effects and side effects of heroin and methadone. In *Proceedings of the 3rd National Conference on Methadone Treatment.* New York: NAPAN, 1970, p. 50.

Williams, H. R.; and Johnston, W. E.: Factors related to treatment retention in a methadone maintenance program. In *Proceedings of the 4th National Conference on Methadone Treatment.* New York: NAPAN, 1972.

Zahn, M. A.; and Ball, J. C.: Factors related to cure of opiate addiction among Puerto Rican addicts. *Int J Addict,* 7:237-245, 1972.

CHAPTER 3

RESIDENTIAL TREATMENT FOR DRUG DEPENDENCE

Vincent P. Zarcone, Jr.

INTRODUCTION

This paper gives the concepts and philosophy of a residential program, Satori, which effectively treats heroin addicts (Zarcone, 1975). Satori's treatment philosophy evolved along with the structures and techniques in the program. They are based on a psychodynamic understanding of individual patients who have been in the program. That understanding has resulted in Satori's evolving as a highly structured program that emphasizes clear expectations, rationality, and a sense of fairness in order to protect the patient and staff against narcissistic injury. It provides a framework for interpersonal interaction in which ego growth can occur by modeling. The goal is to know oneself in action so that motivated behaviors, which are at once satisfying and which protect ongoing interpersonal relationships, can occur.

The chapter begins with a review of psychoanalytic ego psychology, which is concerned with narcissism and the borderline personality. My own observations of intrapsychic problems of addicts, some recent literature in this area, and some social psychological considerations are combined to give a definition of the problems of addicts. A description of Jonesian therapeutic community (T.C.) and the modification that we have made are given. The importance of meticulously designing an interpersonal framework of interactions is emphasized. The use of gestalt therapy approach of Fritz Perls (1973) and Kohler (1947) is then described. The chapter concludes by contrasting Satori with other T.C.s.

THE PROBLEM

Rapoport (1960) indicated in his description of the Jonesian T.C. that angry acting-out characters did not do as well as older more passive patients. To me this implies that the Jonesian T.C. did not specifically focus on the defense mechanisms employed by the younger more difficult patients. Instead, they developed the overall social setting for their work, and focused on conflict-free ego functions in an occupational rehabilitation mode.

I believe that the angry acting-out patients in Jones' T.C. and addicts share at least one very important characteristic: they do not accurately perceive themselves when they are emotional. This ego defect is a very important reason why addicts lack a stable sense of identity. Addicts are known to be very heterogeneous in personality type; however, without exception, the 600-plus addicts treated in Satori lacked a stable sense of identity and were not at all skilled in accurately perceiving themselves or others in emotional situations.

The gestalt-psychoanalytic approach is based on Erikson's (1959) definition of ego identity, that is "a successful alignment of basic drives, synthetic and executive functions of the ego, and the opportunity in the situation." Ego identity results in a sense of continuity of the self in the situation and a sense of order. A "good" ego identity, a reassuring sense of self in action, is based on ego defense mechanisms that work successfully. Ego defense mechanisms result in a particular style or synthesis of actions in interpersonal situations in which the other(s) have emotional and motivational value(s) for the self.

These characteristic modes are largely determined by memories and fantasies derived in various stages of childhood development, and elaborated throughout life. Situations in the here and now are always in some way similar, but not identical to prior childhood experiences. I am convinced that addicts suffer from confusion created by the similarities and need a demonstration in a T.C. that adult life is not identical to childhood. In order for a T.C. to be successful with addicts, an understanding of the particular defense mechanisms they employ is vital.

Many reports in the literature describe psychopathology in addicts. Almost all of these reports can be very usefully subsumed or translated into terminology developed by Vaillant (1971).

Addicts use what Vaillant terms immature character defenses, and they use them more frequently and inflexibly than normals. These immature character defenses described by Vaillant are projection, schizoid fantasy, passive-aggressiveness, hypochondriasis, and acting-out. They are normal in the development period between the ages three and sixteen. The fact that most addicts begin significant drug use around the age of twelve suggests why they may become fixated or frequently regress to this type of character defense. This level of immature defense is the level which they have reached before drug use begins to have a significant effect in their lives and in essence is the only thing they know how to do. The choice of particular drug life-styles and immature defenses is made on the basis of availability of drugs and modeling by the peer group. Vaillant's description overlaps extensively with that used by Jones to describe the patients that he treated in his original therapeutic community (i.e., aggressive, emotionally insulated, conforming, somatically ill or physically withdrawn) and with the Grinker et al. (1968) description of four clusters of borderline personality (i.e., the psychotic borderline, neurotic borderline, as-if personality, and the angry or true borderline). The reports in the literature indicating psychopathology in addicts reviewed by Kaufman (1974) can also be summarized as describing a continuum of patients who use immature defenses with two poles: the angry, acting-out and the angry-withdrawn, passive type.

The actual incidence of borderline syndrome among addicts is as yet unknown because researching the question is quite difficult (Guze, 1975). Indeed, the whole concept of borderline personality is a controversial one. It is common in the literature to see the question "borderline of what?" Historically, the borderline personality has been a kind of "waste basket" category in which patients who are neither neurotic nor psychotic, nor clearly obsessional or hysterical personalities, are lumped together. However, Gunderson and Singer (1975) have created a better operational definition of borderline syndrome. They identify six features they believe determine the borderline personality: predominant angry affect; history of transient psychotic episodes, which, in the light of remarks later in the paper, can be interpreted as regressions to a state of grandiosity and archaic selfobjects described by Kernberg (1976) and Kohut (1975); the appearance of normal social skills, but with the characteristic of brittleness and shallowness in adjustment; a history of manipulation, degradation, and hostility in interpersonal relationships; a disparity between normal performance on personality tests such as the WAIS and Bender-Gestalt (in which the subject interacts with the examiner in a "normal" way) and evidence of considerable conflict and tendency for psychological regression to childlike cognitive process when given projective tests such as the Rorschach or TAT; and, finally, the presence of acting-out behaviors such as drug use, violence, anti-social acts, etc. These criteria are more closely related to the behavior characteristics observed by Grinker et al. (1968) in their study of the borderline personality. They describe the borderline personality as an angry, depressed, lonely individual who has difficulty maintaining affectionate relationships and who has a markedly weak sense of identity. The Grinker work, of course, did not include a study of patients who had an addiction history. They were specifically ruled out for the purposes of the study. However, Grinker et al. do note that many of their patients had episodes of drug use, and that many more subjects who could have been included in their study and who met all the other criteria were also addicted.

THE DEVELOPMENT OF IMMATURE DEFENSES AND THE ADDICTION LIFE-STYLE

Most addicted patients have histories resembling those given in Grinker et al. (1968) for borderline personalities. These histories of addicted patients do indicate that their childhood development played a part in their interpersonal problems long before their drug use began.

Addicts report that their parents were frustrated and angry much of the time. They alternated between "good" care and neglect, brutality, rejection, coldness, and hostility. When these parents made demands or denied gratification, they tended to be too angry. They were coercive, manipulative, and denegrative. In other words, the transaction was "you give me this or I'll be enraged. You do as I say or I'll reject you." The addict was left with the feeling that he did not have any recourse except to understand what the parent was demanding, and to give it to him at the same time he suppressed his own hostile rage. This suppression was necessary in order to avoid fear that the situation would deteriorate and result in a complete catastrophic rejection with brutal punishment or smothering. It also resulted in a tendency for massive perceptual distortion in any emotional situation.

Later in life, in interpersonal encounters, the addict continued to project and externalize his own anger in order to control the level of fear. He very readily recreated these angry encounters or finds himself in them because he knows no middle ground in which he can have mixed feelings about another person. They are either all good when he wants something from them, and has some expectation of getting it, or they are all bad when he does not get what he wants. Most addicts report that "life on the street" was characterized by a defensive attitude of warding off other people to maintain separateness, and to protect oneself against angry encounters that could be lethal. At the very least, life on the street certainly did not offset any abnormal development beginning in childhood.

Alan Wheelis (1958) points out that our culture does not have clear, strong values, and that our society does not create strong ego ideals and realistic super-egos. This observation is important in understanding the characteristics of addicts. A relatively realistic super-ego can force the defective ego "back on itself" by limiting the use of acting-out defenses. This can lead to an increased use of more realistic ego defenses. Identification with a respected older person who teaches strong values results in a more normal development of the sense of identity in adolescence and can offset previously abnormal trends. A coherent set of cultural values, however, depends on a stable environment, and even in the more normal nonghetto parts of our society, let alone the ghettos, there are many forces that result in decreased coherence and strength of values (Toffler, 1970). On the streets, instead of a coherent humanistic value system, there is a cold marketplace philosophy that defines people as the "ultimate consumers," i. e., the addict is victimized by pushers who help create a totally artificial need and then fill it for him.

In interpersonal interactions, in which the addict begins to feel angry, he always preconsciously remembers that it takes two to make a fight. In order to control the level of fear that he is experiencing, and put some control on the situation, he projects his anger, and then manipulates the other person so that he or she will demonstrate some controlled level of anger that is less intense, such as irritation or a mild reprimand. This, then, serves as an explantion of the interaction and as an excuse for separating oneself from it before it gets worse.

Another way to review these transactions is an attempt to avoid guilt or blame for angry feelings by blaming the other person. In other words, in this type of re-enactment, the patient is saying, in effect, that it is the other person's fault, and not his, that the situation is deteriorating and resulting in angry feelings.

Addicts do note that they like to keep angry feelings outside themselves, and almost always give some external chain of events or set of causes for what happens to them. They do this so that they will not have to experience fear in interpersonal situations.

Kohut (1975) gives a description of psychodynamics in narcissistic characters that is also highly relevant and is a good description of a type of behavior that resembles projection in its effects. Following his system of description, the addict is seen as avoiding insults or blame at all costs. This avoidance exists because of a sensitivity acquired during childhood.

There is a vertical split in the personality between a grandiose self, which seeks frequent, intense narcissistic gratification because it received a similar type of gratification during childhood, and the rest of the ego, the reality ego, which integrates reality demands, current impulses, and cultural prohibitions and which seeks the best possible solution to the problems that these three psychic entities present. Since the realistic ego does not have any of the energy used to maintain the vertically split-off grandiose self, it does not enjoy making sense of the real world and finding realistic sources of gratification. In effect, the addict has not learned to be realistically satisfied because he has not had adequate models of working through frustration with a loved one who protects his sense of self-esteem.

I have frequently noted that addicts "regress" to a state in which they are grandiose and extremely sensitive to narcissistic injury. During these regressions, the realistic ego is indeed afraid because it realizes that there is very little chance that the grandiose self can in fact get what it needs, since, from early childhood experiences, it remembers that frequent large scale disappointment of such needs. It is possible to side therapeutically with the realistic ego when it experiences this fear of the grandiose self by making statements to the patient that simultaneously build up his sense of self-esteem and confront him with the current reality issues he experiences. If this is done with some degree of warm empathy, the patient can be worked out of his preoccupation with his vertically split-off grandiosity.

This grandiosity manifests itself in a sensitivity to insults and to subsequent angry outbursts directed at the person who has insulted the patient. The episodes have a strong resemblance to those created when the patient projects in order to avoid fear in a deteriorating, angry situation. When the patient does retreat into this grandiosity, it is in effect a psychiatric emergency. It the patient feels insulted at this point by a statement he interprets as rejection, for instance, "we have already put a lot of energy into trying to help you, and we do not want to try to help you any more," he will surely remove himself from the situation as soon as possible, and attempt to seek narcissistic gratification elsewhere. Oftentimes, the only statement that helps him to avoid this despite his anger and fear is a gentle but firm confrontation with the reality that he is in a life and death struggle with his addiction, and that the T.C. presents the best alternative and the most opportunity to learn despite the pain that is involved.

THERAPEUTIC PROCESS IN A GESTALT-PSYCHOANALTIC THERAPEUTIC COMMUNITY

Many of the papers describing analytic work with borderline patients suggest techniques useful in a T.C. for addicts. Chessick (1972) described a sequence in which feelings of affiliation are often associated with anger. This is followed by projection and manipulation, and a return of the anger by the therapist. In order to prevent this from happening, so that relationships can be maintained in a therapeutic community, much structure is necessary. As Chessick suggests, a gradual, orderly approach has to be taken in interactions with patients displaying these characteristics. Limits must be set so that the therapist can interact with the patient without feeling too angry or too hurt. Zetzel (1971) and Lewis (1968) make similar suggestions. Vaillant (1975) and Adler (1973) suggest that a staff working with borderline patients must develop techniques so that they can avoid reconfirming the projections that the patients are expert in eliciting from people. The staff has to handle its own retaliatory fury towards the patient's provocative acting-out behavior and has to be able to set limits in a firm, nonpunitive way. Reed, Bale, and Zarcone (1974) made similar observations pointing out that a common countertransference phenomenon was for the staff to meet the patient's externalizations with their own. Establishment of internal controls, in both patients and staff, must be the goal. For the staff repeated work on this is mandatory in T-groups if such programs are to be effective.

Adler (1973) indicates structure to be critical in the treatment of hospitalized borderline patients. There is a tendency to regress to a primitive defensive style. The patient depends on the limits previously set by the therapist. Without them, the regression in fantasy becomes too real.

Friedman (1969) noted that the borderline patient's disruptive behavior is often justified in an intensive treatment milieu that fails to set limits on their wish for gratification. The patient easily can be led to expect too much.

Lewis (1968) points out that the major goal of the psychotherapy of the borderline state should be a clarification of the patient's *perception of himself*. The patient must be trained to increase his sense of *separateness and individuality*, and to form a clear picture of the meaningful people in his life.

The model of a T.C. as developed by Jones (Rapoport, 1960), Wilmer (1958), and Glasser (1965) had to be modified in two major ways to help addicts with the problems indicated above. First, clearly defined structures that set limits on acting-out behaviors are critical in order to control the level of anger and the use of externalization and to protect the addicts' self-esteem. The second modification is a very active use of Gestalt therapy to carry on the work of modifying perceptual style in the real emotional living-learning situations created by the structures of the program.

Jones' system consists basically of an ideology of a therapeutic culture in which democracy, permissiveness, reality confrontation, and communality are highly valued, a regimen of organized activity, and well-defined role relationships. Jones' approach operates in a rehabilitation mode that attempts to focus on improvement in specific social roles. It resembles moral therapy as practiced in the eighteenth and nineteenth centuries in various psychiatric settings. This is a combination of a kindly attitude, regular habits, self-control, diversion from previous deviant behavior, and constructive work. This kind of moral therapy works well with "yeomen farmers" but not with poorly socialized, angry, acting-out individuals. It can also fail because of too large differences in the cultural background of the patients and staff or because of psychotherapeutic nihilism on the part of the program directors and hospital administrators (Rapoport, 1960).

In the Jonesian T.C., reality confrontation did result in personality changes *despite* the rehabilitative mode (Rapoport, 1960). This occurred while the patients were being trained to recognize the social roles required in their life situations. They learned the behavioral components required to fill various roles but did not systematically examine their perceptions of themselves or others while actually interacting. There was not enough emphasis on increasing the power of the synthetic functions of the ego by making those functions highly valued skills that could be learned.

These skills can be learned if there are frequent reality confrontations; but, these confrontations must be planned and controlled so that the addict can undergo a gradual orderly successive approximation of the role models provided by the staff and senior members.

Detre, who led the Tompkins program at Yale New Haven Hospital, significantly advanced the application of social learning and behavior modification principles in a therapeutic community. Almond's (1974) analysis of Detre's work emphasizes the importance of charismatic leadership in the Tompkins Program. A wide variety of psychiatric patients were successfully resocialized in a seven- to ten-week period. Considerable improvement in their family and work interactions was achieved at the same time that medical management of their psychopathology was done. However, working with a wide variety of patients for a relatively short time probably precluded significant change in their use of immature ego defenses.

In a therapeutic community, social learning situations must be frequent and intense enough so that modeling can occur. Jones' statement that the ego grows in a series of successfully resolved crises, that it is in a moving steady state, is extremely important. Addicts can be given some feel for this process going on inside themselves. Obviously, just telling them about it is not enough, neither is telling them a list of things wrong with them, and what they could do as alternatives. They have to *live* through the crises in order to get a feel for this process. However, in the Jones T.C., forums and techniques were not systematically planned considering the particular defenses of the patients. Rapoport was critical of Jones' therapeutic community for this reason. However, the fact remains that his system is an excellent beginning. It results in an open communication system that prevents covert disagreements. The staff is thereby able to give each other support. The values of communality and democracy and sharing power with the patients protect the staff against being split and victimized by the patient's externalizations.

CONTRACTS

In *Satori,* clear expectations and limits are achieved by making contracts. The concept of a contract comes from transactional analysis and behavior therapy. It is an agreement between the individual patient and his team, that is, the staff and other patients who form a group of ten to twelve people on each of three teams in the program. The contract is an agreement to behave differently in some sphere of action, most often interpersonal. However, it can be in a contract to change speech habits, to do something about medical problems, to learn a new form of recreation, to seek employment, to make a videotape of a particular kind of interview that gives the person trouble, etc. The number of possibilities for contracts is virtually unlimited. It contains a statement of what behavior is to be done, when it is to be attempted, and who is involved. It is preceeded by a discussion of the odds that the contract can fail to be completed. These contracts clearly set the limits of the realistic relationship between the individual and the members of the team. Making contracts and trying to follow through with them creates emotional reactions in the patients, which are then explored both during the contract sessions (called a Progress and Planning Meeting in *Satori;* they are held at phase changes and every three weeks during a phase), and in group and individual psychotherapy.

These contracts create a paradoxial situation: the addict begins to value negative emotional states as opportunities. To quote a patient: "If you stuff feelings, you don't have a chance to learn what's happening." He develops a tougher ego that can face narcissistic blows and the dictates of reality because the therapists (including the senior patient members of the T.C.) do not give him too much to handle at one time. Also, they are careful to protect his self-esteem at the same time they are confronting. Patience and real caring are communicated. The staff and senior residents serve as models of a clear perception process. Although this is something of a complimentary (one down) position for the addict, every attempt is made to get him to change it to a symmetrical position. He learns to modify his perception process when emotional and internalizes a sense of responsibility for doing this in "heavy" situations in the future. He holds himself in the program because he has challenged himself to "do something" about his dangerous life-style. In *Satori*, patients typically go through mood changes corresponding to the phase they are in.

In the first phase, the patient most often becomes depressed because he has given up his acting-out defenses, schizoid fantasies, hypochondriasis, and drug effects, and faces his loneliness and dissatisfactions with his own identity. He experiences low self-esteem and begins to believe that his style has got to change.

In the later phases of the program, this depression gives way to anxiety and repeated episodes of anger, because of the difficulty in fulfilling the contracts and because maintaining relationships becomes quite intense. The patient is very vulnerable when he first comes into the program. His projection of a strong need to be cared for is met by real concern, and the clear message that, if he meets the community halfway, he will get something of genuine value.

In the last phases of the program, the anger and anxiety give way to a milder irritability and feelings of rebelliousness, because the patient has changed his sense of identity and yet still has to make contracts with the community. The feelings about these contracts are different because he has an increased awareness of how he can cope with the problems of life. He has a clearer idea both of the difficulties that he will face and of the strength and capabilities that he has acquired. The patient believes that he is, and in fact is, much stronger. He is excited and ready to prove himself, but he is anxious and depressed over having to leave the program and the stability and the relationships that it provides. Transition to the community has much the flavor of separation of an adolescent from his family.

Throughout the phases of the program, there is a constant preoccupation of the patient with his contracts, his position in the community, and his changing sense of identity. A sense of order and continuity of the personality is created with every successfully resolved confrontation around the issues of fulfilling the contracts. There is repeated chance to imitate others who are good models, in the sense that they set limits, maintain the relationship, and do not accept externalizations, and yet do not get too angry about them either since they are not in a life and death struggle with the patient. Thus, internalized models help the patient to create a sense of identity.

Phases and contracts are very important in establishing group cohesion. They provide structures so that the patient can say "I am in a group in which each member behaves according to a plan. I will attempt to adopt these ways of behaving. These ways include learning to wait, and a stronger sense of responsibility for myself over the long run. I can learn to take care of myself when I get emotional." In other words, there is an inhibition of action and habits, and an increase in the time taken to perceive clearly, so that more varied plans for action, rehearsal, and effective feedback can be used. The patient realizes that this is an advantage, and bcomes proud of his contracts and his ability to live up to them. As noted previously, the words of Adler (1973) and Wolberg (1973) and others emphasize that the protection of the patient's self-esteem is critical. The addict has to be protected against narcissistic blows from the staff as much as a schizophrenic patient has to be protected against too much anxiety. By providing structures that set clear limits and expectations, the staff is helped to avoid antitherapeutic interactions. The structures and value system function as an external ego that is easily synchronized with the egos of individual staff and patients.

Structure enables the staff to prevent the reenactment of childhood conflicts. The effect of this reenactment is to split the staff. The patients frequently project and manipulate the staff as though they were engaged in a life and death struggle with their parents. The quality and the intensity of the neurotic reenactment became transparent. Early in the program it was a clue that we were dealing with the psychodynamics of people frozen in early adolescence in which intense affect leads to misperception of reality, splitting, and the use of projection and manipulation to verify the projection. It is important to take this kind of ego defense very seriously. Without some concept of the intrapsychic life of the addict, the patient often succeeds in simply getting better at the use of immature character defenses. It is very easy for addicts to "ride over the top" of an approach that limits itself to the modification of behavior.

As is true in any T.C., a system of open communnication provides considerable dilution of the externalization since it allows the staff to give each other support. It is much harder for the patient to retain this habit of externalization because the staff is constantly on guard against it and is able to decipher the "grain of truth" in an externalization and to prevent angry retaliation if a patient succeeds in "pushing a button" of a staff member. Without this kind of staff support, the therapeutic process quickly deteriorates to a life and death struggle, a neurotic reenactment that does the patient no good.

The structure of the program creates frequent living-learning situations in which the addict can increase his awareness of his own perceptural processes. In order for the situation to be realistic, it is of vital importance that the administrative and therapy functions be located in the same people. In order to do this, the various meetings in which behavioral contracts are made are directed by the same people who are responsible for the therapy. This gives frequent opportunity for staff and senior patient members of the community to act as models. If the process is not realistic, the patient will quickly lose interest in it, and the staff will more easily fall prey to a particular important problem for them, namely, their use of intellectual defenses. The staff can then react with a permissive attitude and get vicarious satisfaction from acting-out behaviors of the patient or rationalize a "moral" attitude toward acting-out defenses. This loss of interest can be prevented only if real work can be done in the planning meetings. Making contracts is certainly real work.

THE GESTALT APPROACH IN THE T.C.

The above considerations lead then to the creation of structures that limit acting-out behavior and provide the context for social learning while emotional; i.e., the structure of the program leads to the living portion of the "living-learning situations" described by Jones.

There were many reasons why the gestalt approach was chosen as the mode of *learning* in the many living-learning situations that arise.

The gestalt approach works because it is fairly easy to communicate the basic dynamics involved. This consists of a definition of successful closure, which means a mutually satisfying outcome in action, that is, two or more peope doing something they simultaneously want and feel good about. This requires clear perception of the "I" and the "You" in terms of wants, feelings, and current action. This idea, coupled with the idea of separating out memories and fantasies that get in the way of successful closure so that "real" action can occur between two people, is essentially a working definition of the gestalt approach as given by Fritz Perls (1973) and has been easy to communicate to patients. Operating in that mode within a therapeutic community generalizes to a similar mode of operating in the community outside of the hospital.

It is important to note that gestalt therapy calls for the inhibition of action while clarifying perception. This is crucial in working with impulse ridden addicts. It emphasizes the necessity of making plans before one responds, or at least taking time enough to understand what is going on. The emphasis of gestalt therapy on "I" statements is a direct attack on the tendency to use projection and externalization. This basic approach can be easily worked into various meetings, discussions of contracts, and therapy sessions in the program.

The here and now orientation of gestalt therapy is particularly important in treatment of patients with immature character defenses. They fail to make a connection between successive emotional states. Each emotional state results in fantasies and memories that deflect the person from mutually satisfying interaction with another person. The gestalt techniques of staying with the confusion, shuttling, and role plays specifically focus on understanding the process of fantasy and memory that occurs whenever one individual interacts with another so that there can be clear messages between people. In the process of doing this over and over again, the patient can learn the relationship between successive emotional states and his fantasies and memories.

Gestalt techniques help the addict to place himself in the process of living. The patient learns to differentiate the environment in terms that he can understand. Therefore, it is very important that gestalt techniques start with a real situation where the patient has wants and feelings; confusion with overintellectualization is avoided. He then is helped to learn to focus on the clarification of his own perception and to make his own model of the world, or a particular subset of the world involving the person with whom he is interacting. In the gestalt-psychoanalytic T.C., two or more people actually redefine each other in a here and now process in contrast to receiving theories about other people, how to communicate with other people, etc.

It is a simple fact that the gestalt approach does not *require* the patient to do anything specific in the real world. It focuses entirely on the process of perception, and is therefore an open-ended, relatively institutional-value-free kind of therapy. The patient can be asked to engage in this kind of therapy simply because he is inherently interested in his own process of perception and realizes without any doubt, in most cases, that there is something wrong with it. The approach emphasizes an instrumental value, the value of "know thyself."

Perhaps the most important advantage of the gestalt approach lies in the fact that its techniques can be used publicly. It is therefore possible to publicly positively reinforce the use of the approach by the patients, i.e., it is modeled (Bandura, 1969). When this is done in the various meetings with the T.C. the effects are powerful both for the patient and the community. A therapeutic value system is created that can be transmitted by modeling from one generation of patients to the next. This is the sine qua non of a T.C. which I believe leads to the cohesiveness of the group. In turn, this cohesiveness as Yalom (1970) suggests holds the main therapeutic benefit for the patients in any kind of group process. This has some of the quality of a "perpetual motion machine" or of "pulling oneself up by one's own boot straps." Once a therapeutic value system can be modeled by older members of a T.C., it will seem to the staff to start running by itself as though it has a life of its own.

Another advantage of the gestalt approach lies in its relatedness to psychoanalysis. Both are based on assumptions familiar to most professionals undertaking this kind of work. Both the gestalt approach and psychoanalysis emphasize the importance of memory-motive systems and ego defenses in determining behavior. To clinicians, these phenonenon seem obviously important and are not to be ignored because they are too difficult to conceptualize.

There are a number of reasons why the gestalt approach should be used in a T.C. instead of psychoanalysis. Because of obvious time and manpower considerations neither individual nor group psychoanalytic psychotherapies can be employed in a T.C.

Second, the psychoanalytic approach is somewhat static in the sense that it focuses ultimately on core neurotic conflicts, and the genesis of those conflicts. It is not a dramatic enough technique and does not appear realistic to people unless they are psychologically quite sophisticated. However, people with very little educational background in psychology are able to use the terms employed in gestalt therapy.

The third reason against a psychoanalytic approach is the difficulty of making a large number of interpretations concerning crisis situations in the patient's recent past. Most of those involved acting-out in the drug culture. These are not easily worked with since the drug effects confuse the recall and deaden the emotional responses which are to be interpreted.

Psychoanalytic psychotherapy can be divided into four modes: confrontation, clarification, interpretation, and working through. The gestalt approach with its frequent small psychodramas can be viewed as a substitute for interpretations. Alexander et al. (1946) and others have suggested that corrective emotional experiences as they occur in the analysis of transference can be viewed as a substitute for interpretations. Greenson (1967) suggests that, while interpretation is important, working through the transference and actually experiencing the self using more adaptive ego defenses in the relationship with the analyst (who is more and more accurately perceived as the analysis progresses) is of equal importance. To say the least, this is a controversial issue since most psychoanalysts believe that without creating a verbal simulation of core conflicts and their derivatives and a transference neurosis, no change is likely to be maintained. Analysts might argue that unless changes in defense mechanisms that occur during corrective emotional experiences in a T.C. are verbalized in some way, they cannot be encoded in memory sufficiently to have lasting benefits. It is difficult not to agree at least partly with the criticism, and addicts do seem to need to make some intellectual sense out of what happens to them in a T.C. However, the gestalt approach does employ a character typology that is useful in this connection. The patients can build on the description of their characteristic mode of interpersonal interactions. They can use the description to verbalize the contrast with the new ways that they learn to manage their own perceptual process when emotional. In fact, successful graduates do report that they are able to achieve a considerable degree of intellectual understanding of the process of change. They can describe it to others important in their lives and find it useful to do so. The process of change in a gestalt-psychoanalytic T.C. is similar to the resolution of a transference neurosis, which can be described as a process in which freedom from perceptual distortion of the analyst is achieved. This then generalizes so that the analysand can see his transference reactions in the relationship of everyday life.

An added advantage of the gestalt approach is the avoidance of the development of intense transference reactions with any one individual therapist in the program; transference is to the team, senior patients members, the value system, and the entire community. Many times, successful graduates of the program return to visit after months or even years. At these times it is sometimes slightly disappointing for the therapist to learn that the former patient is just as interested in finding that his team and the community is still there and going well as he is in seeing him. The dilution of the transference not only protects everyone involved against narcissistic injury and a life or death quality of interacting but it also avoids the development of maladaptive dependency.

CONTRASTS

The gestalt-psychoanalystic T.C. is an intense process that needs considerable modification to work with patients who can psychotically regress. It would have to focus more on the attention defects and executive function defects present in these patients. More effort would be necessary to teach the potentially psychotic patient to decipher communications, to clarify reality on an almost moment to moment basis, and to tell the difference between communication and meta-communication.

In order to treat more neurotic individuals, the approach would have to be modified so that neurotic and normal defenses that worked for the individual in the past could be reinstituted. Most therapeutic communities are for more neurotic patients and take a crisis intervention stance in which the medical-psychological model is employed. There is really very little attempt to move the patient from the use of neurotic defenses to the use of mature or normal defenses such as altruism, humor, sublimation, suppression, etc., because most therapeutic communities that treat neurotic depressive reactions, etc., do not have time to do this.

The gestalt-psychoanalytic T.C. is certainly not nondirective and does not use a rogerian approach. This approach would probably fail with addicts and would result in the staff's getting "run over" emotionally. Rogers' techniques do not allow for enough limit-setting so that the staff can feel comfortable and able to control the level of angry manipulation.

A collection of learning theory techniques, as a program, would probably not be useful with addicts. For instance, a program could combine assertion techniques, relaxation therapy, classes to improve social skills and sexual performance, increased cognitive understanding of the world around him, and a system of behavior control by the use of punishment and reward.

This would probably be viewed as cold and rejecting, and would result in many patients leaving therapy too soon. It would be difficult for the staff to ignore the kinds of psychodynamics described above, and the staff might "burn out" quickly. This kind of system would be terribly complicated to execute because of the skill the patients have acquired in their life on the street in getting around the criminal justice system.

The only systematic use of these kinds of techniques with character disordered patients was successful as described by Arthur Coleman (1971); however, the criterion for success was functioning on a job in the Army after leaving the unit. The life-style that was taught the patient was an Army life-style, so it not yet clear to me that a collection of behavior modification techniques would really be effective in an ordinary environment outside the institutional setting.

The Synanon approach can be contrasted in many ways. Perhaps the most important is that it has very powerful reinforcers such as money, sex, and power at its disposal, which are not present in a gestalt-psychoanalytic T.C. There is a definite opportunity in this type of treatment program for the patient to move from a neophyte position to a position of authority by rising to a senior position on the staff. Also, in the Synanon approach, he gains in status by being a leader in the games. Association with an elite group is a powerful reinforcer for some people. For others, it means very little, if anything and for that reason, such programs will not appeal to many patients whose value system emphasizes autonomy, individuality, and primary family affiliation. Also, some addicts see the leaders of this type of program as part of the "Establishment." They appear to act at times like lawyers and businessmen who concentrate on the output of business, i.e., the auto repair shop, restaurant, etc., and are constantly worried about their "labor relations."

The Synanon model provides frequent opportunities for confrontation games in which "ritualized externalized" within set limits occurs. The games serve a catharsis function, and at the end the patient is given the feeling that he is still accepted in spite of the hostile obscene attacks. However, the process alone is not likely to be enough because it has an unrealistic quality. It is very difficult to imagine using ritualized externalization in any sort of everyday life. There is not enough modeling of an alternative perceptual style, and the Synanon game often violates what should be an axiom: too much anger can make learning impossible. This type of confrontation reminds one of the Western movie in which two men engage in a life and death struggle in a bar room fight and emerge life-long friends because they respect each other's ability to survive hand to hand combat. That outcome is probably not as frequent as the people who run Synanon would like to believe. The games are particularly hard for a patient who has difficulty paying attention because of anxiety or depression.

SUMMARY

The gestalt-psychoanalytic therapeutic community described in this paper is a modification of a jonesian therapeutic community to fit the immature character defenses of many addicted patients. The program emphasizes structures, that is, rules, policies, staff roles, therapeutic forums, program phases, and clear expectations, to create living and learning situations in which addicts can model after staff and senior residents in the program. This modeling results in a development of a new perceptual style so that the addict patient is better able to clearly perceive his own behavior and the behavior of others when involved in an emotional situation.

The structures also protect the staff and patients against externalization and narcissistic injury. The program has developed out of consideration of recent psychoanalytic work with borderline and narcissistic personalities. A gestalt therapeutic approach is employed because of its focus on perception of here and now social learning situations, ease of communication of the basic concepts and techniques, and most importantly because it focuses on clear perception when emotional.[1]

REFERENCES

Adler, G.: Hospital treatment of borderline patients. *Am J Psychiat, 130(1)*:32-36, 1973.
Alexander, F., et al.: *Psychoanalytic Therapy.* New York, Ronald Press, 1946.
Almond, R.: *The Healing Community. Dynamics of the Therapeutic Milieu.* New York, Jason Aronson, 1974.

---

[1]Editor's note: For a comparison of T.C. approaches in terms of effectiveness, the reader is referred to Chapter 13.

Bandura, A.: *Principles of Behavior Modification*. New York, Holt, Rinehart and Winston, Inc., 1969, pp. 120-143.

Blachly, P. H.: *Seduction. A Conceptual Model in the Drug Dependencies and Other Contagious Ills*. Springfield, Thomas, 1970.

Chessick, R. D.: Externalization and existential anguish in the borderline patient. *Arch Gen Psychiat, 27*:764-770, 1972.

Coleman, A. D.: *The Planned Environment in Psychiatric Treatment. A Manual for Ward Design*. Springfield, Thomas, 1971.

Erikson, E.: Identity and the life cycle. In *Psychological Issues, Vol. 1, No. 1, Monograph 1*. New York, International Universities Press, Inc., 1959.

Friedman, H. J.: Some problems of inpatient management with borderline patients. *Am J Psychiat, 126(3)*:47-52, 1969.

Glasser, W.: *Reality Therapy. A New Approach to Psychiatry*. New York, Harper and Row, 1965.

Greenson, R. R.: *The Technique and Practice of Psychoanalysis. Vol. I*. New York, International Universities Press, 1967.

Grinker, R. R., Werble, B., Drye, R. C.: *The Borderline Syndrome. A Behavioral Study of Ego-Functions*. New York, Basic Books, 1968.

Gunderson, J. G.; and Singer, M. T.: Defining borderline patients: An overview. *Am J Psychiat, 132*:1-10, 1975.

Guze, S. B.: Differential diagnosis of the borderline personality syndrome. In Greenblatt, M. (Ed.): *Borderline States in Psychiatry*. New York, Grune & Stratton, 1975, pp. 69-74.

Kaufman, E.: The psychodynamics of opiate dependence: A new look. *Am J Drug Alcohol Abuse, 1*(3):349-370, 1974.

Kernberg, O. F.: *Borderline Conditions and Pathological Narcissism*. New York, Jason Aronson, 1976.

Kohler, W.: *Gestalt Psychology. An Introduction to New Concepts in Modern Psychology*. New York, Mentor Books, 1947.

Kohut, H.: *The Analysis of the Self. The Psychoanalytic Study of the Child. Mongraph No. 4*. New York, International Universities Press, 1975.

Lewis, A. B.: Perception of self in borderline states. *Am J Psychiat, 124(11)*:49-56, 1968.

Perls, F.: *The Gestalt Approach and Eye Witness to Therapy*. Palo Alto, Ca, Science & Behavior Books, Inc., 1973.

Rapoport, R.: *Community as Doctor*. London, Tavistock, 1960.

Reed, J., Bale, R., and Zarcone, V.: Clinical processes in a residential drug dependence treatment program. An abstract presented at the North American Congress on Alcohol and Drug Problems. San Francisco, December 12-18, 1974.

Toffler, A.: *Future Shock*. New York, Random House, 1970.

Vaillant, G. E.: Theoretical hierarchy of adaptive ego mechanisms. A 30-year follow-up of 30 men selected for psychological health. *Arch Gen Psychiat, 24*:107-118, 1971.

Vaillant, G. E.: Sociopathy as a human process. *Arch Gen Psychiat, 32*:178-183, 1975.

Wheelis, A.: *The Quest for Identity.* New York, Norton, 1958.

Wilmer, H. A.: *Social Psychiatry in Action. A Therapeutic Community.* Springfield, Thomas, 1958.

Wolberg, A.: *The Borderline Patient.* New York, Intercontinental Medical Book Corporation, 1973.

Yalom, I.: *The Theory and Practic of Group Psychotherapy.* New York, Basic Books, 1970, pp. 36-59.

Zarcone, V. P., Jr.: *Drug Addicts in a Therapeutic Community: The Satori Approach.* Baltimore, York Press, 1975.

Zetzel, E. R.: A developmental approach to the borderline patient. *Am J Psychiat, 127*:43-48, 1971.

CHAPTER 4

BEHAVIORAL TREATMENT OF DRUG ADDICTION

STEVEN M. ROSS AND DALE A. CALLNER

Historically, there have been several major philosophical approaches to the problem of chronic drug and alcohol addiction. Treatment intervention based upon behavioral principles represents the fifth and most recent of the major approaches designed to help individuals with this problem.

Initial attempts to intervene in drug addiction were based primarily on the assumption that "enforced abstinence," i.e., prolonged periods within an institution, would permit an individual to free himself from the addiction (Brecher et al., 1972). The second major approach is derived from psychodynamic concepts such as disrupted psychosexual development, oral fixation, and dependent personality (e.g., Fort, 1955; Rado, 1933; Wikler, 1952). The third approach is derived from such psychological concepts as the need for group acceptance, alienation, and existential hopelessness and resulted in the acceptance of the "therapeutic community" as its treatment modality (Nash, 1969; Yablonsky, 1967). Biochemical theories of drug abuse emphasize the role of a substance's chemical effect upon the CNS. Biochemical research has resulted in the fourth major therapeutic approach, namely, such chemical treatment and maintenance procedures as methadone maintenance (Dole and Nyswander, 1967), narcotic antagonists (Chappel et al., 1971), and disulfiram therapy (Lundwall and Baekland, 1971).

The use of behavioral approaches to the problem of drug abuse represents the most recent major "school" or clinical view-

91

point addressing this problem. Although the behavioral approach of aversive counterconditioning for alcoholism has been tried intermittently for the last forty years (Baekland, 1977), these early behavioral interventions were not practiced on a large enough scale until recently to constitute a major treatment approach.

· The contemporary use of behavioral techniques has spread to the treatment of drug addiction after having first established itself with other clinical problems and populations. During this period, behavior therapy techniques became more sophisticated and varied and they continue to do so. Thus, there is no one behavioral approach to drug addiction, but rather a composite of procedures, largely developed with other clinical populations, which are now being used to treat drug addicts.

Just as it would be unwise for the reader to assume that a behavioral approach implies one technique for all addicts, it would be equally unwise and perhaps obvious to assume that the five major approaches are mutually exclusive or that any one of them implies the use of one procedure. Each is frequently used in combination with others and each may have a number of methodologies or treatment procedures depending on the setting, the therapist, and the characteristics of the clients served. Yet, all of these approaches have characteristics that make them unique enough to allow a differential classification

The remainder of this chapter will be devoted to a description of various behavioral approaches to treating drug addiction from the perspective of etiology, assessment, treatment techniques, and outcomes both in a general setting and within our own experience in a specific setting. In reviewing behavioral approaches we will briefly describe the major theoretical issues and specific treatment procedures. References will be provided the reader who is interested in greater detail, since there are now several volumes and numerous articles available entirely devoted to behavioral treatment of addictions (e.g., Albrecht, 1973; Boudin et al., 1977; Callner and Ross, 1980; Marlatt and Nathan, 1978; O'Brien and Ng, 1979).

Before proceeding, we need to delineate what substances to include in the term "drug addiction." It has been common practice until recently to exclude alcohol from discussions of drug addictions. The term has been usually limited to narcotics, stimulants, hallucinogens, volatile solvents, and sedative-hypnotics.

Despite convention, there are several important reasons for including alcohol within the scope of this discussion: (a) alcohol *is* a drug; specifically it is commonly classified among the sedative-hypnotics along with the benzodiazopines and barbiturates; (b) it is not uncommon for abusers of other drugs to also abuse alcohol (e.g., Crowley et al., 1974; Kielholz and Battegay, 1967; and (c) there are frequently similar processes operative with respect to the etiology and maintenance of drug-taking behaviors across all drugs of abuse. Consequently, the term "drug addiction" is used in this chapter to refer to all classes of commonly abused licit and illicit substances.

Although there are inevitable problems in defining drug addiction, a precise definition of the term is actually of secondary importance. A precise definition is not important because one of the essential elements of a behavioral approach lies in a highly individualized assessment of the behaviors and context in which they occur. That is, the detailed assessment of the antecedent cues that set the stage for drug-taking, the act of drug-taking itself, and the total context of consequences for each individual serves to define the problem (Miller, 1976). The definition of drug addiction therefore becomes operationalized as part of a highly specific *functional analysis* of that individual's idiosyncratic drug-taking behaviors. In conducting this form of highly individualized assessment, the definition of drug addiction becomes a function of each person's physical, psychological, and interpersonal totally idiosyncratic style.

ETIOLOGY AND MAINTENANCE

The Role of Learning

A behavioral approach to drug addiction views etiology as dependent upon three interacting areas of learning: (a) observational learning and imitation; (b) classical conditioning; and (c) operant conditioning. Although this is not to say that genetic and metabolic factors do not play a significant role in predisposing some individuals to addiction, even such vulnerable individuals must learn to use the chemicals that are especially reinforcing for them. The etiology role of each of these forms of learning will be discussed as they relate to drug addiction.

Observational Learning

It is doubtful that most addicts had their first drug experiences by reading a description of how to administer their drug of choice or by trial and error. It is more likely that peers demonstrated "how to do it" and the more ritualized and complex the drug-taking behaviors (procuring, cooking, and injecting heroin versus drinking beer, for example) the more plausible this likelihood becomes. Indirect evidence for this hypothesis is provided by Albrecht's (1973) review of studies on teenage drinking in which the single most important determinant of teenage drinking was drinking by peers. Similar evidence for use of narcotics, stimulants, marijuana, depressants (including alcohol), inhalants, and hallucinogens is provided by Stumphauzer (1976). Thus, peer models not only exert pressure to engage in the drug-taking, but also demonstrate specifically how to do it in terms of response typology, duration, and quantity to be consumed per unit of time.

While other sources of observational learning such as observing parents, television, and movies undoubtedly exist, there are few data that contribute to our understanding of the potency of these models and the extent of their influence on actual drug-taking behavior. Some recent indirect evidence is provided in a laboratory study by Caudill and Marlatt (1975) in which male college students classified as heavy drinkers were exposed to "warm" peer or "cold" peer models or a no-model control condition. Models who exhibited light or heavy drinking exerted significant control over subjects' drinking behavior regardless of whether or not they were perceived as interpersonally "warm" or "cold." Results consistent with these have also been obtained by Baker et al. (1975).

The implications for etiology are clear. The initial drug-taking behaviors may be learned and practiced by observing others who frequently are very willing to demonstrate "proper technique."

Classical Conditioning

As a result of classical conditioning, innate responses or reflexes come to be elicited by new stimuli. Withdrawal symptoms such as nausea, gooseflesh, and running noses are all innate physiological responses that are typically elicited by stimuli associated with flu viruses or the abrupt cessation of chronic narcotic use. If these innate abstinence responses are paired with external stimuli a sufficient number of times, the external stimuli themselves (drug paraphernalia, familiar locations, specific individuals) may, in fact, elicit these same responses. Wikler (1971) has termed this phenomenon the *conditioned abstinence syndrome.* In addition to external stimuli it seems likely that, at least for some individuals, internal states such as fear and destructive thoughts such as "I'm" getting sick and it's going to be unbearable" can also become conditioned stimuli (CCs), which now elicit withdrawal symptoms in opiate addicts (Lynch et al., 1973; O'Brien et al., 1977) and alcoholics (Ludwig et al., 1974).

In terms of etiology, classical conditioning factors probably play a major role in increasing the frequency of drug use during the latter stages of the addiction process. In addition, they probably account for a significant amount of sustained drug use and the strong tendency toward relapse in abstinent individuals.

Operant Conditioning

This type of learning introduces new responses into an individual's repertoire. By emitting a new response under favorable conditions the response is strengthened by immediately rewarding consequences and the chances for the new response to be emitted under similar conditions in the future are improved. For example, a tired truck driver may try amphetamines in order to become more alert and to finish his trip on schedule. The immediate consequences, subjective feelings of well-being, energy, and alertness reinforce the drug-taking behavior.

Even in situations where the immediate consequences appear to be unpleasant, a careful analysis will usually reveal rewarding consequences or a strong *expectation* for reward with persistence. For example, few individuals enjoy their first injection of heroin or even their first taste of alcohol. The heroin injection may, for example, have resulted in nausea and diarrhea. With these unpleasant consequences, what would reinforce continued drug-taking? First, peers probably reinforced it with approval and by telling the individual that these consequences are only temporary. With another "hit" or two the nausea will go away and the person will get a super "rush." The mere gesture of injecting the drug may also have had the powerful reinforcing properties of peer group acceptance and approval. Finally, some of the unpleasant consequences exert less powerful control over drug-taking behavior because they are not as immediate as the pleasant consequences of euphoria, relaxation, and peer approval. The more remote the consequences in time, the less the behavior is usually affected by them. Almost all of the unpleasant consequences for behavioral excesses (e.g., smoking, overeating, drug-taking) do not typically occur until hours, days, or even years later (e.g., lung cancer, hypertension, divorce).

Five powerful and immediate reinforcing consequences to drug-taking have been identified (cf., Cahoon and Crosby, 1972; Callner and Ross, 1980; Copeman, 1975; Crowley, 1972; Jaffe, 1970; Wikler, 1973) and can be generally listed as (a) positive social reinforcement from peer addicts, as well as such reinforcing aspects of the drug culture as music, language, and the excitement of a hedonistic and manipulative street life-syle; (b) primary positive reinforcement derived from the pharmacological properties of the drugs, e.g., euphoria, relaxation, alertness, sensory hallucinations; (c) primary negative reinforcement resulting from termination and/or avoidance of aversive physiological withdrawal symptoms; (d) primary negative reinforcement that results from aversive physical states which are not drug related, e.g., pain due to trauma or illness; and (e) secondary negative reinforcement that occurs when the aversive aspects of one's internal or external environment are reduced, e.g., guilt, anxiety, stress, boredom, and rejection.

As with observational learning and classical conditioning, the implications for etiology and continued drug use are fairly obvious and pervasive. Clearly, an individual who begins using drugs to relieve boredom or obtain peer approval may continue using for entirely different reasons at a later time. e.g., to avoid withdrawal, to act out against authority figures, to obtain an identity, etc.

Most commonly these five sources of reinforcement interact with one another. Rarely does one find an addict who uses only one source of reinforcement. Similarly, operant, classical, and observational learning processes are typically all involved in the etiology and maintenance of drug-taking behavior for a given addict. For example, an individual may be clearly motivated to try a drug to gain peer approval and social acceptance or to avoid an unpleasant marital or work environment (operant conditioning). The individual quickly learns the precise procedures as well as the intricate social behaviors involved in drug procurement, actual use, and even part of the subjective experience itself largely by observational learning. Throughout this process, an enormous variety of internal and external stimuli become repeatedly paired with many of the innate responses to drug use and the influence of classical conditioning exerts a strong influence on sustained drug-taking.

INTERVENTION

Assessment

Behavioral assessment is still in its infancy both as a general methodology and in relation to drug abuse in particular. In 1977 to 1980, however, four texts and two behavioral assessment journals were introduced. While there is still a great deal of overlap, the major differences between traditional assessment and behavioral assessment lie in their respective emphases.

A complete discussion of the similarities and differences between traditional and behavioral assessment of addiction would take us far afield from our primary interest in treatment. Indeed, one may wonder why a section on assessment is even included in a chapter on treatment. The answer lies in one of the fundamental differences between traditional and behavioral assessment, namely, the continuity between behavioral assessment and behavioral treatment compared with the discontinuity between traditional assessment and treatment. While the primary function of assessment in the traditional sense is the diagnosis and inferential description of personality dynamics, traits, or states that are norm-related across individuals, behavioral assessment attempts to determine the specific actions of individuals and the *context* in which the actions occur (antecedent conditions and consequent events). Rather than norm-referenced, the actions are typically criterion-referenced and the criteria themselves are usually operational definitions of levels of self-management or interpersonal skills. Perhaps most important for our present purposes, the raison d'etre of behavioral assessment is to collect information on intraindividual differences (as opposed to the traditional interindividual approach), which will enable us to design and implement treatment interventions. Finally, behavioral assessment is concerned, in an ongoing fashion, with all stages of treatment: planning, implementation, progress checking, and evaluation, while more traditional assessment is usually concerned with pretreatment diagnosis.

Our brief discussion of behavioral assessment will also be limited to assessing drug use per se rather than the broader inclusion of psychological, physical, and social functioning. While important in any treatment intervention, these other factors go beyond the present discussion and are included only to the extent they permit a functional analysis of drug-taking. Several recent texts on behavioral assessment provide a more thorough discussion of these and other related issues (Cone and Hawkins, 1977; Ciminero et al., 1977a; Hersen and Bellack, 1976; Mash and Terdal, 1976).

Sobell and Sobell (1973) divide the literature on behavioral assessment of drug-taking into four general categories: (a) basic research in a controlled or laboratory setting; (b) basic research in a less controlled or more natural setting; (c) applied research in a laboratory setting; and (d) applied research in a more natural setting. Within each of these settings and types of research, assessment has consisted of measures of physiological functioning, self-report, self-observation, and observation by others. Miller (1977) and Nathan and Lawson (1979) organize this literature along similar lines.

The majority of behavioral assessment has been conducted with male alcoholics in controlled settings, and contrary to treatment planning relevance, many of the assessment methods have been outcome rather than treatment oriented. This has prompted Nathan and Lawson (1979) to state that ". . . most assessment of alcoholic drinking in the real world continues to be distinctly non-behavioral." For example, the use of direct observation of drinking behavior, i.e., number of sips, amount consumed per unit of time, straight versus mixed drinks, has direct treatment relevance if one is attempting to train different drinking behavior per se as in the training of controlled drinking. However, for the goal of abstinence such information is only indirectly related to treatment. That is, such information can verify that the individual drinks or does not drink like an alcoholic prior to or after treatment but it does tell us how to assist the individual in achieving abstinence.

An alternate way of discussing behavioral assessment of addiction, which allows a briefer and more clinically relevant overview, would be in terms of what is typically done within each treatment phase, i.e., pretreatment, during treatment, and posttreatment. The following behavioral methods illustrate how assessment can be used during all phases of treatment.

Self-report Measures

Included in this category are questionnaires, surveys, interviews, and the more traditional psychological tests and schedules. Self-report refers to retrospective estimates of either specific or more global concepts or behaviors, e.g., marital satisfaction, circumstances of drug use, number of daily injections of heroin, etc. Furthermore, it is usually assumed that the self-report is a measure of some other observable event falling within the overt motor, physiological, emotional, or verbal-cognitive response mode.

In clinical practice self-report constitutes the most widely used assessment method in all phases of the treatment cycle. Behavioral self-report measures differ from more traditional measures such as the MMPI, WAIS and Rorschach in the content that they seek to measure rather than the way they seek to measure it. Behavioral self-report most often seeks to determine what occurred, how often, and under what circumstances rather than why or as the result of what dynamics or traits.

Thus, initial behavioral assessment of narcotic addicts typically includes a "broad band" appraisal to determine suitability for treatment and behavioral assets and liabilities. Areas such as current and past drug use (and the need for detoxification), legal status, employment, living arrangements, cultural factors, religious beliefs, family situation, medical problems and social-recreational involvement are typically assessed in order to begin to focus on the drug-taking as well as the contexts, including antecedents and consequences, in which it occurs. This data base also contributes to the construction of a mutually agreed upon problem list for which treatment intervention can be designed. Again it should be emphasized that questions of quality and quantity, i.e., how pleasant or aversive and how frequently, are of major interest rather than efforts to determine why a drug is taken. A useful example of this approach is the Drinking Profile (Marlatt, 1976). This profile is a nineteen-page questionnaire completed during an interview, which attempts to provide specific information pertaining to both drinking behavior per se (e.g., preferences, rates, patterns, settings) as well as the antecedents and reinforcing consequences for drinking. This information can be collected before, during, and after treatment in order to assess treatment needs, progress, and outcome.

While self-report is the most commonly used data collection modality, one may wonder how reliable and valid self-report data are. Recent studies of the veracity of self-report are encouraging, at least for drug-related events verified by official records and significant others (e.g., Callahan and Rawson, 1980; Homer and Ross, 1977; Sobell and Sobell, 1975). In order to maximize the veracity of self-report data, however, several guidelines may be abstracted from the available literature:

(1) Use trained interviewers who can establish rapport and mutual trust.

(2) Since there is variability in the reliability and validity of self-report information, especially when there is environmental pressure to respond in a desired way to avoid aversive consequences such as jail or program termination, checks should be

made on the veracity of self-report. These can include multiple collateral sources of information (friends, relatives, employers), official records (e.g., hospital, welfare, military, driver, police), and more objective corroborative evidence to be described below in terms of observation by others and physiological measures (e.g., urinalysis).

(3) For heroin addicts (and possibly other substance abusers) there are data which indicate that reliability and validity may be lowered during actual heroin use, since addicts may become increasingly withdrawn and angry (Babor et al., 1976). Cox and Longwell (1974) found those using the most heroin were most likely to lie about it. Homer and Ross (1977), however, found no differences in the veracity of self-report between nonusing drug abusers and dry alcoholics.

(4) Heroin addicts tend to give more reliable responses to questions seeking dichotomous information (have you ever used heroin?) versus those that seek continuous information (how often have you used this past month?) (Maddux and Desmond, 1975).

(5) Use specific, measurable terms and make sure the client understands what the consequences for truthful answers will be. There is a greater chance for accurate self-report if the client knows ahead of time that you will be verifying what he or she says against official records or the reports of significant others.

(6) For evaluating treatment outcome, frequent follow-up intervals, e.g., every three or four weeks, will enhance the veracity of self-report especially if other sources of information (including probes utilizing breathalyzers or urinalysis) are also used (Sobell, 1978).

Observational Methods

Self-observation. Self-observation is not a new phenomenon in the sense that people have always attempted to observe themselves via the use of introspection and diaries. Self-observation differs from self-report in the immediacy and systematization of the report. With self-report measures, the individual typically attempts to recall whether or not a response occurred over the course of elapsed hours, days, weeks, or months. With observational methods, however, the individual's behavior is monitored at the time and the discrimination is made in situ as to whether the response in question occurred and may also include noting the context in which it occurred.

This procedure is advantageous for several reasons: (a) it provides baseline data to determine the nature and extent of a problem; (b) it is less expensive and more convenient than using trained observers; (c) some private or covert behaviors are not readily observable by others (urges to use drugs) or, if they are observable, the presence of observers may change the response into a reactive measure of behavior (Ciminero et al., 1977b); (d) it is less vulnerable to the frailties of human memory and judgment.

Reactivity may not only be a problem for observation by others, however, as self-observation may also change the frequency, intensity, latency, or duration of the response being monitored. This may be either an advantage or a disadvantage of the method. For example, if self-monitoring is being used to obtain highly accurate pretreatment data, reactivity may be a nuisance that lowers the reliability of the data obtained. On the other hand, if we are interested in changing the behavior or its context, reactivity may, in fact, be therapeutic and the use of self-observation can become a viable treatment intervention under appropriate circumstances. The latter point also demonstrates the continuity between assessment and intervention upon careful use of behavioral self-observation techniques.

Ciminero et al., (1977b) discuss the advantages and disadvantages of various procedures that may be employed in self-observation. For most drug-related behaviors these procedures can probably be distilled into a few practical approaches. Employing "urges-to-use-drugs" as an example, several procedures can be used depending on individual factors. If the client experiences discrete urges of short duration (lasting several minutes at most), then a simple frequency count on a data sheet or wrist counter will probably suffice. To simplify the procedures even more, the individual can be asked to use a time sample when urges are typically most likely to occur. For example, the client may typically have the urges upon awakening, in midafternoon, and late in the evening. In this case the client can record the number of urges per hour at three distinct time intervals, e.g., 8 to 9 AM, 2 to 3 PM and 10 to 11 PM. In addition, the client can be asked to record the intensity of each urge recorded. Intensity can be recorded on a scale with one representing a very slight intensity, two being slight, three being medium, four being strong, and five being a very strong urge. If the urges are of a longer duration and/or have less discrete starting and stopping times the individual can either record the actual duration of the urges or simple occurrence or nonoccurrence.

In an effort to simplify the self-recording and increase the chances for compliance, it would probably be best to use a time-sampling procedure to record the duration or occurrence. In the example outlined above, the client could self-record at morning, afternoon, and evening times, but instead of counting the number of urges during each of those three intervals, the client could time how long each urge lasted or whether an urge was occurring during these times. The reader is encouraged to consult Ciminero et al., (1977a) for a more detailed discussion of the mechanics and pitfalls of self-observation.

In addition to urges, of course, actual drug use can be recorded. Sobell and Sobell (1973) employ daily Alcohol Intake Sheets that require their clients to record the date, specific type of drink, percentage alcohol content, time the drink was ordered, number of sips per drink, amount of the total drink consumed, and the environment where the drinking occured. These data sheets contain a lot of information pertaining to specifically how the alcohol was consumed because these investigators are interested in changing the drinking behavior per se for selected individuals rather than eliminating it entirely.

Boudin et al. (1977) provide another example of self-monitoring with drug abusers. Specific behaviors that appeared to be functionally related to heroin use were determined by the client and treatment team. These were called "pinpoints" or dependent variables and included such responses as heroin urges, ability to relax, feelings of frustration, and number of "tokes" of marijuana. The data obtained from self-monitoring were then used to evaluate daily functioning by comparing these pinpoint variables with daily logs of social adjustment, such as daily work or school attendance.

Several caveats are suggested by the available literature, e.g., Ciminero et al. (1977a), in order to increase both the accuracy and thereapeutic reactivity of self-observation. These include such things as providing the client a sound rationale for the procedure, reinforcing for compliance, adequate training and rehearsal, providing spot checks for accuracy with the client's knowledge that this will occur, keeping the recording simple, graphing the data with the client, and using positive behaviors (e.g., perhaps the absences of urges or number of urges not acted upon rather than urges to use per se).

The use of self-observation warrants further attention as an assessment and treatment tool. While holding great promise, these procedures are currently minimized in most drug treatment programs.

Observation by Others. As with self-observation methods, the use of trained observers can result in objective information gained from recording the occurrence of target behaviors as they occur in a given situation. There is also considerable overlap concerning both the methods used (e.g., time-sampling, counting frequencies) as well as issues of reactivity. Unlike self-observation methods, however, it is possible to obtain more unobtrusive measures using observation by trained individuals.

The observation of addiction behaviors has been most developed thus far with the laboratory study of drinking behavior of alcoholics. These reports typically include operant measures of the potency of alcohol as a reinforcer by itself or in comparison to other records, and ad libitum measures that assess the strength and typology of the drinking behavior. The latter has been shown to be useful in developing drinking norms, conducting pretreatment assessment, and in predicting response to treatment (e.g., Caudill and Marlatt, 1975; Mello and Mendelson, 1972; Nathan and O'Brien, 1971; Skoloda et al., 1975). Several recent studies have attempted to observe drinking behaviors in more natural settings such as homes and bars (Cutler and Storm, 1975; Kessler and Gomberg, 1974; Reid, 1978; Sommer,

1965). These studies have demonstrated the feasibility and usefulness of systematically observing the drug-taking behaviors as well as the contexts in which it occurs. For example, data were consistent across settings in terms of interobserver reliabilities, drinking rates of solitary versus group drinkers and alcoholics versus social drinkers, the effects of a model's drinking behavior, and the emotional climate of the setting.

For the most part these data were obtained unobtrusively via inconspicuous trained observers. An additional assessment device for obtaining an obstrusive measure of preference for drinks containing alcohol is the taste-rating task, which may be conducted in a treatment or laboratory setting. In this procedure the client is told that he or she will be asked to rate the various drinks on their pleasantness, sweetness, strength, bitterness, etc. (Caudill and Marlatt, 1975; Miller and Hersen, 1972). Rather than determining the sensitivity of the individual's palate, however, the real purpose, of course, is to determine how much alcohol the person will drink given the opportunity in a nonjudgmental setting.

While the majority of the work to date that employs direct observation by others has been done with alcoholics, a few reports have appeared in which heroin use has been systematically observed. In the earliest of these reports, Wikler (1952) conducted a laboratory study at Lexington and employed one subject. Later studies have been reported by Haertzen and Hooks (1969) using self-administered morphine, and by Babor et al. (1976) during stages of heroin use, detoxification, and antagonist administration. These studies are significant because of the consistency of increasing anger, depression, and social isolation with continued use. As Callahan and Rawson (1980) point out, however, it is difficult to determine if these results were due to paradoxical long-term drug effects, the result of a hospital environment, or classically conditioned responses to prolonged drug-taking since considerable stress often accompanies street use as the dose needs to be maintained and increased. The implication for treatment is that precise observation of individual use and signs of distress may be just as necessary a prerequisite for treatment of heroin addiction as Nathan and O'Brien (1971) claim it is for alcoholism.

Finally, the use of observers can also entail the measurement of byproducts of substance abuse including the official legal documents mentioned earlier as well as such physiological changes typically measured through urine analysis for metabolites, breath tests, and medical examination for induced liver enzyme production, liver damage, track marks, and collapsed veins.

Treatment

Behavioral treatment of addiction can be discussed according to which of the three components of the functional analysis are modified by the intervention: the antecedent cues that set the stage for drug taking (the A component), the behavior itself (the B component), or the reinforcing consequences that maintain the drug-taking (the C component). Any treatment modality addresses one or more of these components.

Previous sections on etiology made reference to several treatment implications based upon the specific reinforcers and consequences maintaining the drug-taking behavior. Consequently one general treatment strategy to be discussed below is to modify the C part of a functional analysis, i.e., changing the reinforcing consequences in some way so that the usual reinforcers for drug-taking are either eliminated or modified and the client is taught to obtain these and other reinforcing consequences without the use of drugs. Focusing on the C portion of an A B C functional analysis paradigm then provides five treatment strategies: (a) aversive counterconditioning of new physiological responses to drug-taking, e.g., equating drug use with tension or nausea rather than relaxation or euphoria; (b) training in social skills to achieve other competing reinforcers, e.g., training behaviors for job prestige rather than respect as a hustler; (c) chemical blockade or antagonist to remove the drug "high"; (d) medical detoxification to avoid withdrawal; and (e) training in alternate ways of dealing with aversive aspects of one's environment, e.g., training a variety of drug-free highs to relieve boredom. Each of these five general treatment strategies will be reviewed below in terms of the important research utilizing the method in question as well as the overall effectiveness of the intervention.

Treatment Addressing the Consequences of Drug-taking Behavior

Counterconditioning. To date, the majority of behavioral treatment approaches to drug abuse have attempted to condition either incompatible or aversive consequences with the action of drug-taking. The conception of counterconditioning entails temporal pairing of incompatible or aversive stimuli with problem-related responses such that the thought or act of engaging in these responses elicits aversive consequences instead of the usual pleasant sequelae (Bandura, 1969). The behavioral drug treatment research literature includes instances where aversive chemical, electrical, and covert stimuli have been used in the presence of drug use. Relaxation, accomplished through tension-discharge exercises, has been most commonly used as an incompatible response paired with anxiety-provoking stimuli (systematic desensitization). Because the use of aversive counterconditioning has been generally applied to the act of drug injection or ingestion and systematic desensitization has been applied to behaviors *leading to* drug use, aversive counterconditioning methods will be reviewed here and the use of desensitization will be discussed in the Antecedents section.

The application of aversive counterconditioning through chemical action has been broad (see reviews by Eysenck and Rachman, 1965; Franks, 1958, 1963; Rachman, 1961, 1965; Rachman and Teasdale, 1969). Chemical aversion therapy involves giving an individual chemical compounds that eventually produce such noxious physiological effects as nausea, vomiting, or temporary respiratory paralysis. Once the time for the onset of these effects is determined, the individual is instructed to begin actual drug-taking behaviors, i.e., injecting or ingesting the drug. A wide range of problem behaviors are therefore temporally consequated by the onset of a chemically induced aversive experience.

Chemical aversion techniques were initially researched with alcoholic patients (Lemere et al., 1942; Voegtlin, 1940, 1947).

Nathan and Lipscomb (1979) have recently reviewed this literature, which has shown some encouraging results. Weins et al.,
(1976), for example, reported that 63 percent of 261 alcoholics
were abstinent one year after emetine conditioning. These results are similar to those obtained earlier by Thiman (1949) and
Lemere and Voegtlin (1950). One cannot assume that a pure
conditioning procedure alone is the behavioral treatment of
choice since many of the subjects in these studies were exposed to
other treatments during and after conditioning (personal and
family counseling, AA, supportive aftercare), were subject to
expectation effects, and came from a higher socioeconomic
group than many other alcoholics (Nathan and Lipscomb, 1979).
How many of these subjects actually developed a conditioned
aversion to alcohol is not known since it has only been in the last
year that anyone has demonstrated a conditioned aversion to
alcohol. Using a modified Lemere and Voegtlin (1950) procedure
in which emetine dosage was reduced and syrup of ipecac added,
Baker and Cannon (1979), working at the Salt Lake City V.A.
Medical Center, demonstrated a conditioned aversion in terms
of behavioral, attitudinal, and psychophysiological measures.

In sum, chemical aversion techniques appear promising for
alcoholism treatment when supplemented with other interventions.

Efforts to reduce drug abuse through chemical aversion
methods closely resemble these initial studies on alcoholic patients. With chronic drug users, Raymond (1964) and Liberman
(1968) paired apomorphine with self-administration of drugs to
produce a conditioned nausea and vomiting response. Thomson
and Rathod (1968) used the compound scoline to produce temporary respiratory paralysis timed to coincide with heroin injection. Although these efforts were obviously designed to reduce
the final act of the drug-taking chain, i.e., drug injection or ingestion, it was also hoped that the unpleasant responses produced by the chemicals would generalize to other related behaviors and thoughts in the drug user's repertoire such as
thoughts of drug use or observing another person using drugs.

The use of electroshock as the noxious event paired with drug use has the advantage of enhanced stimulus control, versatility, and physiological safety in comparison to noxious chemical agents. It can be precisely controlled to occur directly after the troublesome behavior is shown and the use of portable shock units permit in vivo counterconditioning within the naturalistic environment.

The earliest attempt to employ electrical aversion to treat alcoholism was reported by Kantorovich (1930). This early report was encouraging (70% abstinent from 3 weeks to 20 months posttreatment). More recent attempts to employ electrical aversion techniques have been disappointing or have shown conflicting results (Blake, 1965, 1967; Hsu, 1965; MacCulloch et al., 1966; McGuire and Vallance, 1964; Miller and Hersen, 1972; Vogler et al., 1971). These results may be due, in part, to factors which are similar to those relevant to chemical aversion, i.e., the lack, until very recently, of a demonstrated conditioned aversion and the need to use the technique in conjunction with other therapeutic modalities such as family therapy and supportive aftercare. An additional variable has been suggested by Wilson and Davison (1969) and Garcia et al. (1974), namely, that chemical aversion produces a more biologically appropriate response, nausea, than electrical aversion, which produces a largely unknown response, if any.

The application of electrical aversion techniques to the problem of drug use follows its initial application with alcoholic patients. In what appears to be the first use of the technique with drug patients, Wolpe (1965) trained a patient to operate a portable shock apparatus and to apply brief shocks to a variety of environmental and internal stimuli. Lesser (1967), O'Brien and Raynes (1972), and Spevack et al. (1973) have also used electrical shock as important therapeutic ingredients in combination with other behavioral treatments. Boudin (1972) and O'Brien et al. (1972) have also employed electroshock, but not as their primary intervention to drug abuse. Finally, Blachly (1971) has designed an "electric needle" designed to deliver a shock to one or more patients through an electrically charged syringe when the plunger is pressed.

The counterconditioning technique of covert sensitization

(verbal aversion, aversive imagery) uses imagined noxious scenes as aversive consequences related to drug use. The behavior to be eliminated or reduced (alcohol ingestion, drug use) is often also represented in an imagined scene. The use of covert sensitization has been used in this manner to reduce a variety of clinical problems relating to "excessive use" such as obesity and smoking.

While covert sensitization appears to have a number of theoretical advantages over chemical and electrical aversion techniques such as mobility and direct association between the aversive stimulus and the drinking behavior and the context in which it occurs, covert sensitization has not been used very much with alcoholics (Nathan and Briddell, 1977). Only one study (Ashem and Donner, 1968) employed a control group to assess the effectiveness of covert sensitization in reducing drinking by alcoholics. Only 40 percent (6 of 15) of their subjects were abstinent at a six-month follow-up.

In the treatment of drug abuse, Anant (1968), Steinfeld (1970), and Steinfeld et al. (1974) have all employed covert sensitization in an effort to introduce an imagined.aversive consequence to many of the thoughts and behaviors involved with drug seeking, preparation, and actual use. Specifically, these patients were asked to imagine a series of scenes in which they first feel like taking a drug, then travel to the place where they obtain the drug, prepare to inject it, actually inject it, feel sick, vomit, and then gradually begin to feel better as they progressively move farther away from the place where they took the drug.

Covert sensitization is often preceded by progressive muscle relaxation to enhance the patient's ability to vividly imagine scenes. It requires no special apparatus or chemicals and the patient can be trained to include many of the specific and idiosyncratic elements of their own drug-taking style and experience. It can also be used to augment other behavioral techniques (see O'Brien and Raynes, 1972; Wisocki, 1972). The validity of the patient's self-reported images and the ability to vividly imagine scenes, even if they are clearly described in great detail by the therapist, are obvious problems inherent in this form of counterconditioning.

Treatments Addressing the Antecedents of Drug-taking

Although the use of chemical, electrical, and imaginal aversive events has been used to negatively consequate the behavior of taking drugs, the preceding complex of behaviors in the chain, the antecedent conditions and behaviors, can also be strongly affected by counterconditioning. If, for example, one can clearly identify some of the major cognitive and behavioral steps leading to the culminated behavior of drug use such a chain may look broadly as shown in Figure 4-1.

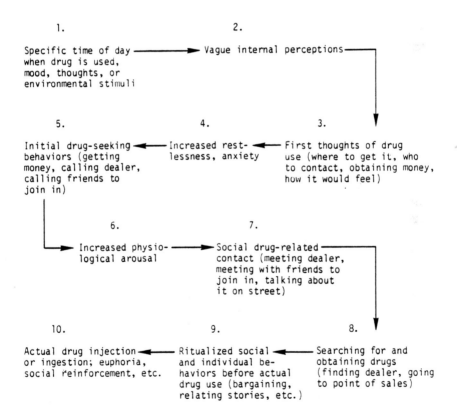

Figure 4-1. Hypothetical chain of drug seeking and drug taking behaviors.

Although obviously simplistic, this ten-step cognitive behavior chain offers many points before actual drug ingestion or injection that may respond to counterconditioning. In this sense, many of these preceding behaviors, thoughts, and even internal perceptions can be thought of as the "behavior" (B) portion of the functional analysis. Similarly, noxious events timed to closely follow the occurrence of these steps early in the chain may serve to stop or significantly alter the patient's well-practiced drug-taking sequence. In this sense, many of the behaviors, thoughts, and feelings preceding actual drug ingestion or injection can represent the "behavior" targeted for counterconditioning. The key to the success of counterconditioning earlier events in the drug-taking chain, however, is reliability with which these events occur in the chain and the power that the aversive events have for the individual in particular.

The use of counterconditioning addressed to the antecedent events preceding and typically leading to actual drug use is exemplified by the application of systematic desensitization. Rather than using aversive consequences, desensitization procedures seek to pair relaxation with anxiety-provoking stimuli often associated with eventual drug use. Patients are first relaxed by verbal muscle relaxation methods, by minor tranquilizers, or by hypnosis. Situations identified by the patient that elicit anxiety are then identified and rank ordered into a hierarchy as a function of the amount of anxiety they elicit. Finally, relaxation is systematically paired with each of the anxiety-provoking items on the hierarchy by asking the patient to imagine each situation while maintaining a high degree of relaxation. As with the use of covert sensitization, the effectiveness of this counterconditioning strongly relies on the patient's ability to identify reliable thoughts, feelings, and behaviors that are associated with anxiety, his ability to vividly imagine such events, and his ability to become and maintain a state of physical relaxation.

Although the use of systematic desensitization for many clinical problems associated with anxiety is wisespread (see reviews by Bandura, 1969; Paul, 1969) the use of this method for the treatment of drug abuse has been most extensively studied by Kraft (1968, 1969, 1970). Kraft suggests that "social anxiety" (i.e., inability to relate effectively in general, inability to turn down drug offers, fear of peer interaction) is the major factor associated with drug use. Treatment is therefore aimed at reducing anxiety in social situations by (a) desensitizing the patient to being around progressively larger groups of people and (b) having the patient spend progressively greater periods of time away from the therapist while practicing in vivo desensitization in his natural environment. Spevack et al. (1973) also used systematic desensitization with an individual to reduce the fears associated with an unpleasant LSD experience.

Only two uncontrolled studies (Kraft and Al-Issa, 1968; Kraft, 1969) have appeared in literature reporting on the use of systematic desensitization alone to treat alcoholism. The eight subjects reported on were felt to have shown improvement in terms of reduced consumption of alcohol.

Two final ways of addressing the antecedents of drug-taking are either to teach the client to avoid the antecedents, e.g., avoiding dope houses, bars, street friends, and/or to teach the client to respond differently if the antecedents are unavoidable, e.g., assertive refusals to use drugs, employ meditation when nervous, call an AA member when having urges to drink. These are discussed more fully in the section which discusses prosocial skill development.

Once again, the use of any counterconditioning technique seeks to reduce or eliminate the occurrence of a "target behavior" by pairing its occurrence with an incompatible or aversive event. Because the process leading to actual drug ingestion or injection is highly complex and inextricably bound to an enormous variety of internal sensations, thoughts, and behaviors, the careful identification of each patient's idiosyncratic drug-taking chain is critical. The multitude of points on this chain can never be thoroughly identified, but reliably occurring events are all important foci for counterconditioning. In this framework, counterconditioning addresses events acting as both antecedents and consequences of drug use.

Treatments Addressing Actual Drug-taking Behaviors

Another general category of treatment methods is primarily

addressed towards the "B" portion of an ABC functional analysis, i.e., techniques designed to change the specific drug-taking behavior or behaviors themselves. Included in these treatment approaches are approaches designed to reinforce specific prosocial behavior contingent upon a prearranged program. This prearranged program outlines the specific behaviors that are required from the patient in order to obtain desired reinforcers. When contingent reinforcement programs are used on an individual basis, the technique of contingency contracting specifies the contractural agreement between the patient and the therapist involving both the behaviors required of the patient as well as the reinforcing or aversive consequences to be received. When designed on a group level, such as on an inpatient treatment program with several patients having a similar contractural program, token economy techniques are often used to reinforce behaviors with tokens or points that can be later exchanged for desired reinforcers.

The use of highly specific contracts outlining appropriate and inappropriate behaviors and corresponding consequences has been widely used with students (Homme, 1969), delinquents (Stuart, 1971), and married couples (Knox, 1972). In the drug treatment literature, Boudin (1972), Boudin et al. (1977), Sammons (1972), and Ross and Jones (1973) have designed specific contingency contracts connecting drug-related behavior to reinforcing and aversive consequences. Examples of actual target behaviors include decreasing unpleasant subjective feelings, increasing self-care behaviors, increasing physical activity, and decreasing non–drug-related peer contacts. Music, opportunity to participate in sporting events, money, food, and television and movies are often used as reinforcers for appropriate behavior.

The use of large-scale token economy programs within hospital inpatient programs have been successfully used with chronic psychotic patients (Atthowe and Krasner, 1968; Ayllon and Azrin, 1968; Montgomery and McBurney, 1970), juvenile delinquents (Fineman, 1968; Tyler and Brown, 1968), and mentally retarded individuals (Lent, 1968). In the treatment of drug abuse, Glicksman et al. (1971) designed a system whereby patients could earn a hospital discharge by accumulating points based upon program performance. Using the Premack Principle (Premack, 1959), O'Brien et al. (1971) reinforced narcotic patients with such things as passes, televison and radio privileges, and visitors for successful adherence to a variety of lower frequency program behaviors (punctuality, compliance to rules, cleanliness).

Although these studies specifically identified drug abstinence as the target, many other problem behaviors commonly found on inpatient programs are addressed. The use of highly individualized contingency contracts, designed to specify behaviors that may be competing and/or conflicting to drug use can, of course, be written between patient and therapist.

A combination of other behavioral techniques have been used to train new behaviors that are either not within the drug user's repertoire or are seldomly practiced. For example, problems related to poor assertive skills and inappropriate or maladaptive communication styles make it very difficult for drug users to break out of the drug "street life" and enter the world of "straight" people.

Callner and Ross (1976, 1978) developed a social skills assessment and intervention program based around several important areas of "straight," non – drug-related life (e.g., finding a job, meeting and maintaining nondrug-using peers, refusing drug offers). Specific situations requiring training in assertion skills as well as adaptive interpersonal communication were discussed, modeled, then practiced through role playing, and finally videotaped and reviewed by a small group of drug abusers. Although the target of drug-taking was not specifically addressed in this program, it was felt that many of the assertion-communication situations likely to confront the drug user when he attempts to return to a nonaddict environment may significantly contribute to relapse if not handled successfully.

Recommendations for a Model Program

Obviously the ideal program would be based upon many of the more promising techniques and assessment procedures that have comprised the bulk of this chapter. Such a program would only be limited by the skill and numbers of the staff available to implement the program. There would still be a need for an underlying philosophy that would direct the timing and sequencing of interventions, appropriativeness of admission, lengths of treatment, staff composition, and other administrative and clinical matters that profoundly affect the day to day functioning of a program regardless of the clinical techniques employed.

The unifying core of the program would be a curriculum of learning experiences to enable clients (a) to cope with stress and be able to problem solve in specific and general contexts; (b) to obtain drug-free highs and meaningful reinforcers; and (c) to be reasonably free of debilitating problems which interfere with (a) and (b), e.g., anxiety, insomia, infections, loneliness. The underlying assumption would be that if life without drugs is "a drag," then why be "straight"?

Assets and deficits in each of the components would be comprehensively assessed via a semistructured interview and would include all areas of functioning: vocational, marital/family, cultural/religious, legal, military, social/recreational, medical, and psychological. Baseline data would be obtained via self-monitoring, self-report, or observation by others for problem areas.

The program would be multidisciplinary in its approach to teaching social skills and would employ a curriculum to teach the appropriate skills. Individuals would take the necessary "courses" based upon the results of the assessments. Criteria for completing courses, advancing in the program, and being discharged would be explicit, and measurable, and a copy would be given to new admissions. Individual performance would be monitored not only by staff but by clients themselves and by peer committees who would monitor progress, and rule violations and act as group coteachers for modeling skill acquisition.

Coping with stress and problem solving would be addressed via stress inoculation training (Meichenbaum, 1977) and problem-solving skills training (D'Zurilla and Goldfried, 1971). Both skills would be taught in a group format with individual tutoring as needed. The groups would have both a didactic and an applied element with emphasis on using the skills in the community after basic proficiency had been demonstrated in the group. Advanced clients and recovered addict staff would play an important role in helping neophytes identify problems in these areas, learn the skills, and *practice them in the comunity.* This emphasis would apply to all parts of the program.

Obtaining drug-free highs and meaningful activities are difficult in many cases because of the antithesis of the street ethic to the "square" life-style. Therefore, clients would be expected to sample various reinforcing activities from an extensive menu. Program resources and community volunteers would make it possible to sample such diverse activities as different sports, creative arts, volunteer helping with children or the elderly, etc. Again, basic skills would be taught in areas chosen by clients as especially appealing with much emphasis on performing these activities on a regular basis in order to get the client "hooked."

Another critical goal in conjunction with rewarding activities and the social-interpersonal area would be helping clients form new friendships with individuals who, even if not totally drug-free themselves (i.e., they may smoke or drink to a light or moderate degree) would be supportive of abstinence or greatly reduced drug-taking.

Being free from debilitating problems would entail medical and psychological treatment. While a substantial number of psychological problems would be helped or eliminated though components (a) and (b), additional interventions would be needed for some. Two examples, depression and psychopathy, will illustrate the point. Component (a) would allow depressed individuals to better cope with stress as they alleviate the feeling of helplessness many depressed individuals experience. Component (b) would attack the feelings of loss of pleasure and fatigue by increasing participation in pleasant activities. However, there may still be family, physical, or cognitive problems that contribute to the depression. Such thoughts as "I must be perfect," "everyone must like me," "I am a terrible person" (Ellis, 1973; Beck et al., 1979) must be detected and directly modified.

Similarly, psychopathic individuals can exert powerfully destructive influences on programs by organizing countercultures that seek other payoffs from program affiliation than the payoffs staff first envisioned, e.g., reduction in the expense of a narcotic habit, hiding from legal authorities, and prestige from manipulating staff, to name only a few. In dealing with substance abusers every program must decide how to manage these types of clients including whether or not to retain them in treatment. A variety of peer confrontive techniques exist for inpatient or outpatient settings. This becomes an issue of management rather than treatment, however, since treatment cannot occur until there is some level of stability. Unless a strong therapeutic community among clients and staff exists, many of these individuals are best treated as outpatients. Long inpatient stays and careful screening (selective dropout, oftentimes) are usually necessary for strong therapeutic inpatient communities to be built and maintained. Many programs are unable to meet these requirements for administrative reasons.

Whether treated as inpatients or outpatients, however, the (c) component is best implemented with this type of client in the form of ironclad contingency contracts having immediate and powerful consequences. Such contracts could be used between the client and the therapist or peer group, his family, his employer, or his parole officer. Such contracts assist both management and treatment by specifying negative consequences for inappropriate behavior and positive consequences for adherence to therapeutic regimen. They may also assist in teaching self-monitoring and self-control by fading staff from the contract writing and gradually turning the entire process over to the client.

Finally, the model program would carry clients in supportive aftercare for an indefinite period of time following active inpatient and/or outpatient treatment. This component would fade the active treatment element by gradually decreasing the amount of contact. Follow-up data for program evaluation purposes as well as therapeutic contact purposes would be collected for up to eighteen months posttreatment.

While many factors make it very difficult to achieve the ideal program in its entirety, many of the components can be added simply by providing a relatively small amount of staff training and supervision and by restructuring existing programs along different lines. To the extent we have been able to move in the proposed model direction, we and our clients have been gratified with the results.

REFERENCES

Albrecht, G. L.: The alcoholism process: A social learning viewpoint. In P. Bourne and R. Fox (Eds.): *Alcoholism: Progress in Research and Treatment.* New York, Academic, 1973.

Anant, S. S.: A note on the treatment of alcoholics by verbal aversion techniques. *Int J Add, 3*:381-388, 1968.

Ashem, B.; and Donner, L.: Covert sensitization with alcoholics: A controlled replication. *Behavior Res Ther, 6*:7-12, 1968.

Atthowe, J. M., Jr.; and Krasner, L.: Preliminary report on the application of contingent reinforcement procedures (token economy) on a "chronic" psychiatric ward. *J Abnormal Psychol, 73*:37-43, 1968.

Ayllon, T.; and Azrin, N. H.: *The Token Economy.* New York, Appleton-Century-Crofts, 1968.

Babor, T. F.; Meyer, R. E.; Mirin, S. M.; McNamee, H. B.; and Davies, M.: Behavioral and social effects of heroin self-administration and withdrawal. *Arch Gen Psychiatry, 33*:363-367, 1976.

Baekland, F.: Evaluation of treatment methods in chronic alcoholics. In B. Kissin and M. Begleiter (Eds.): *Treatment and Rehabilitation of the Chronic Alcoholic.* New York, Plenum, 1977.

Baker, T. B.; Udin, H.; and Vogler, E.: Effects of videotaped modeling and self-confrontation on the drinking behavior of alcoholism. *Int J Add, 10*:779-793, 1975.

Baker, T. B.; and Cannon, D. S.: Taste aversion therapy with alcoholics: Techniques and evidence of a conditioned response. *Behav Res Ther, 17*:229-242, 1979.

Bandura, A.: *Principles of Behavior Modification.* New York, Holt, Rinehart & Winston, 1969.

Beck, A. T.; Rush, A. J.; Shaw, B. F.; and Emery, G.: *Cognitive Therapy of Depression.* New York, Guilford, 1979.

Blachly, P. H.: An "electric needle" for aversive conditioning of the needle ritual. *Int J Add, 6*:327-328, 1971.

Blake, B. G.: The application of behavior therapy to treatment of alcoholism. *Behav Res Ther, 3*:78-85, 1965.

Blake, B. G.: A follow-up of alcoholics treated by behavior therapy. *Behav Res Ther, 5*:89-94, 1967.

Boudin, H. M.: Contingency contracting as a therapeutic tool in the deceleration of amphetamine use. *Behav Ther, 3*:604-605, 1972.

Boudin, H. M.; Valentine, V. E., III; Inghram, R. D., Jr.; Brantley, J. M.; Ruiz, M. R.; Smith, G. G.; Catlin, R. P., III; and Regon, E. J., Jr.: Contingency contracting with drug abusers in the natural environment. *Int J Add, 12*:1-10, 1977.

Brecher, E. M.; and Editors of Consumer Reports: *Licit and Illicit Drugs.* Mt. Vernon, Consumers Union, 1972.

Cahoon, D. D.; and Crosby, C. C.: A learning approach to chronic drug use: Sources of reinforcement. *Behav Ther, 3*:64-71, 1972.

Callahan, E. V.; and Rawson, R. A.: Behavioral assessment of narcotic addiction. In L. Sobell and M. Sobell (Eds.): *Outcome Evaluation in Alcohol and Drug Treatment.* New York, Pergamon, 1980.

Callner, D. A.; and Ross, S. M.: The reliability and validity of three measures of assertion in a drug addiction population. *Behav Ther, 7*:659-667, 1976.

Callner, D. A.; and Ross, S. M.: The assessment and training of assertion skills with drug addicts: A preliminary study. *Int J Add, 13*:227-239, 1978.

Callner, D. A.; and Ross, S. M.: Behavioral treatment approaches to drug abuse. In C. B. Taylor and J. Ferguson (Eds.): *Comprehensive Handbook of Behavioral Medicine* (Vol. 3). New York, Spectrum, 1980.

Caudill, B. D.; and Marlatt, G. A.: Modeling influences in social drinking: An experimental analogue. *J Con Clin Psychol, 43*:405-415, 1975.

Chappel, J. N.; Senay, E. C.; and Jaffe, J. H.: Cyclazocine in a multi-modality treatment program: Comparative results. *Int J Add, 6*:509-523, 1971.

Ciminero, A. R.; Calhoun, K. S.; and Adams, H. E. (Eds.): *Handbook of Behavioral Assessment.* New York, Wiley, 1977a.

Ciminero, H. R.; Nelson, R. O.; and Lipniski, D. R.: Self-monitoring procedures. In A. R. Ciminero; R. O. Nelson; and D. R. Lipniski (Eds.): *Handbook of Behavioral Assessment.* New York, Wiley, 1977b.

Cone, V. D.; and Hawkins, R. P. (Eds.): *Behavioral Assessment: New Directions in Clinical Psychology.* New York, Brunner/Mazel, 1977.

Copeman, C. D.: Drug addiction: I. A theoretical framework for behavior therapy. *Psychol Rep, 37*:947-958 1975.

Cox, T.; and Longwell, B.: Reliability of interview data concerning heroin use from heroin addicts on methadone. *Int J Add, 9*:162-165, 1974.

Crowley, T. J.: The reinforcers for drug abuse: Why people take drugs. *Comp Psychiatry, 13*:51-62, 1972.

Crowley, T. J.; Chesluk, D.; Dilts, S.; and Hart, R.: Drug and alcohol abuse among psychiatric admissions: A multidrug clinical — toxicologic study. *Arch Gen Psychiatry, 30*:13-20, 1974.

Cutler, R. E.; and Storm, T.: Observational study of alcohol consumption in natural settings: The Vancouver beer parlor. *J Stud Alc, 36*:1173-1183, 1975.

Dole, V. R.; and Nyswander, M.: Heroin addiction: A metabolic disease. *Arch Intern Med, 120*:19-24, 1967.

D'Zurilla, T.; and Goldfried, M.: Problem solving and behavior modification. *J Abnorm Psychol, 78*:107-126, 1971.

Ellis, A.: *Humanistic Psychotherapy: The Rational-Emotive Approach.* New York, McGraw-Hill, 1973.

Eysenck, H. J.; and Rachman, S.: *Causes and Cures of Neurosis.* London, Rutledge and Kegan Paul, 1965.

Fineman, K. R.: An operant conditioning program in a detention facility. *Psychol Rep, 22*:1119-1120, 1968.

Fort, J. P.: The psychodynamics of drug addiction and group psychotherapy. *Int J Group Psychother, 5*:150-156, 1955.

Franks, C. M.: Alcohol, alcoholism, and conditioning. *J Ment Sciences, 104*:14-33, 1958.

Franks, C. M.: Behavior therapy, the principles of conditioning and the treatment of the alcoholic. *Q J Stud Alc, 25*:511-529, 1963.

Garcia, J.; Hankins, W. G.; and Rusiniak, K. W.: Behavioral regulation of the milieu interne in man and rat. *Science, 185*:824-831, 1974.

Glicksman, J.; Ottomanelli, G.; and Cutler, R.: The earn-your-way-credit systems: Use of a token economy in narcotic rehabilitation. *Int J Add, 6*:525-531, 1971.

Haertzen, C. A.; and Hooks, N. T.: Changes in personality and subjective experience associated with the chronic administration and withdrawal of opiates. *J Nerv Ment Dis, 148*:606-613, 1969.

Hersen, M.; and Bellack, A. S. (Eds.): *Behavioral Assessment: A Practical Handbook.* New York, Pergamon, 1976.

Homer, A. L.; and Ross, S. M.: The reliability and validity of interview data obtained from drug and alcohol abusers. National Drug Abuse Conference, Fourth Annual Meeting, San Francisco, 1977.

Homme, L.: *How to Use Contingency Contracting in the Classroom.* Champaign, Ill.; Research Press, 1969.

Hsu, J.: Electroconditioning therapy of alcoholics: A preliminary report. *Q J Stud Alcohol, 26*:449-459, 1965.

Jaffe, J. H.: Drug addiction and drug abuse. In L. S. Goodman and A. Gilman (Eds.): *The Pharmacological Basis of Therapeutics* (4th ed.). London, Collier-MacMillan, 1970.

Kantorovich, N. V.: An attempt at associative reflex therapy in alcoholism. *Psychol Abs, 4*:493, 1930.

Kessler, M.; and Gomberg, C.: Observations of barroom drinking: Methodology and preliminary results. *Q J Stud Alcohol, 35*:1392-1396, 1974.

Kielholz, P.; and Battegay, R.: Switzerland's fight against mental illness. *Int J Psychiat, 4*:326-328, 1967.

Knox, D.: *Marriage Happiness: A Behavioral Approach To Counseling.* Champaign, Ill., Research Press, 1972.

Kraft, T.: Social anxiety and drug addiction. *Br J Soc Psychiatry, 2*:192-195, 1968.

Kraft, T.; and Al-Issa, I.: Desensitization and the treatment of alcoholic addiction. *Br J Addict, 63*:19-23, 1968.

Kraft, T.: Successful treatment of a case of chronic barbiturate addiction. *Br J Add, 64*:115-120, 1969.

Kraft, T.: Successful treatment of "Drinamyl" addicts and associated personality changes. *Can Psychiatric Assoc J, 15*:223-227, 1970.

Lemere, F.; Voegtlin, W. L.; Broz, W. R.; and O'Halleran, P.: Conditioned reflex treatment of alcohol addiction: V. Type of patient suitable for this treatment. *Northwestern Med (Seattle), 4*:88-89, 1942.

Lemere, F.; and Voegtlin, W. L.: An evaluation of the aversion treatment of alcoholism. *Q J Stud Alcohol, 11*:199-204, 1950.

Lent, J. R.: Mimosa Cottage: Experiment in hope. *Psychol Today,* pp. 51-58, June, 1968.

Lesser, E.: Behavior therapy with a narcotics user: A case report. *Behav Res Ther, 5*:251-252, 1967.

Liberman, R.: Aversive conditioning of drug addicts: A pilot study. *Behav Res Ther, 6*:229-231, 1968.

Ludwig, A. M.; Wikler, A.; and Stark, L. H.: The first drink: Psychological aspects of craving. *Arch Gen Psychiatry, 30*:539-547, 1974.

Lundwall, L.; and Baekland, F.: Disulfiram treatment of alcoholism: A review. *J Nerv Ment Dis, 153*:381-394, 1971.

Lynch, J. J.; Fertziger, A. P.; Teitelbaum, H. A.; Cullen, J. W.; and Gantt, W. H.: Pavlovian conditioning of drug reactions: Some implications for problems of drug addiction. *Conf Reflex, 8*:211-223, 1973.

MacCulloch, M. J.; Feldman, M. P.; Orford, J. F.; and MacCulloch, M. L.: Anticipatory avoidance learning in the treatment of alcoholism: A record of therapeutic failure. *Behav Res Ther, 4*:187-196, 1966.

Maddux, J. F.; and Desmond, D. P.: Reliability and validity of information from chronic heroin users. *J Psychiatric Res, 12*:95-97, 1975.

Marlatt, G. A.: *The Drinking Profile: A Questionnaire for the Behavioral Assessment of Alcoholism.* New York, Springer, 1976.

Marlatt, G. A.; and Nathan, P. E.: *Behavioral Approaches to Alcoholism.* New Brunswick, Rutgers, Center of Alcohol Studies, 1978.

Mash, E. J.; and Terdal, L. G. (Eds.): *Behavior Therapy Assessment: Diagnosis, Design and Evaluation.* New York, Springer, 1976.

McGuire, R. M.; and Vallance, M.: Aversion therapy by electric shock: A simple technique. *Br Med J, 1*:151-153, 1964.

Meichenbaum, D. B.: *Cognitive Behavior Modification: An Integrative Approach.* New York, Plenum, 1977.

Mello, N. K.; and Mendelson, J. H.: Drinking patterns during work contingent alcohol acquisition. *Psychosom Med, 34*:139, 1972.

Mendelson, J. H.; and Mello, N. K.: *The Diagnosis and Treatment of Alcoholism.* New York, McGraw-Hill, 1979.

Miller, P. M.; and Hersen, M.: Quantitative changes in alcohol consumption as a function of electrical aversive conditioning. *J Clin Psychol, 28*:590-593, 1972.

Miller, P. M.: *Behavioral Treatment of Alcoholism.* New York, Pergamon, 1976.

Miller, P. M.: Behavioral assessment of addictive behaviors. In A. R. Ciminero; K. S. Calhoun; and H. E. Adams (Eds.): *Handbook of Behavioral Assessment.* New York, Wiley, 1977.

Montgomery, J.; and McBurney, R. D.: *Operant Conditioning – Token-Economy.* Camarillo, Calif., Camarillo State Hospital, 1970.

Nash, G.: The sociology of Phoenix House — A therapeutic community for the resocialization of narcotic addicts. Unpublished paper, Columbia University, Bureau of Applied Social Research, 1969.

Nathan, P. E.; and Briddell, D. W.: Behavioral assessment and treatment of alcoholism. In B. Kissin; and H. Begleiter (Eds.): *The Biology of Alcoholism.* New York, Plenum, 1977.

Nathan, P. E.; and Lawson, D. M.: Overview of behavioral efforts to assess alcoholics and their alcoholism. In G. M. Marlatt; and P. E. Nathan (Eds.): *Behavioral Approaches to Alcoholism.* New York, McGraw-Hill, 1979.

Nathan, P. E.; and Lipscomb, T. R.: Behavior therapy and behavior modification in the treatment of alcoholism. In J. H. Mendelson and N. K. Mello (Eds.): *The Diagnosis and Treatment of Alcoholism.* New York, McGraw-Hill, 1979.

Nathan, P. E.; and O'Brien, J. S.: An experimental analysis of the behavior of alcoholics and normal drinkers during prolonged experimental drinking: A necessary precursor to behavior therapy? *Behav Ther, 2*:455-476, 1971.

O'Brien, J. S.; and Raynes, A. E.: Treatment of heroin addiction with behavioral therapy. In W. Keup (Ed.): *Drug Abuse: Current Concepts and Research.* Springfield, Thomas, 1972.

O'Brien, J. S.; Raynes, A. E.; and Patch, V. D.: An operant reinforcement system to improve ward behavior in inpatient drug addicts. *J Behav Ther Exp Psychiatry, 2*:239-242, 1971.

O'Brien, J. S.; Raynes, A. E.; and Patch, V. D.: Treatment of heroin addiction with aversion therapy, relaxation training, and systematic desensitization. *Behav Res Ther, 10*:77-80, 1972.

O'Brien, C.; and Ng, L.: Innovative treatments for drug addiction. In R. DuPont; A. Goldstein; and J. O'Donnell (Eds.): *Handbook on Drug Abuse.* Washington, D.C., NIDA, U.S. Govt. Print. Office, 1979.

O'Brien, C. P.; Testa, T.; O'Brien, T. J.; Brady, J. P.; and Wells, B.: Conditioned narcotic withdrawal in humans. *Science, 195*:1000-1002, 1977.

Paul, G.: Outcome of systematic desensitization. In C. Franks (Ed.): *Behavior Therapy: Appraisal and Status.* New York, McGraw Hill, 1969.

Premack, D.: Toward empirical behavior laws: I. Positive reinforcement. *Psychol Rev, 66*:219-233, 1959.

Rachman, S.: Sexual disorders and behavior therapy. *Am J Psychiatry, 118*:235-240, 1961.

Rachman, S.: Aversion therapy: Chemical or electrical. *Behav Res Ther, 2*:289-300, 1965.

Rachman, S.; and Teasdale, J.: *Aversion Therapy and Behavior Disorder.* Coral Gables, University of Miami Press, 1969.

Rado, S.: The psychoanalysis of pharmacothymia (drug addiction). *Psychoanaly Q, 2*:1-23, 1933.

Raymond, M. J.: The treatment of addiction by aversion conditioning with apomorphine. *Behav Res Ther, 1*:287-291, 1964.

Reid, J. B.: Study of drinking in actual settings. In G. A. Marlatt, and P. E. Nathan (Eds.): *Behavioral Approaches to Alcoholism.* New Brunswick, Rutgers, Center of Alcohol Studies, 1978.

Ross, S. M.; and Jones, C. G.: Contingency contracting with drug abusers. In D. Cannon (Chair.): Social Skills Training in a Drug Rehabilitation Program. Symposium presented at the meeting of the American Psychological Association, Montreal, 1973.

Sammons, R. A.: Contingency Management in a Drug Treatment Program. Paper presented at the first annual Rocky Mountain Conference on Behavior Modification, Denver, 1972.

Skolada, T. E.; Alterman, A. I.; Cornelison, F. S., Jr.; and Gottheil, E.: Treatment of outcome on a drinking-decision program. *J Stud Alc, 36*:365-380, 1975.

Spevack, M.; Pihl, R.; and Rowan, T.: Behavior therapies in the treatment of drug abuse: Some case studies. *Psychol Rec, 23*:179-184, 1973.

Sobell, L. C.; and Sobell, M. B.: Outpatient alcoholics give valid self-reports. *J Nerv Ment Dis, 161*:32-42, 1975.

Sobell, L. C.; and Sobell, M. B.: Outpatient alcoholics give valid self-reports. *J Nerv Ment Dis, 161*:32-42, 1972.

Sobell, L. C.: Critique of alcoholism treatment evaluation. In G. A. Marlatt; and P. E. Nathan (Eds.): *Behavioral Approaches to Alcoholism.* New Brunswick, Rutgers, Center of Alcohol Studies, 1978.

Sommer, R.: The isolated drinker in the Edmonton beer parlor. *Quart J Stud Alc, 26*:95-110, 1965.

Steinfeld, G. J.: The use of covert sensitization with institutionalized narcotic addicts. *Int J Add, 5*:225-232, 1970.

Steinfeld, G. J.; Rautio, E. A.; Rice, H. H.; and Egan, M. J.: Group covert sensitization with narcotic addicts: Further comments. *Int J Add, 9*:447-464, 1974.

Stuart, R. B.: Behavioral contracting within the families of delinquents. *J Behav Ther Exp Psychiatry, 2*:1-11, 1971.

Stumphauzer, J. S.: Social learning analysis of teenage alcohol, drug uses. *Los Angeles County Medical Association Bulletin, 106*:12-13, 1976.

Thinman, J.: Conditioned reflex treatment of alcoholism. I. Its rationale and technique. *N Engl J Med, 241*:368, 1949.

Thomson, I. G.; and Rathod, N. H.: Aversion therapy for heroin dependence. *The Lancet, 2*:382-384, 1968.

Tyler, V. O., Jr.; and Brown, G. D.: Token reinforcement of academic performance with institutionalized delinquent boys. *J Educ Psychol, 59*:164-168, 1968.

Voeghtlin, W. L.: The treatment of alcoholism by establishing a conditioned reflex. *Am J Med Sci, 199*:802, 1940.

Voeghtlin, W. L.: Conditioned reflex therapy of chronic alcoholism: Ten years' experience with the method. *Rocky Mount Med J, 44*:807-812, 1947.

Vogler, R. E.; Lunde, S. E.; and Martin, P. L.: Electrical aversion conditioning with chronic alcoholics: Follow-up and suggestions for research. *J Cons Clin Psychol, 36*:450, 1971.

Weins, A. N.; Montague, J. R.; Manaugh, T. S.; and English, C. J.: Pharmacological aversive counterconditioning to alcohol in a private hospital: One year follow-up. *J Stud Alc, 37*:1320-1324, 1976.

Wikler, A.: A psychodynamic study of a patient during self-regulated re-addiction to morphine. *Psych Q, 26*:270-293, 1952.

Wikler, A.: Some implications of conditioning therapy for problems of drug abuse. *Behav Sci, 16*:92-97, 1971.

Wikler, A.: Sources of reinforcement for drug-using behavior — A theoretical formulation. *Pharmacology and the Future of Man: Proceedings of the 5th International Congress on Pharmacology.* Basel, Karger, 1973.

Wilson, G. T.; and Davison, G. C.: Aversion techniques in behavior therapy: Some theoretical and metatheoretical considerations. *J Cons Clin Psychol, 33*:327-329, 1969.

Wisocki, P. A.: The empirical evidence of covert sensitization in the treatment of alcoholism: An evaluation. In R. D. Rubin; H. Fensterheim; J. D. Henderson; and L. P. Ullman (Eds.): *Advances in Behavior Therapy.* New York, Academic, 1972.

Wolpe, J.: Conditioned inhibition of craving in drug addiction: A pilot experiment. *Behav Res Ther, 2*:285-287, 1965.

Yablonsky, L.: *Synanon, the Tunnel Back.* Baltimore, Penguin, 1967.

CHAPTER 5

GROUP THERAPY WITH DRUG ADDICTS

Robert J. Craig

INTRODUCTION

Whether one views the causes of drug dependence as a metabolic disease, as a psychological disturbance resulting from intrapsychic conflicts, as a sociological phenomena due to societal conditions that disallow minorities the chance to acquire economic and problem solving skills to cope with today's world, as an escape from an hostile and overcrowded environment, as a result of poor family relationships, as a form of adolescent rebellion, as a result of an inadequate personality development, as a result of maladaptive interpersonal transactions, or merely the result of simple curiosity and propinquity with the drug-taking peer group, the ensuing behavior is remarkably similar.

Within the context of therapy, such acting-out patients tend to demonstrate an action-oriented method of handling problems, a willingness to talk to a therapist only when there is a crisis in their lives, poor introspection, manipulation and conning, an "out-of-sight-out-of-mind" approach to problems, saying one thing to a therapist and doing something else outside of therapy, a tendency not to link the past with the present and future, a poor frustration tolerance, tendencies to externalize and deny, self-destructive acting-out behavior, intellectual explanations of behavior to avoid conscious experience of affect, maintenance of self-image, irregular attendance, and premature termination (Borriello, 1979).

The therapeutic modality utilized in most drug treatment programs is individual counseling, often by people most untrained and unprepared to give it (ex-addicts). If counseling services are offered to drug abusers while in jail, brief (one or two sessions) individual counseling is the primary modality offered (Newman and Price, 1977). Family therapy in most drug programs is nonexistent. Coleman and Davis (1978), in a NIDA-commissioned survey of family therapy offered in drug programs nationally, found that only 15 percent of the agencies responding to the survey were providing family therapy. Usually this meant that the primary care therapists were less formally trained family therapists-counselors. The authors concluded that family therapy is given low priority by most agencies. Respondents cited that they did not receive census credit for more than the identified patient in family therapy, but I believe that this is merely an administrative convenience preference. The issue goes much deeper and probably relates to the manifest avoidant behavior seen among drug addicts. Stanton (1977) received a grant that paid families $5.00 per session for family therapy. Even under this monetary incentive it took an average of seventeen contacts with the family before the team could persuade the family to engage in therapy. No doubt the persistent and motivated belief systems of these clinician-researchers interacted with the monetary rewards to facilitate entry into treatment. However, such rewards are usually not present in most drug programs; it is emotionally simpler to deal with the individual than with his primary (family) or secondary (group) relationship. In fact, in my clinical experience, if given a free choice, drug addicts would almost uniformly avoid psychotherapeutic encounters.

Most traditional group therapists exclude drug addicts in their selecting criteria, believing that the compulsive personality characteristics of the addict retards group development. There is near unanimity that drug addicts should be treated within a homogenous group setting but the resulting methods, specific to the group, have been modified and rarely reflect a more traditional method that is used with neurotic and other personality disorders. The purpose of this article is to highlight the various modifications made to accommodate addicts in group therapy, and to discuss issues conducting group therapy on an inpatient and an outpatient basis.

ADDICTS AND GAMING BEHAVIOR

Transactional analysts have been particularly skillful in elucidating and describing the patterns of recurrent interpersonal relationships (referred to as "Games") manifested among people as they engage in human encounters and they have developed a unique and creative language to catalogue these patterns that is easily understood by its patients. Transactional analysis is basically no different when applied to addicts than when practiced among other pathological groups. That is, TA therapists still analyze life positions, rituals, games, scripts, ego states, and the like. However, in the "Games Analysis" it has been observed that addicts play more salient games than other types of disorders, and these have been reviewed by Levine and Stephans (1971):

(1) In the "Junkie-Square" game, the addict claims that the therapist cannot help him becasuse the nondrug abuser cannot understand what its like to be an addict and have to deal with issues of craving, withdrawal, procurement of drugs, and dealing.

(2) "Black-White" is a variant of Junkie-Square with a racial variable introduced to take advantage of white guilt. The implication is that the therapist is a racist and is trying to impose white middle-class values on the addict.

(3) "Cops and Robbers" also emphasizes the inability of the therapist to help the addict because the therapist is on the side of the cops. Thus, the addict can justify to himself the refusal to provide relevant information to the therapist, and circumvent the possibility of therapy ever taking place.

(4) "Courthouse" is a game whereby addicts put the therapist into the role of defendant or counsel for the defense. The behavior of the addict is designed to beat the rap (avoid issues that the therapist deems important). If the addict can manipulate the therapist into defending himself, then he can avoid any emotional responsibility or even discussion of his own behavior.

Let me describe a vignette illustrating how these games are played by addicts in real life. A patient came to my office complaining that he was being discharged from our outpatient clinic because he was caught stealing a television that belonged to one of the staff. The television was placed on a chair while its owner had returned to his office to get his coat. The patient, seeing the television unattended, grabbed it and was caught trying to sneak it out of the door. Staff voted to discharge the patient for violating a clinic rule (no stealing). The patient came to me asking for a reversal of the decision. This conversation went something like this: "You know me, Dr. Craig. You know I am a thief. I came here for help with my problem and you are throwing me out before I can get the help I need. You know if I'm discharged I will have to go out and steal. Is this what you want me to do? Staff should know better than to leave a TV around a guy like me. Look, I gave it back. I made restitution. Now you are throwing me out to steal before I can get help." This game was basically "Poor Me" and attempted to capitalize on therapist guilt to avoid responsibility for his actions.

Addicts play these games because there are certain rewards or payoffs that provide continuing reinforcement. Levine and Stephans list ten such rewards:

   (1) A sense of good craftsmanship.
   (2) Excitement.
   (3) Power.
   (4) Tangible rewards.
   (5) Status among other addicts.
   (6) Security.
   (7) Revenge.
   (8) Personal meaning.
   (9) Avoidance of responsibility.
  (10) Avoidance of punishment.

The thing to remember is that there is a little bit of truth in every game the addict plays — just enough to potentially elicit doubt, guilt, or "nice guy" games by the therapist.

Using "game" understanding implies that the therapist make explicit the games and their ramifications that addicts play and then try to get the addict to relate more honestly in his relationships by identifying new role models and by experimenting with new behaviors. This is accomplished by preventing the player from acquiring the rewards, by verbally exposing the game as it is played, and by setting limits with external controls, such as withdrawal of privileges.

VARIATIONS OF GROUP THERAPY WITH ADDICTS

Confrontation

One does not have to operate from a TA theory to engage in exposing addict games. One can use peer confrontation techniques to accomplish many of the same things that TA espouses and in fact such peer confrontation modalities are the most common ones used in therapeutic communities. The confrontation method with addicts was originally popularized by the Synanon Program and is now almost universally accepted in therapeutic communities. It is also attempted at some detox and some outpatient programs. Van Stone and Gilbert (1972) have described such a group at the Palo Alto VA Hospital where a peer confrontation ward was established for addicts. The program consisted of (1) an individually negotiated treatment contract between each patient and his peers, (2) a twenty-four-hour residential setting away from their original social milieu, (3) a drug and medication free environment, (4) a highly authoritarian, member-control social structure, and (5) group confrontation sessions where addict attempts to play "games" are ridiculed, insulted, browbeaten, and shouted down until he is ready to relate honestly and with appropriate emotions. Authority conflicts, expressed dependency, persistent hostility, and narcissim are treated within an atmosphere of strict control, confrontation, and the emotional warmth of a "super family."

A number of special group therapies have been enumerated for residential treatment programs, each using the variation of the confrontation method (Albert, 1975):

(1) *Hot Seat:* The patient is at the center of the circle and engages in a verbal street fight designed to examine negative behavior and confront his "games."

(2) *Rap Session:* The patient engages in free and light discussion of his problem in a nonpressured atmosphere within a problem-solving context.

(3) *Stroke Group:* Each member tells the other person in the

middle of the circle how he feels about the person and how the person is progressing in his rehabilitation and notes any positive behavior the patient has demonstrated recently.

(4) *Feedback:* The person on the hot seat tells what he thinks of group members. This continues until everyone has taken the hot seat.

Opinions vary as to the extent and the timing of confrontation but there is near unanimity that such confrontation needs to occur with addicts. Most agree that the manipulative behavior and impulse ridden life-style needs to be confronted and dealt with in order to change it. Some advocate that this type of behavior needs to be confronted immediately whenever it is demonstrated, while others advocate an initial stance of requiring the patient to remain peripherally involved until he has overcome his problems with trust and paranoia (Khantzian and Kates, 1978). I believe both approaches are correct. The early confrontation by therapists tells the patient that he is on to their games and will not tolerate or be conned by them. However, early confrontations are more gentle than later ones.

A patient was telling me in an individual session shortly after he was admitted about how he conned the truck drivers on South Water Street and presented this story with a sense of pride and satisfaction. Of course, he said this was all in the past and he was not "into that" any more. One hour later, in group, the patient was demanding to be informed about all the possible benefits he was entitled to and the many sources of money available to veterans so he could choose which one of those sources he would apply to for money. The patient did not need the money for legitimate purposes. Therefore, I handled the matter as follows: "Perhaps you think the VA is just another truck driver." Although the other group members did not understand my train of thought, this gentle confrontation struck a nerve of the patient and forced him to blush, telling the group why I had made the remark. A more constructive session followed.

Marathon Groups

Marathon groups are basically confrontation groups within a time-compressed format. Page (1980) described the marathon group procedure for female drug addicts at a woman's prison. The purpose of the sixteen-hour group was to facilitate discussion of personal problems and to enable the group participant to receive feedback about their interpersonal relationships as they unfolded during the group marathon. Since interpersonal problems mediate or contribute to the development and maintenance of drug-abusing behavior, resolution of these dysfunctional patterns might facilitate patient rehabilitation. The goals of the group were to develop less manipulative life-styles and to decrease their alienation from society.

The format was unstructured and formal exercises were held to a minimum. The coleaders helped the group to express their feelings, encouraged discussion, gave feedback, and avoided defending the prison setting or society. This group passed through the usual stages of marathon groups and the leaders fostered the expression of hostile feelings onto themselves in an effort to work through these "transference projections." As trust evolved, efforts to manipulate the leaders or other group members were often confronted and these self-destructive patterns were analyzed.

Page believes that marathon groups could be used to supplement the gains made in regular group therapy and feels they more intensely focus on the addicts' interpersonal relationship styles and manipulative behavior patterns than traditional group therapies. However, we have no knowledge of whether marathon groups have any affect on the lives of its participants after release from the institution, although such marathon groups receive positive evaluations from the group's members after the experience.

Goal-Oriented Group Therapy

Dell Orto (1975) believes that encounter techniques such as a small group marathon have a short-lived impact due to the random application and lack of skill building. He developed a technique, referred to as goal group therapy, emphasizing the teaching of generalized skills to increase an addict's chance of future success. It relies on the power of group process, the impact of peer pressure, and the setting of realistic and realizable goals.

The structure of goal group therapy consists of four phases, each having three components. Phase I consists of initiation (What group is this?), accountability (Who has goals and who does not?), and exploration (Do you have valid reasons for not having written goals?). Phase II consists of goal presentation (Who wants to get well first?), probe (exploration of stated goals), and feedback (evaluation of past goals). Phase III contains the processes of integration (generalization of goals to other areas), a didactic component (written, audiovisual aid, therapist presentations), and highlights (focusing on key group processes). The final phase emphasizes observations (pre and post gains discussions), questions, and a summary. Goal attainment scaling techniques can be used to supplement this group exercise. Dell Orto sees a goal-oriented group experience as one which focuses on objective outcomes and processes that maximize the attainment of client goals.

Existential Group Therapy

Existenial group therapy has been attempted with addicts on methadone maintenance (Scher et al., 1975). Attendance at these groups is required in order to receive methadone. The group attempts to alter the specific personality traits of low pain tolerance, distorted time perception, hedonic tendencies, and undisciplined life-styles. This requires a high degree of structure within the group. The main rule in the group is no drug talk nor talking about their "junkie past." Patients are expected to deal with here and now and with the future, not with their past. The focus is on what an individual is to become.

Scher notes that four common types of addicts are found in these therapy groups: (1) the noncommunicator, (2) the hostile-disruptor, (3) the superficial verbalizer, and (4) the effective communicator. Such patients need special techniques to deal with such disruptive communication styles. Scher uses a multiplicity of techniques, including group sentence completion items, feedback and challenge sessions, role playing, group fantasy, future time projections, self-evaluations, and attitude exchanges to pace the tempo of the group within an existential orientation.

Comparative Effects

Research on the comparative effects of different group approaches is meager. Abrahms (1979) compared a cognitive-behavioral versus nondirective treatment approach for addicts on methadone maintenance. Fourteen patients were randomly assigned to one of each modality, consisting of ten two-hour sessions. The cognitive behavior approach was designed to teach stress management techniques, control anxiety and depression, negative self-evaluations and nonassertiveness. The sessions use deep muscle relaxation training with imaginal and actual approaches to conflict situations. The sessions are identified and patients practice verbal and nonverbal components of assertiveness. They also used the gradual rehearsal of behavioral units leading to goal attainment. Techniques of thought stopping, covert sensitization, identification of irrational assumptions, and behavioral analyses were further used in conjunction with homework assignments. The nondirective group participated in an equal number of sessions focused around drug-related experiences. Multiple assessment measures and frequent data collection points, including a sixteen-week follow-up, revealed that a cognitive-behavioral approach was more powerful in maintaining short-term behavior changes than the nondirective method.

The peer group confrontation format, emphasizing verbal attack, has received some support in contrast to patients who receive the traditional approaches (Balgooyen, 1974). *Subjects* were thirty-five patients on a group confrontation ward at the Palo Alto VA Hospital. They were compared to a control group of thirty-five patients receiving routine treatment for drug abuse. All subjects were pretested on the FIRO-B SCALE and the Multiple Affect Adjective Check List and then posttested after six weeks of treatment. The confrontation method consisted of three-hour "games" (verbal attack) four times per week. Both psychological measures revealed greater changes in the verbal attack therapy group, especially in areas of interpersonal perceptions and behavior. However, there was no attempt to determine if the changes observed while the patients were hospitalized actually generalized to naturally occurring events following discharge.

STRUCTURAL PROBLEMS IN CONDUCTING GROUP THERAPY WITH DRUG ADDICTS

The purpose of this section is to discuss some common structural problems in conducting group therapy with drug addicts and to present some ideas concerning the therapeutic handling of these difficult issues.

Attendance

Most outpatient (and, for that matter, inpatient) groups with drug addicts require mandatory attendance. Without this proviso, addict groups tend to have sporadic attendance, frequent tardiness, and no shows, and an ephemeral history. Most authors recommend that methadone become contingent upon group attendance in outpatient methadone clinics. Others recommend some type of external punishment or consequences if addicts do not attend their therapy groups (Ben-Yehuda, 1980; Khantzian and Kates, 1978; and Scher et al., 1975).

I believe that the patients in the group need to set limits concerning attendance and to "pull up" members whose attendance is in noncompliance with the therapeutic norms desired by the group leader. Thus, the group therapist needs to "treat the group" when a member's attendance is deficient rather than focusing on the individual member who is violating the norm. The group must come to view such events as their problem and not merely the problem of the group therapist. If the group does not deal with attendance as a "pull up," then the therapist cannot hope for the group to deal with far more important issues that relate to the individual and group functioning. Thus, the therapeutic task in developing such norms is to "pull up" the group for not dealing with the attendance problem and not merely concentrate on the individual member who is acting out or defensive through his attendance posture.

Limit Setting

The issue of attendance is just one form of limit setting. Group therapists will need to maintain a high vigilance and high levels of activity to set and keep limits in working with drug addict therapy groups. Although this will initially revolve around such issues as attendance, tardiness, and time limits, in the later stages of group therapy limit setting will revolve around such behaviors as frequent interruptions, shouting, and everybody talking at once. It would be most helpful and useful for the group norm to develop whereby it is understood that a group member will "pull up" other group members whenever such negative behavior is demonstrated. However, this is not an easy task and the therapist will, sooner or later, have to be the final authority in the setting of limits.

Drug Talk

Some argue that drug talk must not be allowed to enter a therapy group because it is counterproductive (Ben-Yehuda, 1980; Scher et al., 1975). In TA parlance, drug talk is a "pastime" with no intent to change behavior but merely designed to pass the time until the therapy is over. Drug talk in therapy groups is best excluded.

Patients Who Are High

This situation can and does occur, especially in outpatient methadone maintenance clinics. The therapist and the group will need to take a firm stand on his problem. Ordinarily, it is recommended that patients who are high or who are nodding out should not participate in the group for that session (Ben-Yehuda, 1980).

Game Analysis

It is important to confront addict games as they are manifested in the group. Although mere confrontation may not in and of itself be a corrective emotional experience, it does convey to the patient that a different style of relating is expected in the group and indeed his drug abuse will not cease unless the personality factors associated with drug abusing behavior also change. One particular aspect of the addict personality that must change is a manipulative, conning, and role playing behavior that is manifested amidst the drug-taking tendencies. By confronting the patient, either by the group or by the therapist, we convey to the patient that we are "on to their game" and will not reinforce it by passively allowing it to continue in the group. In this approach, the addict is afforded the opportunity of experimenting with new ways of relating in the group in an atmosphere of non-threatened trust and acceptance. Remember, behavior change is a process that takes time. It is a skill that needs practice before it occurs naturally. The group is a perfect place to experiment in these new skills and support their efforts to practice these new skills elsewhere.

Group Norms

Initial goals in a group of acting-out patients is to get the patient to think about himself, feel some curiosity about the way he behaves, inventory his life experiences or a "crisis review," and to demonstrate how it has been "X" number of times that he has experienced a similar crisis, with a goal of internalizing the realization that crises of the past will perpetuate into crises of the future unless the patient does something to change himself (Borriello, 1979). In order to accomplish this task, the following group mores have been suggested: (1) continuous attendance; (2) confidentiality; (3) honesty of relating and the futility of deception; (4) self-investigation and introspection; (5) personal responsibility for my behavior; (6) past-present-future linkage of experience and behavior; (7) tolerance for feelings of being uncomfortable; (8) therapy task diligence; (9) immediacy of affective expression through verbal report; (10) the self-destructiveness of acting-out behavior; (11) futility and consequences of manipulation; (12) the active engagement of attempting to control one's impulses.

Inpatient Groups

Short-term residential programs have special problems in attempting to conduct group therapy. Rapid turnover, ostensibly changing group norms, repetitive questions and challenges, and common attempts to continue initial gaming behavior are common occurrences in such groups. Models of group therapy that exist today are primarily applicable to outpatient groups and have marginal utility in dealing with short-term groups. Such models have never come to grips with the changing group norms and fluctuating group membership of short-term groups. In such instances, the usual practice is to do individual therapy in a group setting and to use group process and group dynamics when it is to the advantage of the group therapist. Norms have to be developed and continually reinforced by the therapist, since group composition changes frequently.

CONCLUSIONS

Group therapy is an important modality in the treatment armamentarium of the clinician. I do not know of a single drug abuse program that excludes group therapy as part of their treatment regimen. However, there are special problems in conducting therapy groups with addicts and some of these special issues have been addressed in this chapter. Group therapy can have dramatic and exciting effects on a drug addict. If the addict can form a therapeutic alliance, it can be the modality that makes the ultimate difference in the patient's eventual rehabilitation.

REFERENCES

Abrahms, J.: A cognitive-behavioral vs non-directive group treatment program for opiod-addicted persons: An adjunct to methadone maintenance. *Int J Addict, 14*:503-512, 1979.

Albert, M.: Administrating residential treatment programs. In R. Coombs (Ed.): *Junkies and Straights.* Lexington, Mass, Lexington Books, 1975, pp. 83-104.

Balgooyen, T.: A comparison of the effect of Synanon "game" verbal attack therapy and standard group therapy practice in hospitalized chronic alcoholics. *J Community Psychol, 2*:54-58, 1974.

Ben-Yehuda, N.: Group therapy with methadone-maintained patients: Structural problems and solutions. *Int J Grp Psychother, 30*:331-345, 1980.

Borriello, J.: Group psychotherapy with acting-out patients: Specific problems and techniques. *Am J Psychother, 33*:521-530, 1979.

Coleman, S.; and Davis, D.: Family therapy and drug abuse: A national survey. *Family Process, 17*:21-29, 1978.

Dell Orto, A.: Goal group therapy: A structured group experience applied to drug treatment and rehabilitation. *J Psychedelic Drugs, 7*:363-371, 1975.

Khantzian, E.; and Kates, W.: Group treatment of unwilling addicted patients: Pragmatic and clinical aspects. *Int J Grp Psychother, 28*:81-94, 1978.

Levine, S.; and Stephans, R.: Games addicts play. *Psychiat Q., 45*:584-592, 1971.

Newman, C.; and Price, B.: *Jails and Drug Treatment: A National Prospective.* Beverly Hills, Calif., Sage Publ., 1977.

Page, R.: Marathon groups: Counseling the imprisoned drug abuser. *Int J Addict, 15*:765-770, 1980.

Scher, J., et al.: Professionally directed existential group therapy in methadone maintenance rehabilitation. An unpublished paper, Methadone Maintenance Institute, Chicago, Ill., 1975.

Stanton, M.: Some outcome results in aspects of structural family therapy with drug addicts. Paper presented at the National Drug Abuse Conference, San Francisco, May, 1977.

Van Stone, W.; and Gilbert, R.: Peer confrontation groups: What, why and whether? *Am J Psychiat, 129*:583-588, 1972.

CHAPTER 6

FAMILY THERAPY OF DRUG DEPENDENT VETERANS*

M. Duncan Stanton

Concomitant with the growing interest in the military family (Goldman, 1976; Segal et al., 1976), attention has also been increasingly directed toward family approaches to dealing with problems of soldiers and veterans (Frances and Gale, 1973; Stanton, 1976b). To some extent this change has been a spinoff from the increased attention families have begun to receive in the larger society, along with a mounting interest in family therapeutic modes within the mental health professions (Stanton, 1975, 1976b). In this chapter the context and some aspects of this trend as it has been manifested in a clinical research program dealing with drug addicted veterans and their families are discussed.

MILITARY ASPECTS

What role do family factors play in a soldier's addiction? Obviously early experience or upbringing plays a critical role in the genesis of such problems. In addition, however, one of the strongest cases for a nonphysiological basis for opiate addiction

---

*An earlier version of this chapter appeared in E. J. Hunter (Ed.), *Changing Families in a Changing Military System*, San Diego, Naval Health Research Center, 1977.

The research portion of this paper was supported by the National Institute on Drug Abuse, Grant No. DA-01119, and the Attorney General of Pennsylvania's Public Health Trust Fund (56772). It was conducted at the Philadelphia Child Guidance Clinic and the Philadelphia VA Drug Dependence Treatment Center. Thomas C. Todd, Ph.D., was Co-principal investigator. Coordination within the VA was primarily handled by Charles P. O'Brien, M. D., George Wood, M. D., and Elton Hargrove.

came from Vietnam in 1971 and 1972 (Stanton, 1976a, 1908b). Data show that 75 to 90 percent of the men who were addicted to heroin in Vietnam had "cleaned up" (detoxified) a few days or weeks prior to their return home (Peck, 1973; Robins et al., 1975). The screenings were clearly a powerful intervention, and, indeed, 90 percent of all Vietnam returnees surveyed by Robins (1974) approved of them. Further, 95 percent of those addicted in Vietnam had not become readdicted 8 to 12 months after return, a phenomenally high rate of remission. The vast majority of these men were not addicted before their Vietnam tour, and the importance of significant others comes to light when reasons given by the men for detoxification are considered.

From all reports, the predominant motive for cleaning up before leaving Southeast Asia was to avoid the stigma, humiliation, and hassle from family and friends of returning home a "junkie" (McGlothlin, 1975; Stanton, 1976a).

VETERANS AND DRUGS

After discharge from military service, what then? A good number of servicemen used drugs heavily in the military — perhaps for the first time — and a certain percentage have subsequently continued use. Those unlucky enough to have been caught while on active duty paid a price, as for example, in 1969-1970, when 16,000 servicemen were punitively or administratively discharged for drug abuse. The majority (11,000) of those men were ineligible for VA treatment, and all of them were at a serious disadvantage when they later tried to obtain jobs. In late 1971 and 1972 the Department of Defense reversed its policy, and these servicepersons were allowed to apply for review of their discharges; however, such a review is not a particularly swift process, and damage had already been done in many instances. Also, in 1972 the Army revised its drug policy to permit honorable discharges for drug addicts and heavy abusers, usually following some attempt at rehabilitation. The importance of these steps was that drug abuse was being de-criminalized and viewed as a social problem, rather than a strictly legal or medical one.

For the veteran with a service-connected drug problem, the Veterans Administration (VA) is an obvious place to turn. Of course, non-VA programs may be deemed more desirable or convenient in some areas, but discussion here will not deal with these. It should be noted that VA psychiatric treatment has tra-ditionally not been family-oriented. Although this policy has been changing in recent years, the VA has generally subscribed to the individual treatment models conventionally applied by most non-VA mental health treatment facilities. Further, a large percentage of its caseload includes older veterans of World Wars I and II, many of whose families-of-origin are deceased. Thus, it is doubtful that a project such as will be outlined below would have been possible ten, or perhaps even four or five years ago. However, times change, and we will describe a program for ad-dicted veterans within a VA setting that highlights family factors in the addiction process and requires family involvement in the treatment plan.

THE FAMILY TREATMENT PROGRAM

This outpatient-oriented program began in 1974 through collaboration between the Philadelphia Child Guidance Clinic, the Philadelphia VA Drug Dependence Treatment Center (DDTC), and the University of Pennsylvania. It was a research program based on the development of new therapy techniques and in testing the efficacy of family therapy with VA drug pa-tients. In this report we will deal partly with the research aspects but mainly with the clinical findings and treatment techniques that have emerged. The family therapy model employed de-rived from the "structural" (Minuchin, 1974) and "strategic" (Haley, 1980) approaches. It involved the therapist being active and maintaining control of the session, using behavioral tasks whenever appropriate, emphasizing symptom change, concep-tualizing the structure of the family as a guide to interventions, setting generational boundaries, and focusing on positive change *in* the session and *between* sessions as the route to more permanent improvement and change (Stanton and Todd, 1979).

The 118 patients involved were all veterans between ages twenty-three and thirty-five (mean = 25.5). Approximately half were black and half white, none had a history of psychosis, and all were addicted to heroin for a period of at least two years (mean = 6.6 years). Thirty-one percent were married. Most were on methadone, at least initially. Forty-four percent had served in Vietnam and three-fourths were Army veterans. All subjects included in the study had two parents or parent substitutes available (e.g., stepmother, stepfather, mother's boyfriend) and saw at least one of them weekly. The extent of contact with family of origin (i.e., parents) is an important phenomenon. In 1972 we undertook a survey of eighty-five patients at the DDTC and found that 82 percent of them were in weekly, and 66 percent in *daily*, contact with at least one of their parents; they either lived at home, or in a downstairs apartment, or just "around the corner." This finding becomes more striking considering that (a) the average age of these individuals was twenty-eight, and (b) they had been away from home in the service for a minimum of several months and had nonetheless returned to their parents afterward. These data are consistent with an increasing number of studies both in the United States and other countries (reviewed in Stanton, 1980a, 1980c, and Stanton et al., 1978) that indicate that the majority of heroin addicts are intimately and regularly involved with their families-of-origin. Thus, the importance of close family-of-origin ties for our patients, both before and after military service, was apparent, and we believe that such forces strongly influenced many of them while they were on active duty also.

When we inspected the structures of these families we found them to be consonant with those of families of other drug addicts, as described in the literature (Harbin and Maziar, 1975; Klagsbrun and Davis, 1977; Seldin, 1972; Stanton, 1979a, 1979b), namely, (a) there was usually a very close, dependent mother-son relationship, (b) father was often distant and excluded, and (c) in a high percentage of the cases, one or both parents had a drinking problem.

Upon initiation of treatment, the function of the symptom for these families became quite clear. In a sense, the addicted member was serving to keep the family, and particularly the parents, together. When he began to improve or clean up, the parents began to talk of separating, or a crisis or fight occurred. When he got "dirty" again, they "rallied around" and resumed a relation with him (Stanton, 1977, 1980a; Stanton et al., 1978). Thus, the family system served to maintain the addiction. This pattern is similar to that described by Haley (1973, 1980) for families of schizophrenics and other "disturbed" young people.

The treatment approach used has been described more specifically in a recent paper (Stanton and Todd, 1979) and a forthcoming book (Stanton et al., 1981). It included all aspects of a drug program, such as counseling, methadone, urinalysis, etc. An important aspect was that the family therapists had control over methadone dosages and other medications. Without such control. the therapy would probably not have succeeded, since these drugs are such a primary part of the reason for seeking treatment; this practice also helped avoid possible struggles between therapist and drug counselor over "turf" and case control. Further, urinalysis results were particularly important because they helped to keep the family abreast of the addict's progress and made change a tangible event.

It became increasingly clear that family treatment must first deal with the triad composed of addict and both parents before proceeding further. If this step is skipped, therapy will falter and possibly fail. In some cases, especially with married patients, we started with the marital pair and found that the treatment process only served to stress or dissolve the marriage; thus, the addict ended up back with his parent(s). Marital therapy (especially when attempted initially and before parents were involved) did not work.

Approximately one month into treatment, we could safely predict that some kind of crisis would occur. As soon as the family system started changing, great anxiety was aroused and disequilibrium ensued. Frequently, it revolved around an attempt by the addict to detoxify. At such time the therapist was called upon to expend great time and energy through telephone calls, home visits, or whatever, to help the family through this period. The therapist attempted to stop the cycle or repetitive pattern and alter its outcome. Such crises, then, became harbingers of effective family change and improvement.

ENGAGING FAMILIES IN TREATMENT

Frequently we are asked how we were able to get these families into treatment. This process required considerable innovation. Addict families are notoriously hard to engage. Other programs have found this a nearly impossible task, especially in getting fathers involved (see Stanton and Todd, 1980a, for a review of the relevant studies). Nevertheless, we were able to engage 71 percent of them (including *both* parents or parent surrogates) in treatment, a percentage that is much higher than other reports in the literature on such patients, and two or three times greater than most reports. This was accomplished through expenditure of (in many cases) considerable time and energy. It took from one to thirty-three direct contacts (telephone calls, interviews, home visits) with addict and family members (median = 5.4), over a median of 20.5 days, to recruit them. The change to having therapists serve in the "dual" role as drug counselors greatly helped to lessen this effort. It reduced the amount of time and the number of home visits required, and also increased our rate of success. Before the dual role, we were successful 56 percent of the time, while with this role the percentage rose to 77 percent. Our calculations show that having therapists serve as drug counselors also *more than doubled the cost efficiency* of the recruitment effort. More detailed analyses of these data and a discussion of the principles and techniques involved are presented in three other papers (Stanton and Todd, 1980a, 1980b; Van Deusen et al., 1981). From our experience in trying to get families of addicts into treatment we have developed a set of twenty-one family recruitment principles. These are set forth below, and are elaborated on in Stanton and Todd (1980a):

(1) The therapist should decide which family members need to be included, and not leave this decision to the index patient.
(2) Whenever possible, one or more family members should be

encouraged to attend the initial or intake interview.

(3) Do not expect the index patient to bring in the family on his own.

(4) Obtain permission from the index patient to contact his family, and then get in touch with them, whenever possible, during the interview.

(5) The closer the family therapist's first contact with the index patient is to the time of intake, the greater are the chances for recruiting the family.

(6) The earlier the family therapist enters the chain of "treaters" encountered by the client, the better are chances for family recruitment.

(7) The sooner the family is contacted the more likely are they to be engaged.

(8) Viewing the family recruitment effort as crisis-inducing can help the therapist in his engagement efforts.

(9) The therapist must get past the index patient and directly contact each family member, or at least both parents; if, prior to the first session, he can obtain from them an agreement to participate, the chances of their actually attending are increased markedly.

(10) The therapist must approach the family with a rationale for treatment which is nonpejorative and nonjudgmental and which in no way blames them for the problem.

(11) Primary focus should be on helping the index patient rather than the family.

(12) The rationale for family treatment should be presented in such a way that, in order to oppose it, family members would have to state openly that they want the index patient to remain symptomatic.

(13) The therapist should adopt the family's goals for the index patient as the primary ones for treatment.

(14) The chances for successful family recruitment are increased if the therapist does the recruiting.

(15) The therapist should be the primary treater of the index patient and his family.

(16) An important recruitment variable is the extent to which the therapist shows interest in the family through his will-

lingness to expend considerable effort in engaging them.

(17) Providing incentives to therapists for each successfully recruited case increases the rate of success.

(18) The program must be structured in a way that does not allow therapists to back down from enlisting whole families.

(19) A mechanical approach to recruitment is insufficient to guarantee success — flexibility and skill are crucial if the therapist is to avoid getting deadlocked.

(20) The treatment agency must have flexile policies to allow therapist flexibility.

(21) The treatment agency must be willing to back up the recruitment effort through commitment of tangible resources.

Finally, a note on the cases we were not able to recruit — the "refusers" — might be of interest. Two-thirds of them were not recruited because the veteran refused to let his family be contacted. With cases in which we were allowed to contact family members directly, we were successful 88 percent of the time.

TREATMENT OUTCOME

The design for this research and some preliminary findings have been presented in an earlier publication (Stanton, 1978). The 118 addicts and their families were divided into four treatment groups. Random assignment was used. The four groups were: a non-family "treatment-as-usual" group; a family movie program; and two types of family therapy — "paid" and "unpaid." The paid condition differed from the unpaid in that family members in paid family therapy received reimbursement for attending sessions to help their addicted member and assist him in staying off drugs; this procedure was included in order to increase their incentive to participate. Movie families also received this reimbursement. Posttreatment interviews, eventually extending over a four-year period, are being gathered by research interviewers on the clients, their parents, and other family members.

A ten-session treatment model was employed with the family movie and two family therapy groups. In general, session attendance was quite good, both in comparison to dropout rates normally seen with addict families and relative to most psychotherapy studies. In the paid family group the mean number of sessions attended (out of the required 10) was 9.4 while it was 5.8 for the unpaid group and 8.7 for the (paid) movie group. The indication is that payment succeeded in keeping families in treatment (Stanton et al., 1979).

As of this writing, we have succeeded in maintaining contact with 97 percent of the patients and their families. In 96 percent of the cases, we have been able to obtain enough information to make judgments about outcome. In particular, we are examining the subjects' extent of drug use, involvement in work or school, and mortality.

An area in which family therapy seems to have had an impact is in the rate at which the addict clients died during the follow-up period. So far, the incidence (over an average of 31 months posttreatment) of deaths for the nonfamily and family movie clients is 10 percent, while for cases that were involved in the two family therapy groups it is only one-fifth as great, i.e., 2 percent. This difference is statistically significant and may be pointing to a preventive component of family therapy.

The four treatment groups have not shown differences in the extent to which their clients have been involved in work or school activities. Days spent working or in school over the first six months after treatment are fairly comparable across groups.

The criterion for measuring drug use that we have used is the *percentage of days* that a client *did not use a particular drug* (or drugs) over the follow-up period. "Days free" from the following nine drugs used as variables have been assessed: (1) legal and illegal opiates; (2) illegal opiates; (3) legal opiates; (4) all non-opiate illegal drugs excluding marijuana; (5) all illegal drugs excluding marijuana; (6) marijuana; (7) all illegal drugs including marijuana; (8) all legal and illegal drugs excluding alcohol; and (9) alcohol. Follow-up results over the first six months after treatment, and comparing *all* cases (whether or not they completed a single family session), revealed a number of statistically significant findings (Stanton et al., 1979). The nonfamily ("treatment-as-usual") and family movie groups showed no differences in the extent to which their clients used drugs of any kind (Duncan's tests). Comparisons between the two family therapy groups showed a difference on only one of the nine drug variables, while both of them produced better results than the nonfamily group. The unpaid family therapy group showed better outcomes than nonfamily on four of the drug variables, while two others were significant at the .10 level. The paid group yielded better results than nonfamily on six of the nine variables, with two others significant at .10. On variables in which significant (p < .05) differences were found, the ratio of days free for the paid group was 1.2 to 4.0 times as great as for nonfamily; the ratios for unpaid (versus nonfamily) were between 1.34 and 2.0 times greater. For example, the mean percentages of days free of "all legal and illegal opiates" (including methadone) were: nonfamily — 25%; movie — 25%; unpaid family therapy — 49%; paid family therapy — 63%. For "all illegal drugs excluding marijuana" the means were: nonfamily — 44%; movie — 50%; unpaid family therapy — 67%; paid family therapy — 74%.

In sum, these data indicate that brief, structural/strategic family therapy can be quite successful in reducing or eliminating drug abuse among opiate-addicted veterans, especially those under age thirty-five. The implications for dealing with similar and related types of family and mental health problems faced by veterans (Stanton and Figley, 1978) would seem apparent.

REFERENCES

Francis, A.; and Gale, L.: Family structure and treatment in the military. *Family Process, 12*:171-178, 1973.

Goldman, N.L.: Trends in family patterns of U.S. military personnel during the 20th century. In N.L. Goldman and D.R. Segal (Eds.): *The Social Psychology of Military Service*. Beverly Hills, Calif, Sage, 1976.

Haley, J.: *Uncommon Therapy*. New York, Norton, 1973.

Haley, J.: *Leaving Home: Therapy with Disturbed Young People*. New York, McGraw-Hill, 1980.

Harbin, H. T.; and Maziar, H. M.: The families of drug abusers: A literature review. *Family Process, 14*:411-431, 1975.

Klagsbrun, M.; and Davis, D. I.: Substance abuse and family interaction. *Family Process, 16*:149-173, 1977.

McGlothlin, W. H.: Drug use and misuse. *Ann Rev Psychol, 26*:45-64, 1975.

Minuchin, S.: *Families and Family Therapy*. Cambridge, Mass, Harvard, 1974.

Peck, M. S.: The role of the military in American society vis-à-vis drug abuse; Scapegoat, national laboratory and potential change agent. In J. P. Lovel and P. Kronenberg (Eds.): *The New Civil-Military Relations: Agonies of Adjustment to Post Vietnam Realities*. New Brunswick, NJ, Transaction Books, 1973.

Robins, L. N.: *The Vietnam Drug User Returns*. Special Action Office for Drug Abuse Prevention Monograph, Series A, No. 2, U.S. Government Printing Office, Washington, D.C., 1974.

Robins, L. N.; Helzer, J. E.; and Davis, D. H.: Narcotic use in Southeast Asia and afterward. *Arch Gen Psychiat, 32*:955-961, 1975.

Segal, D. R.; Segal, M. W.; Holz, R. F.; Norbo, G. J.; Seeberg, R. S.; and Wubbena, W. L.: Trends in the structure of Army families. *J Polit Milit Sociol, 4*:135-139, 1976.

Seldin, N. E.: The family of the addict: A review of the literature. *Int J Addict, 7*:97-107, 1972.

Stanton, M. D.: Psychology and family therapy. *Profess Psychol, 6*:45-49, 1975.

Stanton, M. D.: Drugs, Vietnam and the Vietnam veteran. *Am J Drug Alcohol Abuse, 3*:557-570, 1976a.

Stanton, M. D.: The military family: Its future in the all-volunteer context. In N. L. Goldman and D. R. Segal (Eds.): *The Social Psychology of Military Service*. Beverly Hills, Calif, Sage, 1976b.

Stanton, M. D.: The addict as savior: Heroin, death and the family. *Family Process, 16*:191-197, 1977.

Stanton, M. D.: Some outcome results and aspects of structural family therapy with drug addicts. In D. Smith; S. Anderson; M. Buxton; T. Chung; N. Gottlieg; and W. Harvey (Eds.): *A Multicultural View of Drug Abuse: The Proceedings of the National Drug Abuse Conference – 1977*. Cambridge, Mass, Hall / Schenkman, 1978.

Stanton, M. D.: Drugs and the family: A review of the recent literature. *Marr Family Rev, 2*:1-10, 1979a.

Stanton, M. D.: Family treatment approaches to drug abuse problems: A review. *Family Process, 18*:251-280, 1979b.

Stanton, M. D.: A family theory of drug abuse. In D. Lettieri (Ed.): *Theories of Drug Abuse*. Washington, D.C., National Institute on Drug Abuse, 1980a.

Stanton, M. D.: The hooked serviceman: Drug use in and after Vietnam. In C. R. Figley and S. Levantman (Eds.): *Strangers at Home: Vietnam Veterans Since the War*. New York, Praeger, 1980b.

Stanton, M. D.: Some overlooked aspects of the family and drug abuse. B. Ellis, (Ed.): *Drug Abuse from the Family Perspective: Coping Is a Family Affair*. Washington, D.C., National Institute on Drug Abuse, 1980c.

Stanton, M. D.; and Figley, C. R.: Treating the Vietnam veteran within the family system. In C. R. Figley (Ed.): *Stress Disorders Among Vietnam Veterans: Theory, Research and Treatment*. New York, Brunner/Mazel, 1978.

Stanton, M. D.; and Todd, T. C.: Structural family therapy with drug addicts. In E. Kaufman and P. Kaufman (Eds.): *Family Therapy of Drug and Alcohol Abuse.* New York, Gardner, 1979.

Stanton, M. D.; and Todd, T. C.: Engaging "resistant" families in treatment: II. Principles and techniques in recruitment. *Family Process,* 1981, in press.

Stanton, M. D.; and Todd, T. C.: Engaging "resistant" families in treatment: III. Factors in success and cost efficiency. *Family Process,* 1981, in press.

Stanton, M. D.; Todd, T. C.; Heard, D. B.; Kirschner, S.; Kleiman, J. I.; Mowatt, D. T.; Riley, P.; Scott, S. M.; and Van Deusen, J. M.: Heroin addiction as a family phenomenon: A new conceptual model. *Am J Drug Alcohol Abuse,* 5:125-150, 1978.

Stanton, M. D.; Todd, T. C.; Steier, F.; Van Deusen, J. M.; Marder, L. R.; Rosoff, R. J.; Seaman, S. F.; and Skibinski, E.: *Family Characteristics and Family Therapy of Heroin Addicts: Final Report 1974-1978.* Prepared for the National Institute on Drug Abuse, Grant No. R01 DA 01119, 1979.

Stanton, M. D.; Todd, T. C.; and Associates: *The Family Therapy of Drug Addiction.* New York, Guilford Press, 1982.

Van Deusen, J. M.; Stanton, M. D.; Scott, S. M.; and Todd, T. C.: Engaging "resistant" families in treatment. I. Getting the drug addict to recruit his family members. *Int J Addict,* 15:1069-1089, 1981.

CHAPTER 7

COMBINED TREATMENT FOR ALCOHOLICS AND ADDICTS

RICHARD HEILMAN

Craig (1981) has reviewed the various service designs for the addictions. For most people "combined treatment" still means the treatment of "alcoholics" and "addicts" in the same setting, but distinguishing each as being different and having special problems and requiring different treatment approaches. For others "combined treatment" means treating "alcoholics" and "addicts" in the same setting or program in a fully integrated manner. For a few others involved in "combined treatment," it means treatment without distinction between "alcoholics" and "addicts." More specifically, this means treatment of people of all ages who are periodically or continuously dysfunctionally dependent on the experience of intoxication without primary reference to drug type or types (including alcohol). This latter statement often produces a reaction of confusion. To many it is outright heresy. Society's attitudes, mythologies, prejudices, misconceptions, personal egotisms, and emotionalism still pervades the "alcoholic" and "drug addict" treatment field. This is glaringly apparent at alcohol and drug conferences where the question "Do you treat alcoholics or addicts?" or "Are you alcohol or drug?" is the first question posed after introductions are made and its often the "battle cry."

I will start by sharing my and other experiences in combining treatment over fourteen years. Reviewing this history is crucial and speaks to the very essense of this chapter.

153

LOCAL HISTORY

In March of 1966, the alcoholic patients at this V.A. Medical Center on the psychiatric units were placed in a separate unit of forty-six beds called the Alcoholic Treatment Unit. This was indeed the beginning of an enriching experience in the evolution of the treatment of drug dependency into a specialized service requiring new and remarkably different attitudes and expertise.

Historically, Minnesota traditionally accepted so-called nonalcohol drug dependencies in their alcoholic treatment programs since 1951. However, these cases of narcotic or sedative or stimulant dependencies were relatively uncommon and they were absorbed into the treatment program because there was no other place for them to go unless it was to a psychiatric treatment unit. Even though they were absorbed into the alcoholic treatment program, they and their drug dependency were considered to be quite different from that of the alcoholic and as a result, little was done for them beyond detoxification. They were at best just tolerated. The same was generally true for us in our program between 1966 and 1969, until the Viet Nam veterans were admitted in increasing numbers with nonalcohol drug dependencies.

Around 1969 was the era when discussions of the generation gap were extraordinarily popular. Differences in age, life-style, dress, mythology, taste in music, etc. were maximized and similarities minimized or ignored. In addition, the preference for the young to use illegal drugs and the ensuing public panic reinforced these distorted attitudes. Emotionalism flourished. When the drug dependent Viet Nam era veteran came into treatment in greater numbers, we were geared to think that he was greatly different and would require different and very special treatment. We focused primarily on the kind of drug he was in trouble with and, out of ignorance and confusion, felt it best to minimize the anticipated differences until we knew more about him. In a sense we sat in the weeds studying this "new breed," hoping to learn more about him so we could develop the skill to treat him according to his special needs. In retrospect, it is embarrassing to see how easily we were beguiled into discounting the knowledge we had of human behavior and drug dependency in favor of superficial, ornamental differences. Our program was oriented around the recovery process and philosophy of Alcoholics Anonymous. We were naive enough about the young veteran and his drug problem to tell him to substitute the name of his drug of choice in place of the word alcohol in the first recovery step. "We admitted we were powerless over alcohol, that our lives had become unmanageable." By doing this we reinforced an articifical, social, attitudinal difference that precluded further understanding at that time. This seemed reasonable enough, not knowing we had missed the correct concept entirely. More will be said on this later.

In 1969 we changed the name of the program to Drug Dependency Treatment Program. No effort was made to segregate the patients by age or drug choice. Beds were assigned at random on admission. Our ratio of younger to older patients was 1:2 of forty-six patients. We expected some antagonism between these two groups; however, we observed that they not only tolerated each other, but generally accepted each other and interacted with concern in group therapy and were socially congenial. The older patients helped the younger patients consider their drug dependency more seriously and the younger patients provided stimulation and a greater sense of responsibility in the older patients.

The only conflicts that occurred, of a minor nature, were between the younger patients themselves. Our observation of the younger patients revealed that other than some skepticism of authority, some lack of practical experience, and a greater degree of immaturity, the very special differences from the older patients did not present themselves. The "generation gap" was not apparent in the significant areas of human needs and human relationships. The apparent external differences were washed out by a common problem and the need for help. In fact, we observed that there were greater differences between some of the younger patients than between the younger patients and the older patients and vice versa. We had a few of the young revolutionaries who felt the establishment was no good and needed radical alteration. These revolutionaires were of the 10 percent of the radical group that received so much sensational attention by the media that helped lead us to believe that most of the young people were of this type. We had some of the larger segment of the young who wanted to change the establishment, but just enough to get into it more easily and derive their fair share. The majority of the younger patients were establishment-oriented and by and large accepted it as it was. They generally believed in the American ideals of the right to private property, competition produces excellence, and to work and to produce was of great value. Indeed, it became apparent that any gap was more intragenerational than intergenerational.

At this point we began to believe that a combined program with a therapeutic community orientation was the proper direction. In 1971 guidelines from our central office convinced us to segregate our younger "drug addicts" and our older "alcoholics" with the dictum they needed to be treated differently. This was a frustrating time because we were seeing positive results with a combined community program. The mixture of patients of different ages aided considerably in diminishing stereotyped attitudes. We felt this was a crucial aspect of treatment if our patients were going to learn to live and communicate with all kinds of people in our society. However, under some pressure we segregated our patients on the ward. We felt it was highly probable that artificial problems would result by creating a We-They situation and thus reinforce the stereotype Alcoholic versus Addict. The segregation only lasted about two weeks, primarily because of the resistance of the patients to accept this separation. This surprised our staff that the patients preferred a common program. We received a petition from the patients to recombine. Desegregation took place with considerable relief to the patients and staff. A multigenerational setting and approach finally and lastingly became a truth that works.

During this period between 1969 and 1971 the staff attitudes underwent great change. This was the most crucial factor in our development as a combined program. Our sensitivity to stereotyping became increasingly sharp and we recognized the need to destereotype ourselves as professional people. This clearly was as important as destereotyping the "alcoholic" and "addict." We saw the need to break down the doctor-patient or therapist-patient barrier that interferes with treatment in drug-dependent people who often interpret the therapist as presenting himself as morally, socially, and personally superior. We learned that we must be ourselves and experience ourselves primarily as human beings working with other human beings, that this was our greatest asset and strength, and that our profession of physician, nurse, psychologist, social worker, counselor, clergyman, although very important, needed to be secondary to that. Our frequent biweekly staff encounter groups focused on developing empathy, genuineness, and openness and moving toward becoming creditable role models. We worked on uprooting acquired social attitudes regarding "addicts" and "alcoholics." We learned that sharing ourselves in therapy groups was of far greater value than demonstrating our professional abilities. We learned to greatly diminish the We (staff)–They (patients) obstacle. As was jokingly stated one day, "The only way you can tell the staff from the patients was that the patients improved." We had no casualties or staff dropouts during this process of reorientation or any serious conflicts of belief. With deliberate, structured effort, this required about two years. The staff cohesiveness and high morale created a spirited treatment milieu that contributed the most to patient control, treatment, comfort, and effectiveness. We did indeed learn to acknowledge and respect individual differences among the staff and patients; however, we focused primarily on the more important similarities of humanness and the addictive problem and reality-oriented self-help recovery process.

Working with the younger drug dependent person we learned another startling and crucial factor in understanding the nature of drug dependency. When the so-called heroin dependent person came in, he did not choose to talk about the use of other drugs besides heroin. He was not interested in relinquishing the use of alcohol, marijuana, or other drugs. He seemed to feel that heroin was his problem because that was what he got caught abusing. At that time in our understanding we did not feel greatly different than he did, but felt that the use of other drugs might render him vulnerable to drift back to using the real problem drug, heroin. We actually enabled him to exploit his "specialness." More experience with these people in unraveling more carefully the histories of their drug use taught us that *a particular drug substance was not the problem. The real problem was intoxication with any substance.*

This was indeed an enlightening insight that filtered through the confusion of the so-called different kinds of drug dependencies. It became obvious that the name of the game of drug dependency was intoxication or getting high or whatever special reward intoxication produced. Intoxication was the "hooker." The experience of intoxication was the common denominator. A generic approach was so obvious now. Most "alcoholics" and all the younger drug-dependent patients were polydrug users. They had their drug of choice, but this was secondary in importance to the main problem of the pursuit of intoxication with any drug. This was the pattern of their drug use. They were not in trouble or dependent on a single substance, but actually or potentially dependent on any substance that produced a fairly rapid high or intoxication. It was crucial for the patients to learn that once drug dependent, they could not use any euphoria-producing substance safely again. In our intoxication-oriented society, this was obviously of paramount importance to learn.

We developed the skills to break through their initial resistance to this fact. We learned that you could teach the "heroin" addict that the use of alcohol, marijuana, cocaine, etc., was part and parcel of the problem, and could likewise teach the alcoholic that the use of sedatives, sedative tranquilizers, or any recreational drug was untenable. There was no compromise with the problem of drug dependency. It was clear now that the characteristics of being drug dependent, whatever the drug of choice, were the same. These characteristics were an irreversible, recurrent, uncontrolled, autonomous urge (need) to experience getting high or intoxicated. We then changed the wording of the first step of the recovery process to read "We admitted we were powerless over the urge or need to become intoxicated or get high — that our lives had become unmanageable." Acceptance of this was the beginning of the recovery process of all our patients. Now that we understood the nature of the problem and the once illusive common denominator, we were able to see that the resulting complications from a drug dependency were remarkably similar and predictable. This was especially true of the personality changes they experienced. Now it seemed all of the crucial similarities or common denominators emerged. They were all human beings suffering similar complications from a psychic dependency on intoxication.

A postscript to the above demands attention. Over 98 percent of our younger drug dependent patients gave a history of extensive early teenage use of alcohol. Their commitment to the experience of intoxication as a part of their life-style, in terms of the future, began with alcohol and then the transition to the use of other substances was easily accomplished. This information adds greater significance to the need to have combined treatment programs, especially in view of the increased use of alcohol by today's youth at a progressively earlier age. It needs to be seen that alcohol abuse is not only the major drug problem in our society for many reasons, but that it is or was the common denominator in almost all of the so called "nonalcohol" drug dependencies.

COMBINED AND SEPARATE PROGRAMS

Table 7-I presents a schematic representation of combined versus separate treatment.

Our enthusiasm has been reinforced by hearing about other treatment centers experiencing similar outcomes with combined programs. Some like ourselves are in the V.A. and some are in other public and in private sectors. Of particular note was the Eagleville Hospital and Rehabilitation Center in Eagleville, Pennsylvania. This program developed in the same time frame as ours and had an extraordinary mix of age, sex, color, nationalities, cultures, life-styles, socioeconomic status, alcohol and drug use patterns, etc., evolving under the direction of Donald J. Ottenberg and most dedicated staff (Ottenberg and Rosen, 1971). Their experience and conclusion paralleled ours and is eloquently described elsewhere (Ottenberg, 1980). Their

TABLE 7-I

COMBINED VERSUS SEPARATE TREATMENT

	Advantages of Combined Program	Disadvantages of Separate Treatment
Nature of Addiction	My commitment to intoxication	I'm addicted to a specific chemical.
	Nonsocial or nonprescribed specific pattern of use — common to all chemical dependencies.	I'm in trouble with a chemical not *how* I use the chemical
	Recurrent, tenacious autonomous urge to change my mood chemically.	I must stay away from my drug of choice but other chemicals or alcohol are no special problem.
	Common humanness — needs, problems, adventures in living.	My drug experience is unique, as I am.
	Drug dependency and recovery process in common.	I'm legal, he's illegal, or my problem is superior to his problem.
Patient's Changes	Self-concept — I'm a person who is chemically dependent.	I'm a speed freak.
	Diminish my stereotype of self and others.	Reinforce stereotype of self and others. Need special treatment. My case is different.
	Focus on similarities: deep feelings, values.	Focus on superficial differences: chemical, age, social,.and life-style.
	Utilize and build on individual differences.	Emphasize differences between groups.
	Aware of my chemical dependency.	Aware that I'm an "alcoholic" or "addict" only.
Staff	Have learned to respond to and stretch people.	I work with "alcoholics," do you work with "addicts"? or vice versa.
	Build on similarities.	Treat as different from others.
Ward Living	Divided into four groups called families in one ward community.	2 separate programs (Addicts versus Alcoholics) foster group differences and intergroup problems.
Program	One program — numerous alternate program elements.	Two programs — fewer alternative program elements.

experience of the rapid increase in polydrug abuse in "Alcoholics" and "Addicts" paralleled ours (with Viet Nam veterans mentioned above). In their research in 1974, 43 percent of "alcoholic" admissions were polydrug abusers and 97 percent of "addicts" were polydrug abusers (Ottenberg and Rosen, 1971; Ottenberg, 1975).

Another paper documents the primary role alcohol played in the addiction of the narcotic addict (Green and Jaffe, 1977). The paper documents the addict's commitment to intoxication with alcohol as an integral part or dimension of their life-style at the average age of thirteen and adding heroin at average age of sixteen. From that point forward, any available "recreational drug" (including addictive "pharmaceutical" drugs) was used by most in their relentless pursuit of intoxication as a central function of their lives.

An exceptional study of 31,964 subjects from 267 drug abuse treatment facilities demonstrated that the only difference between separate and combined clinics was that combined clinics offer a wider range of services. The data indicated that it makes little difference in treatment process in separate or combined facilities, and demonstrated the favorability, sensibility, and efficiency of combined treatment and for budgetary and managerial efficiency (Green, 1979). Such studies encouraged President Carter and Congress to consider reorganizing NIDA and NIAAA into a National Institute of Substance Abuse, a move clearly long overdue.

Freed's (1973) paper is an extraordinarily massive review of the literature of drug abuse by alcoholics (150 references in his bibliography), going back to 1924. He took license in combining the studies and found of 15,447 cases about 20 percent or 3,041 used both alcohol and drugs. That is, one-fifth revealed conjoint or sequential use of alcohol and other drugs. Even as early as 1969, he points out, three times as many younger "alcoholics" as older ones admitted using other drugs. As we know, that era was the beginning of a geometric rise in drug abuse and alcohol abuse at an earlier age. Clearly the statistics today show 70 percent of younger alcoholics (under 30) are polydrug abusers (Ottenberg and Rosen, 1971). This certainly seems to dictate adaptations over time of combined treatment for the majority of drug-dependent people. This latter statement reflects the conclusions of Carroll and Malloy (1977) reviewing combined treatment program reports. They found only one program (Spring Hill Foundation) that did not give a positive report. They also presented in their paper many questions that need addressing before combined treatment can become popular as a treatment model of choice. The questions reflected primarily political, social, fiscal, and special interest considerations, not the reality of the true nature of the problem and what would be in the best interest of the patients for recovery. Their report points out also how separate treatment adherants ignored or were not or are not aware of the World Health Organization proposals published in 1967. To quote from WHO's paper (1967), "While recognizing that there are differences between types of drug dependence, the (WHO) committee recommends that problems of dependeny on alcohol and dependency on drugs should be considered together, because of similarities of causation, interchangeability of agent in respect of maintenance of dependence and, hence, similarities in measures required for prevention and treatment" (pg. 41). While the extent and nature of the problem vary from country to country, the relatively frequent transfer from one drug of dependence to another, the not infrequent abuse of drugs in combination, the complex and changing patterns of, and the rapid development of, new drugs with potential for abuse make it important that dependence on alcohol and other drugs be considered as facets of one problem, psychic dependency being the common factor (pg. 8).

Joel Fort, also in 1967, saw clearly the trend during this time and recommended, without reservation, "a unified approach" in treatment and its importance in prevention of drug abuse and dependency.

The V.A. implemented a Pilot Alcohol and Drug Abuse Treatment (PADAT) Project in 1974. Ten "Combined Treatment" modalities were compared in treatment outcome with seven alcohol and seven drug programs. All settings produced sizable improvements in patients. Separate programs had a small edge in recovery rates; however, they were not practically significant to warrant separate over combined treatment programs. Yet, disappointingly, there still remains within the 186 V.A. Medical Centers, 100 "alcoholic" treatment programs and fifty-six "drug" programs and a scant ten "combined" treatment programs. The V.A. Central Office has for years favored "combined" programs. Federal policies, national ideology, policy and funding restraints, and local medical center's resistance to change has made this remarkably prohibitive. It would seem the cliche "don't confuse me with the facts" is tenaciously operative. As long as NIDA functions under its opiate dependency modalities and environments, and NIAAA supports their exclusionary view of alcoholics, the current configuration of treatment resources will remain the same.

In summary, combined generic, multigenerational programs do shatter dehumanizing and self-defeating stereotypes in patients and staff. They effectively call a spade a spade and sometimes lovingly call it a bloody shovel. Heterogeneity as in genetics has a very powerful therapeutic influence. It indeed brings out and nourishes the best and strongest characteristics.

Finally, it is unconscionable to be still planning primarily almost exclusively separate alcohol and drug programs in the face of evidence to do otherise. Especially frustrating is the complacency of separate programs in not even doing research or writing papers defending or demonstrating their position of exclusivity. I have seen none! Continuing to promote two dynasties, if you will, and creating the enormity of cost, waste of time and energy, and reinforcement of dangerous, life-threatening mythologies betraying the perplexed patient is immeasurable.

There is nothing so powerful as an idea whose time has come. When will this be?

REFERENCES

Baker, S.; Lorei, T.; McKnight, H.; and Duvall, J.: The Veterans Administration's comparison study: Alcoholism and drug abuse combined and conventional treatment settings. *Alcohol Clin Exp Res, 1*:4, 1977.

Carroll, J.; and Malloy, T.: Combined treatment alcohol and drug dependent persons: A literature review and evaluation. *Am J Drug Alcoh Abuse, 4*(3):343-364, 1977.

Craig, R.: Treating addicts and alcoholics in combined treatment settings: Issues and perspectives. *J Psychiatr Treat Eval, 3*:87–93, 1981.

Fort, J.: Recommended future international action against abuses of alcohol and other drugs. *Br J Addic, 62*:129-146, 1967.

Freed, E. X.: Drug abuse by alcoholics: A review. *Int J Addic, 8*:451-473, 1973.

Green, J.; and Jaffe, J.: Alcohol and opiate dependence: A review. *J Stud Alcoh, 38*:7, 1977.

Green, B. T.: Treating drug and alcohol abuses in the same facilities: Process and implications. *J Drug Issues, 9:*399–412, 1979.

Ottenberg, D.: Combined treatment of alcoholics and drug addicts: A progress report from Eagleville. *Contemp Drug Prob, 4:*1-21, 1975.

Ottenberg, D.: *The Evolution of a Combined Treatment Program.* Eagleville, Pa. Eagleville Hospital and Rehabilitation Center, 1980.

Ottenberg, D.; and Rosen, A.: Merging the treatment of drug addicts into an existing program for alcoholics. *Q J Stud Alcoh, 32:*94-103, 1971.

World Health Organization Expert Committee on Mental Health, Services for Prevention and Treatment of Dependency on Alcohol and Other Drugs, Report 14, Series *363:*1-45, 1967.

Part II

Assessments

Service demands often present an urgency that requires immediate care of the patient based on the level of current knowledge available to the clinician and program administrator. Ideally, such service designs will be based on replicable research with invariant outcomes. Because of the complexities of human behavior, existing and intricate interrelationships and infinite patterns of environmental stimuli, situational demands, and personality traits, such invariant outcomes can never be guaranteed. Thus, clinicians must be guided by their knowledge of the condition being treated (e.g., drug abuse) and their assessments of the person and their continual monitoring of interaction of these two salient dynamisms. In this section, we take a look at three types of assessments, recognizing that, in reality, there are multiple levels of assessment (sociocultural, vocational, physical, interpersonal, etc.) that are performed daily in understanding a drug dependent patient. However, space limitations does not permit adequate coverage of each of these important areas. Therefore, we have chosen two that are frequently assessed to understand the addict as a person (personality characteristics) and one that is often used to monitor his progress and treatment (urine results), and we have selected an assessment area that has been afforded too little attention in our treatment workups (neuropsychological deficits).

In the first paper, Craig summarizes what we know about the personality of drug addicts. This review is a summary of three previous papers published by the author based on 124 empirical studies limited to the specific study of the heroin addict. An important distinction is made here between the "preclinical" and "clinical" personality of the addict. The former consists of those traits and characteristics that predate the onset of addiction, while the latter represents those characteristics seen by the clinician at the time the addict "presents" in our assessment setting. Although Craig presents some research that indirectly suggests the clinical personality traits of addicts may have predated the onset of addiction, he argues that this is merely an academic argument and, in reality, these are the traits that the clinician has to work with at the level of the patient. The paper concludes with some needed directions for future research in this important area.

Penk and Robinowitz offer a much more detailed account of the personality differences of heroin addicts and polydrug abusers, based extensively on their ongoing research at the Dallas VA Medical Center. Beginning with the empirical question "Do heroin addicts differ from polydrug abusers on measures of personality?" they present research strategies and the resulting evidence that summate to the following conclusion: "The drift of this empirical literature is towards the conclusion that heroin users, though maladjusted, are comparatively better adjusted than polydrug abusers." Their paper is written largely from an empirical research perspective and is an excellent summary of our knowledge concerning personality differences between the heroin addict and his/her polydrug abusing cousin. Since the VA, and many other drug abuse programs, treat a wide array of drug dependencies, the material presented in this paper should be an invaluable reference source to those interested in this topic.

While the Penk and Robinowitz paper establishes the salient personality differences between the heroin addict and polydrug abuser *(caveats* notwithstanding), Mider and Lewis call our attention to a neglected area of assessment among the addictions, e.g., neuropsychological assessment. Their paper presents a study of the neuropsychological functioning of young adults with particular reference to the possible historical antecedents (birth and developmental factors and childhood learning disabilities) and the nature and severity of neuropsychological impairment in a group of polydrug (nonnarcotic) abusers. Their findings indicate that polydrug abuse may have been an outgrowth of antecedent CNS developmental dysfunctions, particularly learning disabilities. Such findings, if substantiated, would argue for closer attention to developmental histories that might result in neuropsychological impairments.

The paper by Mider and Lewis is the only research paper included in this compendium. All of the other contributions are summary papers detailing present knowledge in the respective area. Unfortunately, we are not at a consensus state with respect to possible neuropsychological impairment among polydrug abusers, so this individual study is reported here. The study is not without its deficiencies. In point of fact, some methodological problems are extant that need consideration in future research. However, rather than providing a critique of their methodology, interested readers can scrutinize the paper and come to their own conclusions. We present the paper in order to highlight the need for neuropsychological assessments, especially among patients who present the polydrug abusing pattern. An important question is whether such neuropsychological impairments are permanent or whether they can be remediated following the discontinuance of polydrug ingestion.

On the other hand, urine surveillance has become a necessary evil in most drug abuse treatment programs. Wang is both a physician and a psychopharmacologist and presents his views of the major issues and problems in routine toxicologic urine screens. It is written in a relatively nontechnical manner and deals with the many day-to-day issues facing clinicians in the monitoring, assessing, and adjusting their treatment in conjunction with urine results. Wang's paper, as do most of the other papers in this volume, represents one expert's personal opinion. These opinions await substantive research on the issue in question. We include the paper so that the reader can form their opinion on the ideas presented in it.

CHAPTER 8

PERSONALITY VARIABLES IN THE TREATMENT OF HEROIN ADDICTS

ROBERT J. CRAIG

INTRODUCTION

There has been a major resurgence of interest in the role of personality factors in the initiation, maintenance, and general etiology of substance abuse behavior. Several seminal publications have recently appeared illustrating the contemporary relevance of this topic to the total understanding of drug addiction (Barnes, 1979; Cox, 1979; Craig, 1979a,b, 1981; Owen and Butcher, 1979; Pihl and Spiers, 1978; Sutker and Archer, 1979). I believe this resurgence has been due to the general dissatisfaction with biogenic, sociological, and environmental explanations concerning the genesis of drug addiction. For example, a metabolic disorder theory (Dole and Nyswander, 1967) cannot account for the general failure of methadone maintenance as an overall cure for heroin addiction (Dole and Nyswander, 1976; Maddux and Bowden, 1972; Senay and Wright, 1972). Sociological theories (Winick, 1974) do not provide sufficient breadth or depth to predict drug fads, or to explain why one individual experiencing "role conflict" or "identity-confusion" will select one form of drug while another person confronting the same issues will opt for a different form of drug abuse. Also, simple environmental explanations cannot account as to why two individuals, each facing identical poverty, family disruptions, prejudice, and other disadvantaged childrearing conditions, will develop into a drug addict or a political leader of great renown.

Why is it that identical sociological conditions do not lead to heroin addiction among all affected individuals? Hence, the role of the host becomes a critical variable in the eventual equation of drug addiction. Our goal in this paper is to highlight what we know concerning individual factors in heroin addiction, while permeating major sections with important research trends and methodological critiques that attenuate or enhance our empirical conclusions.

THE "PRECLINICAL" PERSONALITY OF HEROIN ADDICTS

Although we may eventually be able to reach a consensus as to the commonly observed personality traits, behavioral patterns, interactional styles, and cognitive and communication processes of heroin addicts, such consensus will be seriously flawed by two factors: sampling bias and drug effects. As to the first factor, most of our research knowledge is based on addicts in treatment (TCs, methadone, detoxification) or addicts in jail. This presents us with a certain bias in measuring personality traits and tells us little about addicts who do not enter treatment or who do not enter the criminal justice system. The second factor is more serious. It can be argued that sooner or later most heroin addicts will find themselves either in jail or in treatment. Thus, perhaps little is lost in not researching them prior to their treatment history, since we will eventually be able to study them in more controlled settings. However, almost all of our present knowledge concerning the role of personality factors in drug addiction comes from studying addicts *after they have become addicted.* Thus, we are not able to determine precisely if we are measuring addict personality or the traits that result from being addicted.

There are two main research strategies that "partial out" drug effects. First, we could randomly select a group of subjects and administer psychological tests to them and then wait to see which ones became addicted and which ones did not. We would then compare these two groups on our measures and determine which personality factors contribute to the onset of heroin addiction. This research design is necessarily longitudinal and requires extensive funding, research commitment, community cooperation, and a myriad of procedural problems that render such an endeavor quite impractical.

Another research strategy is to select a group of drug addicts and look through their files to see if they had been tested prior to becoming addicted. We could then note any changes, which we would attribute to drug effects, and any stabilities, which we would attribute to constancy of personality. We would then inspect our data to determine if any traits contribute to the development of drug addiction.

Unfortunately, I know of no such study with heroin addicts. However, we do have some analogous data in the area of alcoholism and polydrug abuse that may have relevancy to the preclinical personality traits in heroin addicts.

There have been several attempts to identify prealcoholic characteristics of individuals who later became alcoholics. McCord and McCord (1960) followed 510 males from boyhood to adulthood. A minority of the sample eventually became alcoholics. The authors were able to identify a cluster of traits that differentiated the "prealcoholic boy" from their peers, including such traits as fearlessness, self-sufficiency, independence, aggressiveness and manliness, all of which could be interpreted as an overemphasis on masculine traits that defensively hid their more feminine, dependent traits.

Another longitudinal study followed males and females from age 10½ over a thirty-year period. Once again, a subsample became alcoholics and they were compared to their peers on traits and measures obtained prior to the onset of addiction. Those traits which singled out the group that eventually became male alcoholics were extroversion, uncontrollable behavior as children, impulsivity, acting out characteristics, emphasis on masculinity, and an overconcern with the male role. Other traits were found for female "prealcoholics" and some common "prealcoholic" traits were found for both males and females (Jones, 1968, 1971).

A third longitudinal investigation identified 503 children who were seen at a Mental Health Clinic for behavior problems and later developed alcohol problems at folllow-up, some thirty years later (N =84). Inspection of their childhood records revealed that those who later became problem drinkers had significantly more antisocial characteristics as children than the nonproblem drinker behavior-disordered controls (Robins, 1966; Robins, Bates and O'Neal, 1962).

A few studies investigated college students who later became alcoholics. These students were given the MMPI during routine collegiate testing about fifteen years prior to the development of alcoholism. A total of thirty-eight males were so identified and were compared to 148 males who were classmates while in college. Results of these studies showed that the prealcoholics scored higher on the MMPI scales 4 (Psychopathic Deviation) and 9 (Hypomania), although at subclinical levels, reflecting greater gregariousness, more impulsivity, and less social conformity than their peers. They also scored higher on the content scales of Authority Conflict and Poor Health. The MacAndrews Alcoholism Scale scores were above the suggested cutoff indicative of problem drinking, both at the college level and later when they entered treatment for alcoholism (Hoffmann, Loper and Kammeier, 1974; Kammeier, Hoffmann and Loper, 1973; and Loper, Kammeier and Hoffmann, 1973).

These studies summate to suggest that some personality differences found in alcoholics that are not present in nonalcoholics were also present long before the onset of the development of alcoholism and may, in fact, be predictive of subsequent problem drinking. Thus, we have reason to believe that at least some of the traits found in alcoholics at the time they enter treatment are not ephemeral and, in fact, predated their problem drinking.

Unfortunately, this type of research has not been prevalent in the field of heroin addiction. I am aware of only one similar study, which found that college students who later became heavy drug users were impulsive, extroverted, and adventurous during their predrug histories. Also noteworthy was the fact that their preaddictive personality patterns resembled that of the prealcoholic patterns reviewed above (Goldstein and Sappington, 1977).

While we cannot conclude that such individuals are "addiction prone," those with such traits and patterns may be more easily recruited into alcohol and drug use than others (Owen and Butcher, 1979).

CLINICAL PERSONALITY OF HEROIN ADDICTS

This section attempts to review the salient traits of heroin addicts. It is obvious by now that we are not certain if these traits antedated drug addiction. What is certain is that these traits are probably the ones that the addict "presents with" at the time of treatment. It is what the clinician has to work with and so it really becomes irrelevant or academic whether these traits preceded drug addiction.

In a review of the empirical literature concerning personality characteristics of heroin addicts, Craig (1979a,b) reached the following conclusion:

> In summarizing the results of 77 empirical studies that span a period of over 41 years of research, several facts have emerged. While it is not presumed that all addicts display the characteristics noted below, it is contended here that the following traits are manifested by a majority of addicts: Heroin addicts have consistently demonstrated an internal locus of control contrary to the general expectation that would expect drug addicts as viewing drug taking and other reinforcements as beyond their personal control. While internality may be susceptible to temporary environmental or situational fluctuations, locus of control remains relatively stable and moves towards greater internality following treatment that includes methadone maintenance and therapeutic communities.
>
> Addicts also manifest impulsive behavior on a variety of measures and have pre-conscious concerns with death. This latter characteristic is reality based in view of the addict's lifestyle and degree of risks involved in maintaining it. Depression and anxiety exist in addicts at greater levels than in other groups, but these traits are susceptible to treatment. No characteristic list of psychological needs has emerged for addicts, except they show greater needs for aggression and heterosexuality. Most studies have shown addicts to score in the normal range in sexual identification and sexual interests. Addicts desire more sensation seeking experiences, have lower pain thresholds, tend to be perceptually field dependent, and are more self-actualizing; they are not differentiated with respect to extroversion-introversion. Except for the extroversion-introversion, the traits identified in the last sentence are based on single study findings and have not been replicated. Addicts are often hostile individuals, and their hostility tends to increase during heroin use and they tend to withdraw socially during detoxification. The value structure of addicts has been shown to be different from those of other groups, and the differences that exist

may be attributed to cultural and socio-economic rather than drug taking explanations.

Most addicts have traits that have been traditionally associated with psychopathy. These include demanding immediate gratification, lack of impulse control, demanding attention, low frustration tolerance, impatience, tending to act out aggressively, poor socialization, difficulty in profiting from experience, somewhat egocentric, disrespects authority, difficulty in forming warm and lasting relationships, hostile, somewhat irritable and irresponsible, and has underlying feelings of insecurity and inadequacy. The evidence of these traits comes from MMPI studies, but many of these singular traits have been confirmed by other tests as well. Only the presence of considerable anxiety in addicts is contraindicative of "classical psychopathy". However, the presence of many psychopathic-like traits in addiction suggests a close affinity between drug addiction and psychopathy. Of major importance is the fact that no treatment program has been able to show a reduction in psychopathic-like traits.

Female addicts show traits similar to male addicts, primarily in the area of psychopathy. Addicts have consistently been differentiated from alcoholics with the Heroin (He) Scale derived from the MMPI, but this fact is not presently useful for individual predictive purposes. Some personality traits have been shown to be malleable with treatment experiences, but the psychopathic traits have been impervious and refractory to treatment.

In a subsequent paper reviewing an additional forty-seven studies appearing between 1976-1979, Craig (1981b) found much corroborating evidence for the above conclusions as well as some modifications; specifically:

(1) Heroin addicts consistently present large amounts of psychopathology, especially psychopathy, on the MMPI, irrespective of subgroup status, demographic/subject variables, or conditions of assessment.

(2) The Heroin (He) Scale of the MMPI continues to show promise as a general screening battery for drug abusing tendencies.

(3) Addicts continue to demonstrate an internal locus of control when control groups are used.

(4) Heroin addicts are more field dependent than control groups, but these differences are not large enough to distinguish addicts from other clinical groups who are also field dependent.

(5) Addicts are not differentiable with respect to

extroversion-introversion.

(6) Hostility has been shown to be a major part of the symptom picture of different types of drug clusters associated with different personality types among narcotic users irrespective of the type of test used to measure it.

(7) Heroin addicts tend to score higher on measures of sensation seeking than control groups, although there may be important ethnic differences on this variable. However, there does not appear to be any gender differences noted to date.

(8) The effects of volunteering for treatment need to be seriously considered when assessing traits of heroin addicts as addicts may exaggerate the extent of psychopathology in order to gain admission to a program.

The reader is referred to these articles for a more in-depth presentation of the empirical status of these traits and personality picture.

CHARACTERISTICS OF ADDICTS, POLYDRUG ABUSERS AND ALCOHOLICS

Given the possibility that heroin addicts may be described according to modal personality characteristics that represent the clinical personality of the addict (while recognizing wide individual variations and uniquenesses as well), another question is whether such traits are specific to heroin addicts or whether they represent a general substance abusing personality, independent of drug choice. Two main populations have been studied to answer this question, e.g., polydrug abusers and alcoholics.

Much of the research concerning personality characteristics of polydrug abusers has been conducted by the Penk group in Dallas and their work is summarized in Chapter 9 of this volume (Penk and Robinowitz, 1981). These authors and an independent review by Craig (1981b), have concluded that polydrug abusers are more maladjusted than heroin addicts. For example, polydrug abusers show greater levels of disturbance across comparisons on both MMPI clinical and content scales (Penk et al., in press), and polydrug abusers obtain higher scores on the Heroin (He) Scale of the MMPI (Lachar et al., 1979). Of course, this may be somewhat of a simplification since it is well known that heroin addicts are also multiple drug abusers. However, these studies usually compare heroin addicts with polydrug abusers who do not take heroin and they try to screen out heroin addicts who are into heavy polydrug abuse. Nevertheless, it is important to realize that polydrug abusers may represent a different and perhaps "sicker" type of client. Such knowledge could have important implications for treatment outcome.

A second area to explore is similarities and differences among substance abusers, particularly contrasting the traits of alcoholics and addicts. There is an increasing realization that alcoholics and heroin addicts represent part of a continuum of addictions. The evidence for the theoretically hypothesized psychodynamics, commonalities of mutual experience with the addiction cycle, common areas of overlap in family backgrounds, extensive drug and alcohol use by addicts and alcoholics, personality traits, and the diagnostic similarities of both groups of substance abusers have recently appeared in the literature (Craig, 1981a). The alcoholic personality has been described by Barnes (1979) as having a neurotic component characterized by anxiety, depression, hysteria, and hypochondriasis; a field dependent component characterized by passivity and dependency; a stimulus augmentation component characterized by fears of death and increased sensitivity levels; and a weak ego component including weak sexual identity, negative self-concept, psychopathy, hostility, immaturity, impulsiveness, low tolerance for frustration, and an orientation in the present. The similarities of these characteristics to those of heroin addicts is obvious. Both seem to share a passive-aggressive personality style, with alcoholics tending to show more of the passive side and heroin addicts more of the aggressive component. Both share low frustration tolerance, poor self-esteem and low self-concept, immature demands for attention and impulsive behavior. However, alcoholics tend to manifest more neurotic-like components, while heroin addicts tend to manifest more psychopathic-like traits.

SUBSETS OF ADDICTS

Another interesting question is whether there are meaningful similarities and differences in personality among subsets of addicts. For purposes of this chapter, we will look at the special populations of female addicts, military addicts, incarcerates, black-white addicts, volunteer-nonvolunteer addicts, and physician addicts.

Female Heroin Addicts

What knowledge we have concerning the personality attributes of heroin addicts comes almost exclusively from the study of males. Hence, this research may have little utility in making generalizations about female heroin addicts. However, there has been a recent spate of interest in female addicts and a picture is beginning to emerge suggesting that female addicts show considerable pathology compared to the general population and share many traits in common with their male counterparts. Both male and female addicts obtain MMPI peak scores on Psychopathic Deviation (PD) and both have an internal locus of control (Craig, 1979b). They describe themselves as emotionally dependent, temperamental, impatient, impulsive, ambitious, and energetic (Kilmann, 1974), have different need patterns than male addicts (Steer et al., 1978); yet one study found gender had limited value in predicting personality patterns of male and female addicts (Sutker, Archer and Allain, 1978). The studies on female heroin addiction have not been as well controlled as other studies in this area, and researchers are only beginning to become interested in the topic of female addiction. Much of the research is confounded, and it is unknown if the obtained results are due to the fact that the samples are female or because they are female addicts. Adding normal male/female control groups will help clarify the issue. Ultimately the question of whether there are personality differences between male and female addicts is complicated by the question of whether there are personality differences between males and females in general. Before we can answer the first question, we may have to wait for basic research to be done on the second question.

Military Addicts

The Viet Nam experience dramatically highlighted the effects of heroin availability, peer group acceptance, and stressful conditions on the use and abuse of opium, even among those soldiers who probably would not have taken heroin under ordinary circumstances. Thus, personality variables are only one factor to consider when treating the addict. Yet, a large portion of GIs did not take opium, even under the special conditions created by Viet Nam. Most of the research comparing addicts in the military to civilian addicts has not found any appreciable differences between these populations and found them to be comparable to civilian addicts in personality traits and psychopathology (Black, 1975; Hampton and Vogel, 1973; Kojak and Canby, 1975). Studies in this area have been poorly controlled with major problems in sample methodology, definition of heroin addiction, and other sampling biases to preclude definitive conclusions.

Incarcerates

The use of incarcerates as a control group has been a frequent strategy among researchers (Craig, 1979b). Such a population controls for psychopathy and criminality but is most appropriate when the researcher is interested in comparing addict with nonaddict prisoners. Researchers have been less interested in examining whether incarcerated addicts represent a specific type of addict. One study found that personality measures were able to differentiate successful addicts from nonsuccessful addicts, who were later rehabilited, while still in prison (Platt and Scurra, 1974) and another study found that the personality traits of addicts did not change while in prison (Skolnick and Zuckerman, 1979).

Volunteer and Nonvolunteer Addicts

There have been some suggestions that volunteer addicts show more levels of psychopathology and greater personality disburbance than nonvolunteer addicts. At issue is whether volunteers exaggerate their problems to gain admissions to treatment programs. Studies in this area have been summarized elsewhere (Craig, 1979b, 1981b). For purposes of illustration, two studies will be highlighted.

Sutker's group on the Atlantic seaboard consistently find no differences between volunteers and nonvolunteers and attribute any observed differences not to volunteering, but to the conditions of testing or the hassles of street life. In one of their studies, volunteers and nonvolunteers were given MMPI tests based on three conditions of assessment, e.g., either prior to program assessment in a program that selected its clients, during routine evaluation in an open admission program, or following acceptance into a drug treatment program. The reasearchers found that volunteering had no consistent effect on self-reported psychopathology (Sutker, Archer and Allain, 1979).

The Penk group in Dallas consistently find differences based on volunteer-nonvolunteer status, irrespective of race. In a particularly intriguing study, these authors gave MMPIs to addicts who were initially in their program as nonvolunteers and who later returned as volunteers and found that former nonvolunteers increased their scores upon second admission (as volunteers), while the volunteers produced no significant differences upon returning again as volunteers (Penk and Robinowitz, 1980).

Needless to say, the results are contradictory, despite two excellent research groups and well-designed studies. We are left to conclude that volunteers may exaggerate their status, so the conditions of assessment and the admission status of the patients need to be considered in evaluating the personality traits of heroin addicts.

Black and White Addicts

A rather clear picture has emerged that reveals greater malajustment and psychopathology among white addicts than among blacks (Craig, 1981). White addicts seem to have intense individual difficulties, generalized social maladjustment, experience more parental conflict, and have more neurotic-like concerns than black addicts. In fact, some studies show that ethnicity is among the best predictors of drug status, drug preference, and level of personality disturbance (Kaestner, Rosen and Appel,1977; Penk et al., 1978; and Sutker, Archer and Allain, 1978).

Physician Addicts

Addicted physicians represent a particularly unique subset of addicts and a group not generally considered when one speaks of addict typologies, yet physicians are at high risk for the development of drug addiction due to the accessibility of narcotics, occupational stress and the high demands and expectations placed upon them by the public. Studies of drug dependence among physicians have generally shown that they possess traits more in common with addicts than with their physician peers. Addicted physicians tend to remain in their occupation and tend to remain married. At follow-up, about half of them are still addicted.

Hill, Haertzen, and Yamahiro (1968) compared MMPI profiles of addicted physicians undergoing treatment at Lexington to the MMPI profiles of nonaddicted physicians and hospitalized white addicts. Forty-two addict physicians were compared to eigthty-one hospitalized white addicts and 115 nonaddicted physicians. Results showed that the nonaddicted physicians obtained normal MMPI elevations, while the addicted physicians scored in the intermediate position between the normal physicians and the general addicts. In eight of ten clinical MMPI scales, the addict physician scored significantly higher than normal physicians, with the scales of Psychopathic Deviation and Masculinity/Femininity reaching the highest deviations in the addicted physician group. These results reflect the general maladjustment of the addicted physicians, especially in the areas of sexual adjustment, low frustration tolerance, difficulties in postponing gratification, and some difficulties in interpersonal relations. Since prolonged use of narcotics could have altered the personalities of the physicians, the study could not determine the extent to which the physicians possess these traits prior to the development of their addiction. However, a study by Modlin and Montes (1964) showed that addicted physicians were generally irresponsible before the addiction and another study showed that addicted physicians have more in common in terms of personality structure with criminal addicts than with other physicians (Hill, Haertzen, and Glaser, 1960).

A ten-year follow-up study of sixty-eight addict physicians discharged from Lexington in 1952, compared with sixty-eight other physicians, indicated that the attrition rate from the AMA directories among the control group was 21 percent over a ten-year period, while the same rate for the addicted physicians was 43 percent. The study showed that even while addicted, the physicians maintained their practices as well as their marriages. The addicted physician group showed more geographic mobility and location changes than the control physician group. An inspection of the addicted physicians revealed that many were self-injecting either morphine or meperidine for self-treatment of organic disease or induced stress. Of the sixty-eight subjects, fifty-one were given a psychiatric diagnosis reflecting a personality disorder. The authors cited previous works demonstrating higher rates of mortality, either to preexisting disease or suicide, reported hospitalizations, occasional imprisonment, loss of medical licenses and marginal social and economic adjustment for the physicians who were chronically addicted in comparison to those who were only hospitalized once for their addiction (Putman and Ellenberg, 1966).

CONTEMPORARY RESEARCH PROBLEMS

This rather sketchy presentation is an effort to acquaint the reader with the state of empirical knowledge of the heroin addict personality as viewed from the standpoint of science. This view would not be complete without a brief glimpse of some of the problems and needs facing the researcher in this area.

(1) Unfortunately, most of the research in this area has relied on "cup of coffee" approaches to testing. A researcher gives a paper and pencil test or a self-report inventory to a patient and then "goes for a cup of coffee." The patient is then given another similar instrument and the researcher goes for another cup of coffee. Thus, the most popular test, using this approach, has been the MMPI and much of our knowledge comes primarily from this single test. However, recent research has begun a more broadened assessment base that includes different kinds of tests, tapping different layers or levels of personality. This is an extremely important step, since a veridical addict trait should be

independent of its assessment source. Thus, hostility, if it is a salient addict trait, should be manifested, whether it is measured by the MMPI, TAT, Adjective Checklist, peer group ratings, or scores on a hostility scale. A broad assessment base will add consensual validation to our present findings and may disconfirm others or at least present a more contextual understanding to the appearance of a given trait.

(2) Our research has utilized a static approach to testing. We have strong evidence that the more psychopathic traits have been impervious to change (Craig, 1979b, 1981b), and we have clinical lore to suggest that some of these traits become sublimated or rechanneled only later to appear in different contexts, but we have little research to tell us what really happens to personality traits over time.

(3) It is no longer an acceptable approach to simply measure the presence or absence of a given trait. Rather we need to develop typologies within an interactional framework that systematically relates traits to other variables of interest, particularly such things as recidivism, treatment retention, outcome, and etiology.

(4) We have inappropriately relied on limited approaches to assessment. No one has bothered to determine how the addict personality is seen by a significant other (family, friends) and few have identified high-risk subjects (children of addicts) or longitudinally determined which traits mediate the transition into addiction and which traits immunize against it. The major contemporary issues in personality research, such as androgeny, repression sensitization, achievement motivation, attribution theory, and self-concept approaches, have rarely been considered or assessed. This results in a somewhat stagnant picture of the addict that lacks vitality and perhaps even usefulness.

(5) Personality theory is the result of the integration of characteristics, traits, structure, adjustment, dynamics, development, and change. We have too long researched the trait approach and too often ignored the other aspects of personality.

(6) Consistent with the functional approach that has dominated the field of psychology in recent times, research in the addictions has proceeded without the benefit of underlying

theoretical premises upon which to generate and test hypothesis and to build models of addiction. Few researchers have utilized theory or tested their postulates. Thus, theories perpetuate the field without the benefit of validation.

CONCLUSION

Much and little is known about the personality of the heroin addict. At the level of the client-clinician, it is factors of personality that tend to dominate clinical case discussions and the development of treatment plans. As one drug abuse counselor put it at a team meeting, when discussing his client:

"That's the way he is. That's his psychology. If he doesn't change that, he won't change at all."

Can we as clinicians and researchers help the patient to understand himself, help the counselor to define what needs to change, and help both to work together in the process of change? That is what we are all about.

REFERENCES

Barnes, G.: The alcoholic personality: A reanalysis of the literature. *J Stud Alcohol, 40:*571-634, 1979.

Black, W.: Personality characteristics of Viet Nam veterans identified as heroin abusers. *Am J Psychiat, 132:*748-749, 1975.

Cox, W.: The alcoholic personality: A review of the evidence. In B. Maher (Ed.): *Progress in Experimental Personality Research,* Vol. 9. New York, Academic Press, 1979, pp. 89-148.

Craig, R.: Personality characteristics of heroin addicts: A review of the empirical literature with critique — Part I. *Int J Addict, 14:*513-532, 1979a.

Craig, R.: Personality characteristics of heroin addicts: A review of the empirical literature with critique — Part II. *Int J Addict, 14:*607-626, 1979b.

Craig, R.: Treating drug addicts and alcoholics in combined treatment settings: Issues and perspectives. *J Psychiat Treat Eval, 3:* 87–93, 1981.

Craig, R.: Personality characteristics of heroin addicts: Review of empirical research 1976-1979. *Int J Addict,* 1981b (in press).

Dole, V.; and Nyswander, M.: Heroin addicts — a metabolic disease. *Arch Intern Med, 120:*19-24, 1967.

Dole, V.; and Nyswander, M.: Methadone maintenance treatment: A ten year perspective. *JAMA, 235:*2117-2119, 1976.

Goldstein, J.; and Sappington, J.: Personality characteristics of students who later became heavy drug users: An MMPI study of an avant-garde. *Am J Alcohol Abuse, 4:*401-412, 1977.

Hampton, P.; and Vogel, D.: Personality characteristics of servicemen returned from Viet Nam identified as heroin abusers. *Am J Psychiat, 130:*1031-1032, 1973.

Hoffman, H.; Loper, R.; and Kammier, M.: Identifying Future Alcoholics with MMPI Alcoholism Scales. *Q J Studies Alcohol, 35:* 490–498, 1974.

Hill, H.; Haertzen, C.; and Glaser, R.: Personality characteristics of narcotic addicts as identified by the MMPI. *J Gen Psychol, 62:*127-139, 1960.

Hill, H.; Haertzen, C.; and Yamahiro, R.: The addict physician: An MMPI study of the interaction of personality characteristics and availability of narcotics. In A. Wikler (Ed.): *The Addictive States.* Baltimore, Williams & Wilkins, 1968.

Jones, M.: Personality correlates and antecedants of drinking patterns in adult males. *J Consult Clin Psychol, 32:*2-12, 1968.

Jones, M.: Personality antecedants and correlates of drinking patterns in women. *J Consult Clin Psychol, 36:*61-69, 1971.

Kaestner, E.; Rosen, L.; and Appel, P.: Patterns of drug abuse: Relationships with ethnicity, sensation seeking and anxiety. *J Consult Clin Psychol, 45:*462-468, 1977.

Kammeier, M.; Hohman, H.; and Loper, R.: Personality characteristics of alcoholics as college freshman and at time of treatment. *Q J Studies Alcohol, 34:* 390–399,-1 1973.

Kilmann, P.: Personality characteristics of female narcotic addicts. *Psychol Rept, 35:*485-486, 1974.

Kojak, G.; and Canby, J.: Personality and behavior patterns of American servicemen in Thailand. *Am J Psychiat, 132:*246-250, 1975.

Lachar, D., et al.: A heroin addiction scale for the MMPI: Effectiveness in differential diagnosis in a psychiatric population. *Int J Addict, 14:*135-142, 1979.

Loper, R.; Kammeier, M.; and Hohman, H.: MMPI characteristics of college freshman males who later became alcoholics. *J Abnorm Psychol, 82:* 159–162, 1973.

McCord, W.: and McCord, J.: *Origins of Alcoholism.* Stanford, Calif, Stanford U. Pr, 1960.

Maddux, J.; and Bowden C.: Critique of success with methadone maintenance. *Am J Psychiat, 129:*440-446, 1972.

Modlin, H.; and Montes, A.: Narcotic addiction in physicians. *Am J Psychiat, 121:*358-363, 1964.

Owen P.; and Butcher J.: Personality factors in problem drinking: A review of the evidence and some suggested directions. In P. Owen and J. Butcher (Eds.): *Psychiatric Factors in Drug Abuse.* New York, Grune & Stratton, 1979, pp. 67-91.

Penk, W.; and Robinowitz, R.: A test of the voluntarism hypothesis among nonvoluntering opiate addicts who voluntarily return to treatment. *J Abnorm Psychol, 89:*234-239, 1980.

Penk, W.; and Robinowitz, R.: Personality differences of heroin addicts and polydrug abusers. In R. Craig and S. Baker (Eds.): *Drug Dependent patients: Treatment and Research.* Springfield, Thomas, 1981.

Penk, W.; Woodward, W.; Robinowitz, R.; and Hess, J.: Differences in MMPI scores of black and white heroin users. *J Abnorm Psychol 87:* 505-513, 1978.

Penk, W.; Woodward, W.; Robinowitz, R.; and Parr, W.: An MMPI comparison of polydrug and heroin abusing patients entering treatment. *J Abnorm Psychol,* in press, 1981.

Pihl, R.; and Spiers, P.: Individual characteristics in the etiology of drug abusers. In B. Maher (Ed.): *Progress in Experimental Personality Research,* Vol. 8. New york, Academic Press, 1978, pp. 93-195.

Platt, J.; and Scurra, W.: Peer judgments of parole success in institutionalized heroin addicts: Personality correlates and validity. *J Counsel Psychol,* 21:511-515, 1974.

Putman, P.; and Ellenberg, E.: Narcotic addiction among physicians: A ten year follow-up. *Am J Psychiat, 122:* 745-748, 1966.

Robbins, L.: *Deviant Children Grow Up.* Baltimore, Williams & Wilkins, 1966.

Robins, L.; Bates, W.; and O'Neal, P.: Adult drinking patterns of former problem children. In D. Pittman and C. Snyder (Eds.): *Society, Culture and Drinking Patterns.* New York, Wiley, 1962.

Senay, E.; and Wright, M.: Critique of theories of methadone use. *Int Pharmacopsychiat, 7:* 64-70, 1972.

Skolnick, N.; and Zuckerman, M.: personality change in drug abusers: A comparison of therapeutic community and prison groups. *J Consult Clin Psychol, 47:* 768-770, 1979.

Steer, R.; Gasta, C.; Kotzker, E.; and Schut, J.: Need similarity in husbands and wives who are receiving methadone maintenance therapy. *J Clin Psychol, 34:* 558-561, 1978.

Sutker, P.; and Archer, R.: MMPI characteristics of opiate addicts, alcoholics and other drug abusers. In C. Newmark (Ed.): *MMPI: Current Clinical and Research Trends.* New York, Praeger, 1979.

Sutker, P.; Archer, R.; and Allain, A.: Drug abuser patterns, personality characteristics and relationships with sex, race and sensation seeking. *J Consult Clin Psychol, 46:* 1374-1378, 1978.

Sutker, P.; Archer, R.; and Allain, A.: Volunteerism and self-reported psychopathology among opiate addicts. *J Abnorm Psychol, 88:* 59-67, 1979.

Winick, C.: A sociological theory of the genesis of drug dependency. In C. Winick (Ed.): *Sociological Aspects of Drug Dependence.* Cleveland, CRC Press, 1974, pp 3-13.

CHAPTER 9

PERSONALITY DIFFERENCES OF HEROIN ADDICTS AND POLYDRUG ABUSERS*

WALTER PENK AND RALPH ROBINOWITZ

"**D**o heroin addicts differ from polydrug abusers on measures of personality?" We consider here several aspects of the complex question. The aspects are considered from several vantage points: (1) we operationally define key terms in our question — that is, "heroin addicts," "polydrug abusers," and "personality measures"; (2) we discuss reasons why it is important to compare groups differing in types of drug abused; (3) we examine why we expect heroin and polydrug abusers to differ on personality measures; (4) we review the background literature bearing on the question of heroin-polydrug personality differences; (5) we identify *possible* sources of disagreement in heroin and polydrug personality comparison studies; (6) we summarize our own empirical studies comparing personality scores of heroin and polydrug abusers, presenting evidence both for and against the validity of such differences; and (7) we recommend new directions for clinical observations and research in personality studies of drug abusers.

OPERATIONAL DEFINITIONS OF KEY TERMS

Definitions of drug abusers differ in the scientific literature. Inconsistencies occur across studies because investigators have not standardized their terms in drug-taking histories. Moreover, drug users sometimes will not, and other times cannot, give pre-

*Research conducted by the authors reported in this chapter was performed with support from the General Medical Research Service of the Veterans Administration Medical Center, Dallas, Texas.

187

cise accounts of their drug-taking behavior. The term *polydrug abuser* is the group most fuzzily defined. In a broader sense, all drug abusers are polydrug abusers — even heroin addicts (e.g., D'Amanda et al. 1977). All are polydrug abusers because in the past each has experimented with a variety of drugs during the course of drug-taking careers; all are polydrug abusers because in the present most, if not all, will supplement their primary drug-of-abuse with other drugs, particularly at times when the primary drug is unavailable. As a general rule, it is hazardous to compare personality studies because investigators in different settings use differential behavioral referents for drug-use category classifications and most do not control many other potentially influential variables.

Given problems in operationally defining key terms, we would like to specify from the beginning what we mean by "heroin addicts" and "polydrug abusers." By *heroin addicts* we refer to male veterans who report, at the time they seek to enter a Drug Dependence Treatment Program in a Veterans Administration Medical Center, a daily use of opiates for at least two years. In cases where multiple drug use is reported, use of secondary drugs averages a frequency of once weekly or less. Corroborating evidence of heroin use is obtained from urinalysis in all cases and is further substantiated by other physical signs as rated by trained professional personnel (e.g., withdrawal signs, "tracks," etc.).

By *polydrug abusers,* we refer to male veterans who report daily use, for at least one year, of two or more illicit drugs in combinations. The two most frequently used drugs are amphetamines and barbiturates. Corroborating evidence of polydrug use is obtained from urinalysis in about 60 percent of the cases. Recent use of heroin by those classified as "polydrug abusers" is ruled out in all cases from admission urinalyses. "Polydrug abusers," then, consist of those who use amphetamines and/or barbiturates on a daily basis, who do not regularly use opiates, and whose secondary drug use is restricted to weekly use, or less, for any other drugs (such as alcohol, marijuana, or hallucinogens).

Our samples are distinguished in at least one important dimension from many of the studies reported in the drug abuse literature. We have studied veterans, 20 percent of whom recently participated in military combat. Inclusion of this subset of military combat veterans may limit the extent to which our findings generalize to studies of civilian drug abusers. Some writers already have commented on the possibilities that experiences in the Viet Nam War may contribute a unique factor to this generation of drug abusers among veterans (Baker, 1975a,b; O'Brien et al., 1977). Direct effects from military and combat experiences may interact in the drug-taking experiences of our samples. Indirect effects may arise from selective factors: e.g., civilian samples are more likely to contain drug abusers from the lower levels of intellectual functioning and from the more disturbed extremes of psychological maladjustment; such extremes may not be represented in samples of drug-abusing veterans because preinduction military screening may have precluded service entry. Finally, our groups may differ also from samples gathered in other VA settings because we routinely attempt to assess everyone on a "consecutively admitted" basis, those volunteering for treatment as well as those who do not.

By *measures of personality* we refer primarily to studies using the Minnesota Multiphasic Personality Inventory (MMPI). A comprehensive review of the literature of measures used in studies of personalities of drug abusers is available (Craig, 1979a,b, 1981), as well as a review of his earlier analysis in Chapter 8 in this book. By personality, we refer mainly to the psychometric trait approach in personality measurement. We will introduce, however, data from other traditions in personality meaurement: e.g., data about heroin and polydrug abuser differences from the psychodynamic tradition, cognitive social learning approaches, as well as the psychology of the self, as expressed in measures of anhedonia, family social climates, reasons for seeking treatment, and events which are valued as a function of stopping or continuing drug use. Whereas most previous heroin-polydrug abuser comparisons have been based on the MMPI measures of personality, we will develop a case for the future that clinicians and researchers should compare heroin-polydrug abusers on measures other than traits and should assess at different levels of personality assessment (Leary, 1956). Studies should be undertaken using the latest refinements in personality measurement (Bem and Funder, 1978; Fiske, 1979; Mischel, 1979a).

REASONS FOR COMPARING PERSONALITIES OF HEROIN AND POLYDRUG ABUSERS

Answers for the question of heroin addict-polydrug abuser personality differences should be sought for several reasons. First, there are issues of differential *etiology*. Although it is doubtful that causes of drug addiction can be answered by assessing personalities of drug abusers at the time they seek treatment, nevertheless we must learn the current status of the drug abuser's personality organization at the time in his drug-using-career when he decides to seek treatment (cf. Craig, 1979b, for an analysis of limitations in learning about etiology from personality assessment obtained during the course of treatment). Further, clinicians and researchers not only can generate hypotheses about past causative factors but they also may use data from the present to predict the future course of adjustment. Second, there are issues about *treatment*. Should separate or similar treatment programs be designed for heroin and polydrug abusers? Different treatment approaches already are practiced: i.e., synthetic opiates are substituted in treatment plans of many opiate users whereas a similar chemical substitution treatment strategy does not occur in polydrug abuse treatment, even when psychiatric drugs are prescribed. Third, there are issues of *relapse* and *continuance* of drug abuse after treatment. Do heroin users follow a different course of post-treatment events than do polydrug abusers? Are personality factors implicated? If there are differences, then do such differences mean that aftercare treatment intervention should be specifically tailored for differential courses of post-treatment activities?

WHY EXPECT THAT HEROIN AND POLYDRUG ABUSERS DIFFER ON PERSONALITY?

Considering that our reasons are valid for learning whether or not heroin addicts differ from polydrug abusers, we next should understand the question "Why, in the first place, should we expect heroin addicts and polydrug abusers to differ on personality measures?" There are two theories, at least: (1) compulsive use of illicit drugs is thought to be associated with personality maladjustment; (2) preference for a specific kind of drug is thought to be associated with a specific set of personality problems. We expect heroin and polydrug abusers to differ, then, for an obvious reason, i.e., the *stimulus properties* of the respective drugs are different (Barry, 1977). Since heroin is an analgesic, then persons with enduring physical and/or psychological pain, so it is speculated, should be predisposed to use it. Since amphetamines are a stimulant, then persons who are passive and who negatively value their passivity should prefer this drug as one convenient way to counteract their passivity. Since barbiturates are associated with sedation, then those who are tense and who negatively value their tenseness should prefer a drug that sedates and reduces their tension. Although the validity of such notions have rarely been investigated since the classic studies of Beecher (1959), many clinicians and researchers, particularly those trained in medical settings, operate from such assumptions that people compulsively take drugs because subjective and objective effects meet certain physiological and psychological needs (Solomon and Corbitt, 1974).

Possibly differences in *legal* penalties, more severe for heroin than for other drugs, may be involved directly or indirectly with personality differences among users. Perhaps, the stronger and more intact potential drug users may opt for the "rippin' and runnin'" of heroin use (Agar, 1973) whereas the weaker and more disturbed may settle for the comparatively less demanding and less risky activities by which nonopiate, "soft" drugs are obtained.

Possibly there are *cultural* differences operating to produce personality differences. Heroin, with a longer tradition of drug abuse in poorer urban areas, may be associated more with crime and with antisocial behaviors, whereas amphetamines and barbiturates may be associated more with medically affiliated forms of abuse or with efforts to achieve or sustain the pressures of one's job. Ethnic differences in patterns of drug abused suggest a powerful cultural influence in drug use preferences that interacts with, and may even transcend, biochemistry.

These are but a few examples of the many, constantly evolving personal, social, and chemical forces that may attract certain kinds of people with specific kinds of personality organization to specific kinds of drugs. Such influences, and many others such as variations in drug availability, socioeconomic status, geographic location, etc., all interact to produce addictions. We will not understand "psychic dependence" until the roles of personality, social, and cultural factors are operationalized and specified; a physician who pioneered the study of pharmacological dimensions in drug addiction, N. B. Eddy, in his eightieth year, shortly before his death expressed this point:

> When we first started out we thought only of physical dependence and of dependence as a pharmacological phenomenon. Eventually we had to realize that that was not the case at all, and that from a psychic standpoint the most important thing was the drive towards drug-seeking behavior. Continuing with what I started to say, I wish I could be here 50 years from now to see what degree we would be able to manage psychic dependence (1973, pp. 201-202).

SOURCES OF DISAGREEMENT IN HEROIN-POLYDRUG ABUSER PERSONALITY COMPARISON: *OR* WHAT ARE THE PITFALLS TO RESEARCHING THIS AREA?

Several sources contribute to little research and much disagreement on the question of personality differences between heroin addicts and polydrug abusers. We mention only a few here, the ones more prominent in our personal experience as clinicians working in a treatment center. Others undertaking similar investigations undoubtedly will develop their own catalogue of pitfalls, some of which perhaps may overlap with ours. First, drug abusers usually are not as willing to participate in personality research as are other clinical groups. Perhaps, the more passive, more bored, and/or more captive drug abusers are represented in field studies. Second, moods and attitudes of drug abusers change mercurially during the time they are seeking treatment, which is coincidentally, the time when psychological assessment is most likely to occur. Most tests are given when responses are more likely to be influenced by physical changes associated with changes in drug-taking behavior. Drug abusers are likely to be less cooperative for psychological assessment later in the treatment process when, after a fleeting commitment to treatment, misgivings arise and negativistic aspects of personality reemerge.

Whereas most investigators assume that personality assessment at the time of entering treatment is the most advantageous for obtaining data, data collected at that time may be the more disadvantageous for drawing conclusions about enduring personality traits. Pihl and Spiers (1978) have raised the issue about the preferred time for collecting personality data. Such questions are important for such personality theorists as Mischel (1979a) who calls for greater attention to cross-situational and cross-temporal consistency in personality research (see Sutker and Archer, 1979, for a review of drug abusers' personality changes across time).

Third, most drug abuser field research may be biased by differential attrition rates. Some investigators assess immediately; others wait until "withdrawal" symptoms subside. Those who pause lose many clients, for drug abusers are noted for leaving treatment early (as many as 40% will prematurely terminate treatment within two weeks of entering inpatient programs). Nonrepresentative sampling is the risk of delaying personality assessment.

Fourth, most studies are conducted at one level of personality assessment; many investigators then interpret their findings as if they had tapped deeper structures as well (cf. Leary, 1956, for definitions of levels in personality measurement). Yet, it may be inaccurate to assume that drug abuser studies conducted to date really have much to say about personality predispositions for addiction disorders. As demonstrated in a heroin-polydrug abuser comparison below at two different levels of personality assessment (i.e., Penk et al., 1978), somewhat different conceptualizations of personality types are achieved as a function of differences in level of personality assessment. Perhaps the renewed interest in personality assessment, sounded by such theorists as

Fiske (1979), Mischel (1979a), and Bem and Funder (1978), particularly expressed through a resurgence in the desire to evaluate personality and environment interaction, will produce sound field studies. If clinicians and researchers can implement comprehensive strategies assessing the interaction of personality and environment, then the study of heroin and polydrug abuser differences will receive the complex evaluation it merits. As long as we continue to assess personality solely in terms of traits, so are we likely to remain puzzled about the role of personality in drug abuse.

Fifth, many investigators are asking questions about drug abuse etiology at the time when treatment is sought not when compulsive drug use begins. While one may generate hypotheses about the causes of drug addiction from current personality organization and from retrospective views of the past, nevertheless personality data from the present is better used for answering questions about the present and predicting the course of future adjustment.

Sixth, clinicians and researchers have not settled three important elements of the question, "Do heroin addicts and polydrug abusers differ on measures of personality?" One aspect concerns criteria for determining when a significant difference is clinically relevant (Nathan and Lansky, 1978). Another relates to source of personality differences — demographics or drug preferences? A third arises from the strategy of forming composite profiles. One can readily imagine the same group profile formed by several different combinations of subgroups, each requiring different interpretations. Agreement must be reached about when a significant difference is clinically meaningful. We will illustrate our concerns about composite profiles and the subgroups which compose them later at the conclusion of this paper.

WHAT IS THE EVIDENCE INDICATING THAT HEROIN ADDICTS DIFFER FROM POLYDRUG ABUSERS ON MEASURES OF PERSONALITY?

A review of the literature on heroin-polydrug abuser comparisons yields conflicting results. For excellent, recent analyses of the literature see Craig (1979a, 1979b, and elsewhere in this ·' volume), as well as the chapters by Pihl and Spiers (1978) and Sutker and Archer (1979). Generally, clinical observations and theory-building propose a single core problem at the heart of drug addiction whereas empirical data shows significant personality differences (and, by implication, multiple causality). Unfortunately, the empirical data is beset by methodological defects that compromise any substantive conclusions. Theoretical explanations, on the other hand, have not gathered enough empirical data to confuse or challenge their notions. Consequently, it is worth summarizing both theoretical and empirical forms of explanation about the causes of drug addiction.

The most sophisticated argument favoring an explanation based on a single core problem underlying drug addiction has been developed from a psychoanalytic frame of reference. Otto Fenichel (1945) elegantly speaks for this line of interpretation. He posits the person (and, by implication, the personality) as the place where drug addiction begins. As described in the following section from his classic work, *The Psychoanalytic Theory of Neurosis*, Fenichel writes about addiction in the following way:

> . . . in other words, addicts are persons who have a disposition to react to the effects of alcohol, morphine, or other drugs in a specific way, namely, in such a way that they try to use these effects to satisfy the archaic oral longing which is sexual longing, a need for security, and a need for the maintenance of self-esteem simultaneously. Thus the origin and the nature of the addiction are not determined by the chemical effect of the drug but by the psychological structure of the patient . . . (1945, p. 376).

Fenichel further states that it is persons with similar kinds of core conflicts (i.e., oral dependency) who are predisposed to drug addiction. As illustrated in this passage, Fenichel describes with extraordinary clinical sensitivity the many effects and reactions of drug abusers.

> . . . The effect of the drug rests on the fact that it is felt as this food and warmth. Persons of this kind react to situations that create the need for sedation and or stimulation different from others. They are intolerant of tension. They cannot endure pain, frustration, situations of waiting. They seize any opportunity for escape more readily and may

experience the effect of the drug as something more gratifying than
the original situation that had interrupted by the precipitating pain or
frustration. After the elation, pain, or frustration becomes all the
more unbearable, inducing a heightened use of the drug. All other
strivings become gradually more and more replaced by the 'phar-
macotoxic longing.' Interest in reality gradually disappears, except
those having to do with procuring the drug. In the end, all of reality
may come to reside in the hypodermic needle. *The tendency toward such
development, rooted in an oral dependence on outer supplies, is the essence of
drug addiction.* All other features are incidental (Fenichel, 1945, p. 388,
italics added).

Clinicians working with drug abusers, however, are struck
more by differences than by similarities in personality. Pihl and
Spiers (1978), for example, have faulted psychoanalytic theorists
for having postulated too many explanations of drug abuse.
How do writers such as Fenichel align an array of differing personality types, empirically observed, with a theoretical formulation which conceptualizes drug abuse as a single core problem?
Fenichel explains such variety through the concept of "regression," which holds that the same motive can manifest itself in all
sorts of ways. As Fenichel himself states it, with a freshness, di-
rectness, and relevance which easily spans thirty-five years to
substance abusers of the present day:

> The pre-morbid personality, therefore, is the decisive factor. Those
> persons become drug addicts for whom the effect of the drug has a
> special significance. For them it means the fulfillment, or at least the
> hope of fulfillment, of a deep and primitive desire, more urgently felt
> by them than are sexual or other instinctual longings by normal per-
> sons. This pleasure or the hope for it makes genital sexuality unin-
> teresting for them. The genital organization breaks up, and an ex-
> traordinary regression begins. The various points of fixation deter-
> mine which fields of infantile sexuality — Oedipus complex, mastur-
> bation conflicts, and especially pregenital impulses — come to the
> fore, and in the end the libido remains in the form of an "amorphous
> erotic tension energy" without "differential characteristics of form of
> organization" (Fenichel, 1945, pp. 376-377).

The psychoanalytic persuasion has produced the most elaborate statement for understanding drug abuse. The theory enables the clinician and researcher to go deeper than surface variations and resolve seeming contradictions in overt behaviors. Un-

fortunately, empirical measurement is lacking; it is difficult for practitioners to achieve cross-situational and cross-temporal stability. Also, interpretations tend to be stylized, proceeding so much according to formula that the person gets lost in a briar patch of entangling explanations.

Psychoanalysts, however, are not the only clinicians who prefer to conceptualize addiction disorders as consisting of a single, core problem. For example, Graham (1977) argues for the single problem explanation from his review of the descriptive, trait perspective of MMPI research, holding that heroin addicts, gamblers, and alcoholics have similar personalities. Although he recognizes that the prevailing two-point codes differ in each of these groups, nevertheless Graham contends that the core problem is represented by ". . . the *Pd* (Psychopathic deviate) dimension of the MMPI" (1977, p. 21). (Note: the term "two-point code" refers to a system for classifying MMPI profiles based upon the two highest clinical scale scores; see Graham, 1978.) Graham reports that alcoholics obtain more *27* code types (elevations on scales *D,* Depression, and *Pt,* Psychasthenia, suggesting greater psychological discomfort), that gamblers obtain more *49* code types (highest scales being *Pd,* Psychopathic deviate, and *Ma,* Hypomania, indicating more asocial and acting-out behavior), and that heroin addicts obtain more *48* code types (the two clinical scales that are the highest being *Pd,* Psychopathic deviate, and *Sc,* Schizophrenia, revealing a greater incidence of character disorders among this group of addiction disorders). Nevertheless, Graham concludes that the following attributes in part or in toto will characterize all clients classified as "addiction disorders":

> . . . 1. self-centered, narcissistic; 2. tense, nervous, anxious, vulnerable to threat; overreacts to stress; 3. dysphoric, pessimistic, brooding, ruminative; 4. asocial acting-out behavior; impulsive; 5. anger which gains expression in periodic outbursts; 6. guilt and remorse (possible feigned) following periods of acting out; 7. striving; perfectionistic; high need to achieve but fear of failure; 8. frustrated with own lack of achievement; 9. passive-dependent personality style with strong needs for attention and recognition; 10. reluctance to open up emotionally for fear of being hurt; 11. manipulative behavior; and 12.

stated desire to change and "to turn over a new leaf" but poor prognosis for significant change in traditional therapy (Graham, 1977, pp. 20-21).

Results from empirical comparisons of drug abusers, however, do not support the contention that heroin and polydrug abusers have, at base, the same core problem. Beginning with the early literature, when the prevailing experimental tactic was to compare a single drug-using group with normative, T-scaled scores of the MMPI, group profiles already indicated that polydrug users, or users of illicit drugs other than opiates, were more disturbed in personality scales than were heroin addicts (cf. reviews in Craig, 1979a, b; Butcher and Owen, 1978; and Sutker and Archer, 1979; for examples of specific studies, see Burke and Eichberg, 1972; Zuckerman et al., 1975; Stauss et al., 1977). To illustrate with a few representative, single-group studies, Ellinwood (1967) presented group MMPI profiles of amphetamine users that obviously were more elevated than group profiles of heroin users; similarly, Korman (1977) reported highly elevated group profiles obtained from inhalant abusers that differed markedly from heroin users (cf. Hill et al., 1962; Berzins et al., 1974). This experimental tactic, lacking direct comparison of heroin addicts and polydrug abusers, however, did not delineate whether differences in group profiles occurred because of differences in drug abused or because of differences in nondrug-related factors (such as demographic variables — e.g., age — by which samples notably differ).

Even direct comparisons have not always answered the question, as illustrated by one of the few studies directly comparing heroin with polydrug abusers, that is, the MMPI study of Lachar et al. (1979), which was part of the National Collaborative Study on Polydrug Abuse (Wesson et al., 1978). Lachar et al. (1978) found that polydrug abusers score significantly lower on MMPI validity scale L (indicating less openness), and significantly higher than heroin abusers on clinical scales D (Depression), Pd (Psychopathic deviate), Sc (Schizophrenia), as well as higher on content scales (Wiggins, 1966) of Organicity, Depression, and Feminine Interests. These differences cannot be regarded as merely a matter of differences in maladjustment rather than the result of core personality conflict. The authors went on to classify the profiles by Lachar's (1974) automated interpretation system of categorizing broad diagnostic types and found significant differences in major diagnostic classes, not just for separate scales: 40 percent of their polydrug-using sample was sorted into the "psychotic" diagnostic type compared to only 23 percent of their heroin sample. Based on this evidence, and findings from a larger study of polydrug abusers, Lachar et al. (1978) have concluded that, "Polydrug abusers frequently display a core personality characterized by insufficient internal control and social alienation. The literature presents support for similarity between polydrug patients and psychiatric patients as well as an indication of relatively greater psychopathology in the former . . ." (p. 31).

This summary of studies conducted by Lachar et al. (1978; 1979) brings the reader up to date on most of the heroin-polydrug *controlled* comparisons on personality scales — excluding our work which we review below. There have been many studies reporting single comparisons of either heroin *or* polydrug abusers and comparisons of heroin abusers with other kinds of drug abusers (e.g., heroin abusers versus alcoholics, Overall, 1973; heroin abusers versus hallucinogen users, Toomey, 1974; heroin users with amphetamine users, Teasdale, 1972; or heroin addicts with alcoholics on tests other than the MMPI, Carroll et al., 1976). There have been comparisons of demographic measures (e.g., Sells 1976). However, few heroin-polydrug personality comparisons have been published at the present time.

The drift in this empirical literature is toward the conclusion that heroin users, though maladjusted, are comparatively better adjusted than polydrug abusers. Such trends, if substantiated, might be interpreted to support multiple, rather than single, causality in personality conflicts of drug abusers. Unfortunately, all studies have been methodologically flawed, as the investigators themselves have noted (cf. comments by Lachar et al., 1979).

PERSONAL EMPIRICAL STUDIES COMPARING
PERSONALITIES OF HEROIN AND POLYDRUG ABUSERS

Now we turn to our data, having defined our terms, established our reasons for comparing heroin and polydrug abusers, reviewed the sparse literature on the topic, and prepared the reader for possible pitfalls in conducting clinical research on this question. Our first study yielded equivocal results (Penk and Robinowitz, 1974). Although both heroin addicts and polydrug abusers evidenced appreciable maladjustment, nevertheless polydrug abusers presented themselves as more maladjusted by scoring high on K (more defensiveness), Mf (more passivity), and lower on Ma (less impulsiveness), when compared with heroin addicts. Polydrug abusers scored higher on seven of ten clinical scales, a trend in keeping with hypotheses derived from the single-group studies conducted in the past; such differences were considered at best marginal and not clinically relevant since multivariate analysis of variance approached but did not attain acceptable degrees of significance. This comparison had limited generality since it was part of controlled comparison designed to delineate the role of motivational differences (i.e., volunteers versus nonvolunteers for treatment) on MMPI profiles. The samples consisted of younger, white veterans, carefully matched on such confounding variables as age, education, and intelligence. MMPI group profiles presented in Table 9-I, provide group profile data of male veterans. The "nonvolunteer" sample consists of ASMROs — the active duty servicemen participating in VA drug abuse treatment programs under the auspices of the Armed Services Medical Regulating Office (ASMRO). The data demonstrated that personality differences as a function of primary-drug-used (i.e., heroin versus users of nonopiate, illicit drugs) are less pronounced than motivational differences for entering treatment (i.e., volunteers versus nonvolunteers). Scores are similar to those found three years later by Lachar et al. (1979) among civilian drug abusers. Personality differences from two sources — mild differences as a function of drug abused and strong differences as a function of treatment motivation — doubly challenge the theoretical notion that a single personality problem is common in all drugs abused. Notably, such data do not preclude that several different personality types are associated with drug abuse, nor can the notion be dismissed that a bias may be introduced by combining users at different stages in drug-abusing careers.

TABLE 9-I

COMPOSITE MMPI PROFILES OF VOLUNTEER AND NONVOLUNTEER
HEROIN ADDICTS AND POLYDRUG ABUSERS

| *MMPI* | | *Volunteer* | | *Nonvolunteer* | |
Scale		*Heroin* (N = 34)	*Polydrug* (N = 34)	*Heroin* (N = 34)	*Polydrug* (N = 34)
Lie (*L*)	M	47.46	46.70	51.79	53.41
	SD	5.87	6.43	7.07	6.24
Infrequency (*F*)	M	75.76	72.47	58.64	64.41
	SD	12.92	13.51	9.16	12.79
Defensiveness (*K*)	M	45.14	47.50	53.91	58.17
	SD	7.40	8.88	7.96	11.75
Hypochondriasis (*Hs*)	M	72.44	67.64	54.76	61.38
	SD	18.15	13.99	11.33	12.53
Depression (*D*)	M	76.64	74.41	58.00	63.58
	SD	13.21	14.24	11.18	15.43
Hysteria (*Hy*)	M	68.55	69.02	56.50	61.00
	SD	11.25	9.53	8.63	10.90
Psychopathic	M	81.14	82.52	69.29	71.29
deviate (*Pd*)	SD	7.61	13.01	10.03	9.75
Masculinity-	M	63.23	68.55	57.88	58.85
Femininity	SD	7.10	10.33	8.31	11.34
Paranoia (*Pa*)	M	70.58	67.50	56.73	59.38
	SD	12.73	11.82	10.61	12.05
Psychasthenia (*Pt*)	M	73.76	76.02	59.58	62.61
	SD	15.81	15.60	11.49	13.32
Schizophrenia (*Sc*)	M	85.35	83.64	62.32	70.17
	SD	20.75	20.24	10.92	15.45
(Hypo)mania (*Ma*)	M	79.91	76.08	70.02	66.32
	SD	11.00	10.66	8.50	11.41
Social intro-	M	56.23	54.97	48.41	53.32
version (*Si*)	SD	10.29	10.53	6.97	9.43

Note: Means and standard deviations are given for MMPI *T*-scale scores.

Our first study, among the earliest of the controlled comparisons of heroin addicts and polydrug abusers, was limited in several ways. It was *too* controlled. When subjects are matched on some variables, they inevitably are "unmatched" on others, as Meehl (1973) says. Further, the results did not meet our clinical observations that polydrug abusers express more inter- and intrapersonal difficulties than heroin addicts. Our samples were too small to permit statistical control of potentially confounding variables, so we continued to collect additional data until the question could be addressed with multivariate techniques.

Parenthetically, clinicians working with substance abusers may be wondering, by this time, something like, "Why it's obvious that polydrug abusers are more disturbed than heroin addicts! What's all the fuss about?" We begin our answer by noting that we do not know the source of heroin-polydrug personality differences: background characteristics, drug preferences, or what? Seeing differences does not answer why there are differences. We can imagine some of the influences. For example, in our setting, 90 percent of our polydrug abusers are white, compared with 45 percent of the heroin addicts. Moreover, black heroin addicts score significantly *lower* on the MMPI than white heroin addicts (cf. Penk and Robinowitz, 1974; Penk et al., 1978). Apparently, there is a significant cultural parameter influencing drug abuse studies. Now, if indeed white drug abusers are more disturbed than black drug abusers, and if there are disproportionately more white polydrug abusers than black polydrug abusers, then it follows there will be greater psychopathology found for polydrug abusers than for heroin addicts on the basis of cultural factors alone. For this reason, we are limiting our heroin-polydrug comparisons to white drug abusers. When our data pool of black polydrug abusers becomes sufficiently large (and we have detected a noticeable increase in amphetamine and barbiturate use among black heroin users in our region, who are changing from their pattern of heroin use), then we should be able to differentiate sources of cultural variance on MMPI response. It is essential, for such reasons, that drug abuse research be based upon detailed drug-taking histories and complete sub-background information (demographics).

EVIDENCE AGAINST PERSONALITY DIFFERENCES BETWEEN HEROIN AND POLYDRUG ABUSERS

Data analysis for our second study proceeded in several steps (Penk et al., 1980). Systematic efforts are needed to separate potentially confounding background characteristics from drug use factors. We compared, as a first step, all heroin and polydrug abusers who consecutively entered our setting. Such results represent the clinical situation in vivo. Polydrug abusers, as in our first study four years before, scored higher on all clinical scales except *K* and *Ma;* in fact, significantly higher on *F* (atypicality in thinking), *Hy* (Hysteria), *Pt* (Psychasthenia), and *Sc* (Schizophrenia). Again, the multivariate analysis of variance (MANOVA, for measuring overall profile differences) approached but did not attain significance for the clinical scales.

Comparisons were performed also for content scales (Wiggins, 1966) as done by Lachar et al. (1979). The MANOVA was highly significant (p <.003) and univariate *F* tests were significant for Feminine Interests, Poor Morale, Organic Symptoms, and Phobias in which polydrug abusers scored higher (see Table 9-II). We found, looking at the data as a clinician would in vivo, *that polydrug abusers indeed presented themselves as more disturbed than heroin abusers and that this disturbance was registered in a mixture of state and trait characteristics – more depression, more disturbed thinking, more organic-like symptoms, and greater passivity.* The findings of our 1980 study, like our 1976 study, are consonant with re-

TABLE 9-II

MMPI Clinical and Content Scales Scores of
Polydrug and Heroin Abusers

MMPI Clinical Scale	Uncontrolled		Controlled	
	Heroin (N = 160)	Polydrug (N = 156)	Heroin (N = 160)	Polydrug (N = 156)
L	47.79	48.99	47.27	48.95
F*	61.28	64.75	59.32	61.45
K	48.44	47.10	48.03	47.15
Hs	74.41	76.97	73.24	75.67
D	65.84	67.05	64.25	65.90
Hy*	62.51	65.16	61.73	64.22
Pd	87.34	89.12	86.73	87.16
Mf	56.09	58.76	55.98	57.91
Pa	59.97	63.24	59.48	60.35
Pt*	77.15	79.41	76.87	78.13
Sc*	79.40	82.81	78.22	79.95
Ma	72.52	72.20	72.39	70.86
Si	56.56	58.52	56.10	57.35

MMPI	Uncontrolled		Controlled	
Content	Heroin	Polydrug	Heroin	Polydrug
Scale†	(N = 160)	(N = 156)	(N = 131)	(N = 128)
SOC	54.81	55.17	54.44	54.79
DEP	61.40	64.47	61.52	62.89
FEM*	54.50	56.98	54.23	56.87
MOR*	56.06	59.78	56.70	58.81
REL	45.90	47.05	46.36	48.63
AUT*	61.14	59.28	61.32	59.15
PSY	59.82	62.06	59.25	59.45
ORG*	61.67	66.93	60.48	64.92
FAM	65.71	68.37	65.15	67.08
HOS	55.47	55.87	55.34	55.06
PHO*	52.62	55.80	52.07	54.50
HYP	56.76	57.79	57.41	58.11
HEA	60.62	61.76	60.03	60.71

* $p < .05$ on uncontrolled comparisons; only AUT and ORG was significantly different on controlled comparisons when validity and covariates were studied.

† Wiggins' (1966) content scale abbreviations are: SOC, Social Maladjustment; DEP, Depression; MOR, Poor Morale; REL, Religious Fundamentalism; AUT, Authority Conflict; PSY, Psychoticism; ORG, Organicity; FAM, Family Problems; HOS, Manifest Hostility; PHO, Phobias; HYP, Hypomania, and HEA, Poor Health.

sults reported by Lachar et al. (1979); apparently findings from veterans generalize to findings from civilians.

We introduced during the next steps in data analysis a number of controls — e.g., analysis of covariance, MMPI validity scores, etc. — in an effort to differentiate drug effects from background differences. By the time age, socioeconomic status (SES), education, voluntarism status, and invalid profiles had been controlled, heroin addicts and polydrug abusers did not differ on clinical scales in either univariate and multivariate analyses (see column in Table 9-II where validity and covariates are controlled). Only the content scales yielded two significant differences for univariate analyses (with the MANOCOVA approaching but not attaining significance, $p < .09$). Throughout several comparisons, heroin addicts presented themselves as more distrustful of, and experiencing more conflicts with, authorities. Polydrug abusers presented themselves as having more physical symptoms. These differences, however, might be related to situational interactions, physical reactions to drugs, or personality differences. Using the present experimental tactics, it is difficult to decide whether such differences are associated with personalities or with other factors. The differences make intuitive sense: Heroin abuse usually occurs amidst greater legal conflicts and polydrug abuse frequently entails even greater physical risk (note, for example, that Grant et al., 1979, have reported that polydrug abusers evidence more cerebral impairment than heavy alcohol users similar in age; also see Chapter 10 in this volume).

The comparisons given in Table 9-II suggest that whatever differences are observed under in vivo conditions are minimal once background characteristics are controlled. The evidence indicates that heroin addicts and polydrug abusers are similar when group profiles are compared and covariates are controlled.

Data from other personality tests support this notion (Table 9-III).For example, heroin addicts have not been found to differ from polydrug abusers on measures of anhedonia, a new instrument designed to assess an interference in the ability to experience pleasure (Chapman et al., 1976). Moreover, heroin addicts have not differed from polydrug abusers on either the Family Environment Scales (Moos, 1974) nor, notably, on a scale designed to discriminate heroin addicts (the MMPI-based Heroin Addiction Scale of Cavior et al., 1967). The reader is cautioned that these are preliminary findings from studies still in process; verification is needed under both controlled and uncontrolled methods similar to those illustrated in Table 9-II. *We have, at best, tentative indications from personality measures other than the ubiquitous MMPI which show that heroin addicts and polydrug abusers are similar in some personality dimensions.*

EVIDENCE *FOR* PERSONALITY DIFFERENCES BETWEEN HEROIN AND POLYDRUG ABUSERS

We would now like to present evidence to the contrary. Even though we have not found clinically meaningful differences between heroin and polydrug abusers, we still wonder whether the empirical data reflect reality or result from ineptitude in researching a complex question. Despite contradictory data, we

TABLE 9-III

HEROIN-POLYDRUG DIFFERENCES ON OTHER KINDS OF
PERSONALITY MEASURES

Measures	Heroin Addicts		Polydrug Abusers	
	Mean	SD	Mean	SD
Social Anhedonia*	12.00	8.29	11.36	6.76
Physical Anhedonia	7.07	4.53	7.00	4.23
Family Environment Scales†				
Cohesion	41.74	15.43	44.13	12.53
Expressiveness	44.54	14.40	40.44	12.46
Conflict	49.97	12.50	52.91	13.29
Independence	46.05	18.53	38.13	18.96
Achievement	55.85	9.28	53.31	14.91
Intellectual-Cultural	33.36	12.99	38.13	11.04
Active Recreational	34.26	12.38	40.93	14.57
Moral-Religious	49.44	11.55	55.96	9.58
Organization	52.39	11.77	53.64	10.14
Heroin Addiction Scale‡	31.63	5.30	34.92	5.78

* Heroin addicts do not differ from polydrug abusers on Chapman, et al. (1976) anhedonia scales (ns = 63 heroin and 40 polydrug abusers).

† Polydrug abusers score significantly higher on one scale, Moral-Religious Emphasis from Moos' FES scales (ns = 63 heroin and 23 polydrug abusers).

‡ Polydrug abusers do not differ from heroin addicts on Cavior et al. (1967) Heroin Addiction scale from the MMPI.

continue to hold, with Pihl and Spiers (1978) and Fenichel (1945), that personality is a major component in drug abuse. We are not persuaded by the single core problem hypothesis but believe that several different kinds of personality organization may be implicated. We believe that it will take considerable refinement of experimental measures and tactics to resolve this issue. Measures, for example, must be improved. Personality research must go beyond personality trait theory, psychodynamic formulations, behavior theory, to a charting of the contributions of subjective expectancies and goals, as well as cognitive-symbolic processes of the drug abuser as actor, as perceiver, and as constructor of reality. Clinicians and researchers must find ways of measuring how drug-related events are interpreted rather than focus only on drug-related events themselves. Effective treatments, from the biochemical to the social, already are available; the problem is for drug abusers to decide to participate in such treatment. We have begun to develop a new series of instruments and our preliminary efforts are beginning to demonstrate appreciable differences between heroin and polydrug abusers.

Evidence from New Measures

First, we developed a new standardized instrument for drug abuse studies. One is a subjective expected utility (SEU) scale modeled after the work of Mausner and Platt (1971), a forty-five-item questionnaire empirically derived from structured interviews. Heroin users, weighing the consequences of seeking treatment, focus upon the social interaction of their life-style as illustrated by a stated rejection of the excitement of the "street life" and as estimating their chances of discontinuing drug use as highly more likely than do polydrug users. Polydrug users, in deciding to enter treatment, conceptualize their decision to change drug-taking behavior, are more internally oriented, as associated with a crisis in life-style, accompanied by feelings of getting nothing out of life, of having become "loners," of wishing they could become more socially and sexually active, and of feeling constantly depressed and despairing.

Similarly, heroin addicts and polydrug abusers differ appreciably in stated reasons for seeking treatment, as measured by another newly developed set of rating scales designed to tap motivational differences for entering treatment (Penk, Robinowitz, Dolan, and Adkins, manuscript in preparation). Although both groups rated themselves as equally high on a voluntarism scale, nevertheless polydrug abusers, in addition, endorse a greater number and wider range of items indicating outside pressures for entering treatment. Specifically, polydrug users score significantly higher than heroin users on the following reasons for seeking treatment: poorer physical health, more mental problems, greater family pressure, less satisfaction from the drug of current use, and more pressure from drug-using peers to enter treatment. One set of evidence against heroin-polydrug personality homogeneity, then, is obtained from new instruments implemented within a cognitive social learning framework and focusing specifically on questions about drug-related issues, not general personality items.

Evidence from Other Kinds of Drug Abusers Comparisons

Our second reservations about not finding clinically meaningful personality differences between heroin and polydrug abusers comes from other studies in which heroin addicts differ from other kinds of drug abusers even after potentially confounding variables are controlled. Note, these comparisons are not between heroin addicts and users of two illicit drugs with near equal frequency, but comparisons of heroin addicts versus those who use *one* kind of illicit, nonopiate drug.

The three groups were heroin users, amphetamine users, and barbiturate users; all reported daily use for several years of one primary drug and less than weekly use, on the average, of any other drug (Penk et al., 1979). All three groups emerged as significantly maladjusted, with heroin users, however, displaying significantly less maladjustment. Heroin users score significantly lower on scales *Mf* (Less passivity), *Pa* (less suspiciousness), *Pt* (less anxiety), *Sc* (less disturbed thinking), and *Si* (less social introversion), and higher on *K* (more ego strength). These results correspond, particularly for amphetamine and barbiturate users, to findings reported by Trevithick and Hosch (1978). They show, when comparisons are made for drug-abusing groups defined by one *primary* drug of abuse, that heroin users are more managerial, autocratic, and power-oriented in personality organization. This study also underscores the importance of obtaining detailed drug histories that permit differentiating patterns of drug abuse (Braught et al., 1978). Significant differences do not appear when one drug-abusing group who prefers a single drug is compared with another drug-abusing group which prefers multiple drugs with near-equal frequency; significant personality differences are found when groups using one primary drug are compared. Surprisingly, these comparisons did not produce significant differences between amphetamine and barbiturate users. Before concluding that personality organization of these two groups are not different, replications are needed under conditions when drug histories are refined.

We also compared the same three groups at two different levels of personality organization (Penk et al., 1978). Measurement is possible, in Leary's (1956) system, at two levels for MMPI scales: Level I is termed the public presentation of self to others;

Level III is called private perception of self to self, or underlying character structure. We first found, when MMPI profiles were classified nominally at Level I into one of eight interpersonal orientations, that most drug abusers (70%) were categorized into three of eight Leary (1956) octants: aggressive-sadistic, managerial-autocratic, and competitive-narcissistic. Heroin users differed significantly from amphetamine and barbiturate users. For Level III measures (private perception of self), most of the scores fell with the rebellious-distrustful Leary octant, indicating a difference in underlying character structure from public presentation of self to others. The three groups did not differ at Level III in interpersonal orientation. This study demonstrated two points simultaneously: (1) more than one kind of personality organization is implicated in drug abuse; and (2) kinds of personality organization will vary depending on level of measurement. Such findings underscore our contention that the heroin-polydrug abuser personality comparison is an extraordinary complex question for field research in which the "rules" for investigation have not been delineated. From the quality of studies conducted to date, we probably still have not conducted an adequate assessment of the contribution of personality to drug abuse.

Evidence from New Experimental Strategies

We are shifting our research strategies from the static group comparison approach typified by results presented in Table 9-II and 9-III to experimental designs. As Campbell and Stanley (1966) have noted, the static group comparison tactic actually is as pre- or quasi-experimental approach. It is vulnerable to many errors of differential recruitment and data loss, which not even analysis of covariance may be able to overcome. Testing heroin-polydrug personality differences from a prediction study, we have found that MMPI scores, gathered upon the occasion of first inpatient admission, predict return to treatment as a function of differences in heroin and polydrug use. That is, for heroin addicts, multivariate analysis of variance and multiple discriminant function analysis was not significant for either clinical or content scales but was significant for personality type scales

(Gilberstadt's P-code scales, 1975; see also Dahlstrom et al., 1975). Heroin returners ($n = 101$) aligned with schizophrenic reaction code type scales, and nonreturners ($n = 215$) aligned with character disorder and neurotic code type scales. For polydrug abusers, however, multivariate analysis of variance and multiple discriminant function analyses revealed differences in clinical and content scales. Nonreturners ($n = 127$) aligned with social alienation (*Sc* scale), and returners aligned with help-seeking (*F* scale) and somatic concerns (*Hs* scales). Such data underscore the trends reported earlier in this paper; that is, polydrug abusers are distinguished by somatic concerns from heroin users. Polydrug returners and nonreturners were differentiated at a hit rate of 78 percent by the linear discriminant function; heroin addicts were poorly differentiated by a hit rate of 60 percent (Penk, Robinowitz, and Woodward, 1980, manuscript submitted for publication). Cross-validation and refinement of "returner-nonreturner" presently is underway.

As shown in this example, a shift in experimental strategies may yield significant differences between the two groups. The advantages of studying the question with an experimental design, a pretreatment-posttreatment control group design, is illustrated in a second study (Penk and Robinowitz, 1980). Heroin addicts, formerly nonvolunteers, evidenced significant increases in MMPI scores when they returned for treatment voluntarily; matched subjects, volunteers at both first and second admission, actually showed a mild decline in MMPI scores upon the occasion of their second admission. We believe that the introduction of experimental designs, perhaps within the framework of program evaluation studies, can elevate the quality of heroin-polydrug abuser personality research.

Perhaps the most compelling case against the static group comparison as quasi-experimental design can be made by shifting from the "difference test" altogether to simply an examination of the variety of personality code types which constitute an average or composite MMPI profile. Presented in Table 9-IV is such analysis for MMPI profiles classified by D-square procedures developed by Gilberstadt (1975). This comparison, based on the nominal frequency with which a profile may be classified

TABLE 9-IV

MMPI Code Types* for Heroin Addicts,
Polydrug Abusers, and Alcoholics

MMPI Code Type†	Heroin Addicts ($n=558$)		Polydrug Abusers ($n=279$)		Alcoholics ($n=112$)	
	f	%	f	%	f	%
NC‡	61	10.93	28	10.04	24	21.43
123	4	.01	2	.01	3	2.68
132	3	.01	3	.01	1	1.00
1234	24	4.30	14	5.16	13	11.67
1237	0	.00	2	.01	0	.00
137	6	.01	1	.01	1	1.00
138	19	3.40	6	2.15	4	3.57
139	29	5.20	10	3.58	7	6.21
27	3	.01	2	.01	3	2.68
274	26	4.66	12	4.30	5	4.47
278	28	5.02	28	10.04	7	6.26
4	48	8.60	22	7.89	13	11.67
43	22	3.94	8	2.06	5	4.47
49	41	7.35	14	5.02	1	1.00
78	29	5.20	14	5.02	10	8.93
8123	2	.01	3	.01	0	.00
824	64	11.47	43	15.41	7	6.25
86	72	12.90	46	16.49	10	8.93
89	50	8.96	29	10.39	6	5.37
9	27	4.84	20	7.17	2	1.80

* Code types were classified by Gilberstadt (1970, 1-75), using D-square procedures. Samples include, after 2 percent attrition, all black and white first admission heroin addicts and polydrug abusers who volunteered or did not volunteer for in- or outpatient treatment to the Dallas VA DDTP (1972-1979).

† Numbers represent the following MMPI clinical scales: 1, *Hs*; 2, *D*; 3, *Hy*; 4, *Pd*; 5, *Mf*; 6, *Pa*; 7, *Pt*; 8, *Sc*; 9, *Ma*; 0, *Si*.

‡ The code types may be considered as associated with the following Primary Diagnosis (DSM-II), according to Gilberstadt and Duker (1965). The authors caution consideration of alternatives, however: *NL*, "normal limits" profile; *123*, Psychophysiological Reaction; *132*, Psychoneurosis, conversion reaction with depression; *1234*, Personality trait disturbance with alcoholism, anxiety and depression; *1237*, Psychophysiological reaction with anxiety in a passive-dependent reaction; *137*, Psychoneurosis, anxiety reaction; *138*, Schizophrenic reaction, paranoid type; *139*, Chronic brain syndrome, with brain trauma and personality disorder; *27*, Psychoneurosis, anxiety; *278*, Pseudoneurotic or chronic undifferentiated schizophrenic reaction; *4*, Personality trait disturbance, passive-aggressive personality, aggressive type; *43*, Personality trait disturbance, emotionally unstable personality; *49*, Sociopathic personality disturbance, antisocial personality; *78*, Psychoneurosis, obsessive-compulsive reaction; *8123*, Schizophrenic reaction, simple type; *824*, Personality pattern disturbance, paranoid type; *86*, Schizophrenic reaction, paranoid type; *89*, Schizophrenic psychosis, paranoid schizophrenia; and *9*, Manic-depressive reaction, manic type.

into one of eighteen code types and not an averaged scale scores, reveals an extraordinary variety of personality types within any one drug-abusing class. Such variety suggests that addiction disorders cannot be reduced to the *Pd* dimension. Such variety shows that different kinds of personality organization are represented among drug abusers. Such variety is similar for both heroin and polydrug abusers. Such variety, seen also in a smaller sample of veterans with problem drinking as their primary substance abuse difficulty, suggest new directions for research. This new direction is away from the static group comparison studies of the 1970s and toward new systems for classifying various kinds of substance abusers based on the MMPI. Megargee and Bohn (1979) already have begun the needed work on typologies for classifying criminals. Their system can serve as a model for what is needed for the study of personality among substance abusers. After a typology is developed, then work can proceed, in the 1980s, to understand which factors contribute to such differences.

RECOMMENDED NEW DIRECTIONS FOR RESEARCH IN PERSONALITY STUDIES OF DRUG ABUSERS

There are remarkable opportunities within the Veterans Administration to resolve most of the questions attending the complex question, "Do heroin addicts differ from polydrug abusers on measures of personality?", providing, of course, that clinicians and researchers can broaden the narrow limits of their focus upon a single data-collection site and expand their efforts to encompass a number of treatment settings. Other ideas for future research have been suggested by Craig (1981).

The *first step* towards new directions in personality research about drug abusers is to realize that all questions should be asked with one major purpose in mind: Which factors, including personality, improve treatment effectiveness and treatment outcome? The next steps, all subordinated to the question of treatment outcome, follow:

Second, we must add person-by-environment and cognitive measures to measures of personality states and traits.

Third, we must identify factors other than personality that influence treatment outcome (e.g., constitutional and genetic factors, social conditions, types of treatment activities, etc.).

Fourth, we must introduce multiple measures of key constructs.

Fifth, we must change experimental strategies from static group comparisons to studies predicting treatment outcome. Pretreatment-posttreatment control group designs are preferred. Longitudinal, not cross-sectional, studies should be implemented.

Sixth, drug abuse should be conceptualized as occurring, particularly for compulsive users, in developmental sequences and stages (Kandel et al., 1976).

Seventh, refined drug abuse histories must be collected for breaking up the old dichotomies. We must develop new systems for classifying drug-taking behaviors based on psychometric measures of underlying dimensions embedded in our bifurcated constructs of heroin addicts versus polydrug abusers, users versus nonusers, etc.

Eighth, we must identify and delineate the contributions of demographics to substance abuse.

Ninth, we must quantify the dimensions by which treatment activities and treatment programs differ.

Tenth, we advocate, to meet the ideals of a comprehensive and collaborative strategy, the implementation of designs patterned after the work of Cronkite and Moos (1978) — a model for studying treatment outcome in alcohol dependence treatment. An important feature of this work is the use of path analysis for partitioning unique and shared variances among blocks of measures. Such designs permit overcoming limitations in research on single variables.

In summarizing lessons to be learned from the short history of heroin-polydrug abuser personality comparisons, we conclude that the contributions of personality to drug dependence have yet not been properly studied. As N. B. Eddy (1973) reminds us, it took many talented clinicians and researchers fifty years to reach the limits in the parameters of research about the pharmacological dimension in drug dependence (cf. also Krasnegor,

1978). Considerable work is required before we will be able to understand how to learn about the personality dimension in "psychic dependence" and the drive toward drug-taking behaviors.

Drug abuse treatment will forever remain a mystery as long as clinicians and researchers remain stimulus-bound to one treatment technique or continue to consider all drug abusers as alike. The only way to understand the unknown is to maximize the number of dimensions by which drug abuse and abuse treatment is understood. One dimension requiring additional articulation is that of personality variables.

The contributions of personality, however, cannot be understood unless the interaction of other relevant dimensions each are similarly articulated. Clinical study and research about addiction disorders demands measurement of many different dimensions, varying from the physiological and biochemical, through personality, cognitive-symbolic processes, and the imaging and fantasy processing of drug abusers, as well as cultural and situation factors.

SUMMARY

The "state of the research art" in personality comparisons of heroin addicts and polydrug abusers is, then, as follows: we know some of the semantics, a little of the syntactics, but virtually nothing of the pragmatics. There have been energetic and enthusiastic beginnings in the effort to research this question, although, for the moment, there are no definitive, substantive answers. However, the old order is changing; the old dogmas are shifting. Just as in past generations research in schizophrenia was slowed by skewed perceptions about what constituted appropriate areas for psychological studies, so clinicians and researchers have been reluctant to consider the study of heroin addicts and polydrug abusers as meriting scientific investigation. As clinicians and researchers develop new professional skills for working effectively with "borderline personalities" and "narcissistic character disorders," so attitudes and values are rapidly changing about the suitability of addiction disorders as an area fit for study.

Early trends from heroin addict-polydrug abuser personality comparisons are these. One, at a more general level, heroin addicts, though maladjusted, are comparatively less disturbed than polydrug abusers. However, we do not know whether such differences are due to "selection" or "survival" factors or differential attraction by treatment centers of the kinds of heroin addicts and polydrug abusers who become subjects in research studies.

Two, concerning specific kinds of personality problems, the preliminary evidence suggests that, even though the two groups share personality traits in common, there are differences. Both groups are impaired in the basic ability to trust others; both are constantly frustrated and angry in interpersonal interactions, particularly within family of origin; both use drugs as a way of coping with feelings as a means of preventing regression to less' effective modes of adjustment. There are specific personality differences associated with such core problems. Many heroin addicts are more active in their expression of their conflicts, being autocratic and managerial in their styles of relating with others, being negativistic and constantly in conflict, especially with those in authority. By contrast, polydrug abusers are more passive in their expression of conflicts, as shown by more depression, more social-alienation, and more organic involvement and physical problems associated with their use of drugs.

It is readily apparent that such conclusion will be quickly modified as research on personality factors increases. Already, federal agencies are calling attention to the need for further studies on psychosocial factors. Increased attention will be given to the contributions of "psychic dependence." The role of personality will not be understood until its many aspects are measured within the context of social, genetic, ethnographic, and historic conditions.

REFERENCES

Agar, M.: *Ripping and Running*. New York, Academic Press, 1973.

Baker, S. L.: Traumatic war neurosis. In Freedman, A. M.; Kaplan, H. I.; and Sadock, B. J.: *Comprehensive Textbook of Psychiatry, II* (Vol. II). Baltimore, Williams & Wilkins, 1975a, pp. 1618-1623.

Baker, S. L.: Military psychiatry. In Freedman, A. M.; Kaplan, H. I.; and Sadock, B. J.: *Comprehensive Textbook of Psychiatry, II* (Vol. II). Baltimore, Williams & Wilkins, 1975b, pp. 2355-2367.

Barry, H.: Stimulus attributes of drugs. In Anisman, H.; and Bignami, G.: *Psychopharmacology of Aversively Motivated Behavior.* New York, Plenum, 1977.

Beecher, H.: *Measurement of Subjective Responses.* New York, Oxford, 1959.

Bem, D. J.; and Funder. D. C.: Predicting more of the people more of the time: Assessing the personality of situations. *Psych Rev, 85*:485-501, 1978.

Berzins, J. I.; Ross, W. F.; English, G. F.; and Haley, J. V.: Subgroups among opiate addicts — typological investigation. *J Abnorm Psych, 83*:65-73, 1974.

Braught, G., Kirby, M.; and Berry, G.: Psychosocial correlates of empirical types of multiple drug abusers. *J Consult Clin Psychol, 46*:1463-1475, 1978.

Burke, E. L.; and Eichberg, R. H.: Personality characteristics of adolescent users of dangerous drugs as indicated by the Minnesota Multiphasic Personality Inventory. *J Ner Ment Dis, 154*:291-301, 1972.

Butcher, J. L.; and Owen, P. L.: Objective personality inventories: Recent research and some contemporary issues. In Wolman, B. B. (Ed.): *Clinical Diagnosis of Mental Disorders.* New York, Plenum, 1978.

Campbell, D. T.; and Stanley, J. C.: *Experimental and Quasiexperimental Designs for Research.* Chicago, Rand McNally, 1966.

Carroll, J. F. X.; Santo, Y.; and Klein, J. I.: A comparison of personality Research Form. Unpublished manuscript, 1976 (available from J. F. X. Carroll, Eagleville Hospital and Rehabilitation Center, Eagleville, Pa., 19408).

Cavior, N.; Kurtzberg, R. L.; and Lipton, D. S.: The development and validation of a heroin addiction scale with the MMPI. *Int J Addict, 2*:129-137, 1967.

Chapman, L. J.; Chapman, J. P.; and Raulin, M. L.: Scales for physical and social anhedonia. *J Abnorm Psych, 85*:374-382, 1976.

Craig, R. J.: Personality characteristics of heroin addicts: A review of the empirical literature with critique — Part I. *Int J Addict, 14*:513-532, 1979a.

Craig, R. J.: Personality characteristics of heroin addicts: A review of the empirical literature with critique — Part II. *Int J Addict, 14*:607-625, 1979b.

Craig, R. J.: Personality variables in the treatment of heroin addicts. In Craig, R.; and Baker, S. (Eds.): *Drug Dependent Patients: Treatment and Research.* Springfield, Thomas, 1981.

Craig, R. J.: Personality characteristics of heroin addicts: Review of empirical research, 1976-1979. *Int J Addict,* 1981 (in press).

Cronkite, R. C.; and Moos, R.: Evaluating alcoholism treatment programs: An integrated approach. *J Consult Clin Psych, 46*:1105-1119, 1978.

Dahlstrom, W. G.; Welsh, G. S.; and Dahlstrom, L. E.: *An MMPI Handbook: Research Applications* (Vol. II). Minneapolis, University of Minnesota Press, 1975.

D'Amanda, C.; Plumb, M. M.; and Taintor, Z.: Heroin addicts with a history of glue sniffing: A deviant group within a deviant group. *Int J Addict, 12*:255-270, 1977.

Eddy, N. B.: Prediction of drug dependence and abuse liability. In Goldberg, L., and Hofmeister, F. (Eds.): *Psychic Dependence.* New York, Springer-Verlag, 1973.

Ellinwood, E.: Amphetamine psychoses I: Descriptions of individuals and process. *J Nerv Ment Dis, 144*:273-283, 1967.

Fenichel, O.: *The Psychoanalytic Theory of Neurosis.* New York, Norton, 1945.

Fiske, D. W.: Two worlds of psychological phenomena. *Am Psychol, 34*:733-739, 1979.

Gilberstadt, H.: *Comprehensive MMPI code book for males* (Tech. Rep. 1B 11-5). Minneapolis, VA Medical Center, MMPI Research Laboratory, 1970.

Gilberstadt, H.: *An Atlas for the P-Code System of MMPI Interpretation.* Minneapolis, VA Medical Center, MMPI Research Laboratory, 1975.

Graham, J. R.: MMPI characteristics of alcoholics, drug abusers, and pathological gamblers. Paper presented at the 13th Annual MMPI Symposium, University of the Americas, Puebla, Mexico, 1977.

Graham, J. R.: *The MMPI: A Practical Guide.* New York, Oxford, 1978.

Grant, I.; Reed, R.; Adams, K.; and Carlin, A.: Neuropsychological function in young alcoholics and polydrug abusers. *J Clin Neuropsychol, 1*:39-47, 1979.

Hill, H. E.; Haertzen, C. A.; and Glaser, R.: Personality characteristics of narcotic addicts as indicated by the MMPI. *J Gen Psychol, 62*:127-139, 1962.

Kandel, D. B.; Treiman, D.; Faust, R.; and Single, E.: Adolescent involvement in legal and illegal drug use: A multiple classification analysis. *Soc For, 55*:438-458, 1976.

Korman, M.: Clinical evaluation of psychological factors. In Sharp, C. W.; and Brehm, M. L.: *Review of Inhalants: Euphoria to Dysfunction.* Washington, D.C., NIDA Research Monograph 15, 1977.

Krasnegor, N.: *Behavioral Tolerance: Research and Treatment Implications.* Washington, D.C., NIDA Research Monograph 18, 1978.

Lachar, D.: *The MMPI: Clinical Assessment and Automated Interpretation.* Los Angeles, Wester Psychological Services, 1974.

Lachar, D.; Gdowski, C. L.; and Keegan, J. F.: MMPI profiles of men alcoholics, drug addicts, and psychiatric patients. *J Stud Alcohol, 40*:45-46, 1979.

Lachar, D.; Schoof, K.; Keegan, J.; and Gdowski, C.: Dimensions of polydrug abuse: An MMPI study. In Wesson, D.; Carlin, A.; Adams, K.; and Beschner, G. (Eds.): *Polydrug Abuse: Results of a National Colloborative Study.* New York, Academic Press, 1978.

Leary, T. F.: *Interpersonal Diagnosis of Personality.* New York, Ronald, 1956.

Mausner, B.; and Platt, E. S.: *Smoking: A Behavioral Analysis.* New York, Pergamon, 1971.

Meehl, P. E.: *Psychodiagnosis – Selected Papers.* Minneapolis, University of Minnesota Press, 1973.

Megargee, E. L.; and Bohn, J. J.: *Classifying Criminal Offenders.* Beverly Hills, Calif, Sage, 1979.

Mischel, W.: On the interface of cognition and personality: Beyond the person-situation debate. *Am Psychol, 34*:740-754, 1979a.

Mischel, W.: Looking for personality. Paper presented at the annual meeting of the American Psychological Association in New York City, September, 1979b.

Moos, R. J.: *A Manual of Family, Group and Work Environment Scales.* Palo Alto, Calif., Consulting Psychologists, 1974.

Murray, H. A.: *Explorations in Personality.* New York, Oxford, 1938.

Nathan, P. E.; and Lansky, D.: Common methodological problems in research on the addictions. *J Consult Clin Psychol, 46*:713-726, 1978.

O'Brien, C. P.; Nace, E. P.; Mintz, J; Ream, N.; and Meyers, J.: Depression in veterans two years after Vietnam. *Am J Psychiat, 134*:167-170, 1977.

Overall, J. E.: MMPI personality patterns of alcoholism and narcotic addicts. *Q J Stud Alc, 34*:104-111, 1973.

Penk, W. E.; Fudge, J. W.; and Robinowitz, R.: Differences in interpersonal orientation of heroin, amphetamine and barbiturate users. *Br J Addict, 73*:82-88, 1978.

Penk, W. E.; Fudge, J. W.; Robinowitz, R.; and Neman, R. S.: Personality characteristics of compulsive heroin, amphetamine and barbiturate users. *J Consult Clin Psychol, 47*:583-585, 1979.

Penk, W. E.; Gunst, R. A.; Ulrich, G. J.; and Robinowitz, R.: A factor analytic study of values and expectations among compulsive heroin and polydrug abusers seeking treatment. Manuscript submitted for publication, 1979.

Penk, W. E.; and Robinowitz, R.: MMPI differences of black and white drug abusers. *Cata Sel Doc in Psychol, 4*:51, 1974.

Penk, W. E.; and Robinowitz, R.: Personality differences of volunteer and non-volunteer heroin and nonheroin drug users. *J Abnorm Psychol, 89*:234-239, 1980.

Penk, W. E.; Robinowitz, R.; Dolan, M.; and Adkins, G.: Reasons for seeking treatment: A scale for measuring voluntarism in drug abuse treatment. Manuscript in preparation.

Penk, W. E.; Robinowitz, R.; Kidd, R.; and Nisle, A.: Perceived family environments among ethnic groups of compulsive heroin users. *Addict Beh, 4*:297-309, 1979.

Penk, W. E.; Robinowitz, R.; Nisle, A.; and Jones, R. E.: An empirical test of anhedonia in compulsive use of illicit drugs. Paper presented at the annual meeting of the American Psychological Association in New York City, 1979.

Penk, W. E.; Woodward, W. V.; Robinowitz, R.; and Hess, J. L.: Differences in MMPI scores of black and white compulsive heroin users. *J Abnorm Psychol, 87*:505-511, 1978.

Penk, W. E.; Woodward, W. A.; Robinowitz, R.; and Parr, W. C.: An MMPI comparison of polydrug and heroin abusers. *J Abnorm Psychol, 89*:299-302, 1980.

Penk, W. E.; Woodward, W. A.; Robinowitz, R.; and Parr, W. C.: Cross-validation of a heroin addiction (He) scale. *Int J Addict,* 1981, in press.

Pihl, R. O.; and Spiers, P.: Individual differences in the etiology of drug abuse. In B. Maher (Ed.): *Progress in Experimental Psychology* (Vol. 8). New York, Academic Press, 1978.

Sells, S. B. (Ed.): *The Effectiveness of Drug Abuse Treatment* (Vols. I and II). Cambridge, Massachusetts, Ballinger, 1976.

Solomon, R. L.; and Corbitt, J. D.: An opponent-process theory of motivation. *Psych Rev, 81*:119-145, 1974.

Stauss, F. F.; Ousley, N. K.; and Carlin, A. S.: Psychopathology and drug abuse: An MMPI comparison of polydrug abuse patients with psychiatric inpatients and outpatients. *Addict Beh, 2*:75-78, 1977.

Sutker, P. B.; and Archer, R. P.: MMPI characteristics of opiate addicts, alcoholics and other drug abusers. In C. S. Newmark (Ed.): *MMPI: Current Clinical and Research Trends.* New York, Praeger, 1979.

Teasdale, J.: The perceived effect of heroin on the interpersonal behavior of heroin-dependent patients and a comparison with stimulant-dependent patients. *Int J Addict, 7*:533-548, 1972.

Toomey, T. C.: Personality and demographic characteristics of two sub-types of drug abusers. *Br J Addict, 69*:155-158, 1974.

Trevithick, L.; and Hosch, H. M.: MMPI correlates of drug addiction based on drug of choice. *J Consult Clin Psychol, 46*:180-181, 1978.

Wesson, D.; Carlin, A.; Adams, K.; and Beschner, G. (Eds.): *Polydrug Abuse: Results of a National Collaborative Study.* New York, Academic Press, 1978.

Wiggins, J. S.: Substantive dimensions of self-report in the MMPI item pool. *Psychol Monog, 80*:(20, Whole No. 630), 1966.

Zuckerman, M.; Sola, S.; Masterson, J.; and Angelovie, J. V.: MMPI patterns in drug abuse before and after treatment in therapeutic communities. *J Consult Clin Psychol, 43*:286-296, 1975.

CHAPTER 10

NEUROPSYCHOLOGICAL ASSESSMENT OF POLYDRUG ABUSE

PAUL A. MIDER AND JAMES E. LEWIS

INTRODUCTION

The study of neuropsychological (NP) functioning, as an assessment technique to infer impairment of the central nervous system (CNS), among chemically dependent individuals has focused primarily on the effects of ethanol (Blusewicz et al., 1978; Hill et al., 1979; Kleinknecht and Goldstein, 1972; Parsons, 1975). Recent landmark investigations have been concerned more exclusively with the effects of polydrug abuse on NP functioning (Adams et al., 1975; Carlin et al., 1978; Grant et al., 1978a,b; Grant et al., 1979). These studies of younger drug dependent patients found more frequent and severe NP impairment associated with polydrug abuse than with ethanol alone. When predrug use, medical and developmental histories were taken into account, strong consideration was given to some underlying antecedent condition previous to onset of adolescent polydrug abuse, at least in a proportion of the population of polydrug abusers.

The nature and dimensions of the polydrug abuse problem itself have been difficult to define (Kaufman, 1976). Reference has been made to polydrug abusers as comprising approximately 14 percent of the admissions to federally funded drug treatment programs, when polydrug abuse was defined exclusive of primary opiate use (Sample, 1977). The conclusion of a study of drug abuse clients in a Veterans Administration (VA) treatment program suggested that the characteristics of the addict seeking treatment have changed from a single primary drug of abuse (e.g., ethanol or opiates) to multiple drug abuse (McLellan et al., 1979). While this phenomenon has been addressed at a definitional level by Kaufman, the scope of the problem of polydrug abuse remains an issue open to controversy.

In attempting to specify antecedent conditions to adolescent polydrug abuse, the role of specific learning disabilities (LD) has been given increased attention (Adams et al., 1975; Grant et al., 1978a). Other studies have suggested a more global "link" between childhood LD and later high risk for juvenile delinquency and various emotional disorders (Bachara and Zaba, 1978; GAO, 1977; Levine and Kozak, 1979; Wright, 1974). Further investigations have been conducted into the correlates of NP dysfunction and LD (Austin, 1978; Doehring, 1968; Reed, 1976; Rourke, 1975; Satz et al., 1978; Selz and Reitan, 1979).

The purpose of the present study was to conduct an exploratory investigation of possible historical antecedents of polydrug abuse including birth and developmental factors and evidence of childhood learning disabilities. A second focus of the study was on describing the nature and severity of NP impairment according to type and pattern of drug use.

METHOD

Subjects

The fifty-two subjects evaluated in the study were offspring of veterans of the Armed Forces and were referred for psychological evaluation because of academic, behavior, or emotional problems. They were thirty-three males and nineteen females who ranged in age from sixteen to twenty-two years (mean age equaled 18.2). Highest grade completed in school ranged from ninth grade to three years of college (mean education equaled 10.3±2.8). Subjects lived in suburban or semirural areas exclusively with the following distribution by ethnicity: caucasian, 27; black, 14; hispanic, 7; and oriental, 4.

Procedure

Developmental History

From a structured parent interview and/or through military health records, historical data were gathered that have been suggested as having possible relationships to early CNS development (Corah et al., 1965). Birth complications including prematurity by weight (<5.0 lbs.) or prematurity by term (<38 weeks) or anoxia at delivery were noted. Descriptions of childhood histories focused on occurrence of extended periods of high fever, head injuries with loss of consciousness, and unusual delays in motor or language developmental milestones. No subjects were included who had definitive neurological disorders or histories of CNS abnormalities (e.g., seizures, cerebral palsy, etc). Frequencies of occurrence of the above historical antecedents are shown in Table 10-I.

TABLE 10-I
FREQUENCIES OF POSSIBLE CNS INSULTING CONDITIONS

Birth Complications	*Number of Occurrences*[*]
Prematurity by Term	9
Prematurity by Weight	4
Anoxia at Delivery	8
Childhood History	
Extended Periods of High Fever	16
Head Injuries with Loss of Consciousness	3
Unusual Delay in Motor Developmental Milestones	10
Unusual Delay in Language Developmental Milestones	13

[*] 5 subjects had 3 occurrences, 3 subjects had 2 occurrences.

Type and Pattern of Drug Use

Previous investigation of drug use patterns in the geographical suburban area where this study was conducted revealed a low incidence of the abuse of opiates and/or synthetic narcotics. However, a high incidence of recreational drug use has been reported (Wunderlich et al., 1975). In the present sample, no subject admitted to the use of heroin, morphine, or methadone. Abuse patterns were determined through subject self-report and were recorded on the following scale: never used, experimental use (<5 occasions in lifetime), light regular use (<5 occasions per month), moderate regular use (between 5 and 10 occasions per month), and heavy regular use (more than 10 occasions per month). Categories of drugs surveyed were ethanol, marijuana and hashish, LSD and psilocybin, amphetamines, barbiturates, cocaine, phencyclidine piperidine (PCP), and inhalants. PCP was included because of the high incidence reported in the suburban areas by local news media. Table 10-II shows the distribution of subjects according to type and frequency of drug use.

TABLE 10-II

DISTRIBUTION OF SUBJECTS BY TYPE AND FREQUENCY OF DRUG USE*

	No Use	Experimental Use	Light Use	Moderate Use	Heavy Use
Ethanol	0	5	77	13	5
Marijuana/hashish	6	58	17	11	8
LSD/Psilocybin	71	22	3	4	0
Amphetamines	12	78	7	2	1
Barbiturates	18	72	6	3	1
Cocaine	91	9	0	0	0
PCP	73	18	4	2	3
Inhalants	88	7	4	1	0

* Cells reflect percent of subjects responding affirmatively in each category.

Educational Diagnosis

An educational diagnostician, blind to subjects' drug use histories and neuropsychological test results, classified subjects as having no learning disabilities (LD) or as having one of three types of LD. Those determined to have LD were categorized as Language LD — primarily involving a disorder of letter or word recognition or reading comprehension; Perceptual-Motor LD — primarily involving a disorder of copying, manuscript or cursive handwriting (visuographic) skills; or Numerical LD — primarily involving a disorder of mathematics concepts, problem-solving, or calculation. The relationship of this category system to neuropsychological deficits has previously been demonstrated (Lewis, 1980). The educational diagnosis was performed using the diagnostician's clinical judgement, school records where available (73% of subjects), and results of at least one achievement test battery (Wide Range Achievement Test, Metropolitan Achievement Tests and Gates-MacGinitie Reading Tests).

Neuropsychological Evaluation

Subjects were administered the Wechsler Adult Intelligence Scale (WAIS) and selected subtests of the Halstead-Reitan Neuropsychology Battery for Adults: Categories test, Speech Sounds Perception test, Seashore Rhythm test, finger tapping (dominant and nondominant hands), Smedley Hand dynamometer (grip strength dominant and nondominant hands), tactile finger localization (dominant and nondominant hands), and the Lateral Dominance examination. On the basis of the WAIS and neuropsychological test results, each subject's performance was rated according to the category system described by Grant et al. (1979) in their study of young polydrug abusers: above average, average, borderline or atypical performance, mildly impaired, moderately impaired, or severely impaired.

RESULTS

Educational Diagnosis

Table 10-III shows the distribution by sex of the educational diagnostic procedure. Nearly 52 percent of the males had LD diagnoses as compared with 42 percent of female subjects. Comparison of subjects with LD diagnoses by developmental history yielded an incidence of possible CNS insulting conditions at birth or in early childhood nearly twice as great for those with LD as for those with no evidence of prior learning disorder. The distribution by educational diagnosis and developmental history was as follows: prematurity by weight or by term — LD, ten subjects, no LD, three subjects; extended high febrile illness in infancy or early childhood — LD, eleven subjects, no LD, 5 subjects; anoxia at delivery — LD, six subjects, no LD, two subjects; head injuries with loss of consciousness — LD, two subjects, no LD, one subject; delay in language or motor developmental milestones — LD, thirteen subjects, no LD, ten subjects; total of all possible CNS insulting conditions — LD, forty-two subjects, no LD, twenty-one subjects.

TABLE 10-III
CLASSIFICATION OF SUBJECTS BY EDUCATIONAL DIAGNOSIS

	Male	Female
Language LD	9	4
Perceptual-Motor LD	4	2
Numerical LD	4	2
No LD	16	11
Total	33	19

Neuropsychological Status and Pattern of Polydrug Abuse

Clinical rating of subjects' NP functioning using results of the WAIS and neuropsychological measures yielded the following distribution (reported as the number of subjects in each category): above average — three; average — twenty-two; borderline or atypical performance — eleven; mild impairment — nine; moderate impairment — four; severe impairment — three.

For purpose of clinical description, the six categories were collapsed into three: unimpaired NP functioning (above average and average), borderline NP functioning (borderline and mild categories), and impaired NP functioning (moderate and severe categories). Table 10-IV shows mean performances of subjects in the three NP categories on the WAIS and neuropsychological subtests.

Analysis of variance (ANOVA) of the main effect of diagnostic categories by subtest scores revealed significant discrimination of the sample by clinical rating of NP impairment ($F = 4.96$, $p < .05$).

Subjects who were diagnosed as showing definite NP impairment (7 subjects) were further examined with respect to type and pattern of drug use. As a subgroup, these subjects represented 67 percent of the regular PCP users; i.e., six of the nine regular PCP users were rated as having definite signs of NP impairment. Conversely, only three subjects diagnosed as having definite NP impairment failed to admit to regular PCP use. They did, however, all report regular use of barbiturates, inhalants, or both.

Of the twenty subjects having borderline or mildly impaired NP functions, eighteen admitted to regular marijuana use with

TABLE 10-IV
CLINICAL RATING OF NP FUNCTIONING TIMES MEAN
SCORES ON WAIS AND NP SUBTESTS

	Unimpaired	Borderline	Impaired
Information	11.3	11.5	11.1
Comprehension	11.7	11.6	11.4
Arithmetic	10.9	10.2	9.6
Similarities	11.2	11.1	10.7
Digit Span	11.4	10.8	9.9
Vocabulary	11.6	11.3	10.8
Digit Symbol	11.1	10.5	9.3
Picture Completion	11.1	11.3	11.2
Block Design	10.9	10.3	9.4
Picture Arrangement	10.8	10.6	10.7
Object Assembly	11.2	11.1	10.9
Verbal IQ	111.3	109.3	106.4
Performance IQ	107.1	105.4	102.1
Full Scale IQ	110.2	107.2	105.2
Categories (# errors)	46.3	51.5	59.7
Speech Sounds Perception (# errors)	5.3	6.2	7.4
Seashore Rhythm (# errors)	5.8	6.3	6.9
Tapping Speed (Dom.)	53.1	51.8	47.2
Tapping Speed (Non-Dom.)	48.2	46.3	45.4
Halstead Impairment Index	.22	.46	.58
Grip Strength (Dom.)	51.7	49.3	48.4
Grip Strength (Non-Dom.)	46.5	48.7	46.5
Finger Agnosia (# errors Dom.)	1.8	2.7	3.1
Finger Agnosia (# errors Non-Dom.)	2.1	2.3	2.4

lesser frequency of regular use of other drugs (barbiturates, 4 subjects; inhalants, 1 subject; and amphetamines, 3 subjects). Subjects judged as having above average or average NP functioning (25 subjects) had much less frequent regular use of recreational drugs other than marijuana (13 subjects). Of the twenty-five subjects who showed average or above average NP functioning, only one reported light regular use of PCP, one reported light regular use of barbiturates, and three reported light regular use of amphetamines, LSD, or both. Univariate ANOVA revealed significant differences ($p < .05$) among the three diagnostic categories (unimpaired, borderline, impaired) on the following WAIS and NP subtests: Arithmetic, Digit Span, Digit Symbol, Block Design, Categories, Tapping Speed (dominant hand), Halstead Impairment Index, and Finger Agnosia (dominant hand).

Neuropsychological Impairment, LD and Drug Use

Table 10-V shows the distribution of subjects by level of NP functioning and LD versus no LD; 40 percent of the LD group had mild to severe NP impairment as compared with only 22 percent of the no LD group. An examination of the LD, drug use, and NP functioning together indicated that 48 percent of the LD group had regular multiple drug use other than marijuana. *The overall pattern that emerges was that those subjects diagnosed as having LD who also had histories of regular polydrug abuse had the greatest frequency and severity of NP impairment.*

TABLE 10-V

FREQUENCIES OF LD x NP FUNCTIONING

NP Functioning

Educational Diagnosis	Above Average	Average	Border-line Atypical	Mild	Moderate	Severe
Language LD	1	5	4	0	2	1
Perceptual-Motor LD	0	2	1	1	1	1
Numerical LD	0	1	1	4	0	0
No LD	2	14	5	4	1	1
Total	3	22	11	9	4	3

DISCUSSION

An exploratory examination of predrug use, developmental and educational histories of older adolescent and young adult polydrug abusers revealed high frequencies of occurrence of conditions suggested as causing possible CNS insult. Similarly, as with the study by Grant et al. (1979), there was no history of definite evidence of neurological disorder in the present sample, although there was consistent evidence of learning disabilities. In this younger age group (16 to 22 years) of polydrug abusers, the exploratory evidence indicated that a thorough recording of historical/developmental antecedents as well as educational diagnosis yielded evidence of more subtle predrug use CNS anomalies. It is important to note that neuropsychological subtests, such as those incorporated in the Halstead-Reitan batteries, are sensitive to functional CNS impairment that are not typically detected by a standard neurological examination. Specifically, clinical rating of intellectual and NP impairment was found to be associated primarily with deficits of tests of attention/concentration, visuospatial skill, problem-solving, and flexibility of thinking, tactile sense perception, and fine motor skill. These findings are similar to those reported in the above-mentioned study of Grant et al. (1979).

Although interpretation of the results of the exploratory data of this study must be made cautiously, one important finding is that evidence of NP impairment was present despite the concurrent finding of average range (greater than 100 IQ) intellectual functioning. A possible interpretation of this finding, also discussed elsewhere (Lezak, 1976), is that deficient performance on neuropsychological tests precedes the occurrence of intellectual deficits in acute or early stages of CNS damage. This result is particularly important in considering the influence of LD (antecedent to polydrug abuse) on both intellectual and neuropsychological test results. From the exploratory examination of historical antecedents in this study, it was apparent that diagnosis of LD involved increased incidence of NP impairment. However, subjects with LD who reported regular polydrug abuse had the greatest frequency and severity of NP impairment.

The implication from the sample examined here was that polydrug abuse represented an additional "sufficient" condition to produce more frequent and severe NP impairment. Furthermore, examination of subjects with moderate and severe NP impairment revealed that regular use of PCP and, secondly, of barbiturates and inhalants produced the most significant NP impairment. Although the use of PCP has not been reported in neuropsychological studies of polydrug abuse, the distinctive influence of sedative/hypnotic drugs have been reported elsewhere (Grant et al., 1979). More conclusive demonstration of the interaction of LD and drug use must be shown in a multivariate design that includes larger individual cell frequencies than were within the scope of this study (Parsons and Prigatano,

1978). The inclusion of history of PCP use in further studies of polydrug abuse in younger populations is clearly suggested from the degree of associated NP impairment found in regular PCP users in this study and suggested by Balster and Pross (1978) in their major literature review.

NP Impairment and LD

The relationship between the preadolescent condition of LD and the high risk of polydrug abuse beinning in adolescence has been suggested (GAO, 1977). Previous studies have speculated as to the dynamics of delinquent behavior patterns that emerge in LD children (Wright, 1974). Thus, the LD population has been reported to be at high risk to develop later juvenile delinquency, including increased risk for experimental and regular polydrug abuse. While sociocultural and emotional factors for drug abuse have been elaborated on extensively elsewhere (Chein et al., 1964; Ferguson et al., 1974; Gorsuch and Butler, 1976 and Lettieri, 1975), the physical/constitutional correlates of LD have not received similar attention.

The hypothesis suggested in the present study is that (1) certain prenatal, birth, and early childhood conditions affect the development of CNS functioning and create a high risk for incidence of LD; (2) the condition of LD itself involves atypical or impaired NP functioning; (3) LD children become a high risk for later onset of juvenile delinquency of which polydrug abuse is a significant component; and (4) regular polydrug abuse beginning in adolescence exacerbates any antecedent NP anomalies and results in further and more severe CNS insult. These relationships among developmental precursors of impaired NP functioning, childhood LD, and juvenile polydrug use demand further investigation and more substantive analysis than was within the scope of this exploratory study.

IMPLICATIONS FOR TREATMENT

It has been suggested that a growing subgroup of younger polydrug abusers (average age 22 years) is seeking VA drug dependency treatment services (McLellan et al., 1979). The hypothesis has been proposed that this group's multiple drug use has adversely affected the completion of formal education and/or the development of employment skills. The exploratory findings of the present study suggest a different sequence of events. That is, polydrug abuse may be considered an outgrowth of antecedent CNS developmental dysfunction, i.e., LD.

The young polydrug abusers examined in this study were found to have apparent predrug use learning disabilities and various types and degrees of severity of NP impairment. While intellectual functioning was essentially within the normal range (90 to 110 IQ), there were NP deficits on cognitive tests of flexibility of thinking, attention/concentration, tactile sense perception, visual-motor skill, and motor speed and accuracy.

These findings, though exploratory in nature, suggest that the initial treatment of the young polydrug abuser should involve a comprehensive diagnostic assessment. Such an assessment should begin with a structured interview to determine as closely as possible the specific types and patterns of polydrug use. Second, the most productive psychometric evaluation would incorporate educational tests to detect evidence of LD, traditional psychological-intellectual tests, and at least a neuropsychological screening to uncover cognitive, perceptual, and motor deficits that are not determined through educational/psychological evaluation.

A subsequent outcome of such a comprehensive assessment procedure would be the identification of the individual patient's pattern of strengths and weaknesses. Thus, the treatment prescribed for the young polydrug abuser may include remedial educational training to improve functional academic skills that are prerequisites for any successful aftercare vocational placement. Inpatient treatment programs, including recommendations for individual or group psychotherapy, also would be prescribed on the basis of the assessment profile (Diller, 1976). For example, an insight, cognitively oriented, group psychotherapeutic treatment of the young polydrug abuser who has evidence of cognitive deficit may be inherently less successful than a more structured "work orientation" established by the group leader or therapist (Lewis and Mider, 1973).

The above-suggested procedure, that an initial identification of the patient's idiosyncratic pattern of psychological strengths and weaknesses become the basis for specific treatment recommendations, is consistent with the most current thinking on substance abuse treatment (Luborsky, 1979; O'Brien and McLellan, 1979; Sells, 1979). Further studies using multivariate designs to incorporate developmental antecedents to neuropsychological disorders and to evaluate specific academic skills and relationships among new drugs of abuse and degree of NP impairment may increase substantially the efficacy of prescribed treatment of the polydrug abuser and the development of new treatment programs.

REFERENCES

Adams, K. M.; Rennick, P. M.; Schoof, K. G.; and Keegan, M. A.: Neuropsychological measurement of drug effects: Polydrug research. *Journal of Psychedelic Drugs, 7*:151-160, 1975.

Austin, V. L.; Discriminant and descriptive analyses of neuropsychological, electroencephalographic, perinatal, and developmental history correlates of children with math or reading disability. *Dissertation Abstracts International, 38*:5554, 1978.

Bachara, G. H.; and Zaba, J. N.: Learning disabilities and juvenile delinquency. *Journal of Learning Disabilities, 11*:241-246, 1978.

Balster, R. I.; and Pross, R. S.: Phencyclidine: A bibliography of biomedical and behavioral research. *Journal of Psychedelic Drugs, 10*: 1–16, 1978.

Blusewicz, M. J.; Dustman, R. E.; Schenkenberg, T.; and Beck, E. C.: Neuropsychological correlates of chronic alcoholism and aging. *Journal of Nervous and Mental Disease, 165*:348-355, 1978.

Carlin, A. S.; Stauss, F. F.; Adams, K. M.; and Grant, I.: The prediction of neurological impairment in polydrug users. *Addictive Behaviors, 3*:5-12, 1978.

Chein, I.; Gerard, D. L.; Lee, R. S.; and Rosenfeld, E.: *The Road to H*. New York, Basic Books, 1964.

Corah, N. L.; Anthony, E. J.; Painter, P.; Stern, J. A.; and Thurston, D. L.: Effects of perinatal anoxia after seven years. *Psychological Monographs: General and Applied, 79*:No. 596, 1965.

Diller, L.: A model for cognitive retraining in rehabilitation. *The Clinical Psychologist, 29*:13-15, 1976.

Doehring, D. G.: *Patterns of Impairment in Specific Reading Disability: A Neuropsycholigical Investigation*. Bloomington, Indiana University Press, 1968.

Ferguson, P.; Lennox, T.; and Lettieri, D. J. (Eds.): *Drugs and Family/Peer Influence: Family and Peer Influences on Adolescence Drug Use, Research Issues 4.* Rockville, National Institute on Drug Abuse, November, 1974.

GAO. Report to the Congress of the United States by the Comptroller General. *Learning Disabilities: The link to juvenile delinquency should be determined but schools should do more now.* March, 1977.

Gorsuch, R. L.; and Butler, M. C.: Initial drug abuse: A review of predisposing social psychological factors. *Psychological Bulletin, 83*:120-137, 1976.

Grant, I.; Adams, K. M.; Carlin, A. S.; Rennick, P. M; Judd, L. L.; and Schooff, K.: A collaborative neuropsychological study of polydrug users. *Archives of General Psychiatry, 35*:1063-1074, 1978a.

Grant, I.; Adams, K. M.; Carlin, A. S.; Rennick, P. M.; Judd, L. L.; and Schoof, K.; and Reed, R. J.: The neuropsychological effects of polydrug abuse: The results of the national collaborative study. In Adams, K. M.; Carlin, A. S.; and Wesson, D. R. (Eds.): *Polydrug Abuse: The Results of a National Collaborative Study.* San Francisco, Academic Press, 1978b, pp. 223-261.

Grant, I.; Reed, R.; Adams, K.; and Carlin, A.: Neuropsychological function in young alcoholics and polydrug abusers. *Journal of Clinical Neuropsychology, 1*:39-47, 1979.

Hill, S. Y.; Reyes, R. B.; Mikhael, M.; and Ayre, F.: A comparison of alcoholics and heroin abusers: Computerized transaxial tomography and neuropsychological functioning. In Gallanter, M. (Ed.): *Currents in Alcoholism: Volume V. Biomedical Issues and Clinical Effects of Alcoholism.* New York, Grune & Stratton, 1979, pp. 187-205.

Kaufman, E.: The abuse of multiple drugs. I. Definition, classification, and extent of problem. *American Journal of Drug and Alcohol Abuse, 3*:279-292, 1976.

Kleinknecht, R. A.; and Goldstein, S. G.: Neuropsychological deficits associated with alcoholism. *Quarterly Journal of Studies on Alcoholism, 33*:999-1019, 1972.

Lettieri, D. J. (ed.): *Predicting Adolescent Drug Abuse: A Review of Issues, Methods and Correlates, Research Issues 11.* Rockville, National Institute on Drug Abuse, December, 1975.

Levine, E. M.; and Kozak, C.: Drug and alcohol use, delinquency, and vandalism among upper middle class pre-and post-adolescents. *Journal of Youth and Adolescence, 8*:91-101, 1979.

Lewis, J.: Brain-behavior relationships in educational diagnosis of LD. Paper presented at *The Association for Children with Learning Disabilities*, Seventeenth International Conference, 1980.

Lewis, J.; and Mider, P.: Effects of leadership style on content and work styles of short-term therapy groups. *Journal of Counseling Psychology, 20*:137-141, 1973.

Lezak, M.: *Neuropsychological Assessment.* New York, Oxford University Press, 1976.

Luborsky, L. B.,: Matching of patients and treatment in psychotherapy. Paper presented at The Third Annual Conference on Addiction Research and Treatment: Matching Patient Needs and Treatment Methods. Coatesville Veterans Administration Medical Center, 1979.

McLellan, A. T.: MacGahan, J. A.; and Druley, K. A.: Changes in drug abuse clients — 1972-1978: Implications for revised treatment. *American Journal of Drug and Alcohol Abuse,* 6:151–156, 1979.

O'Brien, C. P.; and McLellan, A. T.: Selecting the best treatment for a given patient with substance abuse. Paper presented at The Third Annual Conference on Addiction Research and Treatment: Matching Patient Needs and Treatment Methods. Coatesville Veterans Administration Medical Center, 1979.

Parsons, O. A.: Alcoholism, brain damage, and altered states of unconsciousness. In Gross, M. (Ed.): *Second Biannual International Symposium on Experimental Studies of Alcohol Intoxication and Withdrawal.* New York, Plenum Press, 1975.

Parsons, O. A.; and Prigatano, G. P.: Methodological considerations in clinical neuropsychological research. *Journal of Consulting and Clinical Psychology,* 46:608-619, 1978.

Reed, H. B.: Pediatric neuropsychology. *Journal of Pedriatric Psychology, 1*:5-7, 1976.

Rourke, B. P.: Brain-behavior relationships in children with learning disabilities. *American Psychologist, 30*:911-920, 1975.

Sample, C. J.: Concept of polydrug use. In Richards, L. G.; and Blevens, L. B. (eds.): *The Epidemiology of Drug Abuse: Current Issues, Research Monograph Series 10.* Rockville, National Institute on Drug Abuse, 1977, pp. 19-31.

Satz, P.; Taylor, H. G.; Friel, J.; and Fletcher, J. M.: Some developmental and predictive precursors of reading disabilities: A six year follow-up. In Benton, A.; and Pearl, D. (Eds.): *Dyslexia: An Appraisal of Current Knowledge.* New York, Oxford University Press, 1978, pp. 315-347.

Sells, S. B: Matching clients to treatments, problems, preliminary results, and remaining tasks. Paper presented at The Third Annual Conference on Addiction Research and Treatment: Matching Patient Needs and Treatment Methods. Coatesville Veterans Administration Medical Center, 1979.

Selz, M.; and Reitan, R. M.: Rules for neuropsychological diagnoses: Classification of brain function in older children. *Journal of Consulting and Clinical Psychology, 46*:258-264, 1979.

Wright, P. W.: Reading problems and delinquency. Paper presented at World Congress on Dyslexia. May Clinic, 1974.

Wunderlich, R. A.; Lozes, J.; and Lewis, J.: Recidivism rates of group therapy participants and other adolescents processed by a juvenile court. *Psychotherapy: Theory, Research, and Practice, 11*:234-246, 1975.

CHAPTER 11

ISSUES AND PROBLEMS IN THE TOXICOLOGIC ANALYSIS OF DRUGS OF ABUSE

RICHARD WANG

When the allied forces occupied Germany near the end of World War II, one of the most interesting chemical compounds obtained from the German chemical industry was methadone (Dolophine®). Methadone is a synthetic agent similar to the opiates in pharmacologic activity, including the ability to cause dependence upon repeated use. Investigations of methadone conducted in the United States demonstrated that it has an analgesic potency comparable to that of morphine. Futhermore, methadone was found to have the added advantages of good absorption following oral administration and a longer duration of action than that of morphine. Nevertheless, methadone was not used extensively for the treatment of pain or any other therapeutic purpose.

It was the report of Dole and Nyswander (1965) that dramatically changed the status of methadone. They reported the oral administration of a therapeutic dose of methadone successfully relieved restlessness, withdrawal symptoms, and drug craving in heroin-dependent individuals without producing euphoria and, thereby, facilitated the rehabilitation of these patients. Methadone treatment programs soon developed throughout the country and they are now a mainstay in the treatment of opiate dependence.

Another drug, commonly known as LAAM (levo-alpha-acetylmethadol), has been used to provide pharmacologic sup-

port for opiate dependent individuals. LAAM, which is chemically related to methadone (Fig. 11-1) is still being tested in regard to the safety of its long-term use. The principal advantage
of LAAM is that it has a much longer duration of action than that
of methadone and, thereby, does not have to be administered
daily.

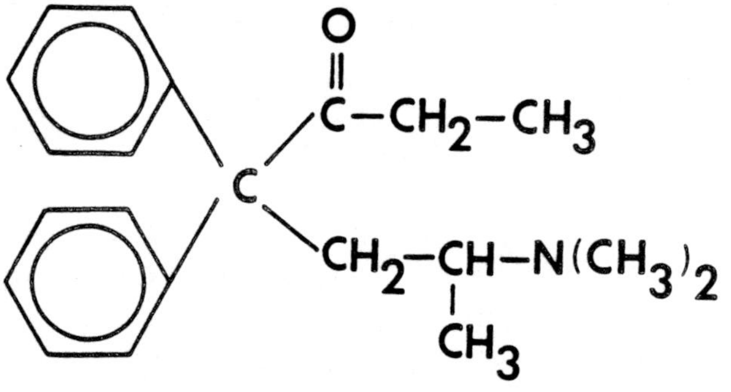

METHADONE

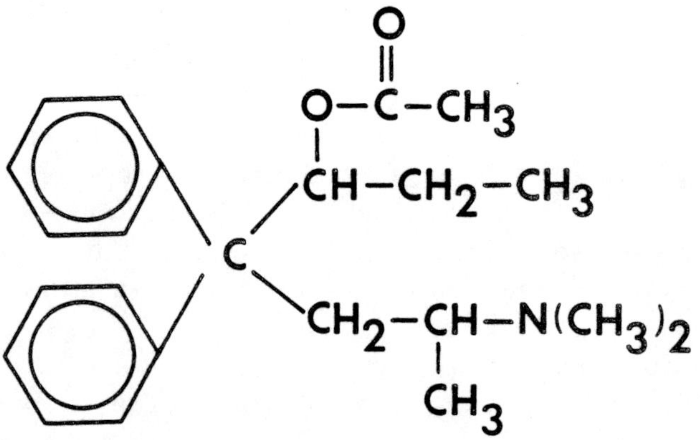

ACETYLMETHADOL

Figure 11-1. Structural formulas of methadone and levo-alpha-acetylmethadol (LAAM).

The phenomenon of dispensing a narcotic to drug abusers — and in effect substituting one addicting drug for another — created the need for new controls designed specifically to regulate narcotic usage for this therapeutic purpose. The FDA responded with a set of stringent rules specifying who may be treated, by whom, in what manner, and with what kinds of controls. These regulations are designed to ensure that individuals enrolled in methadone treatment programs are indeed dependent on an opiate, that the methadone treatment will not worsen a drug abuse problem, and also to prevent (as much as possible) the illegal traffic of methadone. While the FDA regulations require that expensive, tedious, and time-consuming screening and monitoring procedures be performed for each patient seen at methadone treatment clinics, these precautions are unquestionably necessary.

URINE SURVEILLANCE

Included in the FDA requirements is a continuous surveillance of the urine of each patient enrolled in methadone treatment to monitor for the presence of opiates, methadone, barbiturates, and amphetamines. In the early days (about 1965), urine surveillance was fairly unsophisticated. Most laboratories were not well equipped and the laboratory personnel generally had little training or experience in detecting opiates and other drugs of abuse in the urine. Furthermore, there were very few definitive scientific papers on the topic at that time. The urinalysis procedures used then were not only complicated and time- consuming, but they yielded highly unreliable results. It is understandable then that when a positive illicit drug (or "dirty") urine report was issued for a patient who denied the use of any illicit drugs, it was often difficult for the supervising physician to determine if the patient was lying or the laboratory made an error. As the patient population in the drug addiction wards and clinics gradually increased, it became imperative to develop more reliable and simpler methods of analyzing the urine of drugs of abuse. There are now available much improved techniques for analyzing the urine for drugs. These procedures will be discussed in a subsequent section. The use of urine surveillance in drug treatment programs has been reviewed previously (DeAngelis, 1972, 1973).

The Need for Objective Evidence of Illicit Drug Intake

When dealing with both new and existing patients on methadone treatment programs, one cannot rely upon the patient's history regarding his or her intake of drugs. Many times the urine of patients claiming heroin use, cocaine use, and so forth within the last ten hours fail to show the presence of these illicit drugs. With an accurate laboratory method of surveying the urine for drugs and an adequately supervised system for collecting urine samples, one can reliably determine what drugs a patient is taking.

The need for objective evidence of illicit drug use is even more important when dealing with inpatients remaining on the ward or returning from a pass either for job seeking or emergency purposes. Here the patient usually denies using any illicit drugs and some will swear on their mother's grave that they have not used any illicit drugs during their pass or within the last day or two. The most effective method of dealing with such situations is simply to ask the patient to produce a urine sample to be submitted for analysis. Some of our patients, knowing the accuracy of our urine surveillance techniques, will immediately change their story prior to entering the urine collection room. On the other hand, if the patient prefers to go through with the procedure, then urinalysis is the most reliable way of providing objective evidence concerning whether or not the patient has used illicit drugs.

The loss of privileges when the urine report indicates the presence of illicit drugs is an effective deterrent for the use of illicit drugs by patients on the treatment program. It is very hard to determine accurately the progress of patients, particularly outpatients, unless you have a reliable method for monitoring their intake of illicit drugs. Occasionally we see patients in a stuporous condition who still deny any use of illicit drugs. The urine result is very much needed by the staff to counsel the patient and to assess the treatment plan and the patient's progress toward the treatment goal.

The Need for Objective Evidence That the Prescribed Drugs Are Being Taken

It is sometimes even more important for the treatment team to have the urine results of patients, particularly outpatients, in order to determine if they are following the treatment plan and taking the prescribed medications regularly. Occasionally, outpatients who receive take-home doses of methadone, tranquilizers, or antidepressants fail to take them. Certain inpatients also may not take their prescribed medication (a common technique used by the patients is to put the pill in their mouth in front of the nurse but then keep it in the oral cavity without swallowing until they are out of the nurse's sight, at which time they spit out the pill to be sold to another patient or saved for later use). The urine surveillance, thus, should also be designed to monitor for the presence of the drugs prescribed by the physicians. If the urinalysis fails to detect prescribed drugs, the patient is obviously not following the instructions of the treatment team and he should be confronted by the staff regarding this matter.

Negative urine reports for prescribed drugs, in our opinion, are worse than the presence of illicit drugs in the patient's urine. The reason is that the patient who does not take the prescribed medications is deliberate in not following the treatment plan and is abusing the program. The outpatient who is not taking prescribed take-home medications may be selling the drugs. Among the negative urine results, we consider negative methadone to be the most important issue for a number of reasons: (1) The patient should not have any take-home medications and he should remain in Phase I of the treatment regimen, which requires daily pickup of medication, with the possible exception of Sundays. (2) The patient may have taken a small portion of the take-home medication of methadone and sold one of the other methadone bottles. Therefore, the amount of methadone in the urine is so minute that its result is negative in the urine report. This applies to all medication given by the treatment team either in the inpatient wards or the outpatient clinics. After obtaining the negative urine data from the patient, the treatment team can suspend the patient's take-home privileges as well as instruct the nurse or pharmacist to observe very closely the ingestion of the medication.

The absence of prescribed medication in a patient's urine also indicates that the patient probably does not need the prescribed amount of medication and therefore the dose of methadone or other medication can be reduced or even discontinued. Of course, the patient will complain bitterly about this action. Explanation can be given to the patient as to why that action was taken. The patient should be informed that if he follows instructions, his privileges of take-home medication and his original dose of medication can be restored.

Commonly Abused Drugs to Be Examined in Urine

In the early days, methadone and morphine-like compounds were the only drugs tested for in the patient's urine. As patients on methadone maintenance were subsequently found to be abusing barbiturates, cocaine, and amphetamines with increased frequency, these drugs were also added to the list for urine surveillance. In recent years, due to the gradually increased incidence of benzodiazephine abuse, diazepam (Valium®) and chlordiazepoxide (Librium®) have also been added to the list of drugs to be tested for in the patient's urine at our treatment facility. After a restriction on use of *d*-amphetamine was instituted in the last few years, the use of other stimulants, such as methylphenidate (Ritalin®) has gradually increased in our patient population. For this reason, methylphenidate and other stimulants should also be tested for in the patient's urine.

In recent years, patients in the midwest area, particularly Chicago, have shown a marked increase in the use of pentazocine (Talwin®) with or without tripelennamine (Pyribenzamine®). Therefore, our laboratory is now monitoring urine for the presence of these drugs.

Pentazocine is an analgesic with weak narcotic antagonist properties. It is a derivative of one of the opiates, thebaine. Pentazocine has a short duration of action. When pentazocine is injected, it is mildly addictive in emotionally unstable individuals, particularly ex-drug addicts. Tripelennamine (Pyribenzamine®) is a potent antihistaminic that has a long duration of sedative action. The combination of the two drugs reportedly gives narcotic addicts a "high" lasting for six hours. It is known that tripelennamine will produce seizure disorders. For this reason many narcotic addicts experience tremor, even gross seizure-like activity when using Talwin and Pyribenzamine (T's and Blues*). Addiction to T's and Blues can be treated readily even though T's and Blues are easily obtained through prescription channels. While the patients are having a good time injecting T's and Blues, they usually don't come in for treatment. On the other hand, prolonged use of T's and Blues will invariably produce thrombophlebitis or multiple abscesses at the site of injection. Patients who develop these complications are the ones who come in and want to get rid of their T's and Blues habit.

The Issue of Dealing with Patients Who Have Taken Illicit Drugs

The presence of heroin, cocaine, or other illicit drugs in the patient's urine frequently disturbs the treatment team. It is my opinion that the urine data merely tells the status of the patient and the treatment team should not be so alarmed if the patient is exhibiting objective evidence that he or she is in need of a great deal of help. In such cases, it is likely that (1) he is still in very good contact with illicit drug suppliers; (2) if he is employed, he probably uses most of his income for illicit drugs; (3) if he is not employed, one can readily presume that he is dealing as well as using these illicit drugs; (4) the patient is trying to relate to the treatment staff that he is not doing as well as the treatment staff thinks.

The treatment staff should take the attitude that these are manifestations very much similar to those of the patient with hypertension whose blood pressure remains very high; in other words, it is an indication that more vigorous treatment is needed. While we do not use a blocking dose of methadone (high dose of methadone), we consider the presence of heroin in the urine to indicate the patient's continuous need for the use of illicit drugs on top of the prescribed methadone. That means that the dose of

---

*Tripelnnamine (Pyribenzamine ®) tablets are blue in color.

methadone may be inadequate. We usually increase the dose of methadone and the majority of patients will stop using heroin. The only exception to the rule is when the patient uses illicit morphine or Dilaudid® from a practicing physician. In this case, the presence of opiates in the urine is due to a high dose of morphine-like substances and in our opinion the patient will probably continue to use this illicit opiate-like substance from certain unscrupulous physicians. There is no way to greatly increase the methadone dose to match the amount of pure opiate-like medication from such physicians. The only thing to do is to make sure the patient is coming daily and that he has no take-home privileges.

If the patient's urine shows heroin as an outpatient, he may have to be dropped down to a phase that requires more frequent visits to the outpatient clinic. The denial of take-home privileges will motivate some patients to have "clean" urine but it will have a lesser effect on those having ready access to opiates from practicing physicians. For example, an indigent patient on Title 19 receives Dilaudid regularly for pain due to prostatic carcinoma, which was operated on unbelievably more than five years ago. At least with the availability of reliable urine surveillance, the treatment team can counsel the patient more effectively because the status of the patient is very clear. Without an adequate and reliable urine surveillance everything is muddled and the patients usually have very little respect for the treatment team.

Patients found to have cocaine and other central nervous system stimulants such as methylphenidate (Ritalin®), phenmetrazine (Preludin®), and diethylpropion (Tenuate®) in the urine are offered counseling as well as antidepressant drugs.

As far as the presence of barbiturates in the urine, we usually want to know whether the patient was taking short-acting barbiturates such as secobarbital (Seconal®) and pentobarbital (Nembutal®), or longacting barbiturates such as phenobarbital. When the reason for taking barbiturates is ascertained, these patients usually can be detoxified readily. If attempts at barbiturate detoxification fail, the patient can be placed on tranquilizers that have minimal abuse potential.

Techniques Used by Patients to Invalidate Urine Surveillance

Many patients on the methadone maintenance program still have the urge to use illicit drugs including heroin, cocaine, methylphenidate (Ritalin®), amphetamines, barbiturates, and other sedatives, either sporadically or regularly (and particularly on weekends). If the urine surveillance procedure is only designed to detect narcotic drugs such as heroin, dihydromorphinone (Dilaudid®), codeine, Percodan®, and methadone, then other highly sought after drugs of the barbiturate and stimulant groups are missed in the urine surveillance. This type of surveillance is inadequate for obtaining a clear picture of the patient's status and allows the patient to seek drugs and play "doctor" himself. When the patient is abusing these other illicit drugs without being confronted by the treatment staff, then there is no need for him to manipulate his scheduled urine surveillance. On the other hand, if the laboratory is testing for a variety of drugs and the patient is being confronted and warned by the treatment staff of the illicit drug use, then the patient's natural instinct is to invalidate the urine surveillance by some means.

There are many techniques used by the patients. The most common ones follow: (1) They will bring in an old sample of their own urine (collected when they were not using illicit drugs) or a drug-free sample of a friend's urine hidden inside their jacket or taped on their thigh; behind a closed door, they will take out this false sample to hand in for analysis. (2) They will dip the urine cup into the toilet water so that the drug concentration of their urine is minimal. If the urine sample is sufficiently dilute, no drugs will be detected during laboratory urinalysis. (3) Without close supervision of urine collection, the labels on the urine cups can be switched by patients. (4) They will give less than 30 cc of urine claiming that they voided just prior to coming to the clinic and cannot give any more urine. With a small volume of urine it is more difficult to detect drugs, particularly those drugs present in low concentrations or those drugs consumed more than twenty-four hours prior to the collection of the urine sample. (5) The patient, knowing he was abusing illicit drugs, will drink a lot of coffee, tea, or beer so that by the time he comes to the clinic in the late afternoon he voids a copious amount of dilute urine having a very low specific gravity. Owing to the hypervolemia, the concentration of drugs in the urine is very low and it is difficult for the laboratory to detect any drugs in the urine.

Many patients will use excuses that they have to go back to work or pick up their children and so forth and, therefore, cannot wait to give an adequate urine sample when they visit the clinic. Patients will complain of hardship if the treatment staff insists that they stay until they have dropped an adequate urine specimen. Our treatment philosophy is that such patients generally use illicit drugs continuously so skipping one urine surveillance will only delay confrontation with the patient for one week. Chances are the patient cannot use the same excuse for not dropping on following visits, so the status of his or her intake will be ascertained in one of the next visits to the clinic.

If the urinalysis procedure used requires an adjustment of urine pH to a desired level before the test can be performed, patients may become wise to the fact that they can sabotage the urinalysis procedure by adding vinegar to their urine; the resulting strongly acidic urine does not reach the proper pH level when the laboratory technician performs the standar pH adjusting procedures and, hence, the urine does not respond to the drug analysis. Urinalysis procedures using the XAD-2 resin (to be described in a subsequent section) are not affected by a patient's attempt to tamper with his or her urine pH.

Precautions for Urine Collection

Adequate labeling on both the lid and the body of the urine collection cup are required to ensure proper identification. The urine containers should be handed to the patients rather than allowing the patients to pick up a urine container from the shelf or table. A member of the staff should be there to supervise the collection of the patients' urine. There should be a reflecting mirror installed in the proper corner of the urine collection room, which will allow a minimal chance of undetected alteration of the urine samples. If the urine surveillance observer belongs to the opposite sex and the patient cannot urinate while they are observing, the patient must subject himself to a brief, simple body search and the door to the urine surveillance room can then be closed.

As a further precaution, the warmth of the urine container should be checked by the observer to make sure that no cold urine is being delivered. A coloring agent should be installed in the flushing system so that the water is tinted a light blue color. If the patients dip their container into the toilet, their urine specimen will change to a yellowish-blue color. The coloring agent should not be on the side of the toilet bowl because this can easily be removed and placed back, but should be installed as an integral part of the flushing system.* After receiving the urine samples from the patients, they should be stored in a safe place out of sight and reach of the patients. For long-term storage (more than a day), the urine samples should be kept in a refrigerator that can be locked. The key should be available to a limited number of reliable personnel.

In our treatment program we do not allow drug counselors who were ex-abusers to supervise the urine surveillance. The reason behind this is to avoid unnecessary suspicion and undue pressure on these workers to play favoritism to their own patients. In some treatment programs the patients have admitted that they gave five dollars to the drug counselors to invalidate their urine. It is, therefore, best to have a full-time employee, such as a nurse or nursing assistant supervising urine collection.

Transporting the Urines

Urines should be kept in plastic containers rather than paper cups. This is because most of the paper cups will leak after standing twelve to twenty-four hours. Some have poor covers and will leak around the covers when jarred or tipped over. In our program, the urines are transported in specially made racks in which the plastic urine cups fit snugly; the racks are stacked one on top of another in a locked container or box. They do not spill or leak, even with sudden jarring movement. The urine

---

*We use Sentry Liquid manufactured by Airkem. This system consists of a stainless steel bowl that is attached directly to the plumbing (a specially made wrench is required to install or remove this bowl). Each time the toilet is flushed, six to eight drops of the blue liquid is drawn from a tube attached to the steel bowl and into the toilet water.

containers should be labeled with the patient's last name and first name, as well as the date and the time the specimen was taken. The name of the person supervising at the time the specimen was taken should also be on the label. The reason the first name is included is to avoid confusion when two patients in the same program have the same last name. If urine is collected by different supervisors at different times and one supervisor constantly accepts cold urine, an inadequate amount of urine, urine containing grapefruit juice or urine that clearly is very dilute, then that supervisor should be relieved of the responsibility of supervising urine collection. The first time a patient submits a urine sample for analysis, the laboratory assigns the patient a number that is attached to his or her urine label for all future reporting purposes, thus avoiding the need to copy down the patient's name many times.

Laboratory Methods for Detecting Drugs in the Urine

There are many different methods that can be used to identify drugs in human urine. A detailed description of the technical aspects of these methods are out of the scope of this review, but there are numerous articles published on the subject (Kaistha, 1972; Mulé, 1971a; Mulé et al., 1971b; Roerig et al., 1975a). The most popularly used methods at the present time are: (1) thin layer chromatography (TLC); (2) gas liquid chromatography (GLC); and (3) immunoassay.

In our laboratory at the Wood Veteran Administration Medical Center, we use a TLC urinalysis procedure along with GLC and radioimmunoassay when a confirmatory test is needed. Table 11-I provides a summary of the analysis methods we use for detecting various drugs at the Wood V.A. Medical Center. Table 11-II lists the sensitivity of the analysis procedures for the various drugs, expressed as the minimum concentration of drug or metabolite (μg of drug/ml of urine) that must be present in the urine to make detection possible. We have found TLC to be the most versatile and least expensive urinalysis procedure for our purposes. It requires less equipment and can detect more drugs in the urine than any other method. A reasonably intelligent laboratory technician can be trained to perform this test readily

TABLE 11-I

METHODS USED FOR DETECTING DRUGS IN URINE

Chemical Name	Trade Name	Detected by		
		Thin-Layer Chromatography	Gas-Liquid Chromatography	Radioimmunoassay
Morphine		× (4)		× (1)
Diacetylmorphine	Heroin	× (2)		× (1)
Oxycodone	Percodan		× (4)	
Meperidine	Demerol	× (4)	× (2)	
Methadone	Dolophine	× (2)	× (2)	
Propoxyphene	Darvon	× (2)	× (3)	
Pentazocine	Talwin	× (4)	× (4)	
Barbiturates:				
Amobarbital	Amytal	× (4)	× (4)	× (1)
Pentobarbital	Nembutal	× (4)	× (4)	× (1)
Phenobarbital		× (4)	× (4)	× (1)
Secobarbital	Seconal	× (4)	× (4)	× (1)
Chloral hydrate		× (4)		
Methyprylon	Noludar	× (4)		
Chlorpromazine	Thorazine	× (4)	× (2)	
Hydroxyzine	Atarax	× (2)	× (4)	
Promazine	Sparine	× (4)	× (2)	
Thioridazine	Mellaril	× (2)		
Trifluoperazine	Stelazine	× (2)		
Amitriptyline	Elavil	× (2)	× (2)	
Desipramine	Norpramine	× (2)	× (2)	
Imipramine	Tofranil	× (2)	× (2)	
Methylphenidate	Ritalin	× (4)	× (4)	
d-Amphetamine	Dexedrine	× (4)	× (4)	
Methamphetamine	Methedrine		× (4)	
Diethylpropion	Tenuate	× (4)	× (4)	
Cocaine		× (2)	× (4)	× (1)
d-Brompheniramine	Drixoral	× (4)	× (4)	
Promethazine	Phenergan	× (2)	× (4)	
Trimethobenzamide	Tigan	× (4)	× (4)	
Chlorpheniramine	Teldrin	× (4)	× (2)	
Quinine		× (2)	× (2)	
Benzodiazepines	Valium, Librium, Serax	× (2)		
Glutethimide	Doriden		× (3)	

(1) Parent compound indistinguishable from metabolic product(s).
(2) Parent compound with metabolic product(s) detected.
(3) Detected primarily by metabolic products.
(4) Parent compound only.

Drug Dependent Patients

TABLE 11-II

Sᴇɴsɪᴛɪᴠɪᴛʏ (µg/ml) ᴏғ Tᴇsᴛ Mᴇᴛʜᴏᴅs ғᴏʀ Dᴇᴛᴇᴄᴛɪɴɢ Dʀᴜɢs ɪɴ Uʀɪɴᴇ

DRUG		*METHOD*		
Chemical Name	*Trade Name*	*Thin-Layer Chromatography (50 ml urine)*	*Gas-Liquid Chromatography (5 ml urine)*	*Radioimmunoassay (0.1 ml urine)*
Morphine		0.2	—	0.1
Codeine		0.5	—	0.1
Methadone	Dolophine	0.5	0.2	0.1
Secobarbital	Seconal	0.5	0.2	0.1
Pentobarbital	Nembutal	0.5	0.2	0.1
Amobarbital	Amytal	0.5	0.2	0.1
Phenobarbital		0.2	0.5	0.1
d-Amphetamine	Dexedrine	0.5	0.2	1.0
Methamphetamine	Methedrine	>1.0	0.2	1.0
Cocaine		0.5	—	0.1
Chlorpromazine	Thorazine	1.0	—	—
Thioridazine	Mellaril	1.0	—	—
Trifluoperazine	Stelazine	1.0	—	—
Prochlorperazine	Compazine	1.0	—	—
Glutethimide	Doriden	2.0	—	—

and after several months of repeated exposure to the technique, the technician can become highly competent. The sensitivity of the TLC method is related to the volume of urine used in the test. It also depends on the efficiency of the extraction of the drug from the urine and upon the sensitivity of the chromatography system.

As reported by Fujimoto and Wang (1970), the XAD-2 resin method of extraction has greatly increased the sensitivity, dependability, speed, and economy of the TLC method. This extraction method makes it possible to detect many drugs in low concentration because the entire amount of urine is poured through an XAD-2 resin and all the drugs in the urine sample are then absorbed onto the resin. Using this extraction technique, even 30 ml of a patient's urine can provide a reasonable report of the patient's intake of drugs.

In our laboratory we have found that TLC using XAD-2 resin extraction can detect the presence of opiates (including morphine, heroin, codeine, etc.), barbiturates, amphetamines, methadone, and many other drugs (see Table 11-I) for at least thirty-six hours after the patient has taken the drugs. For example, in our laboratory TLC can detect barbiturate in 90 percent of the urine samples tested on subjects who ingested 100 mg of a barbiturate thirty hours prior to giving the sample. We have also found positive barbiturate in 70 percent of urine samples when barbiturates were ingested two days prior to the urine collection. Thus, the sensitivity of the TLC will provide a good survey of drug use when urine samples are collected and analyzed twice weekly on a randomized schedule. The majority of patients abusing drugs can be identified with this urine surveillance system. Any drug treatment program that would conduct such a urine surveillance would, sooner or later, detect all patients abusing illicit drugs.

False-negative results are reasonably minimal. Unfortunately, TLC does provide a significant number of false-positive results, which mislead the treatment team regarding the patients progress and status in the treatment program. For example, in one survey we found that a number of false-positive results were found in 130 urine samples (Roerig et al., 1975b). Among them were seven false-positives for methadone, one for morphine, three for barbiturates, and two for amphetamines. For this reason, in our laboratory we perform additional tests to confirm any positive results obtained with TLC.

Gas liquid chromatography, which is more sensitive than TLC, is used by our laboratory as a confirmatory test method. GLC is more effective for separating drugs and the method is less prone to result in false-positive data. The use of GLC as a confirmatory test can totally eliminate false-positive results found in TLC, as illustrated in our published data (Roerig et al, 1975b). Besides eliminating false-positive TLC results, GLC is also valuable for identifying or repeating the results of TLC on those urine samples with questionably positive data on certain drugs. Thus, in our laboratory the combination of TLC and GLC have greatly increased the sensitivity of urine surveillance. It should be pointed out, however, that GLC requires slightly more expensive equipment and technical knowledge. The increased time for analysis and the greater cost of GLC have made GLC less attractive and TLC remains the primary method for generalized urine surveillance.

As far as immunoassay techniques are concerned, it should be emphasized that the antibodies contained in these immunoassays do react with some analogues of the parent drug. For example, antibodies produced to react with morphine react better or equally well with codeine. Because of such cross-reaction, the immunoassay procedure of urinalysis cannot be relied upon as absolute evidence of a drug's presence, but only as an indication. Because of the high sensitivity of immunoassay masses, they are used solely as confirmatory tests for TLC results rather than as a primary method in urine surveillance.

At the present time there are four types of immunoassay procedures for detecting drugs of abuse in the urine; (1) radioimmunoassay (RIA); (2) enzyme multiple immunoassay technique (EMIT); (3) free radical assay technique (FRAT); and (4) hemoglutination inhibition. Of these four types of immunoassay procedures we have been using only RIA in our laboratory because it is the most sensitive and has the capability of being used quantitatively (Mule et al., 1974). The morphine RIA has been proven particularly useful because morphine cannot be confirmed easily by GLC. Codeine and other morphinans also are detected with the morphine RIA, but in our opinion this presents no great problem since TLC can distinguish morphine from codeine. In our laboratory practice, RIA is used to confirm all positive and questionably positive results for morphine found in TLC. It should be pointed out that, based upon our past experience, the presence of a large amount of quinine in the urine frequently obscured the identification of opiates in the urine using TLC. For this reason RIA for morphine is routinely run on those samples with the presence of quinine. As stated in the earlier part of this review, occasionally a patient may drink a large amount of fluid or beer deliberately or unintentionally so that dilute urine samples are received (specific gravity of 1.005 or less). If dilute urine samples are obtained in our laboratory, RIA for morphine is routinely performed.

As far as barbiturate determination is concerned, the TLC method is reasonably satisfactory (Wang and Mueller, 1973). However, RIA for barbiturate also has been found to be an excellent method of confirmation (Roerig et al., 1975b). It is as sensitive as GLC but is faster and less expensive. Unfortunately, RIA for barbiturate does not distinguish the kind of barbiturate, whether it is secobarbital, pentobarbital, or phenobarital. To identify different barbiturates, GLC must be used. While different barbiturates cross-react with glutethimide (Doriden®), this poses no problem since glutethimide can be distinguished from barbiturates by the TLC method.

The sensitivity of RIA for amphetamines requires 1000 ng/ml in the urine. This does not compare as favorably to morphine and barbiturates, which can be detected by RIA when present in 60 and 100 ng/ml, respectively (Roerig et al., 1975a). Nevertheless, RIA is a useful confirmatory method for amphetamines. Again, RIA is faster and less expensive than GLC for running confirmatory tests for amphetamines.

Thus, we have concluded that TLC should be used as the primary method for urine surveillance. It is sufficiently sensitive to produce clinically meaningful results in screening a large number of drugs in the drug abuse treatment program (Table 11-II). TLC has the advantage of simultaneously itemizing a large number of drugs at a reasonable cost. However, the possibility of false-positive results is greater with TLC than with other methods. For this reason the need for higher reliability dictates the use of supplemental confirmatory procedures. Confirmation of TLC results by GLC and radioimmunoassay reduces the possibility of false-positive results to nearly zero. Thus, our combined urinalysis program results in a high, overall reliability. While the RIA is faster and less expensive than GLC, GLC is more versatile since it can detect a wider range of drugs. Presently RIA is used in our laboratory only for confirmatory tests for morphine, barbiturates, and amphetamines.

Advantages and Disadvantages of Urine Surveillance

When urine samples are taken on a time schedule unknown to the patients, urine surveillance is an efficient and economical way of assessing the status of the patients' drug intake. When the urine results are reported to the treatment team on a continual basis, it gives the treatment team some objective information as to the status of the patient. Intensive counseling can be provided for the patient with a positive report for illicit drugs with the hope that the patient will discontinue using such expensive illicit drugs. Proper conduction of the urine testing will also add a great deal of confidence on the part of the treatment team concerning the accuracy of the urine surveillance reports. If a patient is on 15 mg of methadone a day or higher, the patient should have positive methadone in their urine. On the other hand, if the methadone dose drops below 15 mg, it will be hard to detect methadone in the urine. A negative result for methadone in the urine of a patient prescribed to take 15 mg of methadone or more relates two important pieces of information: (1) the patient is not ingesting the take-home dose of methadone as he is supposed to; (2) the patient is probably engaging in some illegal activity such as selling the take-home medication. In such cases the take-home medication should be discontinued. This means the patient will have to return to the clinic six times a week with only a take-home dose on Sundays.

Urine surveillance allows the staff to monitor the proper usage of other medications ordered by their physicians. Occasionally, the urine surveillance results are used for medicolegal reasons, such as when the district attorney or a judge wish to know the status of the patient in terms of his illicit drug use. With our urine surveillance it is possible to state categorically if the patient is or is not using illicit drugs on a treatment program. When the urine surveillance indicates the presence of illicit drugs or absence of a methadone dose, it allows the treatment team to have an opportunity to confront the patient in regard to his drug intake and other behavioral problems. When the urine surveillance is done properly in regard to both collection and laboratory procedure, the patient usually develops a great deal of respect for the treatment program because of the extreme sensitivity and accuracy of the urine surveillance.

Some of the patients come to visit the clinic six times a week, even though it is time-consuming and a hardship at times, particularly in inclement weather. Nevertheless, many patients see visiting the clinic, giving a urine sample, and having a session with their counselor as a healthy and positive habit. This is particularly true in the case where the patient is unemployed and has free time on his hands. This creates a bond between the patient and the treatment team. It is interesting to note that in such a relationship the patient will frequently admit that the recent urine will show illicit drugs or that he does not want to give a urine sample because he has used illicit drugs. Based upon our past experience, denial by the patients that they did not take illicit drugs in the face of positive urine results usually turns out to be a con game on the part of the patient. Rarely is the problem due to mislabeling or faulty reporting by the laboratory. This problem can be readily eliminated by saving the urine sample for two weeks so that a repeat analysis can be done should the need arise. Even though the results of the urine surveillance are sent to the treatment team almost three to four days later, it provides weekly information invariably needed by the treatment team.

The disadvantages of urine surveillance are really minimal. If it is done properly, the time spent on the collection of urine and the expense is justified by the many advantages. Treating patients strictly on hearsay is not only unscientific but also potentially detrimental to the patient. Incorrect urine results are a troublesome disadvantage; however, with better trained laboratory technicians, such mistakes have become more and more infrequent. In our laboratory we have 100 percent accuracy in terms of the Community Disease Center (CDC) urine surveillance. We also employ an internal checking system whereby each urine sample is split in two before analysis and coded by the nurse; when the urinalysis results are returned by the laboratory, the nurses and physicians can check to see that the two analyses for each patient are in agreement.

Thus, urine surveillance does not solve the patient's addiction problem but is certainly a positive aid to the treatment team in the rehabilitation of the drug dependent patients. Since we are not only testing for opiates and methadone, but also minor tranquilizers like diazepam, barbiturates such as secobarbital and others, amphetamines, methylphenidate, propoxyphene, cocaine, phenothiazines, and so forth, this type of urine surveillance is not only useful to the physicians but useful to every member of the treatment team.

A survey conducted by Lewis et al. (1972) concluded that urine surveillance is considered a demeaning procedure by many drug abuse patients. Our experience supports this finding to a certain extent. Some of our patients resent the fact that we will not take their word on what drugs they have taken and many others feel that it is degrading to have to produce a urine sample under direct observation. However, we have found that some patients appreciate urine surveillance because there is an added deterrent against illicit drug use when they know that any deviation from their prescribed drug regimen is likely to be detected.

Urine surveillance must be viewed as an integral part of the treatment program. Those who argue that urine surveillance should not be employed because it is degrading to the patient should reexamine their position. The use of urinalysis in the management of drug dependence is just as beneficial and ethical for detecting and monitoring problems of drug abuse as it is for detecting and monitoring other health problems, such as sugar and acetone levels in the urine of diabetics.

The treatment staff should make every effort to respect the dignity of the patients in regard to urine surveillance and every facet of the treatment program. The patient should be made to feel as comfortable as possible, although this may be difficult. In cases where a patient is unable to urinate in front of another individual, the supervising nurse or other member of the treatment staff should conduct a simple body search of the patient and then allow him or her to produce a urine sample behind a closed door.

DETERMINATION OF THE DEGREE OF
PHYSICAL DEPENDENCE

It has been well known that physicians and treatment personnel who work with drug patients have had a problem determining the degree of a patient's opiate addiction. In fact, it is well known that it is difficult to determine whether the patient is actually addicted. The patient's self-reported history of drug intake is very unreliable. Most workers can recall very convincing stories told by patients about their drug habit. Until recently, there has been no effective method for measuring the degree of opiate dependence. Needle track marks on the arms only indicate that the patient has been shooting some substances. Also, fresh needle marks could be due to venopuncture for blood donation or blood chemistry tests ordered by another physician. When a supervised urine collection is conducted and laboratory analysis shows the urine to contain an opiate, we still know little about the existence or degree of dependence. For that reason, in the early days of FDA requirements, several positive urine tests had to be obtained before the patient could be placed on a methadone maintenance program. The shortcoming of this rule was not noticed at first, but became evident when addicts seeking methadone maintenance deliberately went out of their way to shoot several doses of heroin before presenting themselves to gain admission to a methadone treatment program. In other words, in following the FDA requirements, methadone treatment centers were encouraging patients to shoot more heroin just so they could be accepted into the treatment program.

However, when we look back to the earlier years, we recall that there was less problem in determining physical dependence to opiates. This was simply because most patients showed clear-cut signs of withdrawal by the time they came in for treatment. For example, it was quite common to find patients with goose flesh on their chest and arms, extreme chills, severe stomach or muscle cramps, and even vomiting of bile-stained material. Today, most patients seeking treatment find it unacceptable to wait for the development of withdrawal symptoms prior to receiving medication in order to prove the severity of their narcotic deprivation. As one patient said, "if I have to suffer that much to get into a hospital, I might as well go cold turkey in the comfort of my home."

Those who have not been enrolled in any drug dependence treatment programs in the past and, hence, do not have a documented drug history from another treatment facility pose the greatest dilemma in terms of evaluating their degree of dependence. In our group, we have developed a test using naloxone (Narcan®), which is a pure narcotic antagonist, to accurately assess the degree of a patient's opiate dependence (Wang et al., 1974). As a narcotic antagonist, naloxone will rapidly reverse the effects of opiates and, thereby, precipitate withdrawal in dependent individuals. Following the administration of naloxone, then, the signs and symptoms of opiate withdrawal are monitored and rates as a measure of dependence.

The test also provides a scientific basis for determining the initial dose of methadone to be administered to the patient, provided he or she does have a positive reaction to the naloxone test. The test can be very helpful for the patient's peace of mind as well when the results show that physical dependence is either absent or minimal. In our experience, we have found that patients who exhibit little or no dependence with the naloxone test are generally quite relieved.

The naloxone test is administered after the admission of each new patient to our inpatient ward. Each patient has a complete physical examination and routine laboratory tests. The naloxone test is scheduled for the morning following admission. Morphine, 10 mg, can be given intramuscularly (IM) if needed on the evening of admission to alleviate the patient's discomfort due to the onset of withdrawal. However, no morphine should be given after midnight in order to provide a controlled opiate-free period before the naloxone test the next morning. The morning of the test, breakfast is withheld.

Table 11-III illustrates the rating system used in the naloxone test. Briefly, this rating system is designed to account for the specificity of a withdrawal sign as well as the time of its onset. For example, since patients can easily mimic symptoms of acute withdrawal such as restlessness, nervousness, nausea, muscle cramps, and so forth, the rating system assigns less weight to these subjective symptoms than to the more specific signs including goose flesh, gross tremor, vomiting and profuse sweating. To attach appropriate significance to the time of onset of the various symptoms, a withdrawal sign is assigned progressively lower ratings the later it appears naloxone administration.

Withdrawal symptoms are rated just prior to the IM administration of 0.8 mg of naloxone. If this baseline preinjection withdrawal score is greater than 10, the naloxone test is not necessary for the diagnosis of opiate dependence, although it should be useful for clarifying the degree of severity. The withdrawal symptoms are then rated ten, twenty, and thirty minutes after

TABLE 11-III

NALOXONE TEST RATING SYSTEM

Presence or absence of signs and symptoms (circle number)

Signs and Symptoms	Zero time (preinjection) 0 min Present	Absent	Time after injection of 0.8 mg naloxone 10 min Present	Absent	20 min Present	Absent	30 min Present	Absent
Muscle aching	3	0	1	0	1	0	1	0
Stomach pain	3	0	1	0	1	0	1	0
Feeling of change in temperature	3	0	1	0	1	0	1	0
Uncontrollable yawning	4	0	2	0	1	0	1	0
Lacrimation & nasal congestion	4	0	2	0	1	0	1	0
Restlessness	4	0	2	0	1	0	1	0
Profuse sweating	6	0	3	0	2	0	1	0
Tremor	6	0	3	0	2	0	1	0
Vomiting	6	0	3	0	2	0	1	0
Gooseflesh	6	0	3	0	2	0	1	0

Zero time score = _____	Total Postinjection score
10 minute score = _____	Severe 31-45
20 minute score = _____	Moderate 21-30
30 minute score = _____	Slight 11-20
Total postinjection score	Marginal 5-10
(dependence rating) = _____	Absent 0-4

naloxone administration.

It has been found that any sign or symptom present at the ten-minute checkpoint is also present at the twenty- and thirty-minute checkpoint. Therefore, if tremor was present at the ten-minute time interval, it would receive a total thirty minute score of 6 (3 points for being present at the ten-minute checkpoint, plus 2 points for being present at the twenty-minute checkpoint, plus 1 point for being present at the thirty-minute checkpoint). If however, tremor does not appear until the twenty-minute checkpoint, the symptom would receive a rating of 2 plus 1, or 3 points. Each symptom is rated in this manner and then the total thirty-minute score (postinjection only) for all symptoms manifested is tallied and recorded as the dependence rating. Severe dependence is designated by a total postinjection score of 31 to 45, moderate dependence by a score of 21 to 30, slight dependence by a score of 11 to 20, marginal dependence by a score of 5 to 10, and the absence of dependence by a score of 0 to 4.

Appropriate precautionary measures should be instituted during the naloxone test. These include the continual presence of a nurse, or preferably a physician, for the first thirty minutes after naloxone administration. If withdrawal signs and symptoms become severe, such as marked vomiting of bile-tinged matter, one or two 10-mg doses of morphine should be given IM to terminate the naloxone test even as early as the first ten minutes following naloxone administration. This is to prevent unnecessary discomfort to the patient, as diagnosis of the presence of a severe dependence to opiates is established. Prior to the test, the patient should be assured that the naloxone test will be terminated with morphine if he or she becomes extremely uncomfortable.

Based on the thousands of patients who have undergone this test for opiate dependence at the Wood VA Medical Center and Milwaukee County General Hospital, we feel that the naloxone test is both safe and reliable and that it provides an objective assessment of a patient's current physical dependence to opiates (Wiesen et al., 1977). The naloxone test has many advantages. For one thing, many patients seeking treatment for opiate abuse are unwilling to wait for the few weeks necessary to establish a diagnosis of opiate dependence via urine surveillance. Furthermore, these patients are generally not willing to go without drugs for a day or two to develop the withdrawal syndrome naturally as evidence of opiate dependence. The naloxone test provides a rapid diagnosis of opiate dependence and an assessment of the degree of severity. Naloxone is, furthermore, inexpensive and easy to administer. Its main drawback appears to be the momentary discomfort of the precipitated withdrawal syndrome. It should be emphasized, however, that this discomfort is rather brief and can be readily reversed. The value of the naloxone-precipitated withdrawal symptom test should be weighed against the dangers and problems of prescribing methadone to a nonaddicted or lightly addicted patient.

REFERENCES

DeAngelis, G. G.: Testing for drugs — advantages and disadvantages. *Int J Addict,* 7(2):365-385, 1972.

DeAngelis, G. G.: Testing for drugs — II; techniques and issues. *Int J Addict,* 8:997-1014, 1973.

Dole, V. P.; and Nyswander, M.: A medical treatment for diacetylmorphine (heroin) addiction. *JAMA, 193:*646-650, 1965.

Fujimoto, J. M.; and Wang, R. I. H.: A method of identifying narcotic analgesics in human urine after therapeutic doses. *Toxicol Appl Pharmacol,* 16:186-193, 1970.

Kaistha, K. K.: Drug abuse screening programs: detection procedures, development costs, street-sample analysis and field tests. *J Pharm Sci,* 61(5):655-678, 1972.

Lewis, V. S.; Peterson, D. M.; Geis, G.; and Pollack, S.: Ethical and socio-psychological aspects of urinalysis to detect heroin use. *Br J Addict,* 67:303-307, 1972.

Mulé, S. J.: Routine identification of drugs of abuse in human urine. I. Application of fluorometry, thin-layer and gas liquid chromatography. *J Chromatogr, 55:*255-266, 1971a.

Mulé, S. J.; Bastos, M. L.; Jukofsky, D.; and Saffer, E.: Routine identification of drugs of abuse in human urine. II. Development and application of the XAD-2 resin column method. *J Chromatogr, 63:*289-301, 1971b.

Mulé, S. J.; Bastos, M. L.; and Jukofsky, D. J.: Evaluation of immunoassay methods for detection, in urine, of drugs subject to abuse. *Clin Chem,* 20:243-248, 1974.

Roerig, D. L.; Lewand, D.; Mueller, M.; and Wang, R. I. H.: Methods of identification and confirmation of abusive drugs in human urine. *J Chromatogr, 110:*349-359, 1975a.

Roerig, D. L.; Lewand, D.; Mueller, M. A.; and Wang, R. I. H.: Comparison of radioimmunoassay with thin-layer chromatographic and gas-liquid chromatographic methods of barbiturate detection in human urine. *Clin Chem, 21:*672-675, 1975b.

Wang, R. I. H.; and Mueller, M. A.: Identification of barbiturates in urine. *J Pharm Sci, 62:*2047-2049, 1973.

Wang, R. I. H.; Wiesen, R. L.; Lamid, S.; and Roh, B.: Rating the presence and severity of opiate dependence. *Clin Pharmacol Ther, 16:*653-658, 1974.

Wiesen, R. L.; Rich, C. R.; Wang, R. I. H.; and Stockdale, S. L.: The safety and value of naloxone as a therapeutic aid. *Drug Alcohol Dep, 2:*123-130, 1977.

Part III

Outcome

Outcome evaluation and accountability are receiving increased attention among social programs that are competing for scarce funds. From the beginning, program evaluation was considered an integral part of the VA Management Systems in its Alcohol and Drug Abuse Programs and this interest is continuing into the present, where computer technology is being planned and implemented to assist the VA in evaluation activities.

In this section, Ted Lorei describes both the process and outcome of centrally directed evaluation research projects. He summarizes the effects of VA treatment for drug dependence at eleven-month and fourty-four-month follow-up periods, and the effects of VA treatment of alcoholic and drug dependent patients treated in traditional and in combined treatment settings at both six-month and twenty-four-month follow-up periods. Although this chapter is written within a substance abuse framework, the general goal-oriented approach to evaluation research is applicable to any human service program and therefore may be of interest to a broad audience.

Most evaluation research is conducted at the field level. In contrast to multiple program comparison, field research usually evaluates a specific program or components of a particular program. Bale's chapter is written from the field level and reports on a large scale evaluation study of therapeutic communities under the auspices of the Palo Alto VA Medical Center. This study includes an outcome report on the therapeutic community clinically described by Zarcone in this present volume.

Bale reviews previous research studies concerned with outcome results in residential treatment settings, and then reports on the results of comparing three distinct types of treatment approaches among three therapeutic communities. He also discusses ways for other programs to compute the amount of staff time necessary to conduct this type of evaluation research and presents ways of ensuring high return rates on follow-up activities. A particular advantage of his research strategy was the use of random assignment (often difficult in previous research in this area), the use of multiple outcome material and objective assessments, and a built-in follow-up period. Finally, he discusses the importance of presenting research results to program staff.

CHAPTER 12

GOAL-ORIENTED OUTCOME EVALUATION IN DRUG DEPENDENCE TREATMENT PROGRAMS

THEODORE W. LOREI

INTRODUCTION AND OVERVIEW

In this chapter I am concerned with the evaluation of the *outcome* (impact on patient performance) of drug dependence treatment, not of the *effort* expended in such treatment (such as number of programs opened, number of staff hired, or number of services provided). Second, the adjective "goal-oriented" reflects of our special effort to assure the relevance of outcome measures to program goals by first carefully defining these goals. Although this may seem like an obvious step, we felt that evaluation research has too often been attempted without adequate attention to the careful definition of program goals. Finally, the title indicates that our topic is the drug dependence treatment (and to a lesser extent, alcohol dependence treatment) provided by the Veterans Administration (VA). This chapter describes only evaluation research conducted since 1973 under the direction of staff in VA Central Office; it does not deal with evaluation research initiated by field staff.

Often research is of interest primarily to other researchers: however, I do not believe that evaluation research falls into that category. How can administrators and clinicians not be interested in the formulation of program goals and in the measurement of the attainment of these goals? Surely these are issues that are central to the very fabric of rational program administration and responsible treatment. Further, a minute's reflection will convince almost anyone that an informal evaluation process is already an intrinsic component of service planning and delivery. If informal evaluation is good, is not formal evaluation even better?

The four studies described here have been previously reported in greater detail in internal VA documents. Although space limitations here have required some abbreviation (several of the tables in the original reports have been omitted and the description of the statistical procedures has been shortened), this loss is compensated for by the opportunity to have all four studies described in one easily accessible publication. A common outline has been used for each study: Background and Study Questions, Method, and Results. Most of the results are in tabular form and the reader is encouraged to make the modest investment of effort necessary to follow that presentation. To avoid unnecessary repetition, a single discussion section has been written in which the broader meaning of the study results are considered.

STUDY 1 — EVALUATION OF VA DRUG DEPENDENCE TREATMENT (11-MONTH FOLLOW-UP)

Background and Study Questions

This study was initiated in 1973 during the expansion of drug dependence treatment in the Veterans Administration. It was done in response to the increasing interest in evaluation among those in the VA Central Office responsible for the national drug dependence program, as well as in response to requests from the Special Action Office for Drug Abuse Prevention (SAODAP).

The study was intended to answer the following questions:

1. How much had patient performance (relative to the goals of treatment listed below) improved over the eleven months from admission to follow-up?
2. Considered from an absolute perspective, how adequate was patient performance at follow-up?
3. How satisfied were patients with the way they were treated and with the results of their treatment?
4. To what extent was follow-up performance related to: (a) patient background and performance just before admis-

sion, (b) length of treatment, and (c) place of treatment?

Patient performance during the four weeks prior to admission and four weeks prior to the eleven-month anniversary of admission was measured with reference to the following goals of drug dependence treatment:

1. To eliminate the nonprescribed use of drugs in drug-dependent patients.
2. To develop the work skills and attitudes necessary to become or remain self-supporting in the community.
3. To eliminate antisocial (criminal) activities.
4. To enable them to establish and maintain stable living arrangements, that is, arrangements that assure adequate food, clothing, and shelter.
5. To improve and maintain physical condition with respect to drug-related medical problems.
6. To improve abilities to relate to people in their immediate living situations (family, job, etc.).
7. To enable them to experience a sense of psychological well-being independent of the drug culture.

These goals were formulated on the basis of (a) earlier efforts to define goals for all mental health services, including those for the drug and alcohol dependent (Lorei and Caffey, 1978), and (b) intensive discussions with selected field staff from several drug-dependence treatment programs.

Measures of patient performance relative to these goals (plus measures of patient satisfaction) constituted the dependent variables of the study. "Explanation" of the variance in these variables was sought in three major independent variables: treatment (before-after), place of treatment (which of the 49 programs provided treatment?), and length of treatment. Treatment was neither controlled nor defined. It was simply whatever the "program" provided for patients. Sells' comment about treatment program evaluation is helpful here:

> Stated most generally, in treatment program evaluation, the "treatment" is defined, in the logician's terms, by extension; it is the treatment offered at a specific organization (agency, hospital, clinic, or treatment center) and the research is concerned with the results obtained by that organization, measured against its specific goals, in ad-

ministering its particular treatment program to a given population of patients (1974, p. 3).

All follow-up patients were asked how much time they had spent in inpatient or oupatient settings and whether the treatment fell into the following categories: detoxification, maintenance (methadone), maintenance (antagonists), slow methadone withdrawal, drug free, and "others." Although some attempt was made to analyze the resulting data, I do not regard these data as very meaningful. Thus, our study was exclusively a treatment program evaluation rather than a treatment type evaluation. As Sells explains, "In research or treatment type evaluation, the treatments must be defined by intention; that is, any distinguishable difference in treatment processes, purposes, and kinds of presumably therapeutic agents employed" (1974, p. 3). Our resources did not permit the identification and measurement of such differences, and, fortunately, our purposes in doing the study did not require it.

Although our primary interest was in the relationship of patient follow-up performance (and change from admission) to treatment variables, we were also interested in the relationship of these "outcome" variables to patient background and preadmission performance variables. Such relationships have traditionally been of interest to program evaluators (including psychotherapy researchers) because of the possible light they may shed on the mechanisms of patient change and because of their usefulness in identifying control dimensions for more precise evaluation research in the future.

Method

Study Plan: The overall study plan called for clinical staff members to interview patients at admission to either inpatient or outpatient treatment regarding their performance during the four weeks before admission. Contracted survey interviewers were to interview these same patients eleven months after admission regarding their performance in the preceding four weeks. In terms of the classification of research designs suggested by Campbell and Stanley (1963, p. 7), we used a one-group (patients from all treatment programs were pooled) pretest-posttest design. Because we also compared patient follow-up performance (adjusted for admission performance) across forty-nine treatment programs, our study plan could also be viewed as a self-selected version of the nonequivalent control group design (Campbell and Stanley, 1963, p. 47), except that the control groups were really comparison groups in that the patients were receiving treatment at other programs.

Patients: Admission data were collected on 4,946 patients admitted to all fifty-three drug dependence treatment programs as either inpatients or outpatients between July and December, 1973. This report focuses on a subsample of 1,655 who were randomly selected for follow-up eleven months after admission to treatment. Patients who were incarcerated at the time of follow-up were not interviewed due to the difficulty of arranging for privacy in prison.

The average age of the sample of 1,655 was 28.2 years; 57 percent were white, 19 percent had some education beyond high school, 32 percent were on probation or parole, and 61 percent had been admitted to drug dependence treatment at least once before. Heroin was reported as the primary drug of abuse for 58 percent.

A comparison of the admission characteristics of the follow-up sample (N=1,655) with the total admission group (N=4,946) showed no statistically significant differences in age, race, education, number of previous admissions for drug abuse, frequency of arrests, and self-support. The follow-up group did have more stable living arrangements (before admission), were less often referred directly from military service, and were rated as having higher motivation to stop using drugs. With the exception of the 11 percent difference on stability of living arrangements, all other differences were small.

Data Collection Forms: Two forms were devised: the Intake Form and the Eleven-Month Follow-up Form. Both were designed to assess patient performance relative to the seven goals of treatment. In addition, the Intake Form contained items for identifying data and a few patient characteristics hypothesized to be related to treatment outcome. The Eleven-Month Follow-up

Form contained items describing amount of treatment received since admission and patient satisfaction with treatment. The Intake Form was a semistructured interview guide, that is, answers or ratings on fixed alternative items were to be obtained from the patients and from other staff members, but the wording of the questions was not prescribed. The Eleven-Month Follow-up Form was designed for a somewhat more sructured interview to meet the needs of the contractor personnel. However, the original rating scales for each of the goal areas were retained to facilitate the comparison of follow-up performance with admission performance.

Procedure: The Intake Form was completed by clinical staff after interviewing patients within a short time of admission to treatment. The Eleven-Month Follow-Up Form was completed by survey interviewers as close as possible to the eleven-month anniversary of admission date. Urine samples were requested at the conclusion of the interviews and ten-dollar incentives were paid.

Data Analysis: To evaluate changes in patient behavior, we have computed both tests of statistical significance and measures of effect size. These latter measures provide a useful supplement to the tests of significance by giving some indication of substantive importance. As is well known, statistical significance does not necessarily imply practical significance. The reader should not be confused by statements such as "a change was statistically significant but small." This merely means that the change in the sample was large enough to believe that it would "hold up" under repeated study. It is a real change, but not a very large one. The effect size measures used here have been standardized so that they can be compared over variables with different measuring scales. Also, when scale units lack intrinsic meaning, such as those on a four-point rating scale (as opposed to inches, for example), these standardized effect size measures can be interpreted as small, medium, or large, as suggested by Cohen (1969). It should be noted that "effect size" does not necessarily imply causality. It merely refers to "the degree to which the phenomenon is present in the population or the degree to which the null hypothesis is false" (Cohen, 1969, pp. 9-10).

Results

Question 1 (How much improvement?): The data relevant to this question are presented in Tables 12-I through 12-IV.

In summary, the *d* statistics (effect size measure) indicate a close to large decrease in heroin use, a medium decrease of involvement in the drug culture, and a medium increase in ability to feel good without drugs. The proportion who were self-supporting had increased slightly. No statistically significant changes had occurred in frequency of arrests, in establishment of stable living arrangements, in drug-related medical problems,

TABLE 12-I

CHANGES IN INDIVIDUAL DRUG USE

Drug	Admission % using	Follow-up % using	t^a	d^b
Methadone (non-prescribed)	11.0	3.2	−8.96*	−.22
Heroin	55.3	16.1	−28.42*	−.70
Other opiates, opium preparations and synthetics	15.6	4.0	−11.73*	−.29
Cocaine	17.6	6.2	−10.47*	−.26
Barbiturates	24.2	7.7	−14.16*	−.35
Other sedatives, hypnotics and tranquilizers	19.8	9.0	−9.20*	−.23
Amphetamines	21.3	8.3	−11.67*	−.29
Cannabis sativa (marijuana or hashish)	49.7	52.3	1.72	.04
Hallucinogens	10.5	2.0	−10.61*	−.26
Alcohol (to the point of intoxication)	26.1	32.1	4.05*	.10
Others	5.7	3.5	−3.15*	−.08

Note: N = 1,655

[a]Although the percentages of 2's (using drugs, as opposed to 1's, not using drugs) are presented for convenience, *t*'s were computed using the dichotomous scores.

[b]*d* values of .20, .50, and .80 indicate small, medium, and large differences, respectively, between admission and follow-up.

*$p < .01$.

Drug Dependent Patients

TABLE 12-II

CHANGES IN TOTAL DRUG USE

Category	Admission % using	Follow-up % using	t^b	d^c
Used one or more drugs	88.1[a]	69.1	−18.68*	−.46
Used one or more drugs other than alcohol	86.0	61.7	−21.88*	−.54
Used one or more drugs other than alcohol or marijuana	81.0	32.9	−25.63*	−.63

[a]One would expect that this entry would be 100% for patients admitted to drug dependence treatment. The fact that it is not apparently reflects the fact that some patients were not using a drug "on the average of twice a week during the first four weeks" as was required to be checked "yes" on the drug items.

[b]t's were computed using the three types of total drug use scores as the basic observations.

[c]d is a standardized effect size measure proposed by Cohen. Conceptually, it is the mean of the difference scores between admission and follow-up mean divided by the standard deviation of these scores. The computational formula suggested by Cohen $d = t/\sqrt{n}$ (2.5.9) was used. In the absence of any more appropriate standards, he suggests that d values of .20, .50, and .80 indicate small, medium, and large differences, respectively.

*$p < .01$.

TABLE 12-III

CHANGES IN SELF-SUPPORT BEHAVIOR

Item	Admission $\overline{X}$	Follow-up $\overline{X}$	t	d^b
Supported self from employment (1 = No; 2 = Yes)	1.45	1.60	9.94*	.24
Supported dependents, if applicable (1 = No; 2 = Yes)	1.39	1.54	6.74*	.24
Hours of employment per week	17.84	20.93	4.88*	.12
Weekly income[a]	$66.37	$76.32	3.50*	.09
Attended school or job training (1 = No; 2 = Yes)	1.07	1.17	9.21*	.23

Note: N = 1,655

[a]The means for this variable were computed including patients with no income.

[b]d values of .20, .50, and .80 indicate small, medium, and large differences, respectively.

*$p < .01$.

TABLE 12-IV

CHANGES IN PATIENT BEHAVIOR RELEVANT TO OTHER
TREATMENT GOALS

Item	Admission $\overline{X}$	Follow-up $\overline{X}$	t	d^a
Mean number of arrests in last six months	.59	.65	1.24	.03
Stable living arrangements (1 = No; 2 = yes)	1.81	1.83	1.45	.04
Physical distress and disability (1 = Not at all; ... 4 = Severely)	1.71	1.77	2.07	.05
Difficulty in getting along with people (1 = Not at all; ... 4 = Very definitely)	1.98	1.92	−1.75	−.04
Able to feel good without drugs (1 = Not at all; ... 4 = Very definitely)	2.03	2.77	22.77*	.56
Involvement in the drug culture (1 = Not involved; ... 4 = Heavily involved)	2.81	2.05	−22.87*	−.56

Note: N = 1,655
^{a}d values of .20, .50, and .80 indicate small, medium, and large differences, respectively.
*$p < .01$.

or in interpersonal difficulties. There had been a small increase in the use of alcohol. Changes in overall use of drugs are presented in Table 12-II.

Because self-report data, particularly about drug use, are naturally suspect, the reader will be interested in knowing that the average agreement (for the 84% of the follow-up sample who provided urine samples) between reported drug use within the past forty-eight hours and the urinalysis results for the five drugs tested was 95 percent.

Question 2 (How adequate was follow-up performance?): The percentages and means in the "follow-up" columns of Tables 12-I through 12-IV indicate that 69 percent reported using a nonprescribed drug or drinking alcohol (to the point of intoxication) on the average of twice a week during the previous month. Forty percent were not economically self-supporting; 17 percent did not have stable living arrangements; 21 percent had at least moderate interpersonal difficulty; 29 percent were at least moderately involved in the drug culture; 12 percent were unable to feel good without drugs; 19 percent were at least moderately distressed by drug-related medical problems; and 36 percent had been arrested in the six months prior to follow-up.

Question 3 (How satisfied were patients?): Patients were asked at follow-up how satisfied they were with the manner in which they were treated and with the results of their treatment. Eighty-one percent reported being highly satisfied with the physical adequacy and cleanliness of the hospital/clinic; 54 percent with staff consideration and concern for patients; 48 percent with the competence of the staff; and 44 percent with the information received regarding drug abuse. With regard to the results of treatment, 82 percent felt that treatment had helped them cut down on drugs; 75 percent to improve their health; 74 percent to improve their self-confidence; and 63 percent to avoid criminal activity. Forty percent felt that the treatment program had helped them to get more education and 46 percent to improve their employment prospects. The twelve "treatment result" areas, not all of which are reported here, were written to reflect the seven treatment goals presented above.

Question 4 (Was outcome related to background and treatment?): Follow-up performance was not substantially related to a set of relatively independent "background measures" selected by factor analysis (age, type of drug use, antisocial behavior, motivation to stop drug abuse, and self-support). Multiple correlations between this set and the seven dependent variables (follow-up performance measure) ranged from .11 to .24, all statistically significant ($p < .01$) but small (see Cohen and Cohen, 1975, p. 151). The admission ratings on whether patients were self-supporting was the independent variable that was the most generally useful "predictor." Follow-up self-support was the most "predictable" of the follow-up variables.

Follow-up performance was also not substantially related to length of treatment received during the eleven-month period or to which local program provided treatment, even with statistical adjustments having been made for patient background and admission performance. There was a small and statistically significant tendency ($p < .01$) for those who had been in treatment longer to use drugs less, to be in less physical distress, and to report a greater sense of psychological well-being. Likewise, there were statistically significant ($p < .05$) and small differences in the adjusted follow-up performance of patients treated in different programs for all seven variables. There was most variation for Psychological Well-Being and least for Self-Support. Although variations across local programs were of modest size, they were of considerable interest to the staff of these programs.

STUDY 2 — EVALUATION OF VETERANS ADMINISTRATION TREATMENT OF DRUG DEPENDENT PATIENTS (44-MONTH FOLLOW-UP)

Background and Study Questions

When Study 1 had been completed, there was some discussion about conducting an additional follow-up, but no definite plans were made at that time. It was recognized that treatment might produce effects not observable within eleven months of admission and that hence a longer follow-up interval would be desirable. Some time later, it did become possible to contract for an additional follow-up and, although it was hoped to arrange for this follow-up to occur three years (36 months) from the time of admission, a number of delays resulted in a forty-four-month follow-up being conducted. The same firm that conducted the eleven-month follow-up (Macro Systems, Inc.) conducted the forty-four-month follow-up (with a subcontract to Hollander-Cohen Associates).

Study 2 was intended to answer the following questions:

1. How much had patient performance (relative to the seven goals of drug dependence treatment) improved over the forty-four months from admission to follow-up?
2. Considered from an absolute perspective, how adequate was patient performance at follow-up?
3. How satisfied were patients with the way they were treated and with the results of their treatment?

4. To what extent was follow-up performance related to (a) patient background and performance just before admission, and (b) length of treatment and place of treatment?

5. For the subsample of patients for whom data were available at admission, eleven-month follow-up, and forty-four-month follow-up, what trends in performance occurred over the three time points? In other words, how did the sizes of changes between admission and the first follow-up compare with those that occurred between the first and the second follow-up?

Patient performance during the four weeks prior to admission (to Study 1) and four weeks prior to the eleven-month and forty-four-month anniversary of admission date was measured with respect to the seven goals of drug dependence treatment. The independent and dependent variables considered in this study were identical to those considered in Study 1.

Method

Study Plan: Patients were interviewed at the time of (a) the initial admission to treatment for Study 1, (b) the eleven-month from admission point, and (c) the forty-four month from admission point. (As will be seen below, the sample selection procedure did not make it possible to interview all patients at all three time points.) The interviews were directed to assessing patient performance in the four-week periods prior to each of the three time points. The effectiveness of treatment was to be inferred from the average patient changes from admission to the two follow-up points as well as from the absolute level of performance at the two follow-up points.

Patients: The study plan called for the inclusion of all patients who were eligible for Study 1, who were still living, and for whom Intake Forms were adequately completed for Study 1. The application of these criteria resulted in a target sample of 2,269 and, of these, 1,471 (64.8%) were interviewed at the forty-four-month follow-up. The analyses reported here were performed on this group and on a subgroup of 1,182 patients who were interviewed at all three time points.

The average age *at admission* was 27 years; 61 percent were white; 20 percent had some education beyond high school; 31 percent were on probation or parole; and 60 percent had been admitted to drug dependence treatment at least once before. Heroin was reported as the primary drug of abuse for 56 percent. Comparison of the admission characteristics of the forty-four-month sample (N = 4,946) showed that the follow-up group included fewer blacks, were younger, and had more stable living arrangements before admission. With the exception of the 10 percent difference in stability of living arrangements, all other differences were small.

Data Collection Forms: With only minor modifications, the same forms were used that have already been described for Study 1: Intake Form, eleven-Month Follow-up Form, and forty-four-Month Follow-up Form. The latter two forms were identical except for changes in time references and in questions dealing with length of treatment.

Procedure: The Intake Form was completed by a clinical staff member while interviewing patients at or within a short time after admission. The two follow-up forms were completed by contracted survey interviewers as close as possible to the eleven-month and forty-four-month anniversary date. Urine samples were requested at the end of the interviews and ten-dollar incentives were paid.

Data Analysis: The statistical procedures applied in Study 2 were almost identical to those applied in Study 1.

Results

Question 1 (How much improvement?): The data relevant to this question are presented in Tables 12-V through 12-VIII.

The *d* statistics indicate a large decrease in heroin use, a medium decrease in involvement in the drug culture, and a medium increase in ability to feel good without drugs. There were small decreases in the uses of all other drugs, except for marijuana and alcohol. The frequency of use of marijuana did not change; however, the frequency of use of alcohol increased slightly. There were also small improvements in self-support and related variables, in average number of arrests, stability of

TABLE 12-V

PERCENTAGES OF PATIENTS USING SPECIFIC DRUGS AT ADMISSION
AND FOLLOW-UP AND DEGREE OF CHANGE

Drug	Percent Using		t^a	d^b
	Admission	Follow-up		
Methadone (non-prescribed)	11.5	2.9	9.92*	.26
Heroin	53.8	10.1	30.83*	.80
Other opiates, opium preparations and synthetics	15.8	2.6	13.31*	.35
Cocaine	17.4	4.7	11.57*	.30
Barbiturates	24.9	5.5	15.74*	.41
Other sedatives, hypnotics, and tranquilizers	19.9	8.0	9.88*	.26
Amphetamines	21.2	5.5	13.32*	.35
Cannabis sativa (marijuana or hashish)	50.6	50.4	.12	.00
Hallucinogens	11.0	1.6	10.96*	.29
Alcohol (to the point of intoxication)	25.4	29.7	−2.77*	−.07
Others	5.6	2.6	4.22*	.11

Note: N = 1,471

[a]Although the percentages of 2's (using drugs, as opposed to 1's, not using drugs) are presented for convenience, t's were computed using the dichotomous scores as interval data.

[b]d values are standardized "effect size" measures suggested by Cohen (1969). Absolute values of .20, .50, and .80 may be interpreted as indicating small, medium, and large differences, respectively, between admission and follow-up.

*$p < .01$

living arrangements, physical distress, and interpersonal difficulties.

The average percent agreement between reported drug use within the past forty-eight hours and the laboratory results for the five drugs tested was 95 percent.

A comparison of the results for Question 1 in Study 1 and Study 2 shows two striking features: (1) the relative sizes of changes remained very similar, that is, the variables showing large, medium, and small changes were nearly the same in the two studies, and (2) the sizes of the changes in Study 2 were con-

TABLE 12-VI

PERCENTAGES OF PATIENTS USING DRUGS AT ADMISSION
AND FOLLOW-UP AND DEGREE OF CHANGE

	Percent Using			
Extent of Use	*Admission*	*Follow-up*	t^a	d^b
Used one or more drugs, including alcohol to intoxication	87.8[c]	63.9	22.90*	.60
Used one or more drugs other than alcohol	86.0	56.8	26.19*	.68
Used one or more drugs other than alcohol or marijuana	80.7	25.4	28.93*	.75

Note: N = 1,471.

[a]t's were computed using the three total drug scores rather than the percentage shown in the table.

[b]d values are standardized "effect size" measures suggested by Cohen (1969). Absolute values of .20, .50, and .80 may be interpreted as indicating small, medium, and large differences, respectively, between admission and follow-up.

[c]That this entry is less than 100 percent (contrary to what one would expect at admission) may reflect the fact that some patients were not using any drug "on the average of twice a week during the past four weeks" as was required for a "yes" response on the drug use questions.

*$p < .01$.

TABLE 12-VII

MEAN SCORES ON SELF-SUPPORT VARIABLES AT ADMISSION
AND FOLLOW-UP AND DEGREE OF CHANGE

	Mean			
Variable	*Admission*	*Follow-up*	*t*	d^a
Supported self (1 = N; 2 = Yes)	1.45	1.65	−11.52*	−.30
Supported dependents, if applicable (1 = No; 2 = Yes; 3 = No dependents)[b]	1.39	1.64	−9.78*	−.39
Hours of employment per week	17.77	22.88	−6.96*	−.18
Full time employment (0 = No; 1 = Yes)	.42	.47	−3.37*	−.09
Part time employment (0 = No; 1 = Yes)	.06	.11	−4.49*	−.12
Weekly income	$63.74	$103.74	−10.44*	−.28
Attended school or job training (1 = No; 2 = Yes)	1.07	1.18	−9.20*	−.24

Note. N = 1,471.

[a]d values are standardized "effect size" measures suggested by Cohen (1969). Absolute values of .20, .50, and .80 may be interpreted as indicating small, medium, and large

Drug Dependent Patients

differences, respectively, between admission and follow-up.
[b]Patients with no dependents were excluded from this analysis.
*$p < .01$.

TABLE 12-VIII

MEAN SCORES ON OTHER PERFORMANCE VARIABLES AT ADMISSION
AND FOLLOW-UP AND DEGREE OF CHANGE

	Mean			
Variable	Admission	Follow-up	t	d[a]
Mean number of arrests in last six months	.63	.38	5.73*	.15
Arrested (0 = No; 1 = Yes)	.35	.24	7.14*	.19
Stable living arrangements (1 = No; 2 = Yes)	1.81	1.97	−12.27*	−.35
Physical distress and disability (1 = Not at all; . . . 4 = Severely)	1.70	1.60	3.08*	.08
Difficulty in getting along with people (1 = Not at all; . . . 4 = Very definitely)	2.01	1.78	6.96*	.18
Able to feel good without drugs (1 = Not at all; . . . 4 = Very definitely)	2.05	2.97	−26.16*	−.68
Involvement in the drug culture (1 = Not involved; . . . 4 = Heavily involved)	2.82	1.90	26.21*	.69

Note: N = 1,471.
[a]d values are standardized "effect size" measures suggested by Cohen (1969). Absolute values of .20, .50, and .80 may be interpreted as indicating small, medium, and large differences, respectively, between admission and follow-up.
*$p < .01$.

sistently higher than were the changes in Study 1, a very plausible set of findings given the longer time period involved. Four of the variables that did not change sufficiently ($p < .01$) over the eleven-month period (mean number of arrests, stability of living arrangements, physical distress, and interpersonal difficulties) did change significantly over the forty-four-month period. As noted above, one of the reasons for conducting the forty-four-month follow-up was the expectation that changes in some behavior, such as that resulting in arrest, requires a longer period to change.

Question 2 (How adequate was follow-up performance?): The percentages and means in the "follow-up" columns of Tables 12-V through 12-VIII indicate that 64 percent reported using a nonprescribed drug or drinking alcohol (to the point of intoxication) on the average of twice a week during the previous month. Thirty-five percent were not economically self-supporting; 3 percent did not have stable living arrangements; 17 percent had at least moderate interpersonal difficulty; 24 percent were at least moderately involved in the drug culture; 9 percent were unable to feel good without drugs; 16 percent were at least moderately distressed by drug-related medical problems; and 24 percent had been arrested in the last six months. Each of these percentages is somewhat more in the favorable direction than the comparable percentages reported for Study 1.

Question 3 (How satisfied were patients?): As in Study 1, patients were asked at follow-up how satisfied they were with the manner in which they were treated and with the results of their treatment. Eighty-one percent reported being highly satisfied with the physical adequacy and cleanliness of the hospital/clinic; 55 percent with the staff consideration and concern for patients; 51 percent with the competence of the staff; and 50 percent with the information received regarding drug abuse. With regard to the results of treatment, 80 percent felt that treatment had helped them cut down on drugs; 77 percent to improve their health: 74 percent to improve their self-confidence; and 62 percent to avoid criminal activity. Forty-six percent felt that the treatment program had helped them to get more education and 48 percent to improve their employment prospects. The twelve "treatment result" areas, not all of which are reported here, were written to index the seven general treatment goals. The percentages reported here were quite similar to those reported for Study 1.

Question 4 (Was outcome related to background and treatment?): As was true in Study 1, follow-up performance was not importantly related to a set of relatively independent "background measures" selected by factor analysis (age, type of drug use, antisocial behavior, motivation to stop drug abuse, and self-support). Multiple correlations between this set and the seven dependent variables (follow-up performance measure) ranged from .08 to .16, three of which were statistically significant (p < .01). The admission rating on desire to stop drug use was the most generally useful "predictor." Ability to feel good without drugs was the most "predictable" of the follow-up variables.

Follow-up performance (except for degree of physical distress) was not related to length of treatment received during the forty-four-month period, statistical adjustments having been made for patient background and admission performance. There was a very small tendency for those who had been in treatment longer to report a higher degree of physical distress. The length of treatment outcome relationships were, thus, even weaker than those reported in Study 1.

In contrast, the differences in *adjusted* follow-up (by analysis of covariance) performance of patients treated in different programs were somewhat larger (than in Study 1) for several variables (total drug score, self-support, number of arrests, interpersonal difficulty, and ability to feel good without drug use). Interprogram difference for total drug use, self-support, interpersonal difficulty, and ability to feel good without drug use fell into the medium category, using the eta (η) statistics suggested by Cohen (1969, pp. 278-281). The last variable varied most across programs.

Question 5 (What was the trend in patient performance over time?): A series of repeated measures analyses of variance for all of the variables listed in Tables 12-V through 12-VIII was run for the 1,182 patients for whom data were available for admission and both follow-up points. The results suggested that the (a) majority of variables changed most between admission and the eleven-month follow-up and then changed very little after that (most of the drug use variables and economic self-support fell into this category), and (b) a few variables continued to change across all three time points (this group included number of arrests, stability of living arrangements, physical distress, and difficulty in getting along with others). A full display of our results relevant to this question is provided in Tables 12-IX through 12-XII.

TABLE 12-IX

PERCENTAGES OF PATIENTS USING SPECIFIC DRUGS AT ADMISSION
AND AT TWO FOLLOW-UP POINTS AND DEGREE OF CHANGE

Drug	N	Percent Admission	11-Month	44-Month	F^a	ω^b
Methadone (non-prescribed)	1,168	11.4	3.3	2.8	57.52*	.17
Heroin	1,170	53.6	15.0	10.2	519.01*	.44
Other opiates, opium preparations and synthetics	1,168	15.3	3.9	2.9	91.60*	.22
Cocaine	1,169	17.5	5.6	4.5	80.88*	.20
Barbiturates	1,168	24.8	8.0	5.3	142.79*	.26
Other sedatives, hypnotics and tranquilizers	1,168	20.6	9.2	7.6	60.05*	.17
Amphetamines	1,168	21.5	8.6	5.6	95.11*	.21
Cannabis sativa (marijuana or hashish)	1,168	50.6	53.9	49.6	3.26	.03
Hallucinogens	1,168	11.0	2.2	1.3	81.36*	.20
Alcohol (to the point of intoxication)^c	1,169	26.5	33.2	29.2	7.81*	.06
Others	1,151	5.6	3.4	2.7	6.98*	.06

Note. Percentages sharing a common underline do not differ significantly ($p < .01$).
^{a}Although the percentages of 2's (using drugs, as opposed to 1's, not using drugs) are presented for convenience, F's were computed using the dichotomous scores.
$^b\omega$ values of .10, .24, and .37 indicate small, medium, and large differences, respectively.
^{c}The difference between admission and 44-month percentages is not significant, but, since the percentages are not in rank order for this variable, the underlining cannot show this.
*$p < .01$.

TABLE 12-X

PERCENTAGE OF PATIENTS USING DRUGS AT ADMISSION AND AT TWO
FOLLOW-UP POINTS AND DEGREE OF CHANGE

Extent of Use	Percent Using at Admission	11-Month Follow-up	44-Month Follow-up	F^a	ω^b
Used one or more drugs, including alcohol to intoxication	87.8^c	70.7	62.7	251.99*	.33
Used one or more drugs other than alcohol	86.0	62.6	55.8	355.01*	.37
Used one or more drugs other than alcohol or marijuana	80.8	31.6	24.8	455.43*	.43

Note. N = 1,182. Pairwise tests indicated that the percentages at all three time points differed significantly. ($p < .01$)
^{a}F's were computed using the three total drug scores rather than the percentages shown in the table.

[b]ω (or ω^2) is a standardized strength of association or "effect size" measure suggested by Kirk (1969, p. 134) for single factor repeated measures designs. Since this statistic is analogous to η suggested by Cohen (1969) for ordinary single-factor designs, Cohen's suggested standards for interpretation (.10 = small; .24 = medium; .37 = large; 1969, pp. 277-281) may be applied here.

[c]That this entry is less than 100 percent (as one would expect at admission) may reflect the fact that some patients were not using any drug "on the average of twice a week" as was required for a "yes" response on the drug use questions.

*$p < .01$.

TABLE 12-XI
MEAN SCORES ON SELF-SUPPORT VARIABLES AT ADMISSION AND
AT TWO FOLLOW-UP POINTS AND DEGREE OF CHANGE

Mean

Item	N	Admission	11-Month Follow-up	44-Month Follow-up	F	ω^a
Supported self from employment (1 = No; 2 = Yes)	1,171	1.46	1.62	1.66	63.95*	.17
Supported dependents, if applicable (1 = No; 2 = Yes)	460	1.40	1.61	1.66	47.09*	.23
Hours of employment per week	1,182	17.76	22.12	23.13	28.11*	.11
Full time employment (0 = No; 1 = Yes)	1,182	.41	.48	.48	10.73*	.04
Part time employment (0 = No; 1 = Yes)	1,182	.06	.11	.11	14.13*	.08
Weekly income[b]	1,145	$66.19	$80.78	$106.50	57.43*	.16
Attended school or job training (1 = No; 2 = Yes)	1,175	1.07	1.17	1.18	42.99*	.15

Note. Means sharing a common underline do not differ significantly ($p < .01$). The means for this variable were computed including patients with no income.

[a]ω values of .10, .24, and .37 indicate small, medium, and large differences, respectively.

[b]The means for this variable were computed including patients with no income.

*$p < .01$.

STUDY 3 — EVALUATION OF THE PILOT ALCOHOL AND DRUG ABUSE TREATMENT (PADAT) PROJECT

Background and Study Questions

The Pilot Alcohol and Drug Abuse Treatment (PADAT) Project was initiated in 1974 to evaluate the relative effectiveness of treating alcohol dependent patients and drug dependent patients on the same inpatient wards versus treating them on separate wards as has traditionally been done in most treatment settings. To examine this issue, ten combined treatment units

TABLE 12-XII

MEAN SCORES ON OTHER PERFORMANCE VARIABLES AT ADMISSION
AND AT TWO FOLLOW-UP POINTS AND DEGREE OF CHANGE

Item	N	Admission	Mean 11-Month Follow-up	44-Month Follow-up	F	ω^a
Number of arrests in the last six months	1,165	.57	.63	.37	18.53*	.09
Arrested (0 = No; 1 = Yes)	1,182	.33	.34	.23	24.58*	.11
Stable living arrangements (1 = No; 2 = Yes)	1,016	1.81	1.85	1.97	65.61*	.21
Physical distress and disability (1 = Not at all; ...4 = Severely)	1,176	1.71	1.76	1.59	13.24*	.08
Difficulty in getting along with people (1 = Not at all; ...4 = Very definitely)	1,176	2.00	1.92	1.76	22.98*	.10
Able to feel good without drugs (1 = Not at all; ...4 = Very definitely)	1,174	2.05	2.82	2.98	348.04*	.38
Involvement in the drug culture (1 = Not involved; ...4 = Heavily involved)	1,172	2.80	2.05	1.90	330.89*	.37

Note. Means sharing a common underline do not differ significantly ($p < .01$).

[a] ω (omega) values of .10, .24, and .37 indicate small, medium, and large differences, respectively.

*$p < .01$.

(called Pilot Alcohol and Drug Abuse Treatment Units — PADATU's) were formed by admitting alcohol-dependent patients to units that were formerly used exclusively for drug-dependent patients. The follow-up performance of patients treated in these combined units were compared with the performance of patients treated in fourteen "conventional" units, that is, seven Alcohol Dependence Treatment Programs (ADTP's) and seven Drug Dependence Treatment Programs (DDTP's).

Although medical traditions would have drug and alcohol abuses treated in separate treatment settings, there has been a growing interest expressed by clinicians toward providing treatment in combined settings. The Eagleville Hospital and Rehabilitation Center in Eagleville, Pennsylvania has been par-

ticularly well known for its combined treatment program (Ottenberg and Orsen, 1971). This interest in combined treatment
has evolved from both theoretical and practical considerations.
Some theoretical formulations regard alcohol dependence and
other drug dependence as similar behavior used to escape unpleasant affects and to produce more desired emotional states
(Freed, 1973). Behavioral dysfunctions with similar causal
mechanisms would suggest similar forms of intervention. Also,
there may be therapeutic value in having patients with diverse
dependency problems live together.

Practical considerations also make combined treatment potentially desirable. Many patients use both alcohol and other
drugs dysfunctionally, and, in numerous cases, no clear basis
exists for assigning these patients to one substance-abuse treatment setting rather than another. Further, it has been posited
that combined settings would promote more flexible utilization
of hospital space, personnel, and equipment and, thereby, provide more efficient and economical services. For example, if the
population of drug abusers decreased in a given facility, the beds
or clinic spots could be assigned to alcohol abusers. Therefore, it
is both desirable and timely that we reexamine the effectiveness
and efficiency of traditional practices of conventional separation.

The study was intended to answer the following questions:

1. To what degree (if any) did the improvement in the performance (relative to treatment goals) of alcohol dependent patients and drug dependent patients over a six-month
   period from admission to treatment differ according to
   whether treatment was provided in a combined or conventional setting?
2. How much did patient performance improve over the
   six-month period, irrespective of treatment setting?
3. Considered from an absolute perspective, how adequate
   was patient (both alcohol dependent and drug dependent)
   performance at followup (six months after admission)?
4. How satisfied were patients with the way they were treated
   and with the results of their treatment?
5. To what extent was follow-up performance related to (a)

patient background and performance just before admission and (b) length of treatment?

Patient performance during the four weeks prior to admission and prior to the six-month anniversary of admission date was measured with reference to the treatment goals.

The goals reflect further specification of those discussed in Study 1 and their "format" was influenced by considerations borrowed from educational literature on instructional goals (see Lorei, 1979).

Measures of patient performance relative to these goals, as well as measures of patient satisfaction, constituted the dependent variables of the study. Explanation of variance in these variables was sought in terms of type of treatment (combined versus conventional), length of treatment, use of Antabuse® (no or yes), and use of methadone (no or yes). As in the previous two studies, although our prime interest was in the independent variables indexing treatment, we were also interested in the relationship of the dependent variables (outcome measures) to patient background and preadmission performance variables.

The study was naturalistic or observational, that is, no attempt was made to influence assignment of patients to units or to determine the treatment they were to receive. However, treatment staff were instructed to follow these general guidelines:

1. A substantial period of inpatient treatment, usually at least thirty days, should be provided to all appropriate incoming patients.

2. Outpatient treatment should be provided at the completion of inpatient treatment, as appropriate.

3. No attempt should be made to limit admission to "good" patients. Applicants, however, who could not be expected to participate in treatment because of severe medical or psychiatric disabilities should not be admitted (until their condition improved).

4. Combined settings should strive to keep a balanced mix of alcohol-dependent and drug-dependent patients. At no time should the patients in either category fall below 33 percent or exceed 67 percent. Conventional settings

should limit their admission to the appropriate patient
category.

Method

Study Plan: The overall study plan called for clinical staff to
interview patients at admission to inpatient treatment regarding
their performance during the four weeks before admission.
They were also to interview these same patients again six months
later regarding their performance during the four weeks prior
to the interview. The alcohol-dependent patients and the drug-
dependent patients were to be regarded as two separate groups
for the purpose of the data analyses. The changes in each group
over the six-month study period was to be compared between the
two types of treatment centers, combined and conventional. In
terms of the Campbell and Stanley classification of research designs, we were using something like a self-selected version of the
nonequivalent control group design (Campbell and Stanley,
1963, p. 47), except that the control group was really a comparison group in that another form of treatment was being provided.
We also analyzed the data for the two patient groups, ignoring
type of treatment setting. This procedure followed the pretest-
posttest paradigm (see Campbell and Stanley, 1963, p. 7).

Patients: Basic demographic data were obtained for 5,265
veterans who made contact with each of the twenty-four selected
treatment facilities between July and December, 1975. Of these,
2,813 (53%) were admitted to inpatient treatment, and 1,025
(36% of the inpatient admissions) remained in inpatient treatment for at least thirty days. From this group, a randomly
selected sample of 886 patients was designated for follow-up,
and 686 patients from this sample (77% of the targeted sample)
were interviewed at follow-up. This 'follow-up' sample is the
major focus of the present report.

Data Collection Forms: Fixed-alternative card punchable
forms were designed to provide (1) a brief description of the veteran at the first contact (Intake Screening Record), (2) a complete initial assessment of the veteran's background and status
relative to the eight treatment goals listed above, (3) patient
opinion about his or her goals for treatment, (4) a description of

the patient's status at follow-up (six months after admission), with specific reference to the eight treatment goals and a description of the treatment received since admission (Follow-up Interview Record), and (5) the patient's opinions about the extent to which he or she had achieved his or her treatment goals and his or her satisfaction with treatment (Patient's Opinion about Treatment).

The three interview forms were semistructured interview guides, i.e., answers or ratings were to be obtained on a fixed set of items, but the manner of developing the information was not narrowly prescribed. The remaining forms were self-administered questionaires.

Procedure: The basic study procedure involved the following steps:

1. Minimum data were collected on all applicants for VA care.
2. Complete data were collected on all applicants admitted to inpatient treatment.
3. A random sample of inpatients was selected for follow-up assessment six months after admission. Patients had to have completed an inpatient program of at least twenty-one days to be eligible for follow-up.
4. Located and cooperative patients in the designated follow-up sample were interviewed in the hospital or in the community, depending on where they were living at that time.

All interviewing was done by VA staff who had been specifically trained in the use of the data collection forms. Unlike Studies 1 and 2, urine samples were not collected.

Admission data collection began in July 1975 in ten Pilot Alcohol and Drug Abuse Treatment Units (PADATU's), seven Alcohol Dependence Treatment Programs (ADTP's), and seven Drug Dependence Treatment Programs (DDTP's) and continued for six months. Six-month follow-up interviews began in February 1976 and ended in August, 1976.

Results

Question 1 (Was improvement different for combined versus conventional settings?): First, I must point out that, although it is convenient to talk in.terms of relative improvement, the actual statistical analysis used compared the mean levels of patient performance at follow-up, after adjustments were made (by means of analysis of covariance) for level of admission performance. The results are the same, however. Thus, the finding that alcohol-dependent patients treated in conventional settings drank to intoxication less frequently at followup than those treated in combined settings is equivalent to saying that patients in conventional settings, on the average, improved more with respect to drinking than those treated in combined settings. We found similar results, that is better results for the conventional settings for each of the following variables: alcohol problem, perception and thinking problems, financial dependence on friends or relatives, self-support problems, management of own affairs, arrests for assaults, and dangerous behavior problems.

Some of these variables are, of course, highly intercorrelated due in part to their redundancy; some are specific items included in some of the more general variables listed. The following more or less independent dimensions seems to be involved: (a) alcohol use problems, (b) perception and thinking problems, (c) self-support problems, (d) management of own affairs, and (e) dangerous behavior problems.

Although the differences just described were statistically significant ($p < .05$), it should be noted that they were not large. Using eta (η), an "effect" size measure suggested by Cohen (1969), we found the differences were small.

The adjusted mean follow-up performance of the drug dependent patients treated in combined settings differed significantly ($p < .05$) from that of those treated in conventional settings on only four variables: attending school or job training, receiving funds from welfare, number of arrests for drug violations other than for possession, and traffic violations other than driving while drunk.

Although the differences on those variables were statistically significant ($p < .05$), according to the *eta* values, they were quite small. For each variable, patients performed better in conventional settings.

Question 2 (How much improvement, regardless of setting?): Although Question 1 was the primary question motivating the study, the data collected also provided an opportunity to examine patient change (and, by inference, treatment effective-

TABLE 12-XIII

ADMISSION AND FOLLOW-UP PERFORMANCE BY PATIENT GROUP

| Variable | Alcohol-dependent patients (N = 442) | | | | | | Drug-dependent patients (N = 197) | | | | | |
	Admission $\bar{X}$	Follow-up $\bar{X}$	t	d[b]	Percent with significant problems[c] Admission	Follow-up	Admission $\bar{X}$	Follow-up $\bar{X}$	t	d[b]	Percent with significant problems[c] Admission	Follow-up
Goal 1												
Days of use of Methadone (non-prescribed)	.01	.07	-.90	-.04	0.0%	0.2%	1.53	.49	3.09*	.22	10.2%	4.6%
Heroin	.31	.04	1.95	.09	1.1	0.2	15.64	2.55	14.83*	1.05	62.0	17.0
Other opiates, opium, other than heroin or methadone	.00	.01	.00	.00	0.0	0.0	1.71	.28	3.72*	.26	11.7	2.5
Cocaine	.10	.04	1.02	-.06	0.5	0.2	2.19	.24	5.00*	.36	14.7	2.5
Barbiturates	.35	.07	2.64*	.12	2.5	0.7	2.87	.60	4.63*	.33	17.3	2.5
Other sedatives, hypnotics, or tranquilizers	.67	.21	2.49*	.12	4.8	1.4	2.92	.91	3.56*	.25	19.3	5.1
Amphetamines	.11	.06	.73	.03	0.5	0.7	1.41	.35	3.70*	.26	11.7	2.0
Cannabis sativa (marijuana or hashish)	.89	.74	.62	.03	5.2	3.4	9.24	5.98	3.77*	.27	54.0	43.0
Hallucinogens such as LSD	.00	.06	-.96	-.05	0.0	0.2	.16	.16	-.03	-.00	1.5	0.5
Alcohol	18.89	7.15	18.41*	.87	79.0	27.0	9.22	6.46	3.36*	.24	49.0	47.0
Alcohol (to intoxication)	15.15	4.53	17.69*	.83	0.8	0.2	3.75	1.82	3.29*	.23	22.0	12.2
Other drugs	.23	.03	1.65	.08			.42	.22	.82	.06	2.7	1.0
Goal 2												
Medical problem[a]	3.00	2.19	10.56*	.50	40.1	18.8	2.47	1.83	6.11*	.44	22.8	10.7
Goal 3												
Psychological problems[a] Perception and thinking	2.84	1.76	15.19*	.73	35.8	11.4	2.10	1.57	5.90*	.42	18.3	8.7
Mood and self-esteem	4.03	2.69	18.52	.89	74.4	29.5	3.49	2.53	8.56*	.61	59.4	23.0

ness) for the two patient groups prescinding from differences in treatment setting. The results of our analyses are summarized in Table 12-XIII.

As the *d* statistics indicate, the alcohol-dependent patients

TABLE 12-XIII (continued)
ADMISSION AND FOLLOW-UP PERFORMANCE BY PATIENT GROUP

Variable	Alcohol-dependent patients (N = 442)						Drug-dependent patients (N = 197)					
	Admission $\bar{X}$	Follow-up $\bar{X}$	t	d[b]	Percent with significant problems[c] Admission	Follow-up	Admission $\bar{X}$	Follow-up $\bar{X}$	t	d[b]	Percent with significant problems[c] Admission	Follow-up
Goal 4												
Interpersonal problem[a]	3.54	2.27	16.82*	.80	55.9%	19.7%	3.43	2.54	8.31*	.59	51.8%	26.0%
Goal 5												
Total hours worked	43.79	70.54	−6.87*	.20	80.0	63.0	27.18	59.11	−5.27*	−.39	88.0	67.0
Full-time employment (0 = No; 1 = Yes)	.21	.38	−6.63*	−.32	79.2	62.0	.16	.33	−4.37*	−.31	84.0	67.0
Net earnings	$153.94	$256.88	−6.35*	−.31	72.0	56.0	$117.62	$235.49	−4.05*	−.30	79.0	64.0
Funds from:												
Welfare	1.10	1.10	.00	.00	10.0	10.2	1.11	1.15	−1.00	−.07	11.2	14.5
VA compensation/pension	1.26	1.27	−.54	−.03	25.4	26.5	1.15	1.24	−2.70*	−.02	14.2	24.1
Friends/relatives	1.39	1.36	.99	.05	39.0	36.3	1.46	1.51	−1.09*	−.08	45.2	50.8
Illegal activities	1.03	1.02	1.79	.09	3.4	1.6	1.50	1.17	8.72*	.63	50.0	16.8
Self-support problem[a]	3.53	2.45	12.11*	.58	58.4	29.2	3.50	2.73	5.90*	.42	56.1	31.0
Goal 6												
Self-management problem[a]	3.09	2.10	11.12*	.53	45.0	19.0	3.08	2.43	4.73*	.34	44.4	23.9
Goal 7												
Number of arrests for:												
Violation of drug laws — simple possession	.01	.00	1.13	.05	0.7	0.2	.24	.07	3.52*	.25	17.8	6.1
Violation of drug laws — all other violations including possession with intent to distribute	.00	.00	.00	.00	0.2	0.2	.09	.02	2.91*	.21	7.6	1.5
Public intoxication	.40	.13	4.71*	.22	18.3%	7.0%	.07	.03	1.38	.10	4.6%	2.6%
Disorderly conduct or vagrancy	.08	.02	3.71*	.18	5.2	1.6	.08	.03	2.06*	.15	6.1	2.0
Driving while intoxicated	.21	.03	6.85*	.32	16.3	1.8	.09	.02	2.18*	.16	6.6	2.0

made large improvements in regard to frequency of drinking to intoxication, problems in the area of mood and self-esteem, interpersonal relations, and attaining satisfaction from socially acceptable activities. Medium improvements occurred in the areas

TABLE 12-XIII (continued)

ADMISSION AND FOLLOW-UP PERFORMANCE BY PATIENT GROUP

Variable	Alcohol-dependent patients (N = 442)				Percent with significant problems[c]		Drug-dependent patients (N = 197)				Percent with significant problems[c]	
	Admis-sion X̄	Follow-up X̄	t	d[b]	Admis-sion	Follow-up	Admis-sion X̄	Follow-up X̄	t	d[b]	Admis-sion	Follow-up
Other violations of traffic and motor vehicle laws	.10	.04	2.91*	.14	6.8	2.9	.18	.03	2.37*	.17	8.1	2.6
Homicide, manslaughter, forcible rape	.00	.00	.58	.03	0.5	0.2	.03	.00	.00	.00	2.5	0.0
Assaults	.03	.02	.76	.04	2.3	1.4	.13	.02	2.94*	.21	8.1	1.0
Robbery	.00	.00	.00	.00	0.5	0.5	.13	.04	2.31*	.16	8.6	3.1
Burglary, larceny, auto theft	.02	.00	1.89	.09	1.6	0.2	.25	.08	2.58*	.18	14.7	6.6
All other offenses	.05	.01	3.32*	.16	3.6	0.7	.13	.07	1.59	.11	9.2	5.6
Total arrests	.87	.22	6.74*	.32	38.3	11.8	1.41	.36	3.88*	.28	45.2	21.9
Dangerous behavior problem[a]	2.35	1.43	11.97*	.57	24.4	6.3	3.01	1.85	2.61*	.69	43.1	11.8
Goal 8												
Problem in obtaining satisfaction from socially acceptable activities[a]	4.28	2.62	21.14*	1.01	81.9	28.4	3.92	2.85	9.06*	.65	72.1	35.7

[a]Scale points were defined as follows: 1 = No problem; 2 = Minimal problem; 3 = Mild problem; 4 = Moderate problem; 5 = Marked problem

[b]d values of .20, .50, and .80 indicate small, medium, and large differences respectively between admission and follow-up (Cohen, 1969)

[c]A patient was considered as having a "significant problem" on a given variable according to the following standards:
  • Rating scale scores higher than 3 on the variables: Medical problem; Psychological problems; Interpersonal problem; Self-management problem; Dangerous behavior problem; and Problem in obtaining satisfaction from socially acceptable activities.
  • Used drugs or alcohol (to intoxication) four or more days in the last four weeks
  • Worked less than 120 hours
  • Earned less than $200
  • Received funds from welfare, VA compensation, friends/relatives, illegal activities
  • Was arrested one or more times

*p < .05

of physical health, perception and thinking, rated self-support (but, strangely, not in employment), management of own affairs, and dangerous behavior. Small changes occurred in regard to employment and arrests.

The drug-dependent patients made large improvements in regard to only one area, frequency of heroin use. Medium improvements occurred in the areas of mood and self-esteem, interpersonal problems, obtaining income from illegal activities, dangerous behavior, and obtaining satisfaction from socially acceptable activities. There were small changes in several areas of drug use, medical problems, perception and thinking, employment, management of own affairs, and number of arrests.

Question 3 (How adequate was follow-up performance?): The data relevant to this question appears in the two columns labelled "Percent with significant problems — Follow-up" in Table 12-XIII. Before commenting on these results, however, it is of interest to note that 65 percent of the alcohol-dependent patients maintained sobriety for the month prior to follow-up and 52 percent of the drug dependent patients did not use any nonprescribed drugs (other than marijuana) in the same time period (these results are not shown in Table 12-XIII).

Returning to the "significant problems" at follow-up in Table 12-XIII, we see that, for the alcohol-dependent patients, 27 percent had such problems with drinking excessively; 19 percent, with medical problems; 30 percent, with mood and self-esteem; 20 percent, with interpersonal problems; 62 percent, with not having full-time employment; 19 percent, with managing own affairs; and 28 percent, with obtaining satisfaction from socially acceptable activities. Considering the drug-dependent patients, we see that 17 percent had significant problems with heroin use; 12 percent, with excessive drinking; 11 percent, with medical problems; 23 percent with mood and self-esteem; 26 percent, with interpersonal problems; 67 percent, with not having full-time employment; 24 percent, with management of own affairs; 22 percent, with being arrested; and 36 percent, with obtaining satisfaction from socially acceptable activities. As with similar percentages presented for Studies 1 and 2, there is a problem in interpreting their meaning without some kind of standard. In the absence of any other standard, one can compare these percentages with an ideal of 0 percent or 100 percent, depending on the variable, such as heroin use or full-time employment.

Question 4 (How satisfied were patients?): As in the other studies, patients were asked at follow-up how satisfied they were with the manner in which they were treated and with the results of their treatment. Here, however, our interest was more the relative levels of satisfaction in combined and conventional treatment settings rather than with their absolute levels of satisfaction. Alcohol-dependent patients treated in conventional settings were more satisfied on all "manner of treatment" variables than were those treated in combined settings. The differences on all nine of these variables (with the exception of "consideration of non-program facility staff") were of medium size. The difference on the "consideration" variable was statistically significant (p < .05), but small.

In contrast, the differences between all but two of the means on the nine variables for drug-dependent patients treated in the two settings did not differ statistically. Those treated in conventional settings were slightly more satisfied with staff interest in patients and moderately less satisfied with the consideration of nonprogram facility staff.

When satisfaction with the results of treatment (alcohol-dependent patients) in the two types of settings were compared, five of the twenty-six variables examined differed significantly (p < .05), with small effect sizes. *In each case, more of the patients treated in conventional settings felt they had made progress toward their treatment goals than did those in the combined settings.* None of these same variables differed significantly for the drug-dependent patients treated in the two types of settings.

Question 5 (Was outcome related to background and treatment?): In contrast to the previous studies, here we examined the relationships to follow-up performance of patient background characteristics and of preadmission performance separately. As might be expected, the relationships of the latter group were stronger. First, I will summarize the relationships for the two sets of predictor variables for the alcohol-dependent patients.

The background variables selected, based on previous analyses of a much larger set, were as follows: age, race, years of education, recent employment, and previous time in treatment. The multiple correlations with the follow-up performance variables ranged from .05 (p > .05) for dangerous behavior to .30 (p < .05) for problems with health and with managing one's own affairs. The multiple correlations resulting from the use of preadmission performance variables ranged from .21 (p < .05) for severity of alcohol problems to .43 (p < .05) for problems with perception and thinking.

For the drug-dependent patients, the background multiple correlations ranged from .13 (p > .05) for problems with perception and thinking to .36 (p < .05) for medical problems. For the preadmission performance variables, the multiple correlations ranged from .21 (p > .05) for problems in obtaining satisfaction from socially acceptable activities to .46 (p < .05) for problems with perception and thinking.

Length of treatment of the alcohol-dependent patients (adjusted for patient characteristics assessed at admission) was not related at all to follow-up performance, except for one (out of nine) variable. There was a small tendency for those in treatment longer to have less problems with perception and thinking. In contrast, for the drug-dependent patients, all follow-up performance variables, except problems with self-support, were related to length of treatment and the statistically significant (p < .05) semipartial correlation coefficients ranged from − .20 for medical problems to − .47 for problems in obtaining satisfaction from socially acceptable activities. All the coefficients indicated that longer treatment was associated with more favorable follow-up performance.

The use or nonuse of Antabuse by alcohol-dependent patients was correlated with follow-up performance (with adjustments being made for initial characteristics). The resulting semipartial correlation coefficient showed statistically significant (p < .05) and small negative relationships between receiving Antabuse and follow-up severity of problems with alcohol, perception and thinking, mood and self-esteem, and managing one's own affairs.

A similar analysis was done for the receipt of methadone maintenance by drug-dependent patients. Only one small, although statistically significant ($p < .05$), correlation resulted: receiving methadone was associated with less severe interpersonal problems at follow-up.

STUDY 4 — EVALUATION OF VETERANS ADMINISTRATION TREATMENT OF ALCOHOL-DEPENDENT PATIENTS ORIGINALLY INCLUDED IN PADAT PROJECT
(24-Month Follow-Up)

Background and Study Questions

The patients included in Study 3 had to participate in inpatient treatment for at least thirty days to be eligible for inclusion. In identifying this sample, data were collected on many more alcohol-dependent patients who did not remain in inpatient treatment this long. The availability of admission data on this larger group plus a sense of increasing urgency to evaluate alcohol-dependence treatment (among VA Central Office personnel) provided the immediate stimulus for contracting for a twenty-four-month follow-up of these alcohol-dependent patients. This study was regarded as potentially capable of producing information on the results of the VA's treatment of a subset of its alcohol-dependent patients, as well as providing a pilot experience for an eventual system-wide evaluation of alcohol-dependence treatment. The questions this study sought to answer were as follows:

1. How much had patient performance (relative to the eight goals of drug and alcohol dependence treatment listed in Study 3) improved over the twenty-four months since admission?
2. How adequate was patient performance at follow-up?
3. How satisfied were patients with the manner in which they were treated and with the results of their treatment?
4. To what extent was follow-up performance related to (a) patient background and preadmission performance; (b) patient goals for treatment; (c) length of treatment; (d) combined or conventional setting; (e) use of Antabuse, and (f) participation in Alcoholics Anonymous?

5. For the subsample of patients for whom data were available at admission, six-month follow-up, and twenty-four-month follow-up, what trends in performance occurred over the three time points?

Measures of patient performance relative to the eight goals of treatment and measures of patient satisfaction constituted the dependent variables of the study. Explanation of variance in these variables was sought in terms of participation in treatment (before-after), length of treatment, other treatment characteristics, and patient characteristics.

Method

Study Plan: The overall study plan was similar to that described for Study 2, that is, a three point study with initial and six-month patient assessments made by clinical staff and the second follow-up assessment (24 months) made by contracted interviewers. (Unlike Study 1, we did not plan to analyze patient performance by individual program.)

Patients: Some admission information was collected on 5,265 veterans who contacted any of the twenty-four treatment facilities selected for the PADAT study (Study 3). To be selected for the twenty-four-month follow-up, these veterans (a) had to enter inpatient care at the time of initial contact, (b) had sufficient admission data to make comparison with follow-up data possible, and (c) had a primary problem of alcohol abuse. Eight hundred and forty-nine patients met these criteria; 465 (54.8%) were interviewed in person and thirty (3.5%) were interviewed by telephone at follow-up, making a total of 495 (58.3%) with follow-up data.

Data Collection Forms: With only minor modifications, the same forms were used that have already been described for Study 1.

Procedure: The admission and six-month follow-up forms were completed according to the procedures already described for Study 3. The twenty-four-month follow-up interview was conducted by an interviewer employed by the contractor, Kirschner Associates.

Results

Question 1 (How much improvement?): The data relevant to this question are presented in Table 12-XIV.

TABLE 12-XIV

ADMISSION AND 24 MONTH FOLLOW-UP PERFORMANCE

Variable	Admission $\overline{X}$	SD	Follow-up $\overline{X}$	SD	t	d[b]	Percent with significant problems[c] Admission	Follow-up
Goal 1								
Days of use:								
Alcohol	17.29	10.70	6.63	10.02	17.40*	.78	—	—
Alcohol (to intoxication)	13.44	10.76	1.69	5.15	22.97*	1.03	73.0	11.7
Methadone (nonprescribed)	.01	.14	.00	.00	1.00	.07	0.0	0.0
Heroin	.12	1.58	.01	.14	1.54	.07	0.6	0.0
Other opiates	.00	.00	.00	.09	−1.00	.00	0.0	0.0
Cocaine	.01	.14	.01	.19	−0.19	.00	0.0	0.2
Barbiturates	.20	1.85	.01	.23	2.27*	.10	1.2	0.2
Other sedatives, hypnotics, or tranquilizers	.73	3.74	.26	2.48	2.57*	.12	4.8	1.2
Amphetamines	.07	1.28	.01	.11	1.15	.05	0.4	0.0
Cannabis sativa	.69	3.54	.84	3.98	−0.75	−.03	5.1	5.3
Hallucinogens	.00	.00	.02	.36	−1.00	−.06	0.0	0.2
Other drugs	.34	2.97	.17	1.91	1.05	.05	1.4	1.0
Alcohol problem[a]	4.64	.90	1.81	1.35	40.48*	1.84	93.4	16.4
Drug problem[a]	1.27	.82	1.07	.38	5.39*	.24	4.6	0.8
Goal 2								
Medical problem[a]	2.92	1.38	2.26	1.47	8.47*	.39	37.3	25.3
Goal 3								
Psychological problems								
Perception and thinking[a]	2.85	1.41	1.42	.95	19.25*	.88	35.9	6.5
Mood and self-esteem[a]	4.00	.97	1.80	1.16	34.51*	1.56	73.6	11.5
Goal 4								
Interpersonal problem[a]	3.56	1.21	1.48	.93	14.29*	1.44	56.4	6.5
Goal 5								
Total hours worked	41.41	64.10	73.89	80.93	−8.29*	−.38	79.0	61.8
Employment (0 = No; 1 = Yes)	.37	.48	.56	.50	−7.17	−.33	79.0	61.8
Full time employment (0 = No; 1 = Yes)	.20	.40	.38	.49	−6.90*	−.32	79.0	61.8
Net earnings	$152.83	266.41	$285.03	369.85	−7.13*	−.33	71.5	58.5
Funds from: (1 = No; 2-Yes)								
Welfare	1.10	.29	1.10	.31	−0.26	.00	9.9	10.1
Friends and relatives	1.36	.48	1.27	.45	3.14*	.15	35.7	26.9
Illegal activities	1.05	.21	1.02	.16	1.98*	.08	4.7	2.4
Self-support problem[a]	3.42	1.50	2.01	1.42	17.03*	.77	55.4	20.4
Goal 6								
Managing own affairs problem[a]	2.99	1.53	1.67	1.14	16.23*	.73	42.4	11.7
Goal 7								
Number of arrests for:								
Violation of drug laws simple possession	0.01	.11	0.00	.05	1.13	.08	0.6	0.2
Violation of drug laws all other violations	0.00	.05	0.00	.00	1.00	.00	0.2	0.0
Public intoxication	0.29	.91	0.11	.69	4.31*	.20	15.4	6.1

TABLE 12-XIV (continued)

Admission and 24 Month Follow-up Performance

	Admission		Follow-up				Percent with significant problems[c]	
Variable	X̄	SD	X̄	SD	t	d[b]	Admission	Follow-up
Disorderly conduct or vagancy	0.05	.30	0.01	.15	2.37*	.12	4.0	1.6
Driving while intoxicated	0.22	.68	0.06	.48	4.46*	.20	16.4	3.6
Other violations of traffic and motor vehicle laws	0.08	.38	0.04	.27	2.10*	.09	6.1	2.8
Homicide, manslaughter, forcible rape	0.00	.05	0.00	.05	0.00	.00	0.2	0.2
Assaults	0.04	.33	0.00	.06	2.69*	.12	3.2	0.4
Robbery	0.00	.05	0.00	.00	1.00	.00	0.2	0.0
Burglary, larceny, auto theft	0.01	.16	0.00	.06	1.29	.06	1.0	0.4
All other offenses	0.04	.26	0.01	.08	3.02*	.15	3.2	0.6
Total arrests	0.71	1.70	0.29	1.54	4.43*	.20	34.9	12.5
Dangerous behavior problem[a]	2.32	1.42	1.32	.75	14.29*	.65	24.2	3.2
Goal 8								
Satisfaction from socially acceptable sources problem[a]	4.22	1.04	1.69	1.18	37.47*	1.69	80.1	12.1

Note. N = 495.

[a]Scale points were defined as follows: 1 = No problem; 2 = Minimal problem; 3 = Mild problem; 4 = Moderate problem; 5 = Marked problem.

[b]d values of .20, .50, and .80 indicate small, medium, and large differences respectively between admission and follow-up (Cohen, 1969).

[c]A patient was considered as having a "significant problem" on a given variable according to the following standards:
* Rating scale scores (on variables with an [a] superscript) higher than 3 on the variables: Alcohol problem; drug problem; self-support problem; medical problem; psychological problem; interpersonal problem; self-management problem; dangerous behavior problem; and problem in obtaining satisfaction from socially acceptable activities.
* Used drugs or alcohol (to intoxication) four or more days in the last four weeks
* Worked less than 120 hours during the four weeks prior to the evaluation
* Earned less than $200 in the last four week period
* Received funds from welfare, friends/relatives, illegal activities
* Was arrested one or more times during the 6 months prior to the 24 month evaluation.

*$p < .05$.

The d statistics indicate large improvements from admission to the twenty-four-month follow-up in the areas of alcohol abuse, psychological problems, social interaction, and obtaining satisfaction from socially acceptable sources. Medium improvements were made in the area of self-support (a somewhat dubious finding in that rated self-support did not seem entirely consistent with factual measures of employment), managing own affairs, and dangerous behavior. Small improvements occurred in regard to medical problems, full-time employment, and arrests. Statistically significant (p < .05) changes occurred in all eight goal areas, but this is not surprising in view of the relatively large sample size (N = 495).

Question 2 (How adequate was follow-up performance?):
The data relevant to this question was summarized in the column
in Table 12-XIV labelled "Percent with significant problems —
follow-up." In the area of alcohol problems, 16 percent had significant problems at follow-up; medical problems, 25 percent;
mood and self-esteem, 12 percent; arrests, 13 percent; and obtaining satisfaction from socially acceptable sources, 12 percent.

Question 3 (How satisfied were patients?): On the average,
patients were quite satisfied with the manner in which they were
treated, as we have found in all of our previous studies. However, this is apparently a common finding in patient satisfaction
surveys and should not be an occasion for excessive self-
congratulations. Rather, those who are concerned with program
improvement should focus their attention on areas where lesser
degrees of satisfaction are expressed.

In terms of satisfaction with the results of treatment, the areas
in which patients most frequently indicated progress were overcoming dependence on alcohol, increasing self-respect, and
feeling better physically. The goals toward which patients least
frequently felt they had made progress were getting into school
or job training, learning to worry less, and finding or holding a
job. There was considerable agreement, therefore, between the
patients and the contractor interviewers about the areas in which
most and least progress has been made.

Question 4 (Was outcome related to background?): In this
study, we dealt with this question by means of a series of hierar-
chical multiple regression analyses, which enabled us to deal with
all of our predictor variables in "one fell swoop," much as did
Bromet et al., (1977) in their study of the treatment of alcohol
dependence. The results of these analyses are easy to summarize. The multiple correlations between "background" variables and follow-up performance were statistically significant (p
< .01) and small for problems with drug abuse, physical health,
self-support, managing own affairs, dangerous behavior, and
obtaining satisfaction from socially acceptable sources. The
other follow-up variables, such as problems with alcohol abuse,
were unrelated to background variables. The addition of patient
goals for treatment information increased the multiple correla-

tions just described to a significant (and small) extent for only one follow-up variable, problems with dangerous behavior. As would be expected, admission scores on the dependent variable being considered made statistically significant increments in the multiple correlations for several of the follow-up variables (drug use, health, mood and self-esteem, and self-support). Length of first treatment made a statistically significant (and small) increment for the multiple correlation for only one variable, problems with mood and self-esteem. Type of program (combined versus conventional) made no significant increment, nor did receipt of Antabuse nor participation in Alcoholics Anonymous.

It should be noted that the analyses just reported were confined to those patients who had been initially hospitalized at least twenty-one days (N = 408), time enough for the type of inpatient setting (combined or conventional) to have some impact.

To summarize, we found that follow-up performance was only weakly related to patient background characteristics and essentially not related at all to length of treatment, type of treatment setting, receipt of Antabuse, and participation in Alcoholics Anonymous meetings. For all predictor variables except the background variables, which were entered into the regression equations first, we are referring to net or partial relationships with the dependent variables rather than raw relationships. Thus, for example, a given variable, such as attendance of Alcoholics Anonymous meeting, may have correlated significantly with a follow-up variable by itself, but it did not do so when the influence of the other variables mentioned here had been "partialled out."

Question 5 (What was the trend in patient performance over time?): Patient performance at admission, six-month follow-up and twenty-four-month follow-up (N = 263) is described in Table 12-XV. As was found in Study 2, two classes of variables emerged: (a) those that changed between the admission and the six-month follow-up and then changed very little after that, and (b) those that continued to change across all three time points. In the first class are drug abuse, problems with health, perception and thinking, employment, managing own affairs, dangerous behavior, and arrests for public intoxication. In the second class (variables that continue to change over time) are problems with alcohol, interpersonal relations, obtaining satisfaction from socially acceptable sources, and total arrests.

TABLE 12-XV

MEAN SCORES AND DEGREE OF CHANGE FOR SELECTED VARIABLES
AT ADMISSION AND AT TWO FOLLOW-UP POINTS

Variable	*Admission*	*Mean 6-Month Follow-up*	*24-Month Follow-up*	*F*	ω^a
Goal 1					
Days of Use:					
Alcohol (any use at all)	18.86	7.02	7.10	139.06*	.48
Alcohol (to the point of intoxication)	15.12	4.02	1.84	226.11*	.58
Alcohol problem[b]	4.71	2.32	1.88	414.03*	.69
Drug problem[b]	1.24	1.10	1.05	11.27*	.13
Goal 2					
Medical problem[b]	2.97	2.22	2.39	30.44*	.23
Goal 3					
Psychological problems:					
Perception and thinking[b]	2.73	1.67	1.49	98.10*	.42
Mood and self-esteem[b]	4.04	2.61	1.86	284.63*	.61
Goal 4					
Interpersonal problem[b]	3.60	2.25	1.48	274.81*	.61
Goal 5					
Total hours worked	40.25	68.99	70.37	21.74*	.18
Full-time employment (0 = N; 1 = Yes)	0.20	0.35	0.37	15.09*	.16
Net earnings	153.50	260.29	284.87	21.24*	.17
Self-support problem[b]	3.47	2.41	2.10	83.66*	.37
Goal 6					
Managing own affairs problem[b]	3.03	1.96	1.72	90.11*	.39
Goal 7					
Number of arrests for:					
Public intoxication	0.35	0.10	0.16	10.86*	.13
Driving while intoxicated[c]	0.22	0.02	0.08	9.08*	.14
Total arrests	0.78	0.16	0.33	12.30*	.16
Dangerous behavior problem[b]	2.21	1.37	1.37	61.98*	.35
Goal 8					
Satisfaction from socially acceptable sources problem[b]	4.30	2.53	1.76	330.56*	.65

Note. N = 263. Percentages sharing a common underline do not differ significantly ($p < .01$).

[a] ω values of .10, .24, and .37 indicate small, medium, and large differences, respectively.

[b] Scale points were defined as follows: 1 = No problem; 2 = Minimal problem; 3 = Mild problem; 4 = Moderate problem; 5 = Marked problem.

[c] Because the means for this variable were not in rank order, it was not possible to indicate the significance of pairwise differences by underlining (it was possible to do this for some variables because of the particular pattern of differences). For this variable, the admission and six-month follow-up means differed significantly, but the other pairs did not.

DISCUSSION

Among the usual purposes of a discussion section are to evaluate the study results with respect to the original hypotheses or questions, to disclose methodological limitations that circumscribe the inferences that can be made, and to make suggestions for future research. Each of these topics is considered below.

Before commenting on the contribution of the results to answering the study questions, it seems important to comment on the reasons those questions were asked — the underlying goals of the studies reported here. Although the goals of evaluation studies, like the goals of treatment programs, may seem obvious, I do not believe this is so. Just as it is often difficult to discover the real goals of treatment programs, so too it may be hard to know the true purposes of evaluation studies.

Two of the studies (1 and 3) seem to have been done partially in response to the interests of another government agency, the Special Action Office for Drug Abuse Prevention (SAODAP). I have no precise understanding of what kind of evaluation information this agency wanted from the VA, but it seems reasonable to assume that information was desired to justify the expenditure of funds for a group of patients that did not elicit a great deal of sympathy from the general public. The General Accounting Office has also wanted the VA to evaluate its alcohol-dependence treatment program and Study 4 was a substantial move in that direction.

As would seem natural, I believe that the VA Central Office management above the level of the managers of the alcohol and drug dependence treatment programs shared interests similar to those described above. They were concerned that the decision to support the treatment of alcohol- and drug-dependent patients, with the necessary result that the support for other categories of patients would be reduced, was a defensible one.

What has just been said does not imply that the Central Office managers of the alcohol- and drug-dependence treatment program were not intensely interested in evaluating their programs for reasons other than satisfying their superiors. Indeed they were, as was indicated by the fact that Studies 2 and 4 were initiated with very little, if any, outside influence. In fact, these managers appear to be "ahead of the pack" among Central Office program officials in their commitment to evaluation research. They appear to want to establish their accountability for the programs they manage and also to use evaluative information to improve those programs.

As one descends the hierarchy from top agency management to field management to clinical staff, the goals for evaluation probably move from the summative to the formative end of the continuum proposed by Scriven (1967). That is, there is less interest in deciding whether a program is worthwhile and more in learning how to improve it. Of course, it is likely that the goals of the field staff varied a great deal, particularly because the studies were mandated from the Central Office.

Given the purposes just described, what have the studies reported here contributed? I believe that we have established (subject to the important limitations to be considered below) that the VA's alcohol- and drug-dependence programs did produce important improvements in patients. Top administrators could reasonably use our results as evidence of program effectiveness. Further, our data regarding the relative effectiveness of combined versus conventional treatment settings (Study 3) would seem to have relevance to decisions about programming that would be made at high levels. From the standpoint of improving programs, our results provide useful baselines of what can be accomplished and make it possible to formulate quantitative goals for program achievement (e.g., six months after admission to treatment, X% of patients will not have used alcohol to intoxication during the month preceding follow-up). Further, areas of weakness in programs performance have been identified, suggesting that renewed efforts should be made to deal with those areas. Finally, from a methodological point of view, we may have set an example for others in regard to the careful definition of treatment goals and restraint in collecting data by using data collection forms developed to focus closely on these goals.

Having discussed accomplishments, it is now important to comment on the limitation of our studies for two purposes: (a) to assure that the results will not be overinterpreted, and (b) to pinpoint issues that require special attention in future studies carried out under similar circumstances. Incidentally, the rather lengthy detailing of limitations flows from the belief that (a) evaluation research should be an ongoing and recurring activity and (b) therefore, it is particularly important to use past experience to improve that activity.

The major limitations of our studies follow:

1. The overall purposes of the studies should have been clarified further, and there should have been more discussion of the relevance of the study questions to the purposes.

2. Our studies were observational rather than experimental and thus could not provide definitive evidence that changes in patient performance were consequences of treatment. Such hypotheses were strengthened, however.

3. Our response rates at follow-up left considerable room for the possibility of biased estimates of outcome.

4. The ad hoc and superficial nature of some of our measures is certainly subject to criticism.

5. The involvement of clinical and nonclinical interviewers could have contributed to measurement difficulties.

6. Our quality control mechanisms for the data collection by VA personnel were less than optimal.

7. The large scale nature of the study produced a certain "grossness." In terms of treatment, certainly "apples and oranges" were lumped together, but this does not mean that there is no value in study "fruit."

Because of these limitations, it may be that our results made treatment appear more effective than it really is, but it seems unlikely that they exaggerated its weaknesses. For the purpose of finding ways to improve our programs, this is sufficient.

Incidentally, although it is important to acknowledge methodological limitations, it is also important to point out one limitation that could be overemphasized. This concerns the interrater reliability of the interviewer forms. Although we were able to make some formal check on this reliability in Studies 1 and 3, we were not able to do this as adequately as we would have wished. However, the absence of reliability data is not damaging as might first appear. As noted in a review of the *Handbook of Evaluation Research,*

> . . . in much evaluation research, however, the reliability of outcome measures is nearly irrelevant. Often a low coefficient introduces no

great difficulty, mainly because the evaluator's primary concern is with group means. Therefore, it is the measurement error associated with the mean (and not the much larger error associated with individual scores) that offers the pertinent reliability index for the evaluator (Task Force, 1976).

Although it is clearly desirable to maximize interrater reliability, its importance in the present context should not be exaggerated. Indeed, the large number of statistically significant findings attest to the fact that our measures were sufficiently reliable for our purposes. Such findings do not occur when measurement is purely random.

I would like to close with a few thoughts about what I would emphasize if I were to continue work in the area of the evaluation of substance abuse treatment. First, I would give more attention to clarifying the goals of those who requested any future evaluation studies, and I have no illusions that this would be easy to do. Second, I would review the program goals we have already developed to see if they could be stated more clearly and more quantitatively, to assure their importance to program staff, and to try to order them in some priority. Further, I would attempt to develop more intermediate goals that would provide guidance for focusing attention on treatment structures and processes, areas that were neglected in the studies described here.

Incidentally, the clarification of both the intermediate and ultimate goals of treatment should be of as much interest to treatment personnel as to program evaluators. Indeed, they should be of more interest because of their critical role in the planning of treatment. Empirical evidence of the usefulness of formulating both intermediate and ultimate goals for treatment purposes is provided by Hart (1978) who found that psychotherapy patients who participated in setting intermediate goals with their therapists improved more over a three-month period than those who did not.

Finally, if I were engaging in continuing evaluation I would give some attention to the general evaluative questions suggested by Rossi et al., (1979): Is the program reaching the appropriate target population? Is the program being implemented as intended? What does it cost? What is the "intervention model" underlying the program? (These authors also list questions about program impact, which have been our primary focus of concern in this series of studies.)

REFERENCES

Baker, S. L.; Lorei, T.; McKnight, H. A.; and Duvall, J. L.: The Veterans Administration's comparison study: Alcoholism and drug abuse — combined and conventional treatment setting. *Alcoholism: Clinical and Experimental Research,* 7(4):285-291, 1977.

Bromet, E. J.; Moos, R.; Bliss, F.; and Wuthmann, C.: Posttreatment functioning of alcoholic patients: Its relation to program participation. *Journal of Consulting and Clinical Psychology,* 45:829-842, 1977.

Campbell, D. T.; and Stanley, J. C.: *Experimental and quasiexperimental designs for research.* Chicago, Rand McNally, 1963.

Cohen, J.: *Statistical power analysis in the behavioral sciences.* New York, Academic Press, 1969.

Cohen, J.; and Cohen, P.: *Applied multiple regression/correlation analysis for the behavioral sciences.* Hillsdale, New Jersey, Lawrence Erlbaum Associates, 1975.

Freed, E. X.: Drug abuse by alcoholics: A review. *International Journal of Addictions,* 8:451-473, 1973.

Hart, R. R.: Therapeutic effectiveness of setting and monitoring goals. *Journal of Consulting and Clinical Psychology,* 46(6):1242-1245, 1978.

Lorei, T. W.: Formulating therapeutic objectives as a prelude to program evaluation. *Hospital and Community Psychiatry,* 30(4):262-265, 1979.

Lorei, T. W.; and Caffey, E. M., Jr.: Goal definition by staff consensus: A contribution to the planning, delivery and evaluation of mental health services. *Journal of Consulting and Clinical Psychology,* 46(6):1284-1290, 1978.

Lorei, T. W.; Francke, G. N.; and Harger, P. S.: Evaluation of drug dependence treatment in VA hospitals. *American Journal of Public Health,* 68:39-43, January, 1978.

Ottenberg, D. J.; and Orsen, A.: Merging the treatment of drug addicts into an existing program for alcoholics. *Quarterly Journal of Studies on Alcohol,* 32:94-103, 1971.

Rossi, P. H.; Freeman, H. E.; and Wright, S. R.: *Evaluation: A Systematic Approach.* Beverly Hills, Calif., Sage Publications, 1979.

Scriven, M.: The methodology of evaluation. In S. Tyler; R. M. Gagne; and M. Scriven (Eds.): *Perspectives on Curriculum Evaluation.* Chicago, Rand McNally, 1967.

Sells, S. B. (Ed.): *Evaluation of Treatment* (Vol. 1). Cambridge, Mass., Ballinger, 1974.

Task Force of the Stanford Evaluation Consortium. Evaluating the handbook of evaluating research. In V. Glass (Ed.): *Evaluation Studies Review Annual* (Vol. 1). Beverly Hills, Calif., Sage Publications, 1976.

CHAPTER 13

OUTCOME EVALUATION OF THERAPEUTIC COMMUNITIES

RICHARD N. BALE

Therapeutic communities for the treatment of characterological disordered persons have evolved exponentially from their early roots in the self-help Synanon efforts of the late 1950s (Casriel, 1963) and the professionally based model of Maxwell Jones in post-World War II England (Jones, 1953). The residential program has represented a major treatment modality for substance abusers for some twenty years, yet evidence for the effectiveness of therapeutic communities is scarce (Ford Foundation, 1972; Brecher, 1972; Smart, 1976).

In this chapter, we will speculate on some of the possible reasons for this paucity of outcome data, briefly review the existing literature, and outline the various components that are crucial to a comprehensive outcome evaluation of residential treatment. Rather than present an exhaustive "cookbook" of options for experimental designs or instrumentation, we intend instead to raise fundamental questions that should be addressed in the design, planning, and execution of an outcome study. In order to concretely illustrate some of the more abstract points presented, selected results are presented from a comparative follow-up study of three therapeutic communities and a methadone treatment program involving 585 subjects who were randomly assigned to treatment at the Veterans Administration Medical Center in Palo Alto, California.*

*This study was supported in part by a grant from NIDA. Vincent Zarcone, M.D. was the principal investigator and William Van Stone, M.D., John Kuldau, M.D., and Thomas Engelsing, M.D., were co-investigators. Susan Cabrera, M.A., coordinated the follow-up.

Most therapeutic communities have been reluctant to follow up their members after the termination of treatment. An early exception was Synanon, which, though philosophically opposed to outcome evaluation (Casriel, 1963), allowed a few selected professionals to affiliate with the program and complete informal surveys of former members living and working in the community (Volkman and Cressey, 1963; Cherkas, 1965).

Another program to support relatively informal follow-up efforts is the Daytop Program in New York, which studied the progress of both dropouts (Collier et al., 1970; Glasscote et al., 1972) and graduates (Casriel and Amen, 1971), as well as comparisons of both groups in a single design (Collier and Hijazi, 1974; Romand et al.,1975).

The Gateway Program in Chicago has evolved a follow-up component from early anecdotal reports (Slotkin, 1972) to more recent systematic efforts (Holland, 1978b) involving a trained and sophisticated staff. Similarly, the Phoenix House system in New York City has established a skilled "in-house" evaluation team, which has examined the criminal activity of dropouts (DeLeon et al., 1972), the relation of time in treatment to a variety of outcome measures (Chambers and Inciardi, 1974), long-term outcome (DeLeon et al., 1978), and psychological functioning at follow-up (DeLeon and Kowlowsky, 1978).

At the Eagleville Hospital in Pennsylvania, a team has investigated the two-year progress of both addicts and alcoholics, and examined the role of subsequent outpatient treatment (Barr et al., 1973). An unprecedented cost-effectiveness study was completed by Aron and Daily (1974) on two residential communities at the Camarillo State Hospital in California.

While the majority of these follow-up efforts were conducted or sponsored by the treatment programs themselves, a few nationally based projects have involved a number of different therapeutic communities, as well as other treatment modalities. These include the Johns Hopkins study of 673 former therapeutic members (Mandell et al., 1974), the Macro Systems study of former members of therapeutic communities in New York City (Macro Systems, 1975), and the systematic assessment of several treatment modalities conducted by Texas Christian

University (Sells et al., 1976; Simpson et al., in press).

The outcome results of these studies have been reviewed elsewhere (Smart, 1976), as well as their methodological limitations (Bale, 1979a). Briefly, those limitations include the following:

(1) The studies are retrospective. The studies were designed and often conceived after the termination of treatment, so that baseline data was either gathered by a different methodology or assessed retrospectively at follow-up. The latter procedure (employed by the John Hopkins study, for example) encounters substantial problems of selective recall and memory loss. A second major problem encountered is the loss of significant numbers of subjects who cannot be located.

(2) Follow-up location rates are too small. This is in part a result of the retrospective design in which subjects are not prepared for the post-treatment contact (discussed later in this chapter). Completion rates of the reviewed studies varied between 29 and 76 percent, with most reported rates in the 50 to 60 percent range, which makes generalization to the treatment population difficult at best. Furthermore, we do not know much about the unlocatable subject population and cannot assume, as some authors do, that these individuals are doing worse than those interviewed. Because so many subjects are found in treatment centers, jails, probation indices, and coroners reports, it may be that those not found are likely to be functioning better precisely because they have not entered one of those public systems.

(3) Outcome variables are often ill-defined and ambigous (Walizer, 1975). Rarely does a study report the actual instrumentation used in the study or the exact wording used in a question. For example, the following definitions for drug use were among those used in the reports reviewed: "free of narcotic use," and "voluntarily absent for six months or more." The meaning of these outcomes is obviously unclear, or so global, e.g., "abstinent," as to conceal important differences between the drug use of different subjects. Finally, the validity of most data is not systematically investigated, an important consideration given the sensitive nature of many of the outcome variables,

particularly criminal activity and drug use.

(4) The relationship of the research workers to the clinical personnel and to the subjects is rarely defined. As discussed later in this chapter, the identity of the follow-up staff can have an important effect on both unconscious biasing of the data as well as credibility of the results. Furthermore, the subject's understanding of the use of his personal information may affect the answers he provides. Is the individual data to be shared with the clinicians who treated the subjects? Or, is it to be kept confidential to the research group? These basic characteristics of the methodology should be described in any evaluation report.

(5) General rubrics such as "residential program" or "therapeutic community," sometimes along with length of stay, are often the only descriptions of treatment. These terms in fact describe a wide variety of highly divergent treatment processes and structures, as Sells and his associates have pointed out (Sells, 1974). Without some assessment of process we cannot even speculate on dimensions of the subject's experience that might be related to outcome.

THE PALO ALTO STUDY

Each of these five major methodological considerations (prospective design of the study, choice of research personnel, follow-up location strategies, and description of treatment structure and process) will be discussed below, using the Palo Alto study as a working example. Accordingly, we will give a brief overview of that study before proceeding.

In 1972, the Veterans Administration Medical Center Drug Dependence Treatment Unit (DDTU; now the Drug and Alcohol Treatment Unit — DATU) in Palo Alto and its division at Menlo Park were funded by the National Institutes on Drug Abuse (then a NIMH branch) to conduct a comprehensive follow-up evaluation of the treatment of narcotic addicts in both therapeutic communities and methadone maintenance. Some 457 male veterans who had entered a short detoxification program and said they were interested in further treatment were randomly assigned to an outpatient methadone treatment program or one of three quite different therapeutic communities.

The residential communities included the Family, a Synanon-based peer confrontation program; Quadrants, an eclectic program staffed by both professionals and a number of ex-addicts; and Satori, a professionally staffed community based on a model derived from Maxwell Jones. Another 128 were not interested in further treatment but were nevertheless followed up. Most of the 585 subjects were located at the three follow-up points: 97 percent at six months and 94 percent at one year on mailed questionnaires, while 96 percent completed the two-year personal interview. A number of both historical and post-treatment data was gathered, and both anecdotal and systematic descriptions of the residential communities were completed. Our experience in the design and planning of this study, as well as selected results, will be used to illustrate many of the methodological discussions below.

THE DESIGN OF AN OUTCOME STUDY

Selection of Personnel

The choice of persons to do evaluative work reflects the purpose of the project itself and has a potentially important impact on the validity of the data and the credibility of the reported results. Often if the outcome of interest is clear-cut and validity checks are available, clinical staff may be trained and assigned to locate and interview subjects who have completed treatment (Craig, 1979). Generally, however, the data generated by clinical staff is understandably regarded with some suspicion by readers outside the program, particularly if the program's survival is at stake (a poor reason to do a follow-up study). Furthermore, the track record of clinical staff attempting to do careful disciplined location and interviewing is not encouraging; it is much too easy to place or to have supervisors place a higher priority on the (unbounded) needs of current patients. A variation on this plan currently used in the DATU-VAMC at Palo Alto is to hire and train intake workers who also are responsible for follow-up. They have no continued relationship to the residents in treatment but have had the advantage of establishing a preliminary contact, which is later helpful in location. Furthermore, the variable scheduling possible in follow-up location and interviewing (as opposed to fixed treatment program schedules) can be better integrated with the unpredictable flow of admissions.

To lessen questions of possible bias, or when several programs are being compared, program personnel should not be involved in the actual follow-up assessment. Two options are then possible. In the first case, research workers on staff at the larger supporting institution may have a better vantage point for doing evaluation, as well as greater competence, training, resources, and time. They may also be perceived, however, to have a parochial interest in the results of treatment, particularly if their entire professional role is devoted to the continued assessment of a few specific programs.

Alternatively, professionals outside the program or sponsoring institution may be employed on a project by project basis. These staff may, however, have less sensitivity to the special concerns of the clinical staff or subjects themselves and may be substantially more costly. Furthermore, with the incentive of further project funding, such "disinterested" groups cannot be conceivably free of any bias. The only truly effective answer to questions of possible interviewer bias is systematic validity investigations, discussed later in this chapter.

In the Palo Alto study, a combination of research personnel was utilized. The project steering committee was composed of hospital administrators, who hired the project director, a staff psychologist not connected to any of the treatment programs. The subjects were assessed, located, and interviewed at follow-up by personnel hired by the affiliated institution, Stanford University, and who were neither hospital employees nor administratively connected to the VA clinical staff.

Prediction of Staff Time Necessary

The amount of time necessary for the location of subjects and the completion of outcome assessment depends on the care with which the project is designed, as well as the choice of media.

Subjects may be interviewed by mailed questionnaire, by telephone, or in a personal interview. Sometimes, the subject is sent a mailed questionnaire, which he fills out while talking with a trained interviewer over the phone. This procedure offers many of the advantages of a personal interview, in which more complex questions can be clarified and probed, and resistance may be evident. In such a case, for example, the phone interviewer may usefully remind the subject of the confidentiality policy.

Personal interviews are particularly useful, because the interviewer is more able to control the interview and the attention and focus of the subject. Nonverbal cues to confusion or resistance may be read. Physical validation of self-reported data, e.g., paycheck stubs, urine samples, etc., may be gathered.

Of course, it takes considerably more staff time to conduct a personal interview, which requires transportation to and from the interview (unless subjects can be enticed to come to the interviewer, a process with disadvantages as well), repeated visits to broken appointments, and so forth. In the Palo Alto study, it took about twice as long (six hours) to complete a personal interview as it did to complete a mailed questionnaire (three hours). These figures, which include all set-up, telephone work, contact with institutions and families in the location process, and written recording of that process, are *averages*, computed for the high return rates of over 90 percent accomplished. Figure 13-1 shows the relationship of effort to location rate for the one-year mailed questionnaire follow-up.

We were able to obtain a 40 percent follow-up rate with just one hour spent per subject. To increase that rate to 60 percent required twice the effort — two hours — on *those* subjects. Another 20 percent increase to 80 percent required three hours for each of those harder to locate and/or interview individuals. Finally, the last 15 percent or so bringing the overall rate into the 90-plus percent range required an average of more than eight hours per subject. However efficient the staff, the completion rate is likely to be exponentially related to the staff time and effort and a crucial factor in the estimation of staff time will be the follow-up rate deemed acceptable. It should be noted that follow-up rates were not related to time in treatment; at one year they were 88 percent for the methadone group, 94 percent for the therapeutic community subjects, and 94 percent for those not in long-term VA treatment.

Drug Dependent Patients

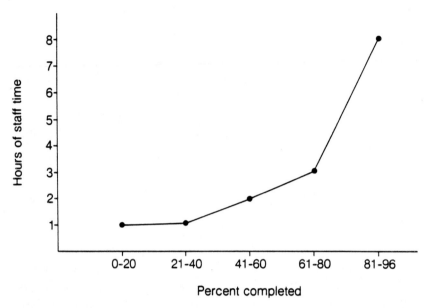

Completion Rate On One Year Mailed
Questionnaire Vs. Staff Time Spent

Figure 13-1. Completion rate on one year mailed questionaires versus staff time spent.

Ensuring a High Return Rate

Achieving a high completion rate depends on the subject's willingness to cooperate, designing questionnaires that will be returned, the collection of adequate information at intake, and the sophistication of tracking techniques at follow-up.

Rapport conducive to follow-up cooperation begins at the initial intake session. In agreeing to participate in the study, the subject should understand that his honest feedback is the project's most valuable source of information, and that there are no "right" or "wrong" answers. He should have a clear expectancy as to when he will be contacted, what the questionnaire or interview will be like, and what confidentiality precautions will be followed. The interviewer should gather at least three names and addresses at this time of friends and relatives (female relatives are often the most stable and reliable sources) who might assist in locating the subject should he not be at his last address.

Any precautions or reluctancies expressed by the subject about even confidential contacting of certain people in his life should be noted and respected. By the end of the interview, the subject should feel that his participation is of real importance to the study and should expect to be contacted by someone who is well trained and respects his privacy. It is hard to overestimate the importance of this relationship between subject and research staff to the willingness of the subject to cooperate at follow-up. The absence of this careful building of rapport in retrospective studies has been a principal cause of the low follow-up rates.

The willingness to return a mailed questionnaire at follow-up — at a time when the subject has perhaps no continuing ties to the treatment program — also will depend on the questionnaire itself. A long questionnaire is less likely to be returned than a short one, and here a decision must be made. It is sorely tempting to gather a large body of "interesting" data given the considerable expense of tracking and location. However, research staff must convince themselves that the addition of items beyond a two-to-three-page questionnaire will be worth the drop-off in returns. Whatever decision is made, the questionnaire should begin with a clear statement to the subject of how long it will likely take him to complete the questionnaire.

It is often argued that monetary incentives are helpful, or even necessary, to ensure a high response rate. Our experience in several follow-up projects has not supported that notion. In the Palo Alto study, for example, location rates were about 95 percent for two mailed questionnaires without incentive, and the same for a personal interview in which the subject was paid $15. We did feel that the small cash amount reasonably compensated the subject for his time, and that it provided a morale booster to staff who felt good about being able to offer the subject something other than personal appreciation.

If both the questionnaire and subject have been properly prepared, and adequate personal information gathered, then the achievement of a high return rate depends only on a few sophisticated tracking techniques.

The author and others (Bale et al., 1977; Goldstein et al., 1977) have described a variety of tracking techniques in operational detail, and they will only be outlined here. Tracking techniques must be utilized in the special case where none of the leads (friends, relatives, personal addresses, work telephones, etc.) assist in location at follow-up. In the Palo Alto study, this was the case about 40 percent of the time.

Because substance abuse and its concomitant problems are often episodic, recurrent events, it is likely that the subject may reenter treatment at a later date. Accordingly, the location worker should be in constant touch with the local admissions office and all related points of possible contact. In a large hospital, such as the VAMC in Palo Alto, for example, former members of programs often come back to the institution for outpatient medical treatment of minor problems. Sometimes program staff will hear from a subject personally or have other indications of his whereabouts. It is helpful to periodically send a note to programs participating in a study listing subjects who have been difficult to locate, and soliciting any information they might have.

The single most useful tool in location is the telephone. Directory assistance can be helpful in providing new listings even when former numbers have been disconnected with no referral. "Reverse" or "Polk" directories, sometimes carried by libraries or Chambers of Commerce, list telephone numbers by street address rather than name. This information is useful when there is indication as to a possible address but no telephone listing.

With proper identification, a State Department of Motor Vehicles will often provide the subject's most recent address, which must be given by a driver upon receipt of renewal of a license and anytime an accident or citation occurs. These leads are particularly useful with subjects who abuse alcohol and who are likely to be cited for drunk driving and other motor vehicle citations.

Incarcerated subjects can often be located by calling a state central identification unit, couny jail, probation indices, or the Federal Bureau of Prisons for those in a federal prison system. Once located, a subject may be mailed a questionnaire, and arrangements are often possible for a personal interview. Although policies vary tremendously between penal institutions, we have found it necessary in all cases to assume that anything said in or mailed into a jail or prison is known to the authorities. The content of a follow-up questionnaire must be modified and perhaps limited to exclude anything that would endanger the subject, and the research worker's exact connection to the subject must not be revealed. Identification as "VA survey workers" or "health survey interviewer," for example, are usually adequate and safe ways to represent oneself.

Other possible sources of location information include welfare agencies, rehabilitation programs, schools, employers, and unions (it sometimes helps to know if the subject has a trade). In the special case where the subject apparently is located but appears unresponsive to repeated requests for completion, certified mail with "return receipt requested" and "deliver only to addressee" will retrieve the subject's signature, confirming that he is indeed at the address. A new lead is obtained if someone else signs for the letter. Finally, telegrams or mailgrams may sometimes motivate a reluctant subject to cooperate.

In the Palo Alto study, less than 2 percent of subjects once located refused to cooperate at follow-up. In part this low rate was the result of the relationship between the research team and the subject, and the extreme care with which information about the subject was handled. In each contact in the tracking process, with every public agency as well as families and friends, the subject's history of treatment could have been revealed or implied. Mistakes as to confidentiality protocol would have been in the grapevine of former residents quickly, affecting our reputation and the willingness of our subjects to respond.

Time Period for Follow-up

How soon should a former resident be followed up to ascertain his progress after treatment? The longer the period from discharge to follow-up, the more difficult it is to locate former residents. On the other hand, most clinicians and other interested parties are interested in individual changes that endure over some period of time. Furthermore, some clinicians feel that, following treatment, many persons will experience a few failures before new adaptive mechanisms are learned and mastered. In this view, follow-up should not occur before an adequate amount of time for this adaptation period following discharge has passed. Finally, the choice of interval time between treatment and follow-up is related to the variable of interest and the pattern of past results. For example, a study predominantly interested in an absolute criterion variable such as total abstinence from a specific drug may find over a period of time that nearly all who are going to "relapse" within a two-year period will do so within six months. In this case, the choice of the longer follow-up period and its inherent problems must be carefully weighed against the value of added information.

When beginning a study, however, we generally have very little a priori information about the post-discharge behavior of clients. Ideally, multiple contacts using the same methodology could answer questions about the timing and stability of important life events. In the Palo Alto study we assessed subjects at six, twelve, and twenty-four months. Because there was a high correlation between the six- and twelve-month results for individuals, we probably could have easily made just one contact during that time without losing much information.

An additional important and often overlooked design decision is whether to follow subjects at established periods following discharge or admission. In the Palo Alto study, for example, since we were comparing therapeutic community members with clients in a methadone treatment program — who we anticipated would not be discharged during the two-year study period — we had to determine follow-up from the admission date. The disadvantage of this procedure is that, especially for the first six-month follow-up, some subjects out of treatment only a short time were compared to others who had not been in treatment for nearly six months. While the relative difference between the groups shrank over time, nevertheless the "at risk" periods, e.g., for criminal activity and possible arrest and conviction, were somewhat different.

Control of Treatment Events

In order to assess the effect of treatment on outcome, or to compare the relative effects of different modalities, the outcome investigator would often like to achieve some degree of experimental control. Ideally, this means some form of random assignment to different treatment conditions and/or to a no-treatment control condition. While the variations of experimental and quasi-experimental designs to achieve control over treatment variables are the subject of a massive body of literature (Campbell and Stanley, 1963) a few problems particularly relevant to substance abuse treatment should be mentioned here.

A formidable problem to the execution of any rigerous research design is the attrition problem so endemic to therapeutic communities. That is, most subjects will terminate treatment — alter their own treatment condition — before the program's definition of "completion". Thus, if time in treatment is related to outcome, and a growing body of evidence suggests that it is in therapeutic communities (Bale et al., 1980), the evaluator has lost control of a key aspect of his independent variable.

Characterological subjects often seem to know not only how much treatment is enough but what kind of treatment is best for them. Staff too share a wide variety of myths about the relationship of individual experience, background, and personality to program type, process, and outcome. These are serious barriers to an empirical atmosphere so necessary to the creation and execution of a protocol involving random assignment. Moreover, it may be that these beliefs themselves, when shared by program members and staff, are highly salient factors in determining positive outcome, particularly with clients who primarily utilize defenses involving externalization and the attribution of responsibility to others. The process of treatment choice cannot easily be isolated from the effects of treatment itself.

Even if the researcher is able to gain control over assignment to local programs, the proliferation of programs in many large communities presents a serious limitation: the individual assigned to a particular program not of his choosing and within a given locale or system may easily travel a short distance to obtain a more desirable program.

In the Palo Alto study, the research team evolved a number of compromises with clinical staff and other protocols in designing a random assignment procedure. The anticipated problems were substantial: a multi-modality unit with staff highly committed to their own program ideology and approach to treatment; some patients entering the hospital specifically for residential treatment would be assigned to methadone outpatient treatment and, vice versa, some patients would be assigned to a Synanon-style program historically found unacceptable by most other substance abuse clients; and a surrounding community offering an assortment of similar and dissimilar treatment alternatives. In designing a random assignment procedure, the study adopted a "thirty-day" rule in which subjects assigned to a specific program would not be allowed to enter any other program until thirty days had passed. This period was long enough to encourage subjects and staff to give strong consideration to the assigned program, but short enough to garner support of the clinical staff and discourage transfer to programs outside the local VA system.

Our randomization protocol was indeed compromised, in both of the ways discussed above. Many subjects assigned to a specific program failed to enter that program or left prematurely; others waited the thirty days and entered a different program. What we were able to effectively randomize was the unbiased initial connection of program and subject. Thus, the ability to attract and retain subjects in treatment became an aspect of the program's outcome effectiveness (Jaffe, 1971a).

True experimental control is rarely possible in psychotherapy situations (May et al., 1976) and random assignment to treatment is of sufficient difficulty that only two such attempts have been reported in the field of substance abuse (Bale et al., 1980; Jaffe, 1971b). When experimental control is lacking or is compromised, the evaluator must resort to some sort of post-hoc statistical control.

Outcome Variables

While considerable recent literature on psychotherapy has addressed the variety of outcome measures for individuals, their families, and their environments (Erickson, 1975; Garfield and Bergin, 1978; Moos, 1974), we shall focus here on the special issues related to substance abuse treatment outcome and the three principal variables of social functioning: drug use, employment, and criminal behavior.

Different parties may be interested in divergent and perhaps even unrelated aspects of outcome. In a therapeutic community, for example, those *doing* the therapy may be most interested in changes in interpersonal style, those *in* therapy may be most interested in getting a job, while those *paying for* therapy may be most concerned with reduction in crime. Ironically, no one may be primarily interested in drug use, which may have been the principal criterion for entry. There is good reason to include some assessment of each of these areas, though the relationship between them at follow-up, rarely reported in outcome studies, should be investigated rather than assumed.

The degree to which these various outcomes are related is a central issue for therapeutic community outcome. The residential program is a working laboratory for diagnosing as well as shaping the behavior of its members. The structure of the program is intricately designed to challenge defenses of externalization, projection, acting out, hypochondriasis, and passive aggressive behavior, while building self-esteem and teaching more adaptive ways of handling anxiety and depression. Although some promising work has been recently reported by Vaillant (1977) on the reliability of assessment of these defenses, no study has yet evaluated former members of a therapeutic community on these dimensions of behavior that were the focus of treatment. Instead, cessation of these defenses, which are primarily responses to interpersonal stress, are *assumed* to lead to positive changes in drug use, productive activity, and criminal behavior.

Often drug use is assessed as a simple binary variable, e.g., "abstinent" versus "not abstinent". The difficulty with measures like this is that they obscure differences between substantially different outcomes, e.g., a person who used once versus a person who used every day. It is hard to imagine that neurotic defenses would be so crudely and uncharitably assessed following psychotherapy.

In the Palo Alto study we found it useful to assess the use of various specific drugs (carefully separating their use rather than combining, say, heroin and marijuana) along a variety of dimensions. Did the subject ever use the drug following discharge? What was the highest frequency of use? Did he experience an overdose? What was the longest period of daily use if any? What was the longest time he was totally drug free on the street during the follow-up period? A combination of such variables would begin to sketch a portrait close to the subject's *pattern* of drug use. In comparing treatment groups, we generally used time samples, e.g., an assessment of heroin use during the three months preceding follow-up. While the data from this single variable were not necessarily descriptive of an individual subject — some who were drug free began to use just before follow-up, while others who were using heavily ceased just before the three-month period — such extremes tended to even out in the analysis of larger groups.

Criminal behavior can be assessed in basically three ways. The subject may be asked the nature and extent of actual criminal behavior, an extremely sensitive line of questioning and potentially risky for the subject. For this reason we did not use such measures in the Palo Alto study; however, we did ask how the subject financed his post-discharge drug use, if any. The second and much more common variable is the number and type of arrests. The primary difficulty with this variable is that in our society we assume that arrests do not necessarily indicate criminal behavior, and, in fact, many substance abusers are routinely picked up for questioning by local police. A further problem with arrests is that what the subject may call an "arrest," e.g., a pickup, and what the local authorities list as an arrest on the books may not coincide. This also presents a problem for validity, which is discussed later.

Convictions are a more fair way to assess criminal activity which has resulted in an arrest. However, the evaluator must face two problems. First, a conviction or other resolution of charge may take a long time. Second, the subject may be convicted of an offense that through plea bargaining may be substantially different from the arresting charge, or may be reduced from a felony to a misdemeanor.

The assessment of employment is somewhat more straightforward, but some value decisions are encountered. What of the artist who is not gainfully employed but productive? How does one quantify his productivity? Should subjects attending school be considered "unemployed"? Compensation is often difficult to assess as well when salary is supplemented or replaced by goods or services. Also troublesome is the interval assessment of seasonal work when the subject may be "unemployed" at follow-up but is usually employed during a different time of year or weather period. (A similar problem obtains with students between semesters.)

For employment as well as the other outcome variables, these complex problems of measurement and abstraction require careful thought and discussion among the research team. They should consider the special characteristics of the study population and the treatment programs, any data already gathered, including anecdotal reports if none exist, and the concerns of potential readers of the results as well as sponsors of the study. This process is greatly facilitated by the creation of "dummy data" for analysis, e.g., making up a plausible but only hypothetical collection of data and discussing both the analysis and reporting of results. No other process so quickly reveals the probable problems in the interpretation of the data; if the data gathered is based on self-reports, this is also the time to plan validity studies.

VALIDATION OF SELF-REPORTED DATA

Because substance abusers characteristically employ denial as a defense and are seen to be highly manipulative (Maddux and Desmond, 1975), it becomes critically important to validate particularly sensitive data that is self-reported. In fact, subjects who are engaged in drug use and other criminal activity may fear that legal sanctions or denial of further treatment may result from honest responses, and validation of self-reports becomes paramount.

In the Palo Alto study, we executed two major validation studies of self-reported heroin use, and a related reliability study of self-reports on other variables. Because we felt that police records were much too varied in quality and inconsistent in themselves, a finding of other investigators as well (Nash, 1976; Amsel et al., 1976), we did not systematically assess the self-reports of arrests and convictions. Validation of employment presented a different problem. Our principal means of validation, comparison by groups with formal records of the Social Security Administration, had been reported useful for psychiatric populations (Dirks and Kuldau, 1974). However, a substantial propor-·tion of our subjects at follow-up were employed by the Civil Service, or earning unreported income while employed by themselves or families. In these cases, no social security tax had been withheld, and the SSA validation procedure was rendered inadequate for the total study population.

The validity of self-reported drug use has been investigated by others (Ball, 1967; Stephens, 1972; Amsel et al., 1976), but results indicating a generally high level of truthfulness were compromised by small sample sizes, low percentage returns, and inadequate corroboration. In order to overcome these methodological limitations and investigate the validity of self-reported drug use in the special context of our research design, we undertook two validation studies.

Personal Interviews

Interviews were completed or death certificates obtained for 562 of the 585 subjects in the study (96%). Of this total, 272 lived within a 100-mile radius, were not incarcerated or in a treatment facility, and were interviewed personally. Each of these subjects was asked questions about his heroin use during the interview and was, without prior warning, asked to provide a urine specimen. The research worker did not directly observe the subject urinating, but he or she did take measures to ensure its genuineness including accompanying the subject to the bathroom, shaking the urine bottle (for the presence of bubbles), and noting whether the specimen was warm and of appropriate color. In addition, the interviewer recorded any overt signs of drug use or withdrawal, and noted their subjective confidence in the truthfulness of the self-reported drug use.

Urine specimens were analyzed by the medical center laboratory, whose analysis accuracy was consistently confirmed by rigorous random periodic tests by the Center for Disease Control in Atlanta. An initial screen using thin layer chromatography was followed for all positive results by a confirming radioimmunoassay (Catlin et al., 1973).

The results indicated a fairly high degree of correspondence between the urinalysis results and the self-reported drug use. Table 13-I shows the relationship between the urinalysis and drug use reported for the last week (the longest period of time for which the urinalysis is sensitive).

TABLE 13-I
Urine Results versus Last Week Self-reported Heroin Use

Any Heroin Use in Last Week	Urinalysis Results for Morphine		Total
	Positive	Negative	
Yes	81 (85.3%)	14 (14.7%)	95
No	39 (22.0%)	138 (78.0%)	177
Totals	120	152	272

(Overall chi square = 100.2, 1 df, p < .01)

Of the 177 subjects who claimed no heroin use in the last week, 138 (78.0%) provided urine specimens negative for morphine. A crucial question in a research design comparing treatment modalities was whether these results were related to treatment experience. They were, as can be seen in Table 13-II.

TABLE 13-II
Urine Results by Treatment Group

Treatment Group	Number Reporting no heroin use in past week	Number with negative urines
Detoxification Only	38	26 (68.4%)
Detoxification plus non VA treatment	53	41 (77.4%)
Methadone Outpatient	26	20 (76.9%)
Therapeutic Community	60	51 (85.0%)
Totals	177	138 (78.0%)

Subjects formerly in residential treatment were much more likely to report their drug use truthfully, and a straight reporting of comparative outcome between treatment groups without attention to these results appeared likely to overestimate the comparative functioning of detoxification-only subjects. These results were tempered by the fact that groups analyzed were not random samples of the treatment populations, e.g., many more detoxification-only subjects were incarcerated than the former therapeutic community members.

The validity study design also provided an opportunity to examine some related questions. Results of the interviewer ratings, for example, indicated that, while the researchers could not reliably note objective symptoms of drug use or withdrawal in subjects whose urines were positive for heroin, they themselves were much more likely to rate themselves as less than confident in the veracity of those reports (using, apparently, other evidence or more subjective perceptions).

More detailed description of this validity study, the correspondence of other verbal reports to urinalyses, the relationship of urine results to time since use, and a variety of other data analyses appears elsewhere (Bale et al., in press).

Mailed Questionnaires

In the Palo Alto study, the first two follow-up contacts were completed by mail and/or telephone. Although no previous study had been made of the veracity of self-reports of drug use using these media, there was nevertheless a general sense that subjects would be more likely to be less truthful than in a personal interview. In order to investigate this question, we chose a random sample of fifty-five subjects from a larger group of 216 one-year questionnaires that were completed during the second half of the study, again excluding those who were institutionalized or living outside a 100-mile radius.

As soon as each of the fifty-five subjects had completed his questionnaire, he was contacted by the research team to schedule an immediate personal interview to "gather additional data." In this interview, items in the mailed questionnaire were reassessed and, without prior warning, a urine sample was collected.

The results indicated that most subjects were truthful in both the mail/telephone contact *and* the personal interview. Table 13-III shows the relationship between reported heroin use and the urinalysis results.

Of the twenty-seven subjects who had indicated no heroin use on the questionnaire, twenty-four (89.9%) had urines found negative for morphine. A related result was that eighteen of the twenty-one (85.7%) subjects with positive urines had admitted some heroin use on the questionnaire. The corresponding valid-

TABLE 13-III

Frequency of heroin use during past month on mailed questionnaire	Urinalysis Results for Morphine		
	Positive	Negative	Totals
"Daily"	6 (75.0%)	2 (25.0%)	8
"Several times/week"	7 (87.5%)	1 (12.5%)	8
"Just a few times"	5 (41.7%)	7 (58.3%)	12
"Not at all"	3 (11.1%)	24 (89.9%)	27
Totals	21 (38.2%)	34 (61.8%)	55

ity figures were slightly *less* for the information reported in the personal interview in which the urine sample was collected. That is, the subjects were not quite as likely to give an interviewer a truthful report of his recent drug use as he was to indicate it truthfully in a mail/telephone contact.

These results described elsewhere in greater detail (Bale, 1979b) were encouraging in indicating to us that the substantially less expensive methodology of mail/telephone contact would not result in lowered accuracy of some key data. However, we were also skeptical as to the reliability of information on such items as employment, salary, criminal records, and other more complex data, and whether such material might need to be assessed in a personal interview. Accordingly, each of the fifty-five subjects were asked again in the personal interview a number of key questions from the mailed questionnaire. In this interview, the researcher was able to probe and clarify any of the subject's answers. The degree of correspondence between the two sets of self-reports are given in Table 13-IV.

The reliability results were also encouraging and indicated that the brief data we were gathering did not require the context of a personal interview. It should be noted, however, that our validity and reliability results were related to the serious nature of the study, the good rapport established at the outset with the subjects, and the clear separation between clinical and research personnel. Because the context of the interview and the confidence of the subject in his anonymity can greatly affect the truthfulness of his reporting (Stanton, 1977), we might have expected quite different results with a different methodology, e.g., if program personnel had conducted the interviews.

TABLE 13-IV

CORRESPONDENCE OF SELF-REPORTS

	Mailed Questionaire (Mean or %)	Personal Interview (Mean or %)	Degree of Exact Correspondence of Individual Scores
Length of longest heroin run in year	3.09 months	3.33 months	$t = .73$, $r = .76$ $p < .40$
Average salary during past six months	$686	$744	$t = 1.47$, $r = .92$ $p < .10$
Public assistance at one year	$177	$175	$t = .32$, $r = .95$ $p < .50$
Working at one year	50%	50%	93%
% in school in past 6 mo.	25%	33%	78%
% arrested in past 6 mo.	33%	33%	89%
% convicted in past 6 mo.	15%	15%	78%
% on probation at one year	40%	36%	83%

Key: For length of heroin run, salary and public assistance, degree of correspondence is given as correlations between the scores and T-tests for correlated means. For school, arrests, convictions, and probation data, the degree of correspondence is the percentage of subjects reporting an event who indicated so in both the questionnaire and the personal interview.

Results

Retention Curves

Figure 13-2 shows the time in treatment during the two-year follow-up period for all the therapeutic community subjects and the methadone treatment group. All subjects were in a program at least one week, the minimal stay to be defined as "in treatment."

More than half the therapeutic community subjects dropped out of their programs before two months elapsed, and less than 20 percent had completed the recommended six months for graduation. While these time periods are substantially less than other nonhospital-based therapeutic communities with *average* stays of more than a year, the intensity of the VA programs, freed from many of the maintenance and fund-raising obligations, is manifest in a much more concentrated group and individual therapy schedule (Van Stone et al., 1976).

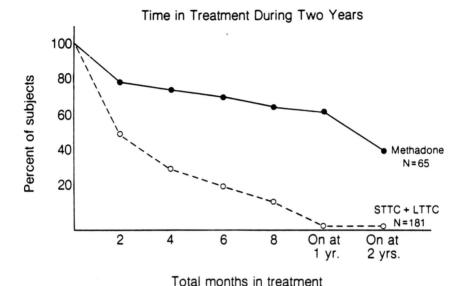

Figure 13-2. Time in treatment during two years.

The three therapeutic communities in the Palo Alto study, in fact, had somewhat different retention curves, as can be seen in Figure 13-3.

Satori, the professionally staffed program, was able to retain significantly more members during the early weeks of treatment. Both the Family and Quadrants had much greater immediate attrition, although after ten weeks the Family equalled and then surpassed Satori in their retention of members.

Interestingly, the first program modification in response to study results was in response to the retention curves. Concerned with its considerable early attrition, the Family developed a two-week "newborn section" specifically designed to intensively orient and incubate new members before exposing them fully to the challenge and stress of confrontation techniques. It is not unusual to find a therapeutic community with severe attrition or census problems that has not even compiled a basic figure like that shown above. The specific characteristics of such an attrition curve can be very useful in suggesting the underlying clinical phenomenon and possible appropriate solutions.

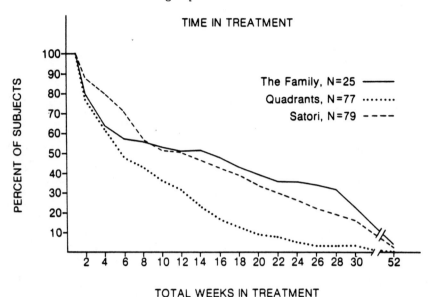

Figure 13-3. Time in treatment.

Therapeutic Communities versus Methadone Treatment

A principal goal of the Palo Alto study was to examine the relative progress of subjects treated in each of these two major modalities, and to compare each of these groups with a non-treated group. In order to facilitate these comparisons, we constructed the following post-hoc cohorts for analysis:

No Treatment subjects (N=150) left the hospital after a five-day detoxification and entered no other program in or outside the VA during the two-year follow-up period.

Non-VA subjects (N=166) entered no VA program beyond detoxification but did enter subsequent treatment outside the VA.

STTC subjects (N=85) were in one of the three therapeutic communities less than fifty days (short term).

LTTC subjects (N=96) were in one of the three therapeutic communities fifty days or more (long term).

Methadone subjects (N=65) were enrolled in the outpatient program during the follow-up period.

Because the randomization protocol had been somewhat

compromised, and we had no control over treatment dropouts, i.e., the no treatment group was in no way a randomly created group, it became imperative to statistically investigate any differences between the groups for outcome analysis. A variety of multivariate classification strategies employed failed to discriminate the groups well (Bale et al., 1980). Table 13-V outlines the demographic characteristics of the treatment groups.

TABLE 13-V

COMPARATIVE DEMOGRAPHIC INTAKE DATA

Variable	N = 150 No Rx	N = 166 Non-VA	N = 85 STTC	N = 96 LTTC	N = 65 Meth	Exact Prob. of Chi Square or F (NS = p .05)	Total
Age	31.6	30.7	27.9	29.3	32.6	.004	30.5
Ethnic Background							
Black	44	40	33	35	46	.01	40
White	35	33	49	57	37		40
Other	21	27	18	14	17		20
Married	23	25	33	22	28	NS	25
High School Grad	69	69	66	76	69	NS	70
Age 1st Heroin Use	20.7	20.7	20.4	21.2	20.4	NS	20.7
Length current run	8.3	8.0	6.9	6.5	8.8	NS	7.8
Ever narcotic free after first run	71	59	69	66	73	NS	67
Use any other illegal drug in previous 3 mo.	69	73	76	71	77	NS	72
Convicted of felony in past two years	45	41	43	46	51	NS	44
Currently employed	16	22	32	21	22	NS	22
Worked or attended school in past 2 years	75	79	86	79	77	NS	78
On probation or parole	37	28	30	36	46	NS	34
In residential treatment program before	5	11	11	19	17	.01	12

There were remarkably few differences on the variables examined in spite of the lack of complete experimental control. Blacks were somewhat more likely to enter the methadone program, as were whites more likely to enter a therapeutic community. The therapeutic community subjects were slightly younger. Both the LTTC and methadone groups had more subjects with previous residential treatment. What a statistical procedure can never tell us is the extent to which the groups were equivalent in terms of more subtle or even unmeasurable qualities, e.g., motivation, a personal sense of readiness for change, or a complex interaction of several variables that would predispose an individual to specific outcome. It is for precisely this reason that statistical control can never fully substitute for random assignment.

Table 13-VI summarizes the outcome results for several key variables and a global variable that combined the variables by assigning one point each to follow-up status of employed or attending school, not using heroin, not using other illegal drugs (besides marijuana), and having no convictions. Incarcerated or deceased subjects (in both cases predominantly drug related) were scored as using heroin. This scoring rule was one of several arbitrary decisions made by the research group, who considered it a fairer picture of outcome than to either separate the data for incarcerated individuals or to score them as drug-free.

TABLE 13-VI
Two-year Outcome

								Specific Comparison		
							Chi Sq	LTTC	Meth	LTTC
Outcome	N = 150	N = 166	N = 85	N = 96	N = 65		Sig. for	vs	vs	vs
Variable	No Rx	Non-VA	STTC	LTTC	Meth	Total	Group	No Rx	No Rx	Meth
Any heroin use during past three months:										
	68	67	68	50	71	65	.02	.003	NS	.01
Any other illegal drug use during past three months:										
	62	52	49	57	40	54	.04	NS	.001	.03
Convicted during two years:										
	69	59	61	48	51	59	.01	.0004	.006	NS
Worked or attended school during two years:										
	73	78	80	90	80	79	.02	.002	.06	NS
Working or attending school at two years:										
	34	41	45	52	45	42	.06	.0005	NS	.07
In jail at two years:										
	34	19	26	12	14	23	.0001	.0001	.01	NS
Global Outcome (means):										
	1.25	1.50	1.47	1.75	1.75	1.49	.008	.001	.003	NS

Note: all figures are percentages except where global outcome, where significance of row ANOVA F is given, and exact significance of t tests for specific comparisons.

Chi squares were computed for the five group comparisons and the specific contrasts between the LTTC, methadone, and no treatment group were reported.

Subjects who stayed in one of the three therapeutic communities longer than fifty days were less likely to be using heroin, less likely to have been convicted or in jail, and more likely to be working or attending school than were subjects who had not engaged in treatment beyond detoxification either in or outside the VA system. Methadone subjects were only less likely to be using other illegal drugs and to have been convicted. Specific contrasts showed the LTTC group to be less likely than the methadone group to be using heroin but more likely to be using other illegal drugs.

The contrasts with the detoxification-only group do not account for probable differences in truthfulness between the two groups as indicated in our validity study, and other reports of outcome have attempted to reflect those results (Bale et al., 1979).

In spite of the apparent pretreatment equivalence of the treatment groups on key variables related to outcome, the possibility exists that these outcome differences might be due to individual differences at the outset of treatment or that, conversely, such differences might mask real posttreatment differences. Accordingly, we employed a stratification analysis (essentially an analysis of covariance for discontinuous variables) as developed by Gart (1971) using parallel admission variables as the covariates. The results for key variables are summarized in Table 13-VII.

In every case the significant group comparison was still obtained when the parallel variable at intake was controlled, except that the methadone group was in this analysis not significantly less likely to be using the drugs when the treatment differences in this same variable were controlled. Moreover, when work or school attendance before treatment was controlled, LTTC subjects were significantly more likely to be working or attending school during the follow-up period than were methadone subjects. This result was obtained even though the therapeutic community subjects had less opportunity in time for school or work because of their period of institutionalization.

An interesting result, rarely examined by other outcome studies, was the only moderate relationship among the major

TABLE 13-VII

STRATIFICATION ANALYSES

		Exact Significance in Main Effect (NS = p .05)		
		LTTC	Meth	LTTC
Outcome	Admission	vs	vs	vs
Variable	Covariate	No Rx	No Rx	Meth
Any heroin use during past 3 mo.	Ever narcotic free after run	.006	NS	.008
Used any other illegal drug in past 3 mo.	Used any other illegal drug in past 3 mo.	NS	.004	NS
Convicted during 2 years	Convicted during previous 2 years	.001	.005	NS
Worked or attended school in 2 years	Worked or attended school in 2 years	.0004	NS	.05
Working/attending school at 2 years	Working/attending school at 2 years	.003	NS	NS

outcome variables, as shown in Table 13-VIII.

Contingency coefficients (analagous to correlation coefficients, but for discontinuous data) were slight to moderate, ranging from .10 to .27. Clearly many subjects were working, but still using drugs, or were not using drugs but also not working. Their use of heroin was only minimally related to the probability of their use of other illegal drugs.

Perhaps these interrelationships are so rarely explored in past studies because they are assumed to be strong. After all, our first contact with subjects is at a time when most or all areas of their lives are failing, and perhaps this negative "halo effect" persists into our conception of post-treatment functioning. In actuality, subjects may choose to enter treatment precisely because they lack *any* remaining sources of competence and self-esteem, and that any follow-up at an arbitrary time in the future will more likely find a mixed pattern of social functioning.

Further analysis of the methadone group, as well as a detailed presentation of design considerations and results, have appeared elsewhere (Bale et al., 1978).

Difference Between the Three Therapeutic Communities

In comparing the residential and outpatient methadone pro-

TABLE 13-VIII

RELATIONSHIP BETWEEN
OUTCOME VARIABLES

	No D	D	
No H	182	41	223
H	133	185	318
	315	226	541

	No WS	WS	
No H	98	126	244
H	201	118	319
	299	244	543

	No C	C	
No H	167	57	224
H	195	124	319
	362	181	543

	No WS	WS	
No D	147	168	315
D	151	75	226
	298	243	541

	No C	C	
No D	223	92	315
D	137	89	226
	360	181	541

	No C	C	
No WS	183	117	300
WS	180	65	245
	363	182	545

H=Any heroin use in last month of first year

D=Any other illegal drug use in last month of first year

WS=Working or attending school at one year point

C=Conviction for a serious offense during the year

All figures are raw numbers; a few values are missing and the total N's range from 541-545.

grams, differences in treatment process were relatively obvious. However, in contrasting outcome from the three therapeutic communities themselves, the Family, Quadrants, and Satori, it became important to systematically differentiate the programs.

We have available descriptions of structure and process for both the Family (Van Stone and Gilbert, 1972; Bale and Potter, 1976; Balgooyen, 1974; Van Stone et al., 1974) and Satori (Zarcone, 1975; Zarcone, in press) as well as the drug unit as a whole (Van Stone, 1974; Van Stone et al., 1976). However, no common methodology had been used to describe all three programs, and we undertook that task in both anecdotal and more systematic efforts.

We noted specific behavioral and structural differences between the programs, e.g., the Family was considerably more separated from the outside world (telephones, television, newspapers), Satori had a much larger and more degreed staff, the residents had much greater power in both the Family and Quadrants, there were strict abstinence rules for the staff of the Family, and so forth. These and other differences on other dimensions such as the nature and positive and negative sanctions, the existence of written versus orally communicated rules, the style of feedback, rules of confidentiality, levels of self-disclosure, criteria for exclusion, degree of physical contact between members, vocational training activities, and the involvement of family members in treatment have been described in detail elsewhere (Bale et al., 1979).

In order to more systematically examine process differences, we utilized a standard instrument that assessed the resident's perceptions of their program: the Community Oriented Program Environment Scale (COPES), a variation of the widely used Ward Atmosphere Scale (Moos, 1974). The scale, which consists of 102 true-false items, was administered in each program three times about four months apart during the study treatment period. The results are presented in Figure 13-4.

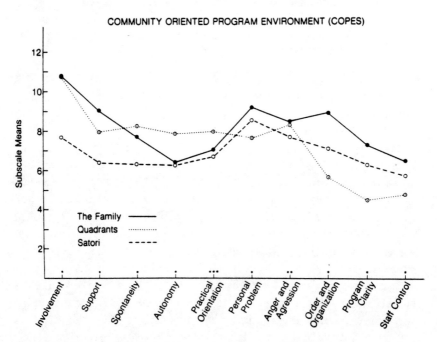

Figure 13-4 Community-oriented program environment (COPES).

There were statistically significant differences on each of the ten dimensions of program process as perceived by the residents themselves. The Family and Quadrants were commonly perceived by their members as higher in "involvement," a measure of how active the residents are in the day-to-day functioning of the program, than was Satori. Similarly, the same two programs were higher than Satori in "Support," the degree to which members feel they are encouraged to be helpful and supportive to other members, and "spontaneity," the extent to which the program is perceived to encourage members to express their feelings openly.

The Family and Satori, both more structured programs than Quadrants, were both seen in comparison to Quadrants as having significantly more staff control, program clarity, order and organization, and offering less autonomy to its residents. These similarities, in spite of overwhelming differences along other dimensions, became especially interesting in the light of outcome data that showed these two programs to be considerably more effective than Quadrants. Those results are summarized in Table 13-IX.

TABLE 13-IX

SUMMARY OUTCOME DATA

Variable		Program		
	Family	*Quadrants*	*Satori*	*Detox Only*
Full group	*N = 25*	*N = 77*	*N = 79*	*N = 166*
(longer term[1])	*(N = 14)*	*(N = 35)*	*(N = 46)*	
No heroin use in	40.0	48.1†	35.4	33.3
past 3 mo.	(42.9)	(60.0)†	(45.7)	
No other illegal	40.0	41.6	53.2**	39.3
drug use in past				
3 mo.	(42.9)	(31.4)	(56.6)	
No convictions in	44.0†	32.5	59.5†	31.3
past 2 years*	(57.1)	(31.4)	(67.3)†	
Working or attend-	48.0†	46.8†	51.9†	34.0
ing school at 2 yrs.	(57.1)	(45.7)	(58.7)†	
Deaths (number)	1	1	1	11

Note: All figures are percentages except where noted.
*Significant chi square p < .05 for row.
†Significant comparison with detox only p < .05.
[1]Longer term subjects were in treatment more than 50 days.

Only former members of Quadrants were significantly less likely to be using heroin at follow-up when compared to the detoxification-only group. However, when these results were analyzed in a stratification procedure controlling for whether the subject had ever been previously narcotic-free after his first period of daily use, the treatment differences were not significant (Table 13-X). It should be noted that the lack of statistical significance is in part a result of the low numbers when the programs are considered separately, and include many subjects who had brief contact with a program.

Satori subjects were significantly less likely to be using other illegal drugs, less likely to have been convicted of a crime, and more likely to be working or attending school than the detoxification-only subjects. Subjects from the Family had a similar result, with the exception of the use of other illegal drugs. All these differences are still obtained in a stratification analysis (Table 13-X), which controlled for the effect of initial differences on parallel variables. Again, Quadrants subjects' differences in working or attending school were not upheld in the covariance analyses.

TABLE 13-X
STRATIFICATION ANALYSES

Outcome Variable	Admission Covariate	Exact Significance of Main Effect (NS = p < .05)		
		Family vs. Detox Only	Quadrants vs. Detox Only	Satori vs. Detox Only
No heroin use in past 3 mo.	Ever narcotic free after first run	NS	NS	NS
No other illegal use in past 3 mo.	Used non-opiate during previous 3 mo.	NS	NS	.05
No conviction in past 2 years	Convicted prior 2 years	.05	NS	.001
Working or attending school at 2 years	Working or attending school at intake	.04	NS	.004

An important finding in the study was that, while three subjects (1.7%) in the residential programs died in the follow-up period (all three had stayed less than fifty days), eleven (6.6%) of the detoxification-only group were no longer alive after two years.

Given the stratification results, Quadrants was not found to significantly exceed the detoxification-only group on any of the major outcome variables, e.g., types of illegal activity among those committing crimes, current access to illegal drugs, suicide attempts, subsequent treatment, medical problems, changes in marital status, social activities, sexual problems, and social stability (credit card, bank account, drivers license, telephone, voting registration).

Because of the relatively successful and similar outcome results of such two radically different programs, Satori and the Family, we were especially interested in any similarities in process that had been evidenced in the COPES data. In four dimensions the programs were most similar to each other and different from Quadrants: a high degree of staff control, clarity of program expectations and rules, high order and organization, and low patient autonomy. That these factors should appear to be salient in working with a population whose primary defenses involve acting out behavior and externalization strategies is not surprising.

Methodological Limitations

Many of the methodological limitations of the study (compromise of the randomization, the absence of a true no treatment randomly assigned control group, and somewhat different follow-up periods "at risk") have been mentioned. These factors limit the extent to which we can ascribe differences at follow-up to treatment. Our results may also be only generalizable to a limited sample of drug abusers, because of the select nature of the study subjects. All were male veterans (with a sufficient premorbid history to qualify them for military service) and the average age of 31.2 years was a few years older than the national average for drug abusers in treatment (Sells, 1974).

A major difference between the Palo Alto study and the design of three major national assessments (Mandell et al., 1974; Sells et al., 1976; Macro Systems, 1975) is the comparison of treated subjects with detoxification-only subjects, rather than with themselves. Such designs using subjects as their own controls pre- and posttreatment are not likely to fail to find improvement for most subjects. For the outcome measures are of essentially episodic events measured at an arbitrary point in time, compared with functioning at treatment entry, which likely occurs at precisely the nadir of most social functioning. (See Campbell, 1969, for a discussion of related social phenomena.) For example, we were reluctant to attribute the 34.5 percent heroin-free statistics in the detoxification-only group (0% were heroin free at admission) to the effects of a five-day hospitalization two years previously. More likely such a figure would be obtained at *any* arbitrary assessment of heroin use in the group later in time (or two years prior to treatment). The performance of the group we felt to be a more realistic baseline for comparisons than the extreme case of admission functioning.

Presentation of Results of Clinical Staff

Typically, a program staff participating in a follow-up study will be totally ignorant of published and even widely cited outcome reports on its former members. While this is in part related to resistance and skepticism of research methodology and results, the usual style in which results are presented to clinical staff is not likely to capture their imagination.

Most clinicians, particularly the paraprofessionals who make up such an important segment of substance abuse treatment staff, are not heavy readers of the research literature. Few are familiar with research methodology, or with questions of design or statistical analysis. However, treatment personnel are not at all unfamiliar with hypotheses about human behavior, speculations about causal relationships, second order interactions among variables, and so forth. Particularly in a therapeutic community, such discussions are the focus of hours of daily formal and informal staff interactions. A researcher with results to present can easily access this energy.

In Palo Alto, we would disseminate research results in a game-like situation. For example, the staff of the detoxification program, from which all transfers to longer term therapy were made, were especially interested in which individual factors were related to the event of transfer. While a few staff were fairly empirical about the question, most in fact felt they *knew* what kind of patients transferred, and which participated only in the short-term detoxification procedures. The study had been able to determine which few individual demographic characteristics were related to treatment and which were not (Bale et al., 1974).

Some variables (previous treatment, alcohol problem, use of other illegal drugs) had, in fact, been found to predict transfer to a longer term program. Other variables not found to be predictive were specifically chosen because the researcher knew they represented certain prevailing myths, e.g., married people *just don't go* into programs, older people *never stay* in therapeutic communities.

Staff members were encouraged to guess whether each variable on the list predicted transfer, no transfer, or did not predict. The price of each guess was to state in one sentence a theory explaining the proposed relationship. Quickly the room was filled with guess and counterguess, a variety of theories, and the staff was surprised by both the variety and heterogeneity, i.e., previously unrealized disagreements, of many of their *beliefs*. When some of those beliefs were not confirmed by the data, they began to discuss other assumptions made about the patients, their validity, and the degree to which those views and unexpressed conflicts about those issues affected the treatment process.

Such modes of presentations, which tap the natural inquisitiveness of a clinical staff, can be very useful in imparting new information as well as challenging old beliefs. In this manner a negative research result — showing no difference — can be useful in engendering a more empirically oriented outlook in the staff.

Clinical Impact of the Study

During the planning stage of the study at Palo Alto, we experienced a good deal of resistance to the study. This resistance stemmed from many sources (Bale, 1979a). Some clinicians were in fact more interested in the quality of life within the therapeutic community and did not believe that a true assessment of a program should be based on the post-discharge behavior of its residents. Others placed little trust in self-reported data and/or felt that the variables of social functioning to be assessed were too far afield from the more complex and subtle changes that were the focus of treatment. Some staff also felt that positive outcome results would probably not be very useful to them, but that evidence of poor outcome might result in the closing of the program.

The crux of the resistance, however, focused on the randomization protocol and the suspicion that such an assignment procedure would substantially lessen the rate of transfer to longer term programs. We too shared these fears, but they were not realized. Pretreatment rates of transfer were doubled during the random assignment period; when the research protocol ended, transfer rates fell some 56 percent within the year. The intense contact between the program and assigned patient required by the protocol, the competition among programs in a comparative outcome design, and the thirty-day rule encouraging entry to the assigned treatment all appeared to have increased the transfer rate.

The research activities also influenced belief systems of both staff and subjects even before the follow-up results were clear. For example, one residential program with a "no one over thirty" rule was required to admit older veterans, who, over time, strengthened and added new dimensions to the program. Further, many persons who had come to the hospital strictly for methadone maintenance and were assigned to a relatively unfamiliar residential modality entered a therapeutic community and were functioning well drug-free at follow-up. Finally, in order to coordinate the study itself, the treatment programs, hitherto unorganized as a functioning unit, began to meet regularly and formed eventually into administrative body, the Drug and Alcohol Rehabilitation Unit (DARU).

Thus, a well-designed research study, rather than compromising therapeutic activities, can engender both an atmosphere of empiricism and a forum for dialogue that is essential to an effective, evolving clinical program.

REFERENCES

Amsel, Z.; Mandell, W.; Matthias, L.; Mason, C.; and Hocherman, I.: Reliability and validity of self-reported illegal activities and drug use collected from narcotic addicts. *Int J Addict, 11* (2):325-336, 1976.

Aron, W. S.; and Daily, D.: Camarillo — Short and long term therapeutic communities: A follow-up and cost effectiveness comparison. *Int J Addict, 9*:619-636, 1974.

Bale, R. N.: Outcome research in therapeutic communities for drug abusers: A critical review 1963-1975. *Int J Addict, 14*:1053-1074, 1979a.

Bale, R. N.: The validity and reliability of self-reported data from heroin addicts: Mailed questionnaires compared with face-to-face interviews. *Int J Addict, 14*:993-1000, 1979b.

Bale, R. N.; Cabrera, L. S.; and Brown, J. D.: Follow-up evaluation of drug abuse treatment. *Am J Drug Alcoh Abuse, 4*:233-249, 1977.

Bale, R. N.; and Potter, B.: Treating drug abuse by treating its causes. In J Krumboltz; and C. Thoresen: *Behavioral Counseling Methods.* New York: Holt, Rinehart and Winston, 1976.

Bale, R. N.; Van Stone, W. W.; Engelsing, T. M. J.; Kuldau, J. M.; and Zarcone, V. P.: The validity of self-reported heroin use. *Int J Addict,* in press.

Bale, R. N.; Van Stone, W. W.; Kuldau, J. M.; Engelsing, T. M. J.; and Zarcone, V. P.: Therapeutic communities vs. methadone maintenance: Characteristics of patients accepting or rejecting treatment in a randomized study. In E. Senay; and V. Shorty (Eds.): *Developments in the Field of Drug Abuse.* Cambridge, Massachusetts: Schenkman Publishing Co., 1974.

Bale, R. N.; Van Stone, W. W.; Kuldau, J. M.; Engelsing, T. M. J.; and Zarcone, V. P.: Preliminary two year follow-up results from a randomized comparison of methadone maintenance and therapeutic communities. In D. E. Smith (Ed.): *A Multicultural View of Drug Abuse.* Cambridge, Massachusetts: G. K. Hall, 1978, pp. 433-441.

Bale, R. N.; Van Stone, W. W.; Kuldau, J. M.; Engelsing, T. M. J.; and Zarcone, V. P.: Three therapeutic communities: A prospective controlled study of narcotic addiction treatment: Process and two year follow-up results. Paper presented at the National Drug Abuse Conference, New Orleans, August, 1979.

Bale, R. N.; Van Stone, W. W.; Kuldau, J. M.; Engelsing, T. M. J.; Elashoff, R. A.; and Zarcone, V. P.: Therapeutic communities vs. methadone maintenance: A prospective controlled study of narcotic addiction treatment: Design and one year follow-up results. *Arch Gen Psych, 37*:179-193, 1980.

Balgooyen, T. J.: A comparison of the effect of Synanon "game" verbal attack therapy and standard group therapy practice on hospitalized chronic alcoholics. *J Commun Psychol, 2*:54-58, 1974.

Ball, J. C.: The reliability and validity of interview data obtained from 59 narcotic addicts. *Am J Sociol, 72*:650-654, 1967.

Barr, H. L.; Ottenberg, D. J.; and Rosen, A.: Two year follow-up study of 724 drug addicts and alcoholics treated together in an abstinence therapeutic community. Paper presented at the Fifth National Conference on Methadone Treatment, Washington, D.C., April, 1973.

Brecher, E. M., and the Editors of Consumers Reports: *Licit and Illicit Drugs.* Boston: Little, Brown & Co., 1972.

Campbell, D. T.: Reforms as experiments. *Am Psychol, 24*:409-429, 1969.

Campbell, D. T.; and Stanley, J. C.: *Experimental and Quasi-Experimental Designs for Research.* Chicago: Rand McNally & Co., 1963.

Casriel, D. C.: *So Fair a House.* Engelwood Cliffs: Prentice-Hall, 1963.

Casriel, D. C.; and Amen, G.: *Daytop: Three Addicts and Their Cure.* New York: Hill and Wang, 1971.

Catlin, D. H.; Cleeland, R.; and Grunberg, E.: A sensitive, rapid radioimmunoassay for morphine and immunologically related substances in urine and serum. *J Clin Chem, 19*:216-220, 1973.

Chambers, C. D.; and Inciardi, J. A.: Three years after the split. In E. Senay and V. Shorty (Eds.): *Developments in the Field of Drug Abuse.* Cambridge, Massachusetts: Schenkman, 1974.

Cherkas, M. S.: Synanon foundation — A radical approach to the problem of addiction. *Am J Psychiat, 121*:1065-1068, 1965.

Collier, W. V.; Hammock, E. R.; and Devlin, C.: *An Evaluation Report on the Therapeutic Program of Daytop Village, Inc.* New York: Daytop Village, 1970.

Collier, W. V.; and Hijazi, M. A.: A follow-up study of former residents of a therapeutic community. *Int J Addict, 9*:805-826, 1974.

Craig, R. J.: Locating drug addicts who have dropped out of treatment. *Hosp Comm Psychiat, 30*:402-404, 1979.

Dealing with Drug Abuse. A report to the Ford Foundation. The Drug Abuse Survey Project. New York: Praeger Publishers, 1972.

DeLeon, G.; Andrews, M.; and Kowlowsky, M.: The therapeutic community for drug abuse: Successes and failures five years after treatment. Paper presented at the American Psychological Association, Toronto, 1978.

DeLeon, G.; Holland, S.; and Rosenthal, M.: Phoenix House: Criminal activity dropouts. *JAMA, 222*:686-689, 1972.

DeLeon, G.; and Kowlowsky, M.: Therapeutic community dropouts: A global index of success and psychological status five years after treatment. Paper presented at the Eastern Psychological Association, Washington, D.C., 1978.

Dirks, S. J.; and Kuldau, J. M.: The validity of self reports by psychiatric patients of employment earnings and hospitalization. *J Consult Clin Psychol, 42*:738, 1974.

Erickson, R. C.: Outcome studies in mental hospitals: A review. *Psychol Bull, 82*:519-540, 1975.

Garfield, S. L.; and Bergin, A. E.: *Handbook of Psychotherapy and Behavior Change: An Empirical Analysis.* New York: John Wiley & Sons, 1978.

Gart, J. J.: The comparison of proportions: A review of significant tests. Confidence intervals and adjustments for stratification. *Rev Interactional Statis Inst, 39*(2), 1971.

Glasscote, R.; Sussex, J. N.; Jaffee, J. H.; Ball, J.; and Brill, L.: *The Treatment of Drug Abuse: Program, Problems, Prospects.* Washington, D.C.: The Joint Information Service, 1972.

Goldstein, P. G.; Abott, W.; Paige, W.; Sobell, I.; and Soto, F.: Tracking procedures in follow-up studies of drug abusers. *Am J Drug Alcoh Abuse, 4*:21-30, 1977.

Holland, S.: Long term follow-up of therapeutic community clients. Paper presented at the National Drug Abuse Conference, Seattle, 1978a.

Holland, S.: Gateway houses: Effectiveness of treatment on criminal behavior. *Int J Addict, 13*:369-381, 1978b.

Jaffe, J. H.: Further experience with methadone in the treatment of narcotics users. In S. Einstein (Ed.): *Methadone Maintenance.* New York: Marcel Dekker, Inc., 1971a, pp. 29-43.

Jaffe, J. H.: A review of the approaches to the problem of compulsive narcotic use. In J. R. Wittenborn (Ed.): *Drugs and Youth.* Springfield: Thomas, 1971b.

Jones, M.: *The Therapeutic Community.* New York: Basic Books, 1953.

Macro Systems: *Three Year Follow-up Study of Clients Enrolled in Treatment Programs in New York City. Phase III. Final Report.* Submitted to the National Institute on Drug Abuse, June 13, 1975.

Maddux, J.; and Desmond, D. P.: Reliability and validity of information from chronic heroin users. *J Psychiat Res, 12*:87-95, 1975.

Mandell, W.; Goldschmidt, P.; and Jillson, I.: Evaluation of treatment programs for drug abusers. In E. Senay; and V. Shorty (Eds.): *Developments in the Field of Drug Abuse.* Cambridge, Massachusetts: Schenkman, 1974.

May, P. R.; Tuma, A. H.; and Dixon, W. J.: Schizophrenia — A follow-up study of results of treatment. *Arch Gen Psychiat, 33*:471-586, 1976.

Moos, R. H.: *Evaluating Treatment Environments: A Sociological Approach.* New York: John Wiley & Sons, 1974.

Nash, G.: An Analysis of Twelve Studies of the Impact of Drug Abuse Treatment Upon Criminality. Monograph, Westchester County, New York, June, 1976.

Romand, A. M.; Forrest, C. K.; and Kleber, H. D.: Follow-up of participants in a drug dependence therapeutic community. *Arch Gen Psychiat, 32*:369-374, 1975.

Sells, S. B.: *The Effectiveness of Drug Abuse Treatment. Vol. 2: Patient Profiles, Treatment and Outcomes.* Cambridge, Massachusetts: Ballinger, 1974.

Sells, S. B.; Simpson, D. D.; Joe, G. W.; Demaree, R. G.; Savage, L. J.; and Lloyd, M. R.: A national follow-up study to evaluate the effectiveness of drug abuse treatment: A report on Cohort 1 of the DARP five years later. *Am J Drug Alcoh Abuse, 3*:54-556, 1976.

Simpson, D. D.; Savage, L. J.; and Lloyd, M. R.: Follow-up evaluation of drug abuse treatment in the DARP during 1969-1972. *Arch Gen Psychiat*, in press.

Slotkin, E. J.: *Gateway: The First Three Years*. Chicago: Gateway Houses Foundation, Illinois Drug Abuse Programs, 1972.

Smart, R. G.: Outcome studies of therapeutic community and half-way house treatment for addicts. *Int J Addict, 11*:143-159, 1976.

Stanton, M. D.: Drug use surveys: Method and madness. *Int J Addict, 12*:95-119, 1977.

Stephens, R.: The truthfulness of addict respondents in research projects. *Int J Addict, 7*:549-558, 1972.

Vaillant, G. E.: *Adaptation to Life*. Boston: Little, Brown & Co., 1977.

Van Stone, W. W.: Treating the drug dependent veteran — perspective from a Veterans Administration Hospital. *Int J Addict, 9*(4):593-604, 1974.

Van Stone, W. W.; Engelsing, T. M. J.; Bale, R. N.; and Zarcone, V. P.: Treating the drug dependent veteran. In J. H. Masserman (Ed.): *Current Psychiatric Therapies* (Vol. 16). New York: Grune & Stratton, 1976.

Van Stone, W. W.; and Gilbert, R.: Peer confrontation groups: What, why and whether? *Am J Psychiat, 129*:5, 1972.

Van Stone, W. W.; Gilbert, R. P.; and Bale, R. N.: Peer confrontation groups — evaluation of a program. Paper presented at the meeting of the Scientific Program of the American Psychiatric Association, Detroit, April, 1974.

Volkman, R.; and Cressey, D. R.: Differential association and the rehabilitation of drug addicts. *Am J Sociol, 69*:129-142, 1963.

Walizer, D. G.: The need for standardized, scientific criteria for describing drug using behavior. *Int J Addict, 10*:927-936, 1975.

Zarcone, V. P., Jr.: *Drug Addicts in a Therapeutic Community: The Satori Approach:* Baltimore: York Press, 1975.

Zarcone, V. P., Jr.: An electric therapeutic community for the treatment of drug dependence. *Int J Addict*, in press.

Part IV

Special Populations

We end this volume with two papers that deal with different ends of the addiction continuum. Hermos and Bachrach deal with the issue of medical patients who become iatrogenically addicted during the course of treatment where psychoactive and analgesic medications are prescribed as part of patient management. The authors provide a number of guidelines that can assist the clinician in dealing with patients' over-reliance on medications with addictive or habituating properties. These techniques are employed not only in the Substance Abuse Treatment Program, where drug addict patients have become hypersensitive to internal bodily changes, but also in pain clinics and stress management programs where similar addict-like behavior is commonly observed. However, they caution that some of these patients may need to be in special treatment programs where their special needs may receive proper attention. Hermos and Bachrach point out that many of the problems described in this paper can be anticipated before they emerge or at least before they get out of hand.

Another end of the addiction continuum is reviewed by Custer, who was instrumental in developing a new program within the VA for patients "addicted" to gambling. Custer shows that the results of pathological and impulsive gambling are as devastating as other forms of addiction. He reviews the various types of gambling, concentrating on compulsive gambling and takes us through the process of onset, prevalence, and treatment opportunities and concepts that have proven useful in the amelioration and rehabilitation of the compulsive gambler. Custer describes the program for compulsive gamblers at Brecksville (Ohio) VA Hospital and presents the issues of legalized gambling and the few treatment programs that exist in the United States and elsewhere for this debilitating problem.

CHAPTER 14

ADDICTIONS TO PSYCHOACTIVE MEDICATIONS: APPROACHES TO MANAGEMENT

JOHN A. HERMOS AND DAVID L. BACHRACH

The number of patients who find difficulty in coping with chronic illness or disability is significant. When the chronic condition is further complicated by dependence on one or more prescribed psychoactive medications, the patient's ability to meet day-to-day problems of living may be even more impaired, and the overall suffering increased. These consequential addictions occur when the prescribed medications possess mood-altering and/or physically addictive properties that are detrimental to the patient's overall ability to function.

Under these conditions patients may become demanding and manipulating, often rejecting or not responding to any of a broad range of therapeutic efforts. The physician then falls short of providing objective and sympathetic care and of promoting effective rehabilitation. Our primary concern is with these problems of patient management, complicated by the addiction rather than with the addiction per se. We are particularly concerned when the unlimited prescription of these medications have substantially contributed to, if not actually having created, the management problem.

PRESCRIBED PSYCHOACTIVE MEDICATION

In medical settings, the most frequently prescribed psychoactive medications are the central nervous system depressant agents, which include the sedative-hypnotics and the minor

351

tranquilizers, and the opiate and other narcotic analgesic agents (see Table 14-I).

TABLE 14-I
PRESCRIBED PSYCHOACTIVE MEDICATIONS
ASSOCIATED WITH MEDICAL ADDICTIONS

OPIATE (NARCOTIC) ANALGESICS

    Oxycodone (Percodan, Percocet, Tylox)*
    Meperidine (Demoral)*
    Hydromorphone (Dilaudid)*
    Propoxyphene (Darvon)*
    Pentazocine (Talwin)
    Morphine
    Codeine
    Methadone (Dolophine)

CENTRAL NERVOUS SYSTEM DEPRESSANTS

Sedative-hypnotics

    Barbiturates (Amytol, Seconal, Nembutol, Tuinol)
    Glutethemide (Doriden)
    Methaqualone (Quaalude)
    Flurazepam (Dalmane)*
    Chloral hydrate
    Paraldehyde
    Methyprylon (Noludar)

Minor Tranquilizers

    Diazepam (Valium)*, Chlordiazepoxide (Librium), Oxazepam
      (Serax) and other benzodiazepine agents
    Meprobamate (Equinil, Miltown)

CENTRAL NERVOUS SYSTEM STIMULANTS

    Amphetamines

*Agents most commonly used by veteran patients referred to authors.

Psychostimulant agents, particularly the amphetamine-type drugs, have only marginal legitimate indications in adult medical practice. Two important types of psychotropic drugs, the antidepressants and the major tranquilizers, appear to have little addictive potential. We will, therefore, focus our discussion on the CNS depressants and narcotic analgesics, which provide the major problems of management.

Whether prescribed for symptomatic relief of anxiety or disturbed sleep (minor tranquilizers and sedative-hypnotics), pain relief (narcotic analgesics), or other medical purposes, e.g., muscle relaxation, these medications are most effective in acute, time-limited, medical or psychiatric situations. In fact, effective long-term therapy with these agents, used either intermittantly or continously, may be accomplished. Major problems emerge, however, in the chronic cases when psychoactive drugs are used in excessive or in progressively increasing doses. Dysfunction may result from unwarranted effects of the medication, medication dependency, or both.

Our clinical experience indicates that the frankly addicted medical patients do not represent a population distinct from the nonconsequential users. The patients, rather, appear to fall on a spectrum exhibiting varying degrees of benefits and consequences attendant to the chronic use of the psychoactive agents, with severely addicted patient being at one extreme of this spectrum.

PILL TAKING BEHAVIOR

Frank addictions to prescribed psychoactive drugs, as with addictions to street drugs and alcohol, are manifest by psychological dependence (habituation), tolerance (metabolic and/or pharmacodynamic), physical dependence (withdrawal or abstinence symptoms), and a substantial rate of relapse to the addicted state, as well as the whole range of psychosocial disruptions. Drug tolerance and physical dependence in medical settings are critical to the extent that they lead to a progressively decreasing efficiency of the prescribed drug, in both intensity and duration of action, and lead to a recurrence of symptoms that are opposite of the intended pharmacologic effects of the drug.

Psychological dependence is evidenced in several ways. It is often articulated by the patient in terms of the need to take a specific medicine to relieve symptoms. In more severe dependency, the medication becomes the only means of obtaining relief and may preclude in the patient's mind alternative methods of treatment or self-care. Such psychological dependency may be further reflected in patient's dread of the very thought of the medication not being available and may elicit the very persistent drug-seeking behaviors of severe addictions.

How does habituation to prescribed psychoactive drugs develop in the medical patient? Are there "signals" that warn of special patient vulnerabilities? One may expect the patients with emotional or behavioral disturbances to gain such profound symptom relief, or to so value the "high," that they will readily increase drug use and develop dependency. Without premorbid psychological assessment, however, one cannot determine whether the psychological state is the precursor or the consequence of the addictive state. The alert primary physician, however, may have knowledge of the patient's style of response to illness and may often recognize the patient's addictive potential in advance.

One can also see the patient as the passive victim, being treated by the unwise or unscrupulous physician whose prescribing habits of psychoactive drugs are unwarranted. A blatant example is found in high compliance settings; for example, the prescribing of sedative or minor tranquilizer drugs to elderly patients in nursing homes or hospitals, where drug accumulation and untoward effects are prevalent (NIDA, 1979).

The importance of the patient's psychodynamics to the problem of iatrogenic addiction ought not be minimized. In the absence of definite information, however, the presumption of a psychopathological precondition is neither justified nor necessary. Consider the patient who presents a nagging, painful orthopedic or neurologic problem that has already caused some impairment in activity as well as a decreased sense of well-being. The physician instructions are typically something like this:

> "Mr. J., your pain has not responded to the medicines I've prescribed. I'm going to give you a stronger medication. However, I must warn you that this is a potentially dangerous drug, and is one to which you could become addicted. Only take one pill when your pain is unbearable." Mr. J. indeed stoically waits until his pain is unbearable, takes a pill, and gets substantial relief.

Two reinforcing processes begin to operate in establishing the habit. Symptom relief and/or pleasant mood change, repeatedly following the pill-taking, begin to serve as reinforcers of that behavior. A second process also emerges, particularly with pain medications. Given the "stoic" instructions, the decision process of when to take the medication becomes stressful. The stress reduction attendant with the decision may then reinforce a tendency on the part of the patient to focus on and elaborate the pain experience, which results in "permitting" the patient to take his pill. Thus, the consequent symptom relief and/or desirable mood change reinforce the pill-taking behavior, which may in turn reinforce the psychological elaboration of the pain experience.

This is usually not all. The next scene in the physician's office generally goes something like this:

> "Doctor, the medicine isn't working anymore. Could you increase the dose?" The physician is suspicious, so he says, "I guess we had better discontinue the medicine since it really is not working." Mr. J. protests, "Well it is better than nothing. At least it takes the edge off the pain."

Sternbach (1974) sees this interaction as part of the patient's game-playing scenario. Indeed, it might well be just that, but there is an alternative explanation, equally reasonable. Narcotic medication has been shown to be far more effective in blocking pain than in relieving it once it has begun. If the patient in fact follows the admonition not to take the pain medication unless he reaches the limits of his endurance, the effectiveness of the medication on the pain may indeed be limited to "taking the edge off." The "stoic PRN" instructions, to the chronic-pain sufferer, may then actually bring about the demand for an increase in dosage, frequency, or both. Thus, the instructions intended to minimize the possibility of addiction may actually "set the patient up."

THE DYSFUNCTIONING MEDICAL ADDICT

Our experience with medical addiction derives, largely, from patients referred to us with chronic pain who have been dependent upon narcotic analgesics. Frequently, these patients are also taking prescribed CNS depressants, which further impair their cognitive and psychosocial functioning. Patients referred to us because they excessively use only minor tranquilizers often present personal characteristics and clinical problems that are distinct from those of chronic-pain patients. In either case, however, the drug dependency itself is but one element, albeit an integral one, of a complex syndrome.

TABLE 14-II

COMMON MEDICAL, SOCIAL AND PSYCHOLOGICAL FEATURE
IN MEDICALLY ADDICTED PATIENTS

Chronic pain, usually of known etiology and/or chronic anxiety-attributed symptoms.

Dependence on Opiate Analgesics, CNS Depressants, or on both.

Psychological discomfort: personal losses, low self-esteem, low activity level, dependent manipulative behavior, fearfulness, free-floating anxiety, sleep and appetite disturbances, decreased sexual activity, poor impulse control.

Unemployment, disability payments, unrealistic rehabilitation and vocational expectations.

Marital, family disruptions; impaired interpersonal relationships, often centered on patients illness, disability.

The personal losses suffered by the patients we see range from the more visible losses of physical strength, employment, and general ability to function to the less visible losses of self-esteem, respect of family and friends, sexual function, as well as interpersonal effectiveness. Characteristically, these patients experience feelings of helplessness and futility. The depressive feelings may be specific, well articulated, and clearly reactive to the situation, or the feelings may be diffuse, poorly articulated, and overlying a depressive condition of long standing. The affective disturbance may be essentially psychologic or it may be pharmacologically intensified, if not induced. Depression may be betrayed by either vegetative or agitated symptomatology, or by both. In any event, the characteristic feelings of helplessness and futility are translated into withdrawal from familial, occupational, and interpersonal responsibilities, as well as from responsibilities of self-care. The burden of responsibility is shifted. The family must provide for personal needs; financial needs are met by family or community; and the physician provides medications for the relief of physical and emotional discomfort. Unless this trend is reversed, the patient becomes crippled as surely as if he were paralytic.

The disinhibitory effects of minor tranquilizers and sedatives may add another dimension to the patient's dysfunction. The effects of these drugs, beyond those of reducing anxiety or facilitating sleep, may disinhibit behaviors that are otherwise controlled, resulting in family, employment, and legal conflicts.

The problem is compounded when the patient is an excessive user of both minor tranquilizers and alcohol. In these cases, the risks for both drug-alcohol overdoses and more flagrant disinhibited behavior are greatly increased. Furthermore, those agents are not likely to be beneficial in cases where depression is implicated. They can, in fact, intensify depressive symptomology (McLellan et al., 1979; Schatzberg, 1978).

EVALUATION AND CARE BY THE PHYSICIAN

The patient who is severely addicted to his medications is a person with an increasingly constricted life-space who is concerned almost exclusively with discomfort — physical, psychological, or both. The patient's methods of dealing with life stresses are now largely limited to the taking of medication and the manipulation of others into taking care of him/her. At this point the psychoactive medications are often only minimally effective and their continued use is very likely to compound the patient's emotional and interpersonal problems. The patient will usually deny the extensiveness of his drug use or try to justify it. In any event, the patient quickly becomes adept at insuring an adequate supply of these medications. Nevertheless, the physician can often help stabilize and redirect the patient's clinical course while continuing to provide objective and sympathetic care. In our consultations with physicians managing patients who are either addicted or who have potential addiction problems, we have found a number of guidelines that prove useful.

(1) **Explore the quality of the patient's life.** Assessment of the patient's somatic or affective complaint (e.g., pain, nervousness) is not enough. The physician must ascertain the patient's level of general functioning, coping-style, and the suffering experience by significant others as well as by the patient. The physician's inquiry is not merely for information gathering. Its primary purpose is to lead the patient to become aware of his/her predicament and its implications for the future. The patient's motivation for change and for involvement in his or her own therapeutic program, we believe, is a function of this self-awareness.

(2) **Accept the patient's somatic complaint as legitimate.** In the case of chronic pain syndromes, judging the legitimacy of the

complaint by correlating it with the severity of the anatomical lesion serves little purpose. It may even prove to be counterproductive where the patient becomes convinced that the physician believes that "it's all in the head." In our experience, challenging the legitimacy of the patient's complaint often serves only to increase the patient's need to demonstrate the severity of the problem, and perhaps to exaggerate or embellish symptoms. This, in turn, often leads to additional procedures and, particularly, to increased doses or strength of medication, or to the increased conviction by the physician of the psychogenic nature of the complaint. These consequences are not necessarily mutually exclusive. An interesting survey of patients who have requested to read their medical records (Altman et al., 1980) has shown that, in the case of chronic-pain syndromes, the patients did so because "they perceived the staff to be skeptical about the validity of their symptoms," and that such requests were indicative of "mistrust" and of "adversary patient-doctor relations." Furthermore, in our experience in the pain clinic, we have found that genuine acceptance of the legitimacy of the patient's complaint facilitates the patient's acceptance or acknowledgement that emotional factors may also contribute to the pain experience.

(3) **Establish in advance the specifics of the treatment plan and the conditions upon which continued treatment is contingent.** Essentially, we are suggesting that the implicit contract between physician and patient be made explicit. In many instances an informal review with the patient of the elements of the agreement will prove sufficient. These include the diagnostic and treatment measures that the physician plans to perform and the behaviors expected of the patient, as well as the reasons behind them. In other instances, a formal review will be appropriate, committed to writing and, perhaps, signed by both physician and patient. The "contract" should include, in addition to the specifics of the diagnostic and treatment measures, a plan of regularly scheduled appointments, commitment to a schedule of medications, doses, and frequencies. Both the physician and patient should also be committed to periodically review the course of treatment and make appropriate modifications of the treat-

ment plan. The specification that only one physician be "in charge" of the case may prove profitable. The objective of this approach is for the patient to be directly involved in his/her own treatment and to accept responsibility for his/her part in it.

(4) **Be alert to the possibility of manipulation efforts on the part of the patient.** Much has been written about the manipulation behaviors of patients with drug dependence, chronic pain, or strong interpersonal dependency needs; i.e., behaviors intended to flatter, intimidate, or to evoke anger, sorrow, or guilt in the physician (Groves, 1978; Sternbach, 1974). Response to such efforts, however, must be restrained. Without such restraint the physician can easily be caught up in competition with the patient for control of the clinical situation. Once caught in this trap, the doctor may ultimately make decisions that are inconsistent with good judgment and the original plans for treatment. On the other hand, we have found a firm focus on the treatment objectives and the plan worked out in advance, as well as a conscious effort to disregard the manipulative behaviors, is the most effective way for maintaining consistently sound treatment and a mutually beneficial doctor-patient relationship.

(5) **Assess the psychoactive medication plan frequently for progress and untoward side effects, making changes as appropriate.** In our discussions with patients, we have found emphasis on the effects of the medications, rather than on the risk or reality of addiction, to be a productive approach. To the typical patients, "addiction" is a high perjorative, emotionally laden word that evokes considerable defensiveness. The patient is usually more amenable to discussions put in terms of "degree of suffering," "level of functioning," and the drug's tendency to be "needed more while helping less." When the decision is made to withdraw or regulate the psychoactive medication, the physician has several alternatives:

(a) *Immediate discontinuation of the drug(s).* This approach is necessary in instances where the effects of the medication impair the safe functioning of the patients, e.g., the accumulating toxic doses of depressants, and where frank physical dependency is not a significant issue. This decision may also prove necessary where the drug-seeking behavior or the drug-induced behavior critically inferferes with the treatment and the safety of others as well as of the patient. Where the situation demands firmness on the part of the physician, he/she must accept the risks of an ugly confrontation, appeals to "higher" administrative levels, and the loss of the patient to continued care by that physician or institution, with the patient turning to other sources for his/her medication.

The widely used, long-acting benzodiazepine minor tranquilizers have been only infrequently implicated in significant withdrawal reactions, and low doses can generally be discontinued safely. Delayed withdrawal signs and symptoms of medical or psychiatric significance can occur, however (Benzer and Cushman, 1980). The critical doses, duration of treatment, and other factors related to withdrawal syndromes from benzodiazepines are not determined. In borderline cases, therefore, discontinuation by successive dose reduction may be more advisable than abrupt discontinuation of these agents.

(b) *Detoxification using a long-acting drug that is crossdependent, e.g., methadone, chordrazopaxide, phenobarbitol, or, in rare instances, the addicting drug itself.* In our experience, detoxification can usually be completed within one week, using a long-acting drug that minimizes discomforting and, in some instances, serious withdrawal symptoms. A supportive but limit-setting inpatient milieu greatly facilitates the process. An immediate advantage of detoxification is that it allows the treatment staff to observe the patient's medical condition and behavior unclouded by the effects of physical dependence and drug tolerance. Often, the result is a dramatic improvement in physical symptoms as well as in emotional state and behavior. The disadvantage of this detoxification procedure is, ironically, the rather brief time it requires. The time may not be long enough for the patient to learn behaviors that are alternative to the drug-taking, much less for them to be adequately reinforced. It may also be too short for the patient to recognize any benefit from new treatment modalities. Where these factors are important to the treatment plan, the modification of the approach discussed next may be appropriate.

(c) *Deliberate phased withdrawal of medication*. A slow "fading out" of the addictive medication is usually to be preferred to an abrupt procedure so long as there are no critical reasons for immediate drug discontinuation or detoxification. This is accomplished by first establishing with the patient a reasonable schedule of dose and frequency. This schedule must be rigidly followed, i.e., a fixed dose, "always and only" at specified hours. Medication then is no longer contingent on the experience of discomfort or pain so that the "learned" component of the discomfort or pain is no longer reinforced. The dose, frequency, or both are then successively reduced according to plan. Extending the time in which the successive reduction of the medication is accomplished thus extends the period of noncontingent medication during which "well" behaviors can be learned and reinforced (Fordyce, 1974a,b). This procedure is usually carried out using the original medication although, at times, an alternative drug may be more appropriate. A long-acting narcotic analgesic (e.g., methadone) can be used in this slow detoxification procedure, so long as indefinite maintenance is not contemplated. In the management of chronic pain, not knowing when the dose is being reduced may help the patient to more realistically evaluate his actual need for analgesics. A fixed size capsule or a "pain cocktail" elixir may be used effectively for this purpose. While "fading" procedures are designed for use in controlled inpatient programs, many patients in our pain clinic have shown sufficient motivation and capacity to carry it out on an outpatient basis.

(d) *Systematic continuation of medication*. Where the immediate objective is regulation of analgesic maintenance rather than detoxification, the "as needed" and particularly the "stoic" PRN instructions must be abandoned. As with the "fading" procedures, the first step is the establishment of a reasonable schedule of medication dose and frequency. The objective of successive reduction of medication in this approach, however, is to determine the minimum effective dose rather than discontinuance. The benefits of this procedure derive primarily from the noncontingent use of medication. First, the reinforcement system is broken as discussed above. The second benefit of the noncontingent medication is due to the greater efficiency of analgesics in anticipating or blocking pain than in suppressing pain that has already become severe. This approach is particularly appropriate in the pain management of patients suffering with cancer.

Where the medical condition of the patient requires continued outpatient medical care, e.g., peripheral vascular disease, sickle-cell disease, and where the patient has not kept to the rigid demands of the fixed schedule, we have found that providing the patient with a fixed quantity of medication for use over a short and definite time span can be a viable alternative. This apparently tenuous arrangement often proves quite workable. This approach can reduce the tension in the patient-physician relationship, lead the patient to assume greater responsibility for his own care, and permit both to redirect attention to the basic treatment objectives.

SPECIALIZED TREATMENT PROGRAMS

Where treatment of the presenting problem, because of its nature or severity, falls outside the scope of the primary physician, treatment alternatives may be available through facilities that specialize in the management of chemical addictions, chronic pain syndromes, as well as psychosomatic, behavioral, and emotional disorders (see Table 14-III).

Programs based on sound treatment philosophies and utilizing effective procedures can offer the following:

(1) a comprehensive approach to assessment, treatment, and management of the presenting problem by a staff specialized in its focus and multidisciplinary in its approach;

(2) special procedures not ordinarily used by or available to the primary physician;

(3) inpatient treatment in an appropriately controlled environment allowing for detoxification, close observation, and limits on drug use and other behaviors that have contributed to the patient's dysfunction and that would interfere with the patient's rehabilitation;

(4) training in cognitive, psychophysiologic, and other methods of behavioral self-control as well as in social skills neces-

TABLE 14-III

SPECIALIZED TREATMENT FACILITIES AND METHOD
FOR MEDICALLY ADDICTED PATIENTS

FACILITIES/PROGRAMS
    Drug Dependence Treatment Programs
    Alcohol Dependence Treatment Programs
    Pain Management Programs
    Behavioral Medicine Programs
    Psychiatric Treatment Facilities
    Rehabilitation Medicine Facilities

METHODS
    Detoxification; with Methadone, Chlordiazepoxide, or other agents
    Dose stabilization, reduction; use of "pain cocktails"
    Nonnarcotic analgesics, antiinflammatory drugs
    Psychtherapy/counseling; group, individual, family
    Antidepressant drug therapy
    Corrective therapy, physical therapy, exercise programs, occupational therapy
    Vocational counseling and training
    Deep-relaxation, editation procedures, biofeedback training, hypnosis
    Social skills training, assertiveness training
    Transcutaneous electrical nerve stimulation, acupuncture

sary for more independent and effective management of physical and emotional problems.

The specialized yet comprehensive approaches to the management of addictions have been met with considerable enthusiasm. The generality of their effectiveness, however, is yet to be determined. Clearly our own experience, and that reported by others (Khatami et al., 1979; Morgan et al., 1979; Swanson et al., 1976; Walker, 1978) indicates that some patients improve dramatically in their ability to function and to cope with life stresses, no longer being drug dependent. The general population of patients entering these treatment programs appear to be heavily weighted with those who have responded very poorly to "traditional" forms of treatment. Their characteristics, however, are so varied and treatment benefits sometimes so tenuous that the overall benefits and cost-effectiveness of such programs are difficult to evaluate. Clearly, the final word is not yet in.

The clinical effectiveness of the more focused management methods designed to treat specific problems is less abiguous. For example, the effectiveness of tricyclic antidepressant drugs, in contrast to the benzodiazepines in the treatment of depression, has been demonstrated (see Hollister, 1978; Schatzberg, 1978). Deep relaxation and biofeedback techniques have been shown to reduce physiological manifestations of stress and abet stress management training (Benson et al., 1977; Miller and Dworkin, 1977; Tarler-Beniolo, 1978), although the question of which of the two techniques is superior is not resolved. While the question of the underlying mechanism involved is far from resolved, the effectiveness of transcutaneous electrical nerve stimulation for the suppression of the range of pain complaints is established (Melzack and Wall, 1965; Shealy, 1974; Wall and Sweet, 1967).

In our Pain and Stress Management Clinic and our Substance Abuse Treatment Unit, we use a variety of procedures and the treatment plan is formulated in terms of the individual addicted patient. For some, the treatment plan includes detoxification with methadone or chlordiazepoxide in a controlled inpatient setting. For patients with chronic pain who we chose to treat as outpatients, the treatment plan may include slow withdrawal from narcotic analgesics and/or minor tranquilizers in concert with psychological counseling, deep-relaxation or biofeedback training, transcutaneous electrical nerve stimulation, and possible occupational rehabilitation. These examples are not exhaustive of the treatment methods or their combinations used.

We offer some guidelines to the physician regarding when to refer the patient, assuming of course the availability of special programs or consultants. In general, many of the addicted or potentially addicted patients can remain under the care of the primary physician, who with patient participation and knowledge of psychoactive drug use can stabilize and redirect patient management. Consultive assistance is appropriate where special expertise is required, e.g., psychiatric evaluation or drug detoxification. Where the patient's overall quality of life, however, has deteriorated significantly and the life-style has become detrimental to self or others, specialized comprehensive assessment and management may be the most effective and efficient means of rehabilitation.

CONCLUSION

We have presented our approach to patients addicted to their medications along with several guidelines for management that have proved useful. We believe that these guidelines will prove useful to others as well. More important to us, however, is our hope that the reader will recognize the implicit concepts of patient care that can be beneficial in anticipating such problems before they emerge, or at least before they get out of hand.

REFERENCES

Altman, J.; Reich, P.; Kelly, M.; and Rogers, M.: Sounding board: Patients who read their hospital charts: *N Engl J Med, 302:*169, 1980.

Benson, H.; Kotch, J.; and Crassweller, K.: The relaxation response. *Med Clin N Amer, 61:*929, 1977.

Benzer, D.; and Cushman, P.: Alcohol and benzodiazepines: Withdrawal syndromes. *Alcoholism, 4:*243, 1980.

Fordyce, W.: Pain viewed as learned behavior. *Advances in Neurology,* Vol. 4. New York, Raven Press, 1974a, p. 415.

Fordyce, W.: Treating chronic pain by contingency management. *Advances in Neurology,* Vol. 4. New York, Raven Press, 1974, p. 583.

Groves, J.: Taking care of the hateful patient. *N Engl J Med, 298:*883, 1978.

Hollister, L.: Medical intelligence, drug therapy, tricyclic antidepressants. *N Engl J Med, 300:*1106-1168, 1978.

Khatami, M.; Woody, G.; and O'Brien, C.: Chronic pain and narcotic addiction: A multitherapeutic approach — A pilot study. *Comp Psychiatr, 20:*55, 1979.

McLellan, A.; Woody, G.; and O'Brian, C.: Development of psychiatric illness in drug abusers. *N Engl J Med, 301:*1310, 1979.

Melzack, R.; and Wall, P.: Pain mechanisms, A new theory. *Science, 150:*971, 1965.

Miller, N.; and Dworkin, B.: Physiology in medicine: Effects of learning of visceral functions — biofeedback. *N Engl J Med, 296:*1274, 1977.

Morgan, C.; Kremer, E.; and Gaylor, M.: The behavioral medicine unit: A new facility. *Comp Psychiat, 20:* 79, 1979.

NIDA, Research Monograph Series: *The Aging Process and Psychoactive Drug Use.* Publ. No. 79-813, U.S. Dept. HEW, 1979.

Schatzberg, A.: Benzodiazephine in depressive disorders. *J South Med Assoc, 71:*Suppl. 2, p. 18, 1978.

Shealy, C.: Six years experience with electrical stimulation for control of pain. *Advances in Neurology,* Vol. 4. New York, Raven Press, 1974, p. 775.

Sternbach, R.: Varieties of pain games. *Advances in Neurology,* Vol. 4. New York, Raven Press, 1974, p. 423.

Swanson, D.; Swenson, W.; Maruta, T.; and McPhee, M.: Program for managing chronic pain, 1. Program description and characteristics of patients. *Mayo Clinic Proc, 51*:401, 1976.

Tarler-Beniolo, L.: The role of relaxation in biofeedback training: A critical review of the literature. *Psych Bull, 85*:727, 1978.

Wall, P.; and Sweet, W.: Temporary abolition of pain in man. *Science, 155*:108, 1967.

Walker, L.: Iatiogenic addiction and its treatment. *Int J Addict, 13*:461, 1978.

CHAPTER 15

GAMBLING AND ADDICTION

Robert L. Custer

GAMBLING BEHAVIOR

Gambling must not be viewed as something unusual or mysterious. It is the playing of a game for money. However, society has divergent philosophical, ethical, moral, and legal attitudes toward play, games, money, and gambling. If one looks at gambling historically, one would be inclined to agree with the National Commission's Report on Gambling (1976) that states "Gambling is inevitable, no matter what is said or done by advocates or opponents of gambling in all its various forms. It is an activity that is practiced, or tacitly endorsed, by a substantial majority of Americans." If gambling is here to stay, a perspective is needed.

There appear to be four broad, distinguishable categories of gamblers, with some overlapping: (1) the *social* gambler, who gambles for recreation — this form is the most common and has the most variability in terms of gambling behavior; (2) the *compulsive* gambler, (3) the *antisocial (criminal)* gambler, and (4) the *professional* gambler. Of all types of gamblers, most are usually men.

The social gambler is paying for his entertainment. Sometimes he wins and most often he loses. Once the gambling ceases to be pleasurable or becomes too painful, he stops the gambling and returns to more satisfying or less uncomfortable behavior. He knows he is playing a game, and he has a totally separate life. He may wish to return to gambling, but his life pressure is to return to his primary or basic life pattern in which he has found a sense of achievement and comfort. The belief that the amount of money or the amount of time spent on gambling is solely indicative of whether or not a person is a social or compulsive gambler is a myth. The reason they gamble is the determining factor. Amounts of time and money are factors, but more important is what they do not do outside of gambling behavior, e.g., family, work, social relationships, etc. *The key to identifying the type of gambler is less by his gambling behavior than by his life outside of gambling.*

The professional gambler approaches gambling as a business. He expects to win but accepts losing. He is a student of the game, highly disciplined, patient, and receives little pleasure from gambling. He will analyze losses and learn from them, not be destroyed by them. He accepts losses as part of his business. They invariably have other business interests as well.

The psychopathic or antisocial person who gambles has unique characteristics. He will cheat whenever possible. He will do anything to win. He feels that losses are due to the cheating of others. If he wants money for gambling, he will take it in any manner possible with no intent of returning the money. He sees himself as a victim. Losing stimulates blaming and violence, rarely remorse and guilt. He has been in trouble virtually all of his life.

COMPULSIVE GAMBLING

Compulsive gambling is a progressive behavior disorder in which an individual has a psychologically uncontrollable preoccupation and urge to gamble. This results in excessive gambling, the outcome of which is the loss of time and money. The gambling reaches the point at which it compromises, disrupts or destroys the gambler's personal life, family relationships, or vocational pursuits. These problems in turn lead to intensification of the gambling behavior. The cardinal features are emotional dependence on gambling, loss of control, and interference with normal functioning (Custer, 1977).

The compulsive gambler does so to minimize discomfort and achieve a state of pleasure. As time goes on, the attempt is more and more to minimize discomfort and less and less for pleasure. The gambling behavior or its anticipation is the relief, excitement, stimulation, and escape from the discomfort. Winning and losing are not the significant factors; the action, or gambling itself, is the essential ingredient. To win is the objective, not to keep the money but to have it to continue gambling. There is no fun, relaxation, or recreation as with the social gambler. The compulsive gambler cannot stop. His life centers around gambling and other aspects of his life gradually diminish in significance and importance. Ultimately, other aspects of his life become intolerable and devoid of emotional concern and response. With heavy losses, there is depression and remorse. The only relief he sees is to return to gambling; the consequences become insignificant. Gambling has become the reality, his world, his existence. To not gamble means despair because he feels he cannot exist without gambling. The compulsive gambler develops an irrational optimism based on previous big wins and bailouts. Big wins establish that they can occur. He is protected from reality by the bailouts, and this gives him the illusion that nothing painful can really happen to him. A rescue fantasy — the bailout — is the "point of no return" for the compulsive gambler. It is similar to the blackout for the alcoholic. Nothing will stop the compulsive gambler, unless the environmental pain surpasses the internal pleasure. Once the environmental pain is gone, so is the stimulus for stopping. The environment can make the compulsive gambler stop for short periods of time, but it will not last for long unless adequate substitutes for the feeling that gambling provides are developed. Punishment is ineffective, since it rarely is as painful as the personal internal discomfort. Punishment also provides no substitute. The rehabilitation of the compulsive gambler is like a three-cornered stool: (1) stop gambling, (2) make restitution, and (3) get treatment. If he does not stop gambling, he can no longer think. By then, gambling impairs judgment so that he cannot make rational decisions. If he does not make emotional and financial restitution, he has no genuine remorse. He is actually encouraged to be irresponsible if he does not make restitution. Treatment is directed toward the search and finding of adequate resources and substitutes for the feelings and escapes that gambling had tried but failed to accomplish. Without the use of these three legs, the compulsive gambler remains exceedingly vulnerable to relapse.

The compulsive gambler, unlike the social gambler, must gamble. It is not a game and he is not just playing. Unlike the professional gambler, the compulsive gambler wants relief not control. Unlike the psychopath, he does not want to hurt others, and he cares what others think of him. The compulsive gambler goes to great lengths to prove he is not a compulsive gambler and that he is in control. As with other aspects of his life, he is constantly acting as defense attorney in his own behalf. As he progresses in his behavior, he gradually develops a gambling life-style along with his gambling activity. He is not only a stress seeker, he becomes a stress creator with his family, work, friends, and his life. He takes irrational risks which seem to fulfill his nongambling time. He takes chances with his family's affection, his employer's consideration, and his friends' kindness. In order to do this, he exaggerates, distorts, lies — all as a defense. He demands honesty, trust, praise, loyalty, affection, appreciation, and admiration. In return he gives criticism of others for not doing more, or not understanding, or gives vague promises so that he can continue his compulsive gambling. He may be successful in the short run, but inevitably, there are long-term negative consequences. As the compulsive gambler becomes more and more alienated from his family, friends, and work associates, his life values become less and less stable. Life risks increase until these values are compromised and he commits acts alien to his basic value system. Unfortunately, he does not really recognize that his course is clearly destructive so he becomes reckless, which leads to more senseless gambling. The whole process is progressive and accelerates to a frantic pace. Thoughts of suicide appear, which is the desire to be away from it all. However, the compulsive gambler is not the only victim. His spouse, parents, friends, employer, and society are hurt as well. By now he has developed a sense of hopelessness and despair.

The climb back is excruciatingly painful, humiliating, depressing, and discouraging. It takes time. The mere cessation of gambling is only the beginning. He must reearn the respect of self and others by a responsible and realistic approach to life.

The only one who can fully understand and share this burden is the recovering compulsive gambler.

Ultimately, the compulsive gambler must make the decision and the commitment to seek and accept help: the painful course of recovery. Often he cannot do this alone. Compassionate and knowledgeable others, like Gamblers Anonymous (GA), offer an alternative approach to life that takes one day at a time.

Prevalence of Compulsive Gambling

"Gambling in America," the report of the Commission on the Review of the National Policy Toward Gambling, contains the only study on the prevalence of compulsive gambling (1976). These estimates show that there are 1.1 million probable compulsive gamblers and 3.1 million potential compulsive gamblers. The Commission has presented other facts useful in education:

1. There are 4.2 million probable and potential compulsive gamblers in the United States.
2. Male compulsive gamblers outnumber females by two to one.
3. Availability of gambling increases the risk of becoming a compulsive gambler.
4. Better educated and higher salaried people bet more, as do single and young people eighteen to twenty-four years of age.
5. One male gambler in four gambles illegally as compared to one female in eleven.
6. Legal gambling facilities seem to stimulate illegal gambling.

The heart of the issue is what will our society do when it becomes fully aware of a serious sociocultural problem such as this. In the past similar problems have been approached indignantly, precipitiously, and vengefully. It is both encouraging and refreshing to see the response of the American Psychiatric Association presented in the *Diagnostic and Statistical Manual (DSM III)* (1978; 1979). They have included the diagnosis of compulsive gambling, listed as Pathological Gambling. The diagnosis is also listed in the *International Classification of Diseases* (1979).

Compulsive Gambling is listed, in DSM III, under Disorders of Impulsive Control, which are characterized by the following:

(1) There is a failure to resist an impulse, drive, or temptation to perform some action harmful to the patient or to others. There may or may not be conscious resistance to the impulse. The act may or may not be planned or premeditated. (2) Prior to committing the act, there is an increasing sense of tension. (3) At the time of committing the act, there is an experience of pleasure, gratification, or release. The act is ego-syntonic in that it is consonant with the immediate conscious wish and aim of the patient. (4) Immediately following the act there may or may not be genuine regret, self-reproach, or guilt.

What is the importance of these diagnostic criteria for compulsive gambling? First it will bring credibility to a problem, not a thoughtless reaction. Also, it will create awareness, alert and inform professionals, encourage treatment, increase knowledge of gambling addiction, direct attention to prevention and research, and will stimulate worldwide thought and the sharing of ideas.

THE VETERANS ADMINISTRATION TREATMENT PROGRAMS

The VA has made major contributions to the recognition, understanding, and treatment of the compulsive gambler. In April, 1972, they pioneered the first inpatient treatment program specifically for compulsive gamblers, and, as far as we know, it is the first in the world.

The Brecksville (Ohio) VA Program idea originated with three GA members. They suggested the idea to the Alcohol Dependent Treatment Program staff in 1971, who studied the possibility and began the program in April, 1972. Much of the success at Brecksville lies with the Cleveland GA groups. It has been their involvement that has given the support to the inpatient component and provided invaluable follow-up treatment (Glen et al., 1975).

The VA interest in compulsive gambling is indicated by the addition of two treatment programs similar to the Brecksville Program, located at Brooklyn and Miami VA Medical Centers. Future plans call for three additional programs elsewhere.

LEGALIZATION

Legalization of gambling must be recognized as not a war to be won or lost. It is merely another area in which we must direct attention. The National Commission on Gambling states that legalization of gambling increases the number of gamblers and the number of illegal bettors. It seems axiomatic that there will be more compulsive gamblers. As of 1980, only 100 thousand dollars (of over 1.2 billion dollars) are currently being realized for treatment of compulsive gambling.

There is no war with those who wish to gamble socially. Honest views must be considered between stimulation and overstimulation. We must look at the issue of the image of governments promoting gambling and at the impact on vulnerable groups such as adolescents, and appropriate limits must be taken to insure fewer casualties.

A compulsive gambler will find a way to gamble if there is no legalized gambling but future studies will likely show that illegal gambling probably creates few compulsive gamblers and legal gambling creates many (Custer, 1977).

Compulsive Gambling and Law Enforcement

Law enforcement is presently concerned with punishment, not with treatment, of the compulsive gambler. The priority needs to be reversed. No true compulsive gambler should go to prison without first having the option to get treatment, to discontinue gambling, and to make restitution. Prison has never cured a compulsive gambler. If it were not for GA in some prisons, the compulsive gamblers would all return to society and be more difficult to treat. Prison, for them, can be disguised bailout. The compulsive gambler, who commits a non-violent act or crime (the vast majority), must stop gambling, make restitution to his victims, and be in GA and other treatment programs. This is not only better for the compulsive gambler but also better for his victims. It is time to correct the imbalance between innocent victims and locked-up offenders. This would require professionally trained and competent probation officers. Those who violate probation conditions could be sent to prison. Our approach demands responsibility, reasonable support, and concern, which is more likely to produce a rehabilitated nongambling citizen (Custer and Custer, 1978).

There is another law enforcement approach that deserves some consideration. Since the compulsive gambler in action patently qualifies as unable to manage his financial affairs and meet personal and family needs, he is by all definitions legally incompetent. Why not declare a compulsive gambler incompetent to manage his own funds for two years contingent upon treatment with GA, restitution, and evidence that gambling has stopped? There would be a furor at the invasion of rights, but think of the rights of the spouse and children and the community. Perhaps this approach would only help the family, but perhaps it would also decrease the likelihood of readily available money. Remember, there is no substance like Antabuse® or methadone available to the compulsive gambler. Actually, about half of the recovering compulsive gamblers turn over all budget controls to their spouse anyway.

TREATMENT PROGRAMS

One should not make the mistake of overemphasizing treatment as the solution to the problem of compulsive gambling. GA and treatment programs are willing to accept the pathological gambler for treatment, but they cannot assume the responsibility for success or failure. All of society must help. This includes judges, attorneys, parents, spouses, employers, banks and loan companies, educators, probation officers, clergy, politicians, unions, and the gambling operators.

For example, GA cannot help the compulsive gambler when the spouse denies the problem, the bank loans the money, and the employer covers up.

Everyone must be involved in treatment. Treatment of alcoholics by AA and physicians alone has not been enough. We should not make the same mistake with compulsive gambling. GA has all the tools to treat but they cannot succeed unless others know how to keep doors closed to the compulsive gambler.

The only treatment program today, outside of the three VA programs, is that established through legislation by the State of Maryland. The Johns Hopkins Compulsive Gambling Counseling Center, which was opened in November, 1979, is the first of its kind among the states that have legalized gambling.

NATIONAL COUNCIL ON COMPULSIVE GAMBLING

The NCCG represents one of the major landmark accomplishments in the efforts to help the compulsive gambler since the birth of GA, September 13, 1957. This organization has become the primary advocate of GA, the public educator, the lobbyist for rational policies on gambling, and the community spokesman.

Historically, the NCCG must be considered a necessity, as is the National Council on Alcoholism. The future will determine its contribution. It may become the main thrust of education efforts about compulsive gambling, GA, Gam-Anon, and Gam-Ateen (Custer, 1980).

RESEARCH

Many questions need to be answered about compulsive gambling. Policies towards compulsive gambling depend upon objective data, which in turn depend upon sound research. The research on gambling has been intolerably meager. Research questions need to be answered. How many compulsive gamblers are there? What is the impact of legalization on the prevalence rate of compulsive gamblers? What are the most effective methods of treatment? What subgroups of gamblers are most vulnerable to progressing into compulsive gambling? How many of our prison population are compulsive gamblers?

The Brecksville VA Program in Cleveland has shed a little light on some of these questions, as a result of their clinical research (Lesieur, 1979). They found that compulsive gamblers can be objectively diagnosed, are treatable with about a 50 percent success rate, that inpatient treatment is valuable for further retention in GA, that a few patients have other serious psychiatric problems that require specialized care, and that not all compulsive gamblers can be helped by GA or by VA Medical Centers. These primarily are criminals who gamble. They are a separate and distinct group. They are not really compulsive gamblers and they tend not to accept the kind of treatment that is available.

GAMBLERS ANONYMOUS

In my opinion, GA is the single most effective treatment modality for the compulsive gambler. It is a voluntary fellowship of compulsive gamblers gathered for the sole purpose of helping themselves and each other to stop gambling. It is not involved in any movement to combat or restrict gambling in general. GA espouses no cause, even ones designed to help compulsive gamblers. This policy does not, however, restrict individual members from becoming involved in community activities or services concerned with compulsive gambling. In fact, GA members are often in the leadership of such efforts.

There is one condition for membership in GA: being a compulsive gambler who wants to stop gambling. Membership is never solicited; when asked, help is given unstintingly. There is one absolute principle. Direction to GA may be given by anyone, but help is given only at the request of the compulsive gambler.

I believe that GA is effective because it (a) undercuts denial, projection, and rationalization, (b) identifies the serious implications of gambling, (c) demands honesty and responsibility, (d) identifies and corrects character problems, (e) gives affection, personal concern, and support, (f) develops substitutes for the void left by the cessation of gambling, and (g) is nonjudgmental.

Gam-Anon

Gam-Anon is a fellowship for the families of compulsive gamblers, who have found that living with a compulsive gambler can be a devastating experience. With Gam-Anon, they can learn to cope with problems in the face of disaster. They hope to and do accomplish many things, including the ability to understand the compulsive gambler, ventilation of feelings, dealing with guilt, doing things for others, setting priorities, planning and meeting some of their own needs. It is a place where they are understood.

They are the largest and most effective group to be of help to GA, as they are also the most effective group to help the families of compulsive gamblers. In fact, they are probably the most effective group, outside of GA, to attract compulsive gamblers to GA.

The family in GA learns how not to hinder the GA member's recovery and growth. They must learn that they can hinder recovery but do not cause the compulsive gambler to gamble. The family member can drive the compulsive gambler toward gambling, but the person must assume the responsibility for the decision to return to gambling.

GA Outside the United States

GA is an international organization. There is much we can learn from GA, Gam-Anon, and the professionals working alongside of GA in countries such as the United Kingdom, Canada, Ireland, Australia, New Zealand, Belgium, and Brazil. Their governments' approach to legalization and treatment can be invaluable to those in the United States. We need to familiarize ourselves with what these countries are doing.

A significant development in treatment of compulsive gambling has occurred since 1971. Gordon House in England is a hostel, like a halfway house, for single, homeless, compulsive gamblers. It was pioneered by the Reverend Gordon Moody. We need to explore other similar types of helping programs, which should simulate healthy competition and sharing.

TREATMENT PRINCIPLES

The initial problem is one of recognition. The compulsive gambler may admit to being depressed and believe it to be due to threatened losses. Gambling may not be revealed. However, if the problem of compulsive gambling is suspected, the spouse can quickly verify the origin of these problems. More commonly, the problem will be admitted. A typical excerpt from an initial interview is: "I feel emotionally beat — and I've thought about suicide. My family has given up on me. I've borrowed thousands from my parents. I've written a letter telling them how sorry I am. I tried to explain that I don't want to gamble, but I can't control it."

Suicidal risk must be determined, and this may easily be done by direct questioning about past suicidal behavior, present feelings and intentions. Inpatient treatment may be necessary for the management of the suicidal patient, particularly those with no family supports. The exhausted compulsive gambler who cannot see any way out of his predicament and who is isolated due to family alienation might be in the process of emotional decompensation and may need a protected environment. Others may be desperate but not suicidal. They may be on the verge of committing a crime as an irrational attempt to resolve their financial problems. Feelings and thoughts about such intentions need to be explored in cases. In essence, such cases represent psychiatric emergencies.

The observations of the staff at Brecksville VA Treatment Program revealed that, if the compulsive gambler had just stopped gambling, it was not at all unusual for symptoms of headache, abdominal pain, diarrhea, cold sweats, tremor, and nightmares to appear a few days after admission to the program. This may represent withdrawal symptoms or they may be due to sleep deprivation. In any event, they respond favorably to sleep, a standard diet, vigorous exercise, ventilation, and reassurance.

In the initial interviews, the gambler will often describe gambling behavior, which has come to dominate his life causing multiple serious consequences, in a manner that almost seems to be bragging. The interviewee is frequently told no one could possibly have such debts. This is done as part of the assessment procedure. One is struck by the inability of these gamblers to control their behavior in spite of consequences and apparent ineffectiveness of either reward or punishment to modify it. These patients may want to change but are unable to do so without help. They have little hope that change is possible. The family history reveals problems of alcoholism or compulsive gambling in their parents in about one-third of the cases. The surprising part of the history is the absence of antisocial behavior as a child or adolescent, with a good school and work performance.

There are four rather consistent defensive postures that gamblers will take and it is wise for the therapist to confront these issues early: (1) they believe that lack of money is the problem, (2) they expect an instant or miraculous cure, (3) they cannot conceive of a life without gambling, and (4) they see complete restitution of debts or stolen money as desirable but impossible.

Compulsive gamblers also face some common concrete problems including spouse-family disruption, immense debts, demands from creditors, loss of job, alienation and isolation, threats from loan sharks, and legal entanglements. Also, the problem of dealing with feelings of hurt, fear, and anger is complicated by a "feeling aphasia" in that they have considerable difficulty recognizing or verbalizing their feelings. However, they are usually quite articulate and can recognize feelings in others. This makes them particularly good candidates for group therapy, especially with other compulsive gamblers who have the same "aphasia."

Compulsive gamblers do have some strengths, including high intelligence, industriousness, high energy level, competitiveness, and a desire for independence. These traits are particularly effective in reestablishing vocational activities. Such efforts are natural and ego-syntonic avenues for these enterprising individuals. Work becomes a time- and energy-consuming activity that substitutes for their drive to gamble. It is not uncommon for them to secure two or three jobs simultaneously. This eases their pressures, and probably more importantly, it is a constructive channel for their energy and provides them with a sense of regaining control of their lives.

Goals of Treatment

No gambling, full restitution, and assistance in development of constructive substitutes for gambling are the main treatment goals. Compulsive gambling is a chronic long-standing disorder that requires long-term care. Since compulsive gambling is impulsive and since stress stimulates their impulsivity, it is wise to develop a system that will provide them with access to someone who can reduce tension any time it might develop. A therapist needs to have a high degree of availability to the gambler. This is one of the advantages of GA. Numerous members are skilled, available, and willing to provide help. The more people available to "talk down" the compulsive gambler who feels driven to gamble, the less chance of relapse. Slips must be watched and treated promptly so that areas of the gambler's life that stimulate gambling can be understood and dealt with appropriately. Marital counseling and assertiveness training are usually quite valuable as protective measures against relapses.

The four personality features that are frequently present and need timely confrontation are hypersensitivity to rejection, inability to express feelings, tendency to lie and manipulate, and reluctance to ask for help in a crisis. Dealing effectively and efficiently with these areas is best done in group therapy with other compulsive gamblers. The concomitant use of GA can often suffice, depending upon the severity of the symptomatology.

Social interactions are usually no major problem after the compulsive gambler returns to work, has resumed or indicated intent to make repayment, has stopped gambling, and has allowed a reasonable amount of time to elapse. Even prior to this time, the social slack is taken up by the GA group.

Recreational activity is occasionally approached fanatically during the recovery phase. Although this can be irritating to spouse and family, it is often a healthy substitute for the gambling behavior. Reassurance of the family that such recreation is beneficial and will run its course is usually all that is required. Still others may need encouragement in recreational pursuits. These vocational, social, and recreational activities can be effective tension replacers, which is the "name of the game" in treating impulse disorders, such as pathological gambling.

REFERENCES

American Psychiatric Association: *Diagnostic and Statistical Manual of Mental Disorders*, Third Edition (Draft). Washington, D.C., 1978.

American Psychiatric Association: *Diagnostic and Statistical Manual of Mental Disorders (DSM-III)*. Washington, D.C., 1979.

Commission on the Review of the National Policy towards Gambling: *Gambling in America — Final Report*. Washington, D.C., U.S. Govt. Printing Office, 1976.

Custer, R.: The Gambling Scene — 1977. Unpublished paper presented at the First International Conference of Gamblers Anonymous, Chicago, Ill., 1977.

Custer, R.: An overview of compulsive gambling. *Carrier Foundation Letter,* No. 59, Belle Mean, N.J., February, 1980.

Custer, R.; and Custer, L.: Characteristics of the recovering compulsive gambler. A survey of 150 members of Gamblers Anonymous. Unpublished paper presented at the Fourth International Conference on Gambling, 1978.

Custer, R. et al.: Syllabus — Treatment of the compulsive gambler. Unpublished paper presented at the AMA Winter Meeting, December, 1978.

Gamblers Anonymous: Gamblers Anonymous, Los Angelos. Los Angeles National Service Organization, undated.

Glen, A.; Custer, R.; and Burns, R.: The inpatient treatment of compulsive gamblers. Unpublished paper presented at the Second Annual Conference on Gambling, June, 1975.

International Classification of Diseases, (9th Edition), *Clinical Modification*, Commission on Hospital and Professional Activities, 1979.

Lesieur, H.: The compulsive gambler's spiral of options and involvement. *Psychiatry, 42*:79-87, 1979.

National Council on Compulsive Gambling: Definition of Compulsive Gambling. Private communication, 1976.

AUTHOR INDEX

SUBJECT INDEX

393